D0365342

W.D. REEKIE, D.E. ALLEN & J.N. CROOK

THE ECONOMICS OF MODERN BUSINESS

SECOND EDITION

The Economics of Modern Business

For Ruth, Barbara and Kate

The Economics of Modern Business

W. D. REEKIE, D. E. ALLEN
and J. N. CROOK

First published 1983
Reprinted 1983, 1986, 1988
Second edition, revised and updated, first published 1991
First published in USA 1992

Blackwell Publishers
108 Cowley Road, Oxford, OX4 1JF, UK

Three Cambridge Center
Cambridge Massachusetts 02142, USA

British Library Cataloguing in Publication Data
A CIP catalogue record for this book is available from the British Library.

Library of Congress Cataloging in Publication Data
Reekie, W.D.
The economics of modern business / W. D. Reekie, D. E. Allen and J. N. Crook
— 2nd ed., rev. and updated.
p. cm.
Includes index.
1. Economics. 2. Microeconomics. 3. Great Britain—Industries.
I. Crook, Jonathan N. II. Reekie, W. Duncan. III. Title.
HB171.5.R29 1991 91–7534
338.5′024658—dc20
ISBN 0–631–17215–7

Typeset in 10 on 12pt Times
by Hope Services (Abingdon) Ltd.
Printed in Great Britain by
T. J. Press, Padstow, Cornwall

This book is printed on acid-free paper

Contents

Acknowledgements

The defects in this text are exclusively our own. However, for the positive qualities our thanks are due to Charles Baird of California State University, Hayward; Falconer Mitchell of Edinburgh University; Brian Summers of the Foundation for Economic Education, Irvington-on-Hudson, New York, and P. J. White of Edinburgh for inspiration and comment. Judith Harvey, desk editor at Blackwell Publishers, and Christine Sharrock of Omega Scientific proved helpful, constructive and fastidious. But our greatest debt is to René Olivieri of Blackwell Publishers, without whose entrepreneurial dynamism this book would never have been begun, and to Tim Goodfellow also of Blackwell Publishers who most efficiently saw it into its second edition.

1

Plan and Purpose

What has been responsible for giving us our present quality of life? The answer is business enterprise. Businessmen perceive the opportunities for making profits, rent the resources they believe are necessary to take these opportunities and hope that the profits materialize.

The economist can help us to understand why resources are allocated in the way we observe between firms, within firms and between consumers. He can deduce how businessmen *should* act given various assumptions, for example concerning their objectives. Thus, as will be explained in chapter 5, given that a firm wishes to maximize profits and with other assumptions concerning the relationships between costs, revenues and output, the economist can *deduce* that the output which the firm *should* produce to achieve this objective is that at which marginal revenue equals marginal costs. Even if the assumptions made are not descriptively completely realistic (indeed the world is too complex for them to be) the economist may find that he can deduce *predictions* about how groups of businesses behave which correspond with what is eventually observed. The particular collection of assumptions that are used to make predictions are those which yield predictions that correspond to reality more frequently than the predictions deduced from other assumptions. Economists may also *describe* how businessmen take decisions such as how they set their prices or outputs or advertising budget.

We live in a world of scarcity. This requires us to make choices between more and less valued ends. Each choice results in forgone benefit. Furthermore, the outcomes of our choices are, in practice, uncertain. All we can hope to do is to make the least bad choices. Thus among other things the economist's role is to emphasize this and to assist the businessman, consumer and government to understand the outcomes of the relevant choices facing them.

It will be enough if in this book we achieve the modest aim of bringing home the ideas that resources are limited, but that trading and commercial activity can, at least potentially, improve our lot. The unsung heroes responsible for our wealth are consumers and producers operating in the market-place. It is to promote appreciation of this fact that we have written the book.

The imperfect engine of wealth creation which is Western industry is our main subject of study. In particular we deal with British business. Chapters 2–7 provide a basic economic tool-kit with which to tackle the rest of the book. The kit includes discussion of why firms are the size they are and why they are members of any given industry. Business decisions and the ways in which they are monitored are covered in chapters 8 and 9. Chapter 10 examines how business is owned by the members of society, either directly, or indirectly through individual savings. In chapter 11 the nature and evolution of modern British industry is discussed; the emphasis there is on manufacturing industry. We discuss the role of public enterprise in chapter 12. In chapter 13 the thrust of the examination returns to the market-place and the consumer; marketing, distribution, trading and exchange again take the centre of the stage. Chapter 14 goes on to consider the relationship between employer and employee. This subject aptly follows chapter 13 since, as emphasized there, both employer and employee are the servants of the consumer. Yet, whenever the topic is treated on its own, this truth is often forgotten. The juxtaposition of these chapters ameliorates but does not excise this conceptual problem. Chapter 15 examines the role of the government: does it hamper or hinder the workings of business for the good of the consumer? We do not attempt a definitive answer, but topics covered include conventional ones, such as monopolies legislation, and less conventional but highly topical issues such as pollution. In that chapter the Coase theorem (notably absent from other elementary textbooks) is introduced.

Wherever possible we avoid abstruse theorizing; we illustrate models with highly relevant practical examples, provide plenty of statistical information, and describe how firms actually take decisions. Business emerges as exciting, interesting and the best (though still imperfect) way of meeting human wants.

2

Setting the Scene

Markets and the Role of Business

Many people believe that only the seller of a good or service benefits from trade. The buyer pays out money which presumably makes him poorer; the seller receives money, which presumably enriches him. Consequently, business is frequently viewed as an avaricious and less than desirable component of society.

There are two fallacies in this reasoning. The first is the claim that one party to a voluntary trade gains while the other loses. This is not so: barring fraud and miscalculations, both parties gain. Individual valuations differ, and trade occurs if, and only if, both parties anticipate receiving in exchange something of greater perceived value than whatever they give up. Voluntary trading is always carried out in the expectation of improving one's lot, be one the buyer or the seller. In short, buyers and sellers have a common interest; they co-operate, not compete, in trade. Buyers may compete against buyers, and sellers against sellers, but sellers and buyers co-operate for the enrichment of both.

The second error is the view that only the person who receives money in exchange for goods becomes richer. Money has no intrinsic value but only as a medium of exchange and a store of value. It is something which may be traded later for other things, to use or consume. The ultimate purpose of voluntary trade is to obtain goods and services to consume. Adam Smith put it succinctly: 'Consumption is the sole end and purpose of all production.'[1]

However, most goods are scarce. If someone gains more of a good then something must be given up (not necessarily by the same person). If half a ton of steel is used to manufacture a car, it cannot simultaneously be used to make five motor-bikes. Very few goods are genuinely free. Even air is scarce if you are a diver or an astronaut, and clean air is scarce to city dwellers.

Given scarcity, three fundamental economic questions arise. What goods should be produced and in what proportions? How should they be produced and with what technologies? For whom should they be produced and how much of each should members of society consume?

In a centrally controlled (sometimes called *dirigiste*) economy the planners can decide on workers' remuneration in a way which ensures that there is a sufficient supply of labour with the requisite skills to complete the tasks required. For example in the Soviet Union until 1989 a tariff–qualifications manual states the qualifications needed to perform a particular type of job and the wage rate to be paid for that job (such as lorry-driver or fitter), although regional differentials are planned to ensure that sufficient workers are available to work there. Product prices are also set centrally (in the Soviet Union historically in a cost-plus manner (see chapter 8) which ignores demand and supply influences) but often are not updated. The aggregate output of goods and services is determined centrally and often allocated by means of queues or political seniority. Labour receives little incentive to be as productive as possible since wage rates are centrally controlled.

In a totally free enterprise economy (i.e. one which is not *dirigiste* but *laissez-faire*) goods are allocated to those who are willing and able to engage in voluntary trade. If in turn those who supply their labour are rewarded on the basis of their productivity then an incentive to be highly productive exists because the most productive gain most and the least productive gain least. Prices adjust so that the amounts of goods and services and of labour which producers and workers are willing to supply equal the amounts demanded. Queues do not form. Unlike a centrally planned economy consumers pay an amount for each unit of good which is sufficient to make it worthwhile for others to produce that unit.

In both types of economies funds are allocated to the invention and innovation of new products and production processes. But there are reasons to believe that the rate of technical progress will be faster in a free enterprise economy because those who invent and innovate directly receive the rewards of doing so whereas in a centrally planned economy they do not. There is therefore a greater incentive to invent and innovate in the former than in the latter. The faster the total output of an economy is increasing the greater the increases in the amounts of goods and services which are available to those who can afford to buy them and the greater the increases in incomes of those who produce. The disadvantaged members of a society can be helped with greater amounts of assistance. This can be provided by voluntary charity or by taxation, thus transferring income from one group in society to another. The more productive can earn ever increasing incomes for themselves (net of tax and charitable donations) and so generate still further wealth for the community. This is the basic rationale for the market economy against a more autocratic system of resource allocation.

The Mixed Economy

The United Kingdom is often called a 'mixed economy'. It is neither wholly *dirigiste* and centrally planned, nor is it one of totally free enterprise. In fact the name is rather misleading since all countries have mixed economies; only the degree of the mixture varies. Thus the Soviet Union has a substantial private sector in taxi-cabs, market-places and agriculture. The USA has significant government interests in health, welfare and social security, as well as the more obvious expenditures on defence and policing. In Britain, general government expenditure (as a percentage of gross national product (GNP)) has risen over the century, as is shown in table 2.1. The impact of the World Wars is clear. Various welfare measures have been responsible for increasing social (e.g. pensions, sickness and unemployment benefits) and educational expenditures.

Table 2.1 *General government expenditure (central and local) as a percentage of gross national product*

1900		14.3
1910		12.2
1920		26.2
1930		25.0
1940		n.a.
1950	37.9[a]	39.1[b]
1960	38.5	
1970	46.6	
1980	52.0	
1989	44.9	

n.a. not available.
[a] *Sources*: *Economic Trends Annual Supplement 1990 edition*, HMSO, 1990, tables 2 and 35; *Monthly Digest of Statistics*, HMSO, April 1990, Table 1.1; *Economic Trends* (April 1990), table 31.
[b] *Source*: *Barclays Bank Review*, 1980.

Table 2.2 illustrates how government expenditure is broken down. Social security payments (plus, of course, their administration) account for over one-quarter. The National Health and associated services, together with education, account for a similar proportion. The national defence budget is the next largest recipient of money from government. The remainder are absolutely large but relatively small. The government sector is, of course, an important ultimate customer of business or industry, through one or other of its programmes (e.g. agriculture, fisheries and food; parts of the defence, housing, industry and roads budgets etc.). Even

Table 2.2 *General government expenditure by function: estimated outturn 1989–1990*

Function	£billion
Defence	20.3
Overseas services including overseas aid	2.4
Agriculture, fisheries, food, forestry	2.3
Trade, industry, energy, employment	7.1
Transport	6.9
Housing	3.7
Other environmental services	7.2
Law, order and protective services	9.9
Education and science	24.9
Arts and libraries	1.2
Health and personal social services	29.4
Social security	53.1
Miscellaneous services	6.9
Privatization proceeds	−4.2
General government debt interest	17.8
Adjustments	7.4
Total	196.4

Source: HM Treasury, *Government Expenditure Plans 1990–1 to 1992–3*, Cmnd 1021, HMSO, chapter 21.

government programmes such as health and education pay not insignificant sums to, for example, the construction, medicine instrumentation and publishing industries.

The mixed economy which exists in Britain is neither ruthless (as autocratic economies can be and have been) nor devoid of concern for others (as totally free enterprise economies theoretically could be). Rather it combines some of the best of both worlds. However, debate can and does exist as to whether the 'mixture' is correct. Is a 'caring bureaucracy' not a contradiction in terms? Would not voluntary charity be more effective? Is government participation too weak? Or too strong? These are legitimate matters of debate, but they will be left to later chapters.

Business in Britain

For the purposes of this book the degree to which the economy is or is not 'mixed' is not of primary importance. Rather, we are interested in modern British business *per se*.

Each activity in the economy is classified into an industry which is ascribed a label known as the Standard Industrial Classification (SIC) number. At the highest level of aggregation of activities only one digit is used in the label. For example metal goods, engineering and vehicles industries is ascribed the number '3'. At each succeeding level of disaggregation of activities another digit is added to that indicating the more aggregated group. For each industry a tree diagram can be constructed to show which disaggregated industries are contained within aggregated ones. Table 2.3 shows such a diagram for the metal goods, engineering and vehicles manufacturing industry. The maximum level of disaggregation possible within the British SIC is at four-digit level.

The current SIC was introduced in 1980. Several factors were taken into account when different activities were classified into the same group. These 'included the nature of the process or of the work done, the principal raw material used, the type of intended use of goods produced or handled, and the type of service rendered'.[2]

Table 2.4 gives an introductory description of the nature of the industries in the United Kingdom and their changes in employment, output and share of gross domestic product (GDP) between 1981 and 1988 (or 1987). It shows, first, that while the numbers employed in the agriculture, forestry and fisheries (SIC 0), manufacturing (SIC 2–4) and construction (SIC 5) industries declined the numbers employed in the service industries (SIC 6–9) increased considerably. The industries with the greatest declines in employment were motor vehicles and parts, metals and mineral products and energy and water supply; while that with the greatest increase was the banking, finance, insurance, business services and leasing industry.

Second, the GDP of almost all industries increased but the increase was greatest for the construction industry followed by the service industries, manufacturing, and agriculture etc. respectively. Within manufacturing the greatest increase in output was from the electrical and instrument engineering industry while the greatest decline was in the other transport equipment industry. In the service sector the greatest increase was in the banking etc. industry with a very large 79 per cent rise. Since in all industries except that of public administration, national defence and compulsory social security the proportionate increase in output exceeds the proportionate increase in employment (in many cases we have noted that employment actually fell) the total labour productivity in most industries has increased. However, by comparing the increase in output with the decreases in employment it can be seen that the greatest increase in labour productivity occurred in the electrical and instrument engineering industry.

Thirdly, the table shows that between 1981 and 1987 the share of GDP produced by agriculture decreased from 1.86 to 1.46 per cent, that of manufacturing from 23.69 to 20.95 per cent, while that of construction remained almost constant and that of the service industries increased from 58.44 to 65.81 per cent. In terms of percentage points the greatest increase in the share of GDP came from the banking etc. industry and the greatest

Table 2.3 *Activities contained with the metal goods, engineering and vehicles industry*

Division	3 Metal goods, engineering and vehicles						
Class	31	32	33	34	35	36	37
	Manufacture of metal goods n.e.s.	Mechanical engineering	Manufacture of office machinery and data processing equipment	Electrical and electronic engineering	Manufacture of motor vehicles and parts thereof	Manufacture of other transport equipment	Instrument engineering

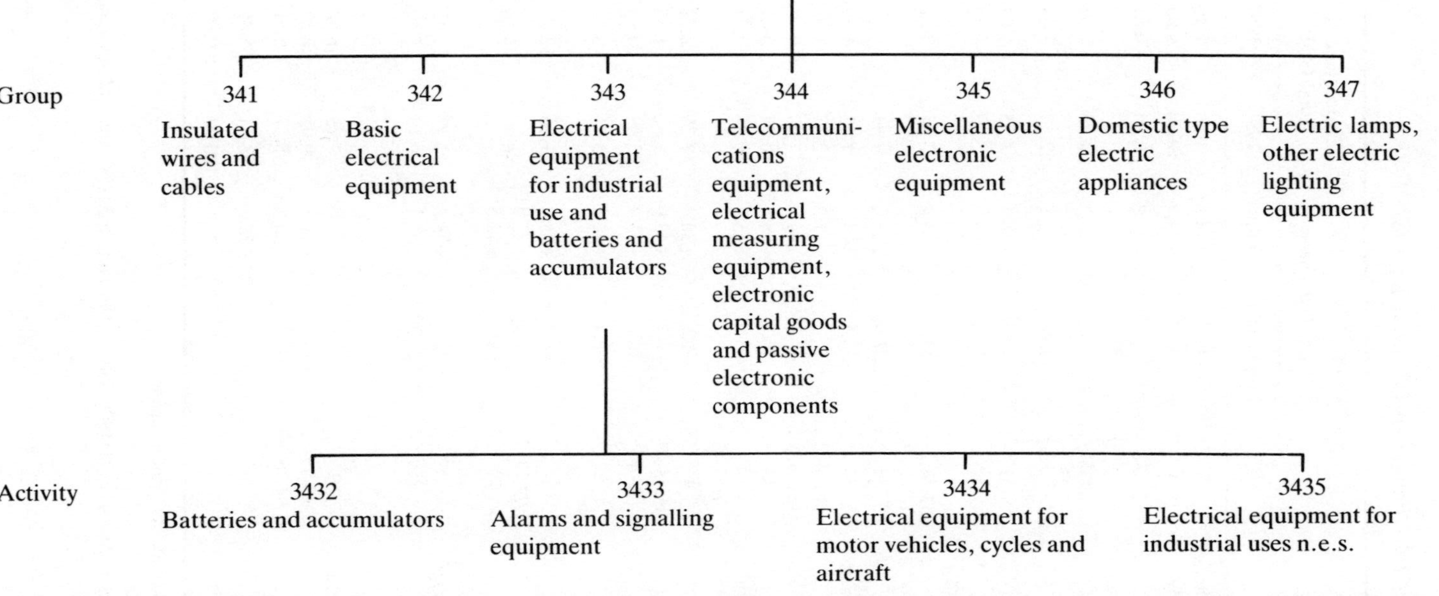

n.e.s., not elsewhere specified.
Source: constructed from *The Standard Industrial Classification Revised 1980*, HMSO, 1979

Table 2.4 *Changes in UK industry 1981–1988*

Industry	SIC	Percentage change: Employment	Percentage change: Output	Percentage of total GDP: 1981	Percentage of total GDP: 1987
Agriculture, forestry, fisheries	0	−11.3	+14.9	1.86	1.46
Energy and water supply	1	−31.3	+14.9	10.30	6.05
Metals	21,22 }	−33.8 (Metals and Other minerals)	+27.8	0.89	0.81
Other minerals and mineral products	23,24 }		+27.9	1.23	1.09
Chemicals	25 }	−15.8 (Chemicals and Man-made fibres)	+35.6 }	2.13 (Chemicals and Man-made fibres)	2.28 (Chemicals and Man-made fibres)
Man-made fibres	26 }		−2.3 }		
Metal goods n.e.s.	31	−19.5	+18.3	1.35	1.09
Mechanical engineering	32	−15.2	+9.9	3.33	2.36
Electrical and instrument engineering	33,34,37	−13.3	+63.4	3.01	2.86
Motor vehicles and parts thereof	35	−26.1	+22.8	1.33	1.19
Other transport equipment	36	−34.1	−4.1	1.43	1.09
Food	410–423 }	−17.2 (Food and Drink and tobacco)	+11.3	2.27	1.98
Drink and tobacco	424–429 }		+1.9	1.05	0.74
Textiles	43	−16.3	+8.8	0.74	0.67
Clothing, footwear, leather	44,45	−6.9	+15.9	0.86	0.74
Paper, printing and publishing	47	−6.8	+30.4	2.25	2.21
All other manufacturing	46,48,49	+4.3	+43.0	1.82	1.85
Total manufacturing	2–4	−16.2	+25.4	23.69	20.95
Construction	5	−8.4	+42.5	5.71	5.73
Distribution, hotels, catering; repairs	6	+6.2	+38.2	11.96	12.27
Transport	71,72,74–77	−9.8	+25.0 }	6.97 (Transport and Communications)	6.50 (Transport and Communications)
Communications	79	n.a.	+42.5 }		
Banking, finance, insurance, business services, leasing	81–84	+42.7	+78.7	11.97	19.42
Ownership of dwellings	85	+28.3	+7.3	6.10	5.40
Public administration, national defence and compulsory social security	91	+2.8	0	7.13	6.82
Education and health	93,95	+10.2	+11.5	9.05	8.89
Other services	92,94,96–99	30.5[a]	+36.8	5.27	6.51
Total services			+28.7	58.44	65.81
Total			+27.1	100.00	100.00

n.e.s., not elsewhere specified; n.a., not available.

[a] Excluding SIC 99 and 00.

Sources: *Annual Abstract of Statistics*, HMSO, 1987, 1990, table 6.2; *UK National Accounts*, 1989, tables 2.2, 2.4.

decrease from the energy and water supply industry. Discussion of the reasons for these changes will be deferred until chapters 4, 5, 8, 9 and 10.

According to some economists whether an industry is state or privately owned is of little importance to an examination of the 'mixed economy'. Rather than the size of the state-owned sector 'it is the public sector activities which do not provide marketed outputs that put particular pressure on the resources of the remainder of the economy . . . . [As these rose] from 41.4 per cent of market output in 1961 to 60.3 percent in 1974 . . . [they reduced] by nearly one third the proportion of output that market-sector producers [state or privately owned] could themselves invest and consume.'[3] In the remainder of this book we shall be concerned with markets and buyers and sellers, whether state, government, private firms, co-operatives or individuals.

Production

The *product transformation curve* (which shows a firm's potential output combinations) highlights the problem of scarcity. The curve is also applicable to a society and is then usually called a *production possibility frontier*.

We shall explain the concept of a product transformation curve by an example (see figure 2.1). Consider a vehicle manufacturing firm which, when operating at full capacity, can only produce at points A, B, C, D or E in a given period. At A it could produce 1000 of the 1.5 litre cars but no 1 litre vehicles in the period. Its manpower and machinery would be fully

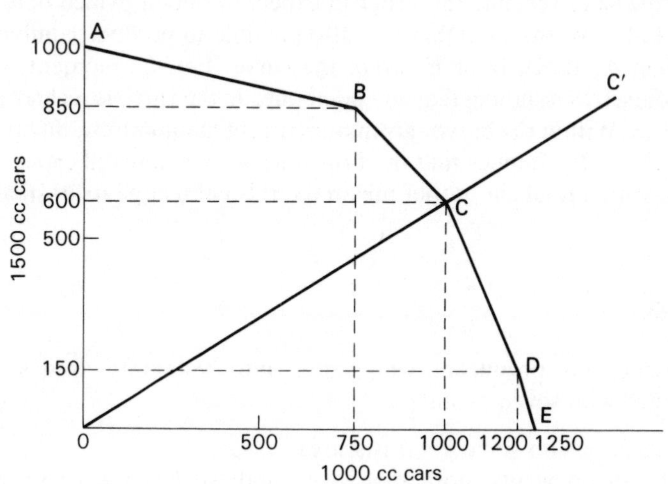

Figure 2.1 *A product transformation curve for a vehicle manufacturer*

utilized. At E, full utilization results in 1250 of the 1 litre cars being produced but no 1.5 litre cars. At points B, C and D different output combinations of the two types of car are possible. But because of technological 'lumpiness' in the equipment available to the firm it cannot move smoothly from A to any point before B. It must switch an entire group of machines over from 1.5 litre vehicles to 1.0 litre vehicles in order to operate efficiently. (A moment of thought will establish the intuitive truth of this. It would be extremely costly to switch the programming of metal cutting, boring, stamping and die-casting machines frequently from one size of car component to another.)

The curve is concave to the origin because of the *law of increasing cost* (strictly, we refer here to 'opportunity' cost, which will be discussed on p. 18 below). This law operates in the presence of heterogeneous inputs. This simply means that some machinery and men are better equipped or skilled to produce larger cars and vice versa. Thus to move from A to B the firm must forfeit the opportunity of producing 150 of the 1.5 litre cars in order to gain 750 of the 1.0 litre cars. Each 1 litre car 'costs' the firm 150/750 = 0.2 of the 1.5 litre cars in forgone production. On the other hand, if the firm moves from C to D it reduces 1.5 litre production by 450 cars and increases 1 litre production by 200 vehicles. Each 1 litre car 'costs' 2.25 of the 1.5 litre cars; there is a substantial cost increase from 0.2 to 2.25. The reason, of course, is that those (differently skilled) men and (differently designed) machines which are best suited to small-car production are transferred first (the A to B shift) and the least suitable (but most suitable for large-car production) are transferred last (the C to D shift).

Where on the product transformation curve the firm will choose to produce depends not only on the curve itself, which illustrates costs, but also on the sales revenue the firm can expect to obtain, which determines profits. Later we shall see that it is also possible to produce combinations other than A, B, C, D or E *within* the curve. For the moment, we will restrict ourselves to noting that any point outside the curve is technologically impossible. Within the curve, given our current assumptions, any point on a ray such as OC′ implies that the firm is working below full capacity, and doing so with a total car output mix in the ratio of 6 large to 10 small cars.

Exchange

Consumers and producers who enter into voluntary trades act in accordance with seven postulates:[4]

1 For each person some good is scarce.
2 Each person wants more than one good; so given scarcity, choice, competition and discrimination are necessary.
3 Each person is willing to give up some, not necessarily all, of one good

to get more (provided that that 'more' is enough) of another. The smallest amount a person would insist on getting of, say, ale to induce him to give up one cake is called the *marginal utility* of that cake measured in ale. It is also the largest amount of ale the other party to the trade would be willing to forfeit to receive one cake.

4 The more a person has of any good, the less valuable is its marginal utility. One glass of ale will quench a thirst. A second will be simply enjoyable. A third may make the drinker feel uncomfortable, and so on. Marginal utility is said to diminish. The reductions in such marginal utility of the cakes and ale are not intrinsic or related to production costs in any way. It may take the same amount of labour to make any one mud cake as it does any one fruit cake. But this is irrelevant in fixing the price at which either type of cake is traded with another person (as under postulate 3). That depends on subjective and *marginal valuations* of the cake in terms of other goods such as ale. Note also that it is the marginal unit which matters to the consumer, not the totality of units.

5 People differ in their tastes and preferences.

6 People are innovative and rational and will try to improve their position by, for example, production and exchange.

7 Decisions taken on the basis of the above postulates may eventually be regretted, or the satisfaction gained may be more than anticipated. No one has perfect knowledge of the future.

Voluntary trade occurs according to these postulates not because people have surpluses to requirements but because people have differing marginal valuations for what they exchange. For example, in figure 2.2.

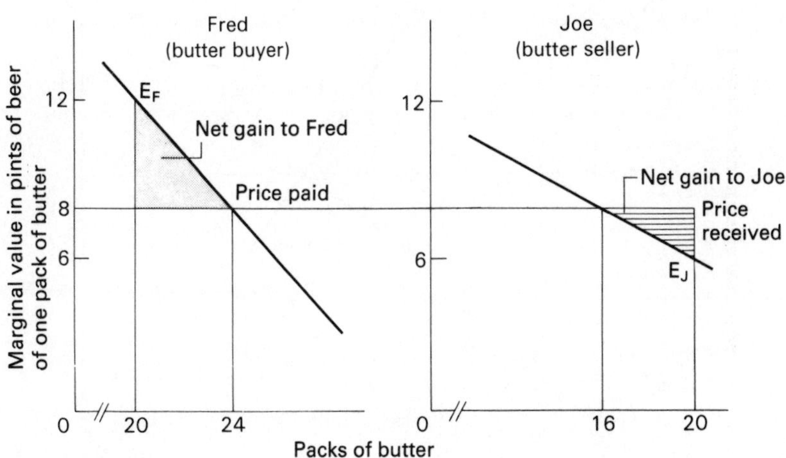

Figure 2.2 *Marginal personal value curves in mutually advantageous trading*

Fred puts a higher marginal value on a pack of butter than does Joe (12 pints of beer against 6) at the initial endowment points of E_F and E_J (12 and 6 pints of beer respectively, and 20 packets of butter each). So mutually advantageous opportunities for trade exist.

Butter will be sold to Fred by Joe until Fred's marginal utility has declined to that of Joe's. Fred values a pack of butter at 12 pints of beer and will gladly buy an extra pack at any price below 12 pints. Joe values butter at 6 pints of beer and will gladly sell a pack for any price about 6 pints. Say Joe and Fred decide to trade at a price of 8 pints of beer. Fred will buy 4 extra packs of butter worth respectively 11, 10, 9 and 8 pints of beer to him, so increasing his stock of butter to 24 packs. Joe will sell 4 packs, reducing his stock to 16. He will receive 8 pints of beer for each pack, although they were worth respectively 6.5, 7, 7.5 and 8 pints to him.

In short, Joe will get more beer (as valued by him) that his butter is worth (to him) and Fred will get more butter (as valued by him) than his beer is worth (to him). Both will benefit by an amount equal to the shaded triangles of the diagram. Trade will have benefited both just as if there had been a magical increase in the quantity of beer. Trade is as 'productive' as is manufacture.

The trading continues until both have the same marginal utilities, when no further gains from exchange are possible. Both place the same marginal value on a pack of butter. This can be seen more clearly if Joe's diagram is flipped over 180° from right to left and superimposed on Fred's in such a way that the total length of the base is the total availability of butter (40 packs) (figure 2.3). It is now easy to see that originally Fred's marginal valuation of butter is higher than Joe's and trading continues until they are equal. The intersection point, at a price of 8 pints of beer, is obviously the

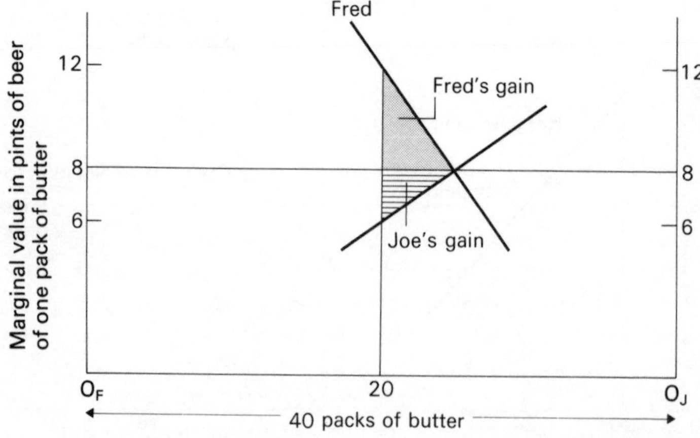

Figure 2.3 *Maximum benefit point and triangles of surplus in mutually advantageous trading*

point of maximum benefit. To the left, the gains from trade are not exhausted. To the right, both Joe and Fred are providing each other with commodities they value less than what they are acquiring. (Joe, for example, gives up a pack of butter for 8 pints of beer, but actually values his fifteenth pack of butter at 8.5 pints; Fred pays 8 pints for a pack of butter but only values his twenty-fifth pack at 7 pints.)

These marginal value lines can be regarded as *demand curves* (i.e. lines connecting points which show how much beer Fred is willing to give up to obtain each unit of the corresponding quantity of butter). In figure 2.3, Joe's demand curve is simply reinterpreted as the *supply curve* of butter to Fred (i.e. a line connecting points which show how much beer Joe must receive to provide each unit of the corresponding quantity of butter).

In conventional textbook analysis, Fred's net gain would then be defined as the *consumer surplus* triangle (i.e. the value from trading obtained over and above what he had paid for the goods). Joe's gain in figure 2.3 would then be *producer surplus*, or *profit* (see later in this chapter). If we now add every individual's demand and supply curves for butter we obtain the *market demand and supply schedules* (figure 2.4). Because barter of butter for beer is inconvenient, time consuming and unrealistic, the vertical axis is expressed in monetary units.

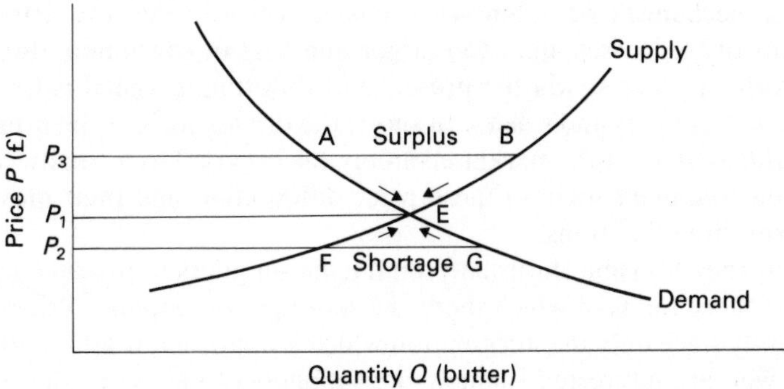

Figure 2.4 *Market demand and supply schedules*

The demand curve slopes down, other things being equal, because more people will buy at a lower price and also existing buyers will buy more. At a lower price, individuals will substitute butter for other goods, such as margarine, cheese and so on. The supply curve slopes up, other things being equal, because more people will sell butter at higher prices and existing sellers will sell more. At a higher price producers will substitute butter production for other activities such as beef production. The increased real price for butter (provided it is high enough) will encourage this substitution despite the presence and operation of either the law of diminishing returns (see chapter 4) or the law of increasing costs (see p. 12).

The Point P_3 in figure 2.4 indicates a position where the price is so high that there is a surplus of AB units of butter. At that price sellers will lower their prices to get rid of inventories; some sellers will then drop out of the market, and additional buyers will be attracted in. This process will continue until *equilibrium* is reached at E, price P_1. This is called equilibrium since below that level, at P_2, a corresponding shortage of FG would exist. The low price is encouraging high consumption but low production. Unsatisfied purchasers will start bidding prices up, some buyers will drop out of the market and the higher prices will encourage suppliers to increase their quantity supplied until equilibrium is again achieved.

It takes little additional thought to imagine what happens in markets where governments impose price floors of, say, P_3 as with equal-wage legislation, or price ceilings of, say, P_2 as with the rented housing market.

Note that the P on the vertical axis of figure 2.4 is relative price, not absolute cash price. That is, the nature of the trade-off must not be forgotten because money is being used. Thus P is not cash P, but rather cash P divided by some sort of average price for all other goods in the economy, such as for example the retail price index (RPI). For reasons of both convention and ease we shall simply label the vertical axis P, not P/RPI which would be both more correct and more meaningful.

This mechanism of voluntary exchange co-ordinates the activities of millions of businesses and even larger numbers of consumers throughout the world. It does so via the presence of differing marginal valuations of products by buyers and sellers. In short, the driving force is the presence of *price differentials*. In a market economy (as opposed to a totally centrally planned *command* society) these price differentials and their movements perform three functions.[5]

First, they transmit information inducing suppliers to produce more (or less) of those items of which there is a shortage (or surplus). Prices do this efficiently since only the information which is important is sent, and only to those who are interested (namely the suppliers of the items, the suppliers of substitutes, the purchasers of the items or the purchasers of substitutes). Traders do not need to know why the price has changed; there could be an infinite number of possible reasons. They only need to know that prices have changed and in which direction. They will then act accordingly.

Second, the information that prices transmit acts as an incentive to producers or to users not only to act but to act efficiently. In order to maximize consumers' surplus or profit, they will use available resources for their most highly valued uses. If the price of a raw material rises, manufacturers will be stimulated to economize on the use of that raw material. They will have an incentive to introduce new and less expensive methods of production. If prices rise, consumers will attempt to shift to other patterns of want satisfaction. If they remain high, resources will move into production of the highly priced (i.e. highly valued) commodity.

Wages will tend to rise and workers will transfer into that industry whose final product's (higher) price has brought this about.

Third, and this is closely related to the second point, the distribution of income will be affected. Workers and firms in industries producing relatively highly valued goods will earn greater wages and profits than labour and capital elsewhere. Admittedly this is not nirvana. All of us would like to earn the income of Sophia Loren or a diver on a North Sea oil rig. But few of us have Miss Loren's beauty or the courage and strength of a diver. In short, supply is limited but demand is relatively high. But would an oil-rig diver risk his life if the rewards were lower? Probably not. The only alternative method of allocation to that of voluntary exchange is by a central authority (see earlier).

Business Objectives

The most obvious objective of business is to maximize profit. Whether this is an end in itself, as the bold statement suggests, or whether profit is a measure of how successful the firm has been in attaining some other objective is another matter. Peter Drucker, in his book *Practice of Management*, argues that 'there is only one valid definition of business purpose: to create a customer.'[6] If a business does not produce what the market wants, it will cease to exist.

Profits, then, are the results of being in business. They test how efficiently a business has 'created a customer' (a topic discussed more fully in chapter 13). All athletes have the sole objective of winning, but different runners aim to run the 100 metres, the 200 metres or the 1500 metres as fast as possible; coming first is the common yardstick of success even though the secondary objectives (the distances) vary. So, in business, the common yardstick of success is profit. The secondary objective is to meet market demand in the firm's selected industry or industries.

What is profit? To the accountant, it is the difference between sales revenues and costs. But the definition of 'costs' can cause considerable problems. In a profit-and-loss account (see chapter 9) the bookkeeper will deduct wages, raw material costs, rent, fuel costs and so on before arriving at some net figure termed 'profit'. This 'profit' or surplus belongs to the shareholders who provided the capital in the first place. The economist would claim, however, that only part of this surplus should be regarded as profit. He would claim that the shareholder's capital, had it not been put into the business, could easily have earned interest as a straightforward risk-free loan to, say, a bank. This interest should be imputed and deducted from the accountant's surplus to give the 'true' profit (or loss).

In short, what the provider of capital would have earned anyway, without incurring any of the risks of uncertainties of business investment, should not be included as business or *economic profit*. What would have been earned anyway is the *opportunity cost* of the capital involved.

This then gives us the first hint as to how economists view profits. They not only reward efficiency in meeting market demand, but also recompense businessmen and shareholders for the assumption of *risk* (see chapters 5 and 9). No firm operates in a sure market. The fruit dealer who buys greengroceries early in the morning must resell the same day or his stock will become inedible. He assumes the risk, for example, that rain will not keep his customers indoors and so leave him with unsold produce. The pharmaceutical firm which engages in research to produce a new drug can spend millions of pounds over ten or more years and finally discover that its new product has an unexpected side-effect and so cannot be marketed (as did Fisons Ltd in 1981 with Proxicromil).

Thus the theory of profit as a reward for risk also merges into the theory of profit as a reward for innovation for being the first to introduce a new product or a new lower-cost process. In such a case, until other firms imitate the innovator, the entrepreneurial firm will earn a profit above those of its competitors. It will have a temporary monopoly until the forces of competition drive down prices and, in the colourful language of Joseph Schumpeter, the 'perennial gale of creative destruction' (i.e. competition from further innovations and imitations) washes away the monopoly profits.

These, then, are some of the theories of the nature of profit. Are they valid? Do businesses maximize profit for these reasons? Indeed, can or should businessmen maximize profits?

In recent years the professional economics literature has been full of articles on why businessmen either do not or should not maximize the profits of their firms. Whether they do is a matter of fact. Whether they should is one of opinion or of judgement. If managers do not maximize profits, even if they wish to, the reasons generally given are that they either cannot (because they do not know how) or they will not (because they prefer to strive for other objectives). If we examine these claims we may be able to judge whether profit maximization is a business goal.

Can business maximize profits?

The earliest attack on the conventional notion of the profit-maximizing businessman came from two Oxford economists, Hall and Hitch, in 1939.[7] They argued, from questionnaire evidence, that managers simply do not have the information to follow profit-maximizing price policies, and that they will accordingly use rule-of-thumb techniques such as the *cost-plus principle* (see chapter 8) to arrive at the price they will charge. In other words, they will not follow the rules of calculus, found in most economics textbooks, to set a price.

But this is not surprising! Businessmen can be successful profit maximizers without either understanding calculus or reading economics primers which purport to predict or explain their behaviour. In everyday life, businessmen make profits because they supply what consumers – you and I – want at prices we are prepared to pay. Businessmen make profits because they understand the market for their products. If they do not, they make losses. Knowledge of the calculus of economics texts is often irrelevant to them. Moreover, since firms produce today for sale tomorrow, it is the knowledge of tomorrow's market which is important to them, not economic theory about today's or yesterday's market data. Tomorrow's market knowledge is entrepreneurial foresight and is available only to those who are alert to the possibility of its existence. Most economists, calculus experts or not, do not even realize that we do not know what information the successful entrepreneur is acting upon.

This type of argument, advanced first by Ludwig von Mises[8] of Austria and latterly by Israel Kirzner,[9] did not quell the enthusiasm of the members of the 'cost-plus' school. Businessmen, they said, were self-confessedly ignorant of their situation. Their admission, in answer to the Oxford questionnaires, of ignorance about the future merely heightened the ardour of the 'they-cannot-maximize-profit' school. Some people might continue to argue that foresight was essential, but businessmen had admitted that they priced on a cost-plus-profit-margin basis.

In 1959, Herbert Simon developed a sophisticated version of this view. He alleged that businessmen operated under conditions of 'bounded rationality' (partial ignorance) and hence 'satisficed' (aimed for a satisfactory profit) and so did not maximize.

Businessmen, of course, had no more read Simon[10] or Mises than they had read or remembered their 'conventional' economics textbooks. It was left to Machlup,[11] of Princeton, to resolve the dilemma. Businessmen, he argued in 1946, could maximize profits *without* full information. Any margin over their accounting costs which they charged was not fixed but varied according to their assessment of the market. In short (successful) businessmen have an intuitive understanding of how to maximize profit even though they cannot articulate it into economists' verbal or mathematical jargon: 'all the relevant magnitudes involved – costs, revenue, profit – are subjective, that is, perceived or fancied by the men whose decisions are to be explained.'

But, said the sceptics, are modern business firms not so large that they have a multiplicity of interests and of competing managers? Do not these individuals in turn have differing personal goals? The 'organizational coalition' which emerges not only results in each manager receiving some adequate personal pecuniary or non-pecuniary satisfaction but also, in turn, forces the firm into a non-profit-maximizing position. Machlup pushed this idea tidily to one side when he compared the entrepreneur, or chief decision-maker in the firm, with a car driver. When a lorry has to be overtaken the car driver neither carries out detailed mathematical calculations nor sits down to argue out the pros and cos of how to do it with his fellow passengers. He can successfully solve the problem of how to overtake the truck subjectively and intuitively because he knows how. So the entrepreneur can maximize profits because he knows how. The unsuccessful driver who does not know how will crash. The unsuccessful businessman will make losses.

Does business maximize profits?

Many have argued that when considering objectives like profit maximization care should be taken to distinguish between the groups of people whose objectives one is considering. Most writers separate the objectives of managers from those of owners. As explained in chapter 8 managers may have goals other than to maximize profits, for example they may wish to maximize the firm's rate of growth, or sales revenue, or perquisites – provided that 'sufficient' profits are made.

When a manager is not the sole owner of a firm the managers of it are often regarded as *agents* making decisions on behalf of the owners or *principals*. The principal rewards the agents for making these decisions out of the profits which result from the agents' decisions. But there are a number of difficulties associated with this relationship as far as the principals are concerned. The agents have far more information about the firm's costs, rivals, market potential etc. than the principals do and so the latter cannot know whether the agents are doing the best possible job of managing the firm which is facing, say, a declining demand or whether the agents are pursuing their own objectives at the expense of the principals. There is information asymmetry.

Certain constraints operate on managers to reduce this loss to principals which results from the agency relationship. One constraint is the threat of takeover. If as a result of the managers' decisions the firm makes less profit than a potential acquirer thinks he can earn from the firm if he bought it, the firm may be acquired and the relatively inefficient managers ejected. However, empirical evidence by Singh[12] and others who have considered the difference between the profit rates of acquired and non-acquired firms suggests that this is a very imperfect constraint. Many non-acquired firms have earned profit rates above those of acquired firms in the same industry. A second constraint is posed by the product market. If the product market in which the firm sells its goods and services is highly competitive then price will be bid down to the level of minimum average costs (see chapter 5) and any managers who do not aim to maximize profits will therefore have costs above price and so make losses and eventually go bankrupt. However, in non-competitive product markets this effect is not so binding. Third, managers may wish to operate in a profit-maximizing way because this will impress their superiors and so may lead them to be promoted more rapidly or to be able to command a higher salary in the managerial job market. A fourth constraint is posed by the shareholders at Annual General Meetings who can vote to dismiss the Board of Directors or to force a significant policy change on them.

Should business maximize profits?

Firms, say many people, have a duty to be 'socially responsible'. They should spend their profits on anti-pollution devices, safety-improving features, 'preserving jobs', the arts or technology. Alternatively they should reduce their profits by being 'patriotic' and buy from high-cost domestic firms rather than low-cost overseas ones. Or, vice versa, profits should be passed up by refusing to sell to customers from nations whose political regimes we do not like, in favour of customers from countries with whose policies we agree.

Some or all of these goals may be laudable, but they can be achieved (if desired) by legislation which treats each firm equally without fear of favour. This is, presumably, what Milton Friedman has in mind when he says that the 'one, and only one, social responsibility of business . . . (is) to increase its profits so long as it stays within the rules of the game'.[13] He goes on: 'Few trends could so thoroughly undermine the very foundations of our free society as the acceptance by corporate officials of a social responsibility other than to make as much money for their stockholders as possible.'

Why does Friedman take this stance? Is it because businessmen would cease to direct their endeavours according to the price signals of the profit-oriented market mechanism? Prices convey messages to entrepreneurs of what is in short supply and what in surplus. If entrepreneurs interpret the price signals correctly, they make profits until prices are driven down. Forgoing the reward of maximum profits might mean taking business decisions based on other criteria. This, in turn, would mean departing from the system which has made free-enterprise economies the wealthiest in history. And this wealth has always percolated all through such societies and makes the wealthy 'mixed economy' possible. Compared with those in Britain in 1900, it is arguably that no 'average working man' had ever been better fed, housed, educated, enjoyed a higher quality of health or longer life expectancy anywhere else in the world or at any other time in human history. This could also be said in 1980 of relatively free-enterprise America.

No. Material welfare alone is not the reason for Friedman's view. Even if men were materially worse off under capitalism, one suspects he would still hold it. Mises argued that not only does equal treatment under the law maximize each individual's productivity and so his private interests; it also promotes 'the maintenance of social peace' if class privileges disappear and so 'conflict over them . . . cease(s)'.

Even more appositely from the viewpoint of the firm, any failure to maximize profit is the equivalent of taxing the shareholder. The use of the profit cushion to fund managerial objectives of any sort other than that which the shareholder, as an individual, would approve of if he had his own money in his own pocket to dispose of is the equivalent of allowing A to spend B's money on B's behalf! This is a privilege generally allowed only to parents and governments.

References

1 A. Smith, *The Wealth of Nations* (1776), book 4, chapter 8, Penguin, 1970, p. 516.
2 Central Statistical Office, *Standard Industrial Classification: Revised 1980*, HMSO, 1979.
3 R. Bacon and W. Ellis, 'How growth in public expenditure has contributed to Britain's difficulties', in *The Dilemmas of Government Expenditure*, IEA Readings 15, Institute of Economic Affairs, 1976, p. 4.
4 This section is adapted from A. A. Alahian and W. R. Allen, *University Economics*, Wadsworth, 1977.
5 M. Friedman, *Free to Choose*, Pelican, 1980, pp. 33–44.
6 P. Drucker, *Practice of Management*, Pan, 1968, p. 52.
7 R. L. Hall and C. J. Hitch, 'Price theory and business behaviour', *Oxford Economic Papers* 2 (1939), pp. 21–39.
8 L. von Mises, *Human Action*, Henry Regnery, 1963.
9 I. Kirzner, *Competition and Entrepreneurship*, University of Chicago Press, 1971.
10 H. A. Simon, 'Rationality as process and as product of thought', *American Economic Review* 87 (1987), pp. 1–29.
11 F. Machlup, 'Marginal analysis and empirical research', *American Economic Review* 36 (1946), pp. 519–54.
12 A. Singh, *Takeovers*, Cambridge University Press, 1971.
13 M. Friedman, *Capitalism and Freedom*, University of Chicago Press, 1962.

Further reading

R. Clarke and T. McGuinness, *The Economics of the Firm*, Basil Blackwell, 1987.
A. Nove, *The Soviet Economic System*, Allen & Unwin, 3rd edn, 1986.

3

Prices and Demand

Although modern understanding of the role of prices and markets has its ancestry, not surprisingly, in the work of many great economists, not least Adam Smith, it bears strong impressions of the work of Marshall.[1] We shall return, therefore, to Marshall's timeless reminder: 'The laws of economics are to be compared with the laws of the tides, rather than with the simple and exact law of gravitation. For the actions of men are so various and uncertain, that the best statement of tendencies which we can make in a science of human conduct must needs be inexact and faulty.'[2]

We need to bear these warnings in mind as we analyse the workings of prices and markets in this chapter. In many senses, price theory is central to the understanding of economic problems. We saw in chapter 2 that the basis of the economic problem is the choice between alternatives, and to solve this choice the following are needed: a preference scale which guides the act of choice; a knowledge of the terms on which alternatives are available: and an understanding of the volume of scarce resources available. Given this information, the problem of 'the scarcity of given means for the attainment of given ends', as Robbins pithily put it, can be solved.[3] Within the mixed economy the price system has a major role to play in providing a solution via the 'higgling and bargaining' of the market-place.

The term *market* is to be interpreted in a broad sense as referring to any mechanism by which the buyers and sellers of a particular *commodity* are brought into contact. It might be a public place, such as the market for vegetable produce in a local area, or it might be the linkage of dealers in commodities such as Stock Exchange securities, money market instruments, precious metals and the like; such linkages, given the advantages of modern communications, frequently stretch around the world. As long as the prices of the same 'goods' tend to equality quickly, and reflect the forces of supply and demand across the market, then the market functions effectively, no matter what the extent of its physical scope.

The Determinants of Demand

At any particular time the demand for a particular good or service by an individual economic agent – be it a consumer, firm or household – is likely to be determined by the complex interaction of a number of factors. These are likely to include the price of the good itself, the prices of other goods, the size of the consumer's income and the nature of his or her taste. These are expressed in the following formulation:

$$Q^{D}_{i,k} = F(P_i, P_j, Y_k, T_k) \tag{3.1}$$

where $Q^{D}_{i,k}$ is the quantity demanded of good i by consumer k, P_i is the price of good i, P_j is the price of good j, Y_k is the income of consumer k and T_k is the taste of consumer k.

The problems arise from the difficulty of simultaneously handling the impact of these factors. The normal practice is to isolate the impact of one whilst assuming that the effects of the others are constant – the economist's famous 'other things being equal' or *ceteris paribus* clause – and to continue in this fashion, examining the influence of each in turn.

Table 3.1 *An individual's monthly demand schedule for apples*

Price of apples (pence per kg)	Quantity consumed (kg per month)
175	0
150	0.5
125	1.0
100	1.5
75	2.0
50	2.5
25	3.0
20	3.5
15	4.0

If we start first with the price of the good, it is probable that, if requested, a consumer could construct a schedule showing how the quantity he would demand of the good would alter as a function of its price, assuming that all the other factors remained constant. In table 3.1 we have constructed a hypothetical individual's demand schedule for apples over a period of a month. It is important to remember that demand is a flow, and measures continuous purchases over a period rather than isolated ones.

The First Law of Demand

The normal pattern we would expect is that the quantity demanded of a good is inversely related to its price: the higher the price the lower the quantity demanded, as shown in figure 3.1. If we added together the individual demand schedule for all the consumers who purchase apples in a particular market, we would have the market demand schedule, and it, too, would display the similar property of sloping downwards from left to right. This is sometimes referred to as the *first law of demand*. It has to be borne in mind that we are concerned here with effective demand, i.e. preferences backed up by purchasing power. Many of us might like to drive round in a Rolls-Royce but not many of us are effectively in the market for Rolls-Royces.

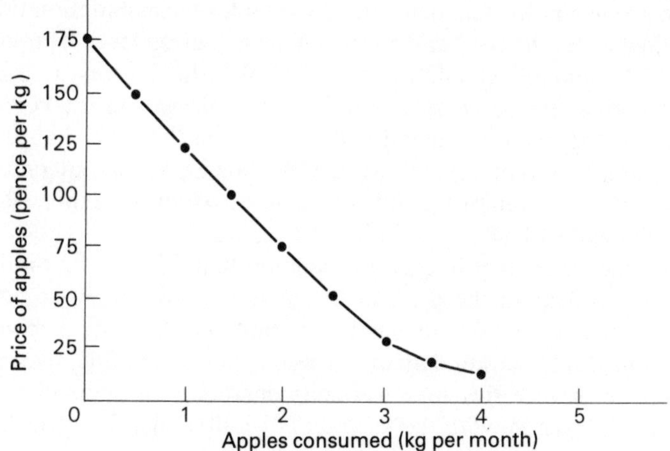

Figure 3.1 *An individual's monthly demand curve for apples*

To return to Marshall's caution about the nature of economic 'laws', do demand curves always slope downwards? Liebenstein has demonstrated that this boils down to a basic question about the additive properties of individual demand schedules.[4]

The additive properties of individual demand schedules

The usual assumption is that individual demand curves can be horizontally summed to produce a market demand curve for the good concerned. This approach assumes that each consumer's satisfaction associated with the consumption of the good is completely independent of the number of other consumers purchasing the same good. Liebenstein terms this approach a functional view of demand, which interprets demand as being based upon qualities inherent in the commodity itself.[5] But what if there are external or non-functional effects? He suggests the following have an impact on utility: (a) the bandwagon effect, (b) the snob effect and (c) the Veblen effect.

Liebenstein's reservations

The bandwagon effect

The bandwagon effect refers to the extent to which the demand for a commodity is increased because other people are purchasing the same good. It represents the desire to be fashionable. Given this assumption, each individual consumer's demand schedule is likely to be influenced by the level of overall demand in the market. We could analyse this by drawing up such individual demand curves under the assumption that each person thinks that the market demand will be at a given level. The summing of all these demand schedules in the usual fashion gives us a market demand such as curve D_a in figure 3.2. D_a is drawn on the consumer's assumption that market demand will be OA. On the other hand, if consumers assume market demand to be OB, then D_b is the outcome. And, likewise, D_n is the sum of the individual curves when consumers assume a market demand of ON.

If consumers are right in their expectation that OA will be the level of market demand, then the price in the market would be P_1 at point E_a. Curve D_a then traces out demand at various market prices, given that assumption. But if market demand turns out to be, say, OB, then as soon as consumers realize this they will start operating on demand curve D_b since this is consistent with the view that overall demand is OB. Again, if

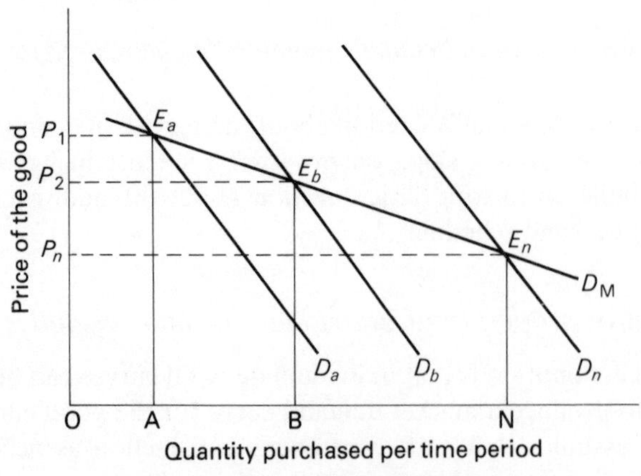

Figure 3.2 *The bandwagon effect*

they are correct in this, there is only one price which is consistent with demand curve D_b and a level of market demand OB and that is price P_2. Given knowledge of market demand, one point only on each of these 'demand curves' is operative, and a line joining these unique points, marked D_M, traces out the true market demand curve taking into account the bandwagon effect.

The effect in this case leads to a market demand curve which is much more responsive to changes in price (i.e. is more elastic; see later in this chapter) than the simple adding of individuals' demand schedules would suggest.

The snob effect

The snob effect can be seen as the reverse of the bandwagon effect. Once again we assume that the demand schedule of an individual consumer is influenced both by the price of the good and by his estimate of the size of the overall market demand. But in this case the relationship between the size of the market and the quantity demanded is reversed. The snob prefers exclusivity and hence the larger the estimated size of the market the less inclined he is to buy. The analysis proceeds exactly as before. It is assumed that it is possible to draw up an individual's demand schedule on the basis that market demand is expected to be at a particular level, and that all such individual curves can be summed to produce a market demand curve. Thus D_a in figure 3.3 represents the market demand for the good given the consumer's expectation that the overall market size is OA, and so on, as previously. Once again only one price is consistent with curves D_a, D_b and

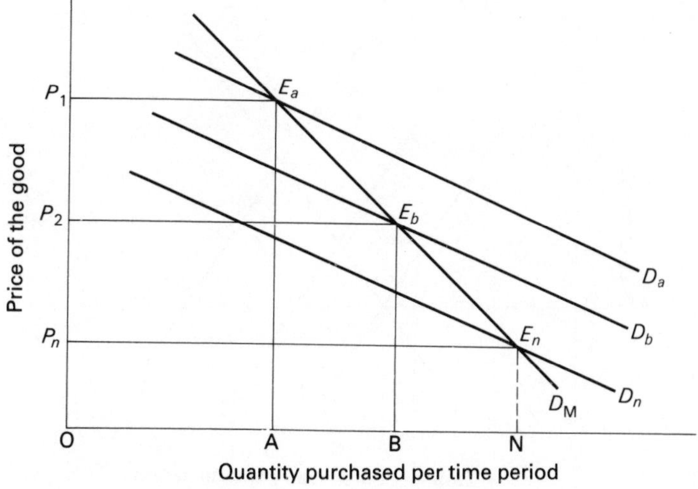

Figure 3.3 *The snob effect*

D_n respectively. This is so since consumers switch to the relevant alternative demand curve once they realize that market size is different from either OA, OB or ON. The only difference from the bandwagon effect is that, as the level of market size increases, the true market demand schedule falls more rapidly, at all prices, as some snobs drop out of the market which they regard as becoming less exclusive.

Once again Liebenstein concludes that simply adding individual demand schedules, ignoring what he calls external effects, leads to an inaccurate estimation of demand and, in this case, demand is less responsive (i.e. less elastic; see later in this chapter) to a price change than otherwise would be predicted.

The Veblen effect

Finally Liebenstein describes the Veblen effect, which is based upon Veblen's theory of conspicuous consumption.[6] Here we distinguish between the good's functional utility and the utility attached to its price; the latter may be considered the conspicuous consumption element. It is the conspicuous component of price which allegedly matters; it is assumed that the higher the conspicuous price the more other people are impressed, and so the greater the satisfaction of the purchaser.

Each consumer has a demand schedule. On the basis of expected conspicuousness of price, prices could be termed P_1, P_2 and P_n, and these curves can be aggregated to produce market demand curves D_1, D_2 and D_n, depending on the conspicuous price. Again, only one point on these aggregated demand curves is relevant, as shown in figure 3.4. If consumers

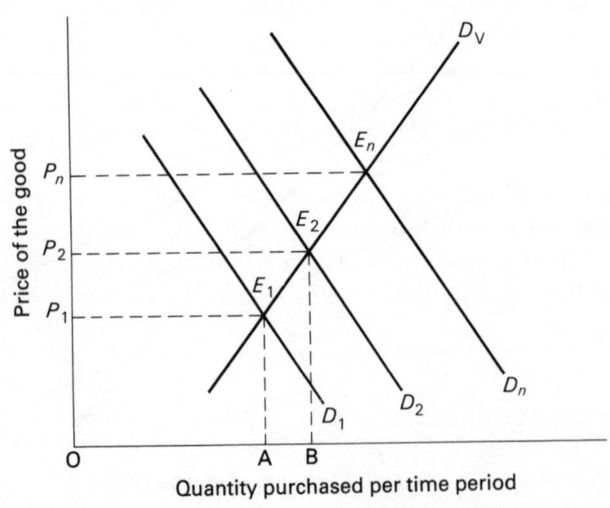

Figure 3.4 *The Veblen effect*

expect the conspicuous price to be P_1, the demand curve will be D_1, but if it turns out to be P_2, they will move up to operate on demand curve D_2, and so on. If conspicuous consumption is an important determinant of demand for the good, the higher the conspicuous price the higher the demand at all price levels. A line can then be drawn through the expected conspicuous price level of each of these demand curves and this produces the 'true' demand curve D_V. The remarkable feature of this demand curve is that it is upward sloping.

This suggests that an upward-sloping demand curve is conceivable, at least for certain ranges of prices on certain luxury goods. If the price of the good is reduced sufficiently we might expect more normal consumers to enter the market; they will not be concerned with conspicuous effects, the Veblen effect will be reduced to zero, and the customary downward-sloping demand curve will emerge.

Does the 'first law of demand' hold?

We have seen that, in certain circumstances, demand curves might indeed slope upwards, that adding individual demand schedules does not necessarily lead to a clear picture of market demand if there are external effects. It is also conceivable that all these external effects might be operating simultaneously and, to a certain extent, counterbalancing. However, these effects explicitly occur only when other things are not equal, so the first law of demand still holds.

It is true also that short-term speculative effects might lead to a temporary increase in quantity demanded, as people lay in stocks in anticipation of a price rise (the useful role of speculators is dealt with more fully in chapter 7). Even here, however, the first law is not violated, since people are buying more today at a lower price than tomorrow's price is expected to be. We are forced into considering again Marshall's previously quoted analogy of economic laws and the tides. Demand curves usually slope downwards and our customary analysis usually holds, although, like the phases of the moon, markets vary and our analysis will have greater or less force. What is critical is to ensure that the conditions required are met. Thus the market response to a drop in price, other things being equal, is an increase in quantity demanded. The responsiveness of quantity demanded to changes in price is termed the *price elasticity of demand* (see later in this chapter).

Utility and the Theory of Demand

Much of the early work on price theory centred on the use of utility theory. Smith, in his famous water–diamond paradox, pointed out the difference between value in use and value in exchange: 'Nothing is more useful than water: but it will purchase scarce anything, scarce anything can be had in exchange for it. A diamond, on the contrary, has scarce any value in use; but a very great quantity of other goods may frequently be had in exchange for it.'[7] The neoclassicals, then, writing 150 years later, concentrated on the concept of utility as an explanation of the force behind individual consumer demand.

The focus was placed on marginal utility, or the addition to total satisfaction derived from purchasing and consuming an additional unit of a good. The view taken was that 'there is an endless variety of wants but a limit to each separate want', and, thus continued Marshall, 'the total utility of a thing to anyone . . . increases with every increase in his stock of it, but not as fast as his stock increases.'[8]

The basis of the *law of diminishing marginal utility* has already been outlined in the seven postulates on personal utility and valuation discussed in chapter 2.

If we ignore the practical difficulties of measuring utility and make the further assumption that the marginal utility of money is constant, we can shift to thinking in terms of the utility of the last pence spent on purchasing the last unit of a good. If overall satisfaction is to be maximized from the purchase of a bundle or collection of goods in a given period, then it follows that the last pence spent on the purchase of the last unit of any of the goods purchased in the period must yield equal marginal utility. If utilities at the margin are not equal, a rearrangement of the pattern of purchases will increase overall satisfaction. The scope for this will continue until equality is achieved at the margin. Thus we have in equilibrium – when an individual's purchases yield maximum satisfaction – the following condition:

$$\frac{\mathrm{MU_Y}}{P_\mathrm{Y}} = \frac{\mathrm{MU_Z}}{P_\mathrm{Z}} = \frac{\mathrm{MU_N}}{P_\mathrm{N}} \tag{3.2}$$

where $\mathrm{MU_Y}$, $\mathrm{MU_Z}$, $\mathrm{MU_N}$ are the marginal utilities of good Y, good Z, good N etc. and P_Y, P_Z, P_N are the prices of good Y, good Z, good N etc.

If we concentrate on the equilibrium conditions for two goods X and Y, we can examine the implications of a change in price of one of the goods. Suppose that initially, at a price of P_X1 for good X and P_Y1 for good Y, the equilibrium conditions are met. So we have

$$\frac{\mathrm{MU_Y}}{P_\mathrm{Y1}} = \frac{\mathrm{MU_X}}{P_\mathrm{X1}}.$$

Then the price of good X falls to P_X2. If this happens our former equality no longer holds and we have

$$\frac{\mathrm{MU_X}}{P_\mathrm{X2}} > \frac{\mathrm{MU_Y}}{P_\mathrm{Y1}}.$$

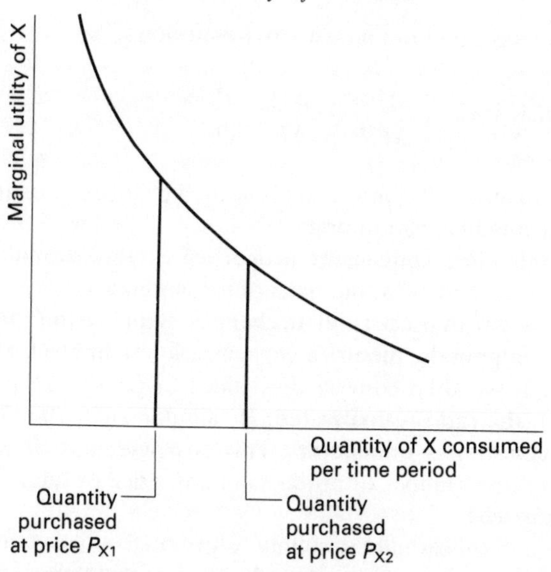

Figure 3.5 *Diminishing marginal utility*

Total utility on the part of our consumer can now be increased by rearranging his expenditure pattern. He can now increase purchases of good X so that its marginal utility falls (as we can see from figure 3.5) until it has fallen sufficiently to restore the equality of

$$\frac{MU_X}{P_{X2}} = \frac{MU_Y}{P_{Y1}}.$$

If a fall in the price of good X leads to an increase in the demand for it by an individual consumer, then, other things being equal, it should also hold for all consumers; once again we have established that demand curves slope downwards from left to right. Given that the marginal utility of each extra purchase of good X diminishes, we are led to wonder to what extent the demand for good X increases following a price fall; this leads us back to consideration of the price elasticity of demand.

Price Elasticity of Demand

Price elasticity of demand, usually symbolized by the Greek letter η, is defined as the proportional change in quantity demanded in response to a proportional change in price.

$$\text{price elasticity of demand } (\eta) = \frac{\text{relative change in quantity demanded}}{\text{corresponding relative change in price}}.$$

Symbolically we could define elasticity as follows:

$$\text{elasticity } (\eta) = \frac{\Delta Q/Q}{\Delta P/P} = \frac{\Delta Q}{\Delta P} \frac{P}{Q} \qquad (3.3)$$

where Q is quantity, P is price, ΔQ is a small change in quantity purchased and ΔP is a small change in price.

One of the most convenient properties of this formula is that it is completely independent of the units of measurement adopted, since it is a ratio concerned with proportionate changes. Suppose the price of the good was initially in pounds; the price change ratio might be, for example, $\Delta P/P = £1/£20$. If we then convert the values to pence, $\Delta P/P = (1 \times 100\text{p})/(20 \times 100\text{p})$; the ratio is unaffected. By similar logic, the unit adopted to measure quantities is immaterial. This is convenient because the price elasticities of any number of products in any price or quantity unit can be directly compared.

Suppose a businessman is selling a product which faces the market demand schedule shown in table 3.2. The graph of this market demand schedule produces the demand curve shown in figure 3.6.

Table 3.2 *Market demand schedule for good X*

Price of X (pence)	Quantity of X demanded in market (kg)
100	0
90	100
80	200
70	300
60	400
50	500
40	600
30	700
20	800
10	900
0	1000

As the relationship between demand for X and its price is a linear one, revealed by the fact that the demand curve in figure 3.6 is a straight line, we could summarize the relationship by writing the appropriate equation:

$$P = 100 - \frac{1}{10}Q. \qquad (3.4)$$

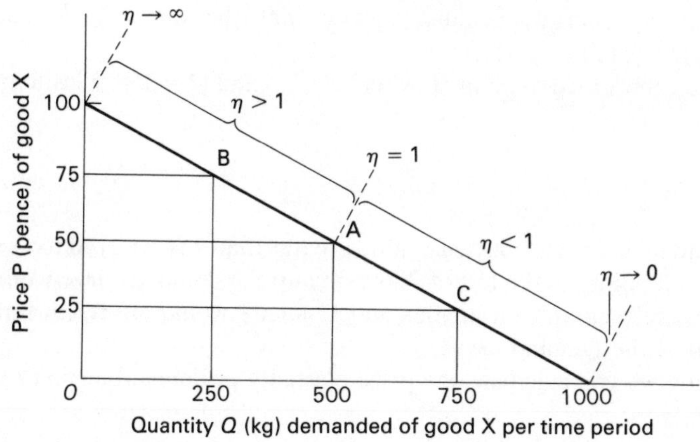

Figure 3.6 *The demand curve for table 3.2, showing elasticity ranges*

In this, admittedly artificial, example we can see that, if nothing is to be demanded, the price will be 100p, and that 1000 kg will be demanded at a zero price. The slope of the demand curve is given by

$$\text{slope} = \frac{\text{change in price}}{\text{change in quantity}} = -\frac{1}{10}.$$

In this case a fall in price of 1p leads to an increase in demand of 10 kg and so the slope is $-1/10$. The slope is negative since the normal relationship is that a fall in price leads to an increase in the quantity demanded. A straight line has a constant slope which, in this case, can be defined as the ratio $\Delta P/\Delta Q$, the change in price divided by the change in quantity demanded in response to that change in price.

If we return to consideration of the elasticity formula in expression (3.3), we see that this formula uses the inverse of the slope, $\Delta Q/\Delta P$, which in this case is -10. This is a constant, but the other constituents of the elasticity formula, P and Q, are inversely related and their values change as we move up or down the demand curve. From this it follows that elasticity is not a constant but varies as we so move. (This is always the case unless we have a demand curve whose slope changes in such a way that changes in the relative proportions of P and Q exactly offset each other.)

Suppose we wish to calculate the price elasticity of demand at point A on the demand curve in figure 3.6; in this case $P = 50$ and $Q = 500$. Reference to our price elasticity formula gives

$$\eta_A = \frac{\Delta Q}{\Delta P}\frac{P}{Q} = -10\ \frac{50}{500} = -1.$$

At point A we see that price elasticity of demand is unitary, i.e. equal to (−)1. (The usual convention is to ignore the minus sign; price elasticity of demand is generally negative, given that the quantity demanded is inversely related to price.)

Let us now move to point B, where $P = 75$ and $Q = 250$. Elasticity at this point is

$$\eta_B = -10 \frac{75}{250} = (-)\ 3.$$

Demand at any price elasticity value greater than 1 is referred to as elastic; in fact, all points to the left of A moving up the demand curve would have progressively greater elasticities and elasticity would approach infinity at the top of the demand curve.

Finally we can calculate the price elasticity of demand at point C:

$$\eta_C = -10 \frac{25}{750} = (-)\ \frac{1}{3}.$$

At point C demand is inelastic, having a value of 1/3. Demand at any elasticity less than 1 is regarded as being inelastic, and as we move down a linear demand curve, to the right of point A, elasticity continually diminishes until it approaches zero at the bottom of the curve.

Well, where does all this get us? The point is that price elasticity of demand has important implications for the changes in revenue that a businessman can expect from revising his prices. The demand curve is often termed the *average revenue curve*, since it depicts the price of the good or average revenue per number of units sold that he can expect from placing a given number of units on the market. Total sales revenue is given by price multiplied by the number of units sold at that price. If we return to figure 3.6, we can see that, at point B, price $P = 75$p and quantity sold $Q = 250$ kg. Total revenue is given by $P \times Q = 250 \times 75 = £187.50$. Total revenue is shown by the rectangle under the demand curve, with its corner touching at point B, linking the price of 75p with the quantity demanded of 250 kg.

Suppose now that our businessman has decided to drop the price to 50p but wonders what the effect on total revenue will be. Total revenue now equals 50p $\times$ 500 = £250. Total revenue has increased, and in fact at point A, where $\eta = 1$, it is maximized. This makes sense when we pause to consider the definition of elasticity; it measures the proportionate response in quantity demanded to the corresponding relative change in price. If price elasticity is greater than 1 there will be a more than proportionate response in the quantity demanded. Thus as long as $\eta > 1$, a price cut will increase total revenue. Where $\eta = 1$ total revenue is maximized, and any further price cutting when $\eta < 1$ will only serve to reduce total revenue. Indeed, in figure 3.6 we can see that at point C, where price has been reduced to 25p, total revenue falls back to £187.5.

It would not be sensible for a profit-maximizing businessman to lower his prices if he is operating in the inelastic range of his demand curve. Some products, such as necessities, will have relatively inelastic demand since they have to be bought whatever the price. Luxury items will have a more elastic demand and so the market will be more price sensitive. Relatively inexpensive products tend to have inelastic demand: if there is a price rise, it is not worth going to the trouble of finding an alternative (if the price of household salt doubled, this would probably not have a very significant effect on quantity demanded). Various extreme examples of demand curves of varying elasticities are shown in figure 3.7.

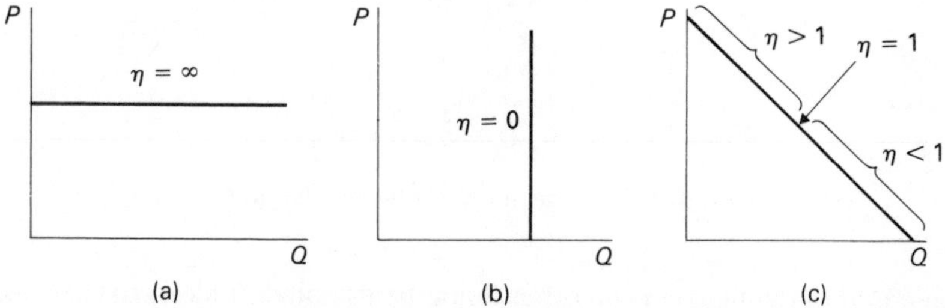

Figure 3.7 *Demand curves of varying elasticity: (a) completely elastic; (b) completely inelastic; (c) varying elasticity (normal case)*

The Second Law of Demand

It is generally accepted that the price elasticity of demand for any product is likely to increase with the time for which a price change persists. There are various reasons why this is likely to be the case. Many purchases are customary or habitual. Consumers have to adjust their spending patterns following a price change, and there will be a certain amount of inertia before they get round to reappraising the relative merits of the various commodities available in the light of the price change. Time is not a free good and there is an opportunity cost for the time spent on seeking market intelligence in terms of the other productive ways in which that time could be spent. Furthermore, markets are imperfect in the sense that information regarding price cuts is not instantaneously available to all, so there will be a lag before the price information seeps through to all potential customers.

A further impact is made by technological considerations. The demand for many products is a derived demand. We do not demand electricity for its own intrinsic merits but for the use to which it can be put in powering electric lights, hi-fi systems, heating appliances etc. There would be a considerable lag before a fall in electricity prices leads to increased consumption via the purchase of electrical central heating, new hi-fi systems and the like.

The *second law of demand* states that price elasticity of demand is likely to be greater in the long run than in the short run. It suggests that the

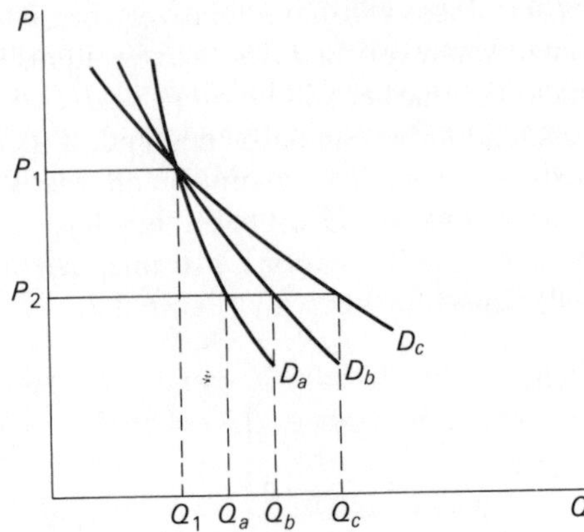

Figure 3.8 *The second law of demand*

behaviour of demand curves, other things being equal, is likely to vary over time as shown in figure 3.8.

In this figure the initial point of equilibrium is P_1, Q_1 on the initial demand curve D_a. The immediate response to a drop in price from P_1 to P_2 is an increase in the quantity demanded from Q_1 to Q_a. After a passage of time the market behaves as if it is now operating on demand curve D_b rather than D_a and the quantity demanded rises to Q_b. After a further passage of time the quantity demanded increases to Q_c.

We now reconsider our original consumer demand function, expression (3.1). We are reminded that so far we have only explored the impact of the price of the good itself on quantity demanded although, in our treatment of the second law of demand, we moved away from this and examined other long-term effects that actually shift the demand curve. Strictly speaking, changes in the price of the good itself, other things being equal, do not shift the demand curve (in the short term) but lead to movements up or down an existing demand curve. The other factors we shall now consider – the prices of other goods, consumer incomes and consumer tastes – all lead to shifts in the actual curve itself. We shall first examine the effects of changes in the prices of other goods.

Changes in the Prices of Substitutes and Complements

Changes in the prices of other goods Y are likely to have an impact on the quantity demanded of the original good X if the other goods are either substitutes or complements. We define X and Y as *substitutes* when an increase in the price of one leads to an increase in the consumption of the other. A typical example would be butter and margarine. On the other hand, some goods – such as petrol and cars – are complements, purchased for joint consumption. We define X and Y as *complements* when an increase in the price of one leads to a decrease in the consumption of the other. An increase in the price of petrol will reduce the demand for cars as more people walk, cycle or use public transport.

The extent to which goods are substitutes or complements can be measured by their *cross-elasticity of demand*, defined as

$$\text{cross-elasticity of demand} = \frac{\Delta Q_X / Q_X}{\Delta P_Y / P_Y} = \frac{\Delta Q_X}{\Delta P_Y} \frac{P_Y}{Q_X} \tag{3.5}$$

where ΔQ_X is the change in quantity demanded of good X, Q_X is the original quantity of good X demanded, ΔP_Y is a small change in the price of good Y and P_Y is the original price of good Y.

Cross-elasticity of demand measures the relative change in quantity demanded of good X in response to a relative change in the price of good Y. Goods which are substitutes will have positive cross-elasticities of demand, since an increase in the price of one will lead to an increase in the quantity demanded of the other. Complements will have a negative cross-elasticity of demand, since an increase in the price of a complement leads to a fall in demand for related goods. If two goods are unrelated, their cross-elasticity will be approximately zero.

Changes in the prices of substitutes can shift the entire market demand curve. An increase in the price of substitutes or a fall in the price of complements should lead to more of the good being demanded at all prices, and therefore the demand curve shifts bodily to the right. This is an increase in demand. A fall in demand would be caused by either a fall in the price of substitutes or a rise in the price of complements. In this case the demand curve would shift bodily to the left.

Changes in Consumer Incomes

The relationship between household expenditure on a good and the level of household income can be illustrated via the use of an Engel curve, shown in figure 3.9. The normal relationship is that increases in income are associated with a rise in expenditure on the good. However, in the case of inferior goods, expenditure on the good might fall as income rises. This was pointed out by the Victorian economist Giffen, who argued that the labouring poor in the nineteenth century subsisted on the cheapest diet available – which might consist mainly of bread. A rise in their income would lead not to an increase in consumption of bread but to the substitution of other preferred foods, such as meat, and a reduction in the consumption of bread.

The relationship between changes in income and changes in a consumer's expenditure on a good is measured by the income elasticity of the good η_Y, defined as

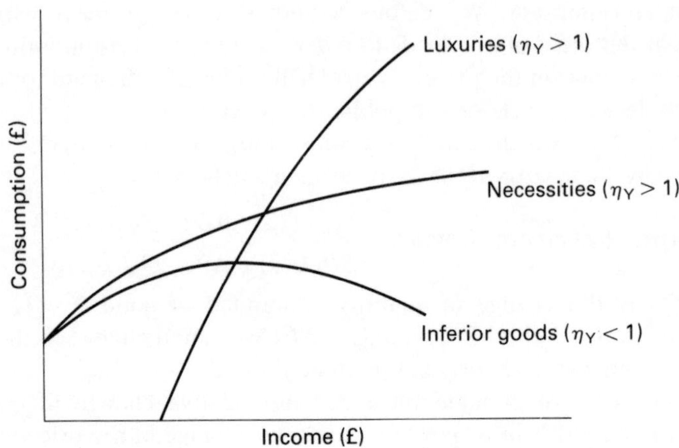

Figure 3.9 *Engel curves for a hypothetical household*

$$\text{income elasticity } (\eta_Y) = \frac{\text{relative change in the quantity of the good demanded}}{\text{relative change in income}}$$

$$= \frac{\Delta Q_X/Q_X}{\Delta Y/Y} = \frac{\Delta Q_X}{\Delta Y} \quad \frac{Y}{Q_X} \tag{3.6}$$

where ΔQ_X is a small change in the quantity of good X consumed, Q_X is the original quantity of good X consumed, ΔY is a small change in the consumer's income and Y is the original level of the consumer's income.

Income and quantity consumed typically move in the same direction, and so in the normal case η_Y is positive. In figure 3.9 we can see that at low levels of income there is no expenditure on luxuries but, once income reaches a sufficient level, expenditure increases on them very rapidly indeed. The income elasticity of demand for cars, audio equipment, air travel, holidays abroad etc. is likely to be positive and high. The income elasticity of demand for necessities such as basic foodstuffs is likely to be positive but it will have a very low value since, for any given individual or household, there is a limit to the amount of these items required. On the other hand, inferior goods will have a negative income elasticity of demand since consumers will switch to other, preferred, goods as their income increases and they can afford them.

The income elasticity of demand for a manufacturer's product is an important piece of information, particularly when he is trying to forecast levels of future demand (see chapter 7). A low income elasticity means that, to a certain extent, he will be insulated from the vicissitudes of the cycle of business activity in the economy. The manufacturer of foodstuffs can rest assured that, even when unemployment is high and increases in the level of incomes are constrained, people still have to eat. The provider of luxuries will have to pay careful attention to forecasts of the future level of economic activity, and, although he is likely to do well on the upswings, times will be hard on the downswings of economic activity.

Income and substitution effects

Now that we have considered the effects of changes in incomes on demand we can digress for a moment and return to the consideration of the effects of a fall in price of the original good. It is suggested that the effect of the fall in price of a good can be divided into an income effect and a substitution effect. If there is a reduction in the price of a good that a consumer habitually consumes, the effect is similar to an increase in his income. He can buy everything that he did previously and still have some money left to spend if he does not change his expenditure pattern. The fact that he still has some financial resources left leads to an income effect, since the result is indistinguishable from an increase in income.

The substitution effect arises from the fact that the good is now relatively cheaper than other commodities. This leads to an increase in the quanitity demanded by the consumer.

The income effect is either positive or negative. We have seen that, usually, increases in income lead to an increase in the quantity demanded, but, in the case of inferior goods, the reverse could happen. Increases in income could lead to the substitution of preferred but more expensive goods. The substitution effect is always positive, but, in the case of an inferior good, the negative income effect could be sufficiently large to overcome this and lead to an overall fall in the quantity demanded after a price fall.

The sum of the two effects will lead to the change in the quantity that the consumer demands in response to the price change.

Changes in Tastes

The factors that shape consumer tastes and preferences are many and varied. They include socio-economic factors – such as age, sex, education, marital status, position in the domestic life cycle (e.g. newly married, a growing family or middle-aged with no child dependents) – and financial factors, such as the disposition of wealth between liquid and illiquid assets. Tastes can change as the result of innovation and advertising (see chapter 13) or, more fundamentally, as the result of changing values and priorities and of rising living standards. Conversely, the existence of stable habits means that the effects of changes in prices, incomes or other variables might be not immediate but subject to a time lag.

Whatever the cause, the effect of a change in tastes in favour of a good is unequivocal; it will move the entire demand curve to the right so that more is demanded at every price level than previously. Conversely, a change in tastes against a good will move the entire demand curve to the left with the reverse effect.

Conclusion

We have now considered all the factors which might affect consumer demand for a good. These included the prices of substitutes and complements, changes in consumer income, and changes in consumer tastes. Their effects are summarized in figure 3.10.

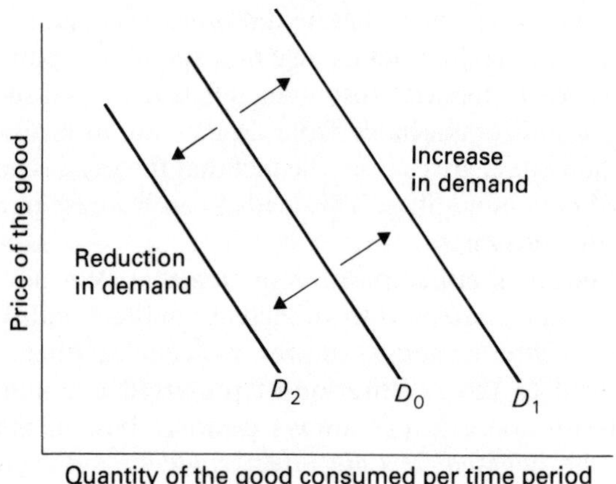

Figure 3.10 *Shifts in demand*

In figure 3.10 the original demand curve is D_0. If there is an increase in demand, it moves to the right, to D_1. If there is a decrease in demand, it moves to the left, to D_2. The factors which could cause such shifts are summarized below:

Decrease in demand	*Increase in demand*
Fall in the price of substitutes	Rise in the price of substitutes
Rise in the price of complements	Fall in the price of complements
Fall in consumer income (normal goods)	Rise in consumer income (normal goods)
Change in tastes against the good	Change in tastes in favour of the good

These effects must not be confused with the effect of a change in the price of the good itself. This leads to movements up and down the original demand curve, not to shifts of it.

There are a few other obvious factors which will also contribute to a determination of the overall size of the market itself. Demographic and socio-economic factors are obviously important: for example, the overall size of the population and its distribution into age groups; the distribution of income and the relative proportions of the various income groups; the age structure of the population; the incidence of marriage; and preferences in family size. All these factors will influence the number of potential consumers in a market.

The geographical area of a market will depend on the price of the commodity and the cost of transportation. The higher the price, the larger the area of supply but the less concentrated the likely demand. The qualities of the product have a major influence. High-value, non-perishable, cheaply transportable commodities – such as financial securities, precious metals, currencies etc. – will have one market which effectively spans the world, in the absence of artificial restrictions. Bulky perishable commodities will have markets that are more localized, but even here advances in transportation and refrigeration mean that Spanish tomatoes and French lettuces can vie with local varieties. Perhaps a better example is given by the housing market, which is usually local. The costs of transportation of tenants is relatively high, yet, even so, commuters travel long distances to London. Nevertheless, there are substantial regional disparities in housing prices, reflecting local differences in supply and demand.

In the next chapter we consider the supply side rather than the demand side of markets. This involves us in considering production and cost. The car markets of Edinburgh and London are considered as separate from the viewpoint of buyers – but not from the viewpoint of manufacturers, who will perhaps have one production plant to serve the entire British Isles. However, the various factors which affect the extent of markets will be considered more fully in chapter 7, which considers demand forecasting.

References

1 A. Marshall, *Principles of Economics* (1890), Macmillan, 9th edn, 1961.
2 Marshall, *Principles of Economics*, book 1, chapter 3.
3 L. Robbins, *An Essay on the Nature and Significance of Economic Science*, Macmillan, 1935, p. 36.
4 H. Liebenstein, 'Bandwagon, snob and Veblen effects in the theory of consumer's demand', *Quarterly Journal of Economics* (1950), pp. 183–207.
5 Ibid.
6 T. Veblen, *The Theory of the Leisure Class* (1899), Allen & Unwin, 1971.
7 A. Smith, *The Wealth of Nations* (1776), book 1, chapter 4, Penguin, 1970.
8 Marshall, *Principles of Economics*, book 3, chapter 3.

4

Production and Costs

The economic theory of production provides a complement to the theory of demand. Given the firm's objectives and given the level of demand, what is the optimum level of output for the firm? Given current knowledge and available technologies, what is the optimal production process? What is the most suitable mix of factor inputs? How will costs vary if output is expanded? Will this involve a change in the use of factors, and how will changes in the prices of factors affect their optimum combination? One of the fundamental rationales for the use of a market system with a pricing process as considered in chapter 2 is that firms compete in their use of factor inputs, react to relative price changes, and continually strive to use their inputs as effectively and efficiently as possible. The theory of production and costs provides an analysis of how price signals should be translated into effective production decisions, so that not only are markets provided with what they demand but also production is by least-cost methods.

Production and the Concept of Value Added

Production is the process of transforming resources into finished products in the form of goods and services. It is an activity which creates or adds value. It applies as much to service, distribution and storage functions as to the process of manufacture. Utility or value can be added by changes in ownership, location or time as well as form. Coal at the bottom of a mine in the middle of summer might not be of much use to you, but once it has been mined, graded, stored until the winter, delivered by the coalman to your door, and ended up sitting at the back of your grate on a frosty night, it has considerable value. To take another example, consider 2 kg of wheat ultimately selling as a loaf of bread to a housewife for 35p. Assume the chain of sales and intervening processes takes place as detailed in table 4.1.

The value to the miller of 2 kg of wheat is 12p. That is what it is worth to him (otherwise he would not willingly part with 12p to obtain it). The

Table 4.1 *Production and value added*

Transactor	Selling price (p)	Value added (p)
Farmer	12	12
Miller	20	8
Baker	30	10
Grocer	35	5
Total	97	35

miller in turn converts the grain into flour. How much effort he spends in doing so is irrelevant. What is relevant is that the baker is willing to part with 20p to get the flour. The baker believes that the miller has added value of 8p to the grain. The baker converts the flour into bread and sells it to the grocer for 30p who in turn sells it to the housewife for 35p. Again, this 5p does not reflect the costs incurred by the retailer; it reflects what the housewife is willing to give up for what the retailer does (otherwise she would purchase the bread from the baker at 30p). She values the retailer's service (convenient opening hours, location, car parking facilities, the provision of convenient selling quantities, the opportunity to purchase other items simultaneously) at 5p. This analysis is exactly in line with our discussion in chapter 2 of marginal personal valuations and the rationale for trade and exchange. In economics, value is subjective and bears little or no relation to production cost.

Value added at each stage equals selling price received at that stage less the amount paid for the intermediate product. More accurately it equals

sales − (material + fuel purchases)

which in turn is identical with

wages + rents + interest payments + profits (gross of corporation tax).

Nevertheless, to keep the arguments straightforward we shall consider production largely in the context of the manufacturing process.

The processes of production add value to goods by transforming them in the manner required by consumers. By this means a fund of value is created, by virtue of which factors can be rewarded. Payments are made for raw materials and components, for labour (in wages and salaries), as well as for rents, taxes etc.

The costs experienced and the production processes adopted will vary both across and within industries. Firms of differing size in the same industry may use different methods of production, have differing combinations of inputs and levels of efficiency and therefore experience

Table 4.2 *Output and costs in UK manufacturing industry, 1974–1988*

	Enterprises	Sales and work (£m)	Gross output (£m)	Purchases (£m)	Increase in value of stocks (£m)	Cost of services (£m)	Gross value added at factor cost (£m)
1974	84,514	80,013	85,153	49,821	1,963	5,950	31,345
1976	89,522	110,485	113,170	67,626	1,773	8,484	38,832
1978	89,203	140,920	142,980	83,001	930	12,269	48,640
1980	90,254	162,381	163,913	90,152	−702	15,929	57,131
1982	85,445	175,268	175,657	95,773	−44	19,039	60,779
1984	120,457	207,543	209,657	117,035	1,174	22,703	71,092
1986	130,297	231,681	232,499	124,742	−210	26,591	80,955
1988	135,474	281,041	283,434	151,356	1,175	32,982	99,934

Source: *Business Monitors*, 1978, 1983, 1986, 1988, cited in *Reports on the Census of Production*, table 1

different costs. A rough outline of the composition of production costs in manufacturing industry is given in table 4.2.

In this table the difference between annual sales and gross output is made up of changes in the value of stocks of finished goods and work in progress. Purchases include the costs of raw materials, components, semi-manufactured goods and workshop materials etc. The increase in the value of stocks shown refers to increases in the value of materials, stores and fuel, not to finished and semi-finished goods. The cost of services includes industrial services, such as payments to other firms for work done, repairs, maintenance and contracts sublet, and non-industrial services, such as rents on property and buildings, hire charges for machinery and vehicles, payments of royalties for the use of patents etc. Thus, by deducting from gross output the purchases and the cost of services, and adding the increase in the value of stocks, we are left with gross value added at factor cost. From this fund wage costs would have to be met, plus all depreciation charges required to maintain the value of equipment, plus payments to providers of capital and to the government in taxation.

The Use of Production Functions

A *production function* is the term given by economists to the technological relationship between the rates of inputs of productive factors and the rate of output of production. To employ production functions it has to be assumed that the state of knowledge and technology is given; if it were not, the relationships between inputs and outputs would be altered by technological advance, leading to more efficient production techniques. It is also assumed that, given production functions, firms utilize their factor inputs at maximum levels of efficiency. The production function could be written as follow:

$$Q = f(A, B, C, D, \ldots). \qquad (4.1)$$

This is simply a symbolic statement of the fact that the output Q is the maximum amount which can be produced for a given numerical set of amounts of factor inputs A, B, C, D etc. The way in which output changes in response to changes in the values, relative and absolute, of these inputs will vary according to the precise numerical formulation of this equation.

The Law of Diminishing Returns

A basic economic assumption underlies the production function. This is the *law of diminishing returns.* It states that as more and more units of one factor are applied, all other inputs being held constant, a point will be reached at which successive additions of that factor will yield diminishing marginal increments to total output.

If we start with a fixed input, say A_1, of factor A, and proceed to add successive units of B, at first production rises very rapidly (see figure 4.1); then the rate of increase slows as diminishing returns set in at b_0. Finally a maximum is achieved, in this case at Q_1, where an optimum combination of A_1 and B_1 units are combined. If further additions of B were made beyond this, total output would not increase and would begin to fall again. This makes intuitive sense. A trite example would be an attempt to increase crop yield from a window box by ever greater applications of labour and fertilizer. Clearly, after a certain point, such foolish efforts would be counter-productive. Figure 4.1 shows the effect of diminishing returns.

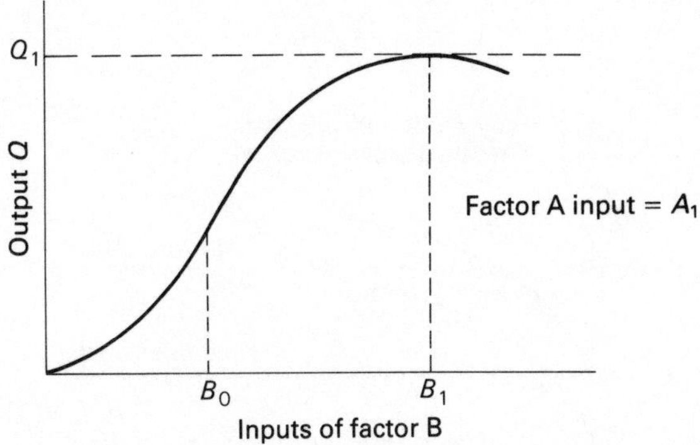

Figure 4.1 *The law of diminishing returns*

This analysis leads naturally on to consideration of the *short run*. This is a conceptual interval of time during which one factor input, usually considered to be capital, is fixed, whilst other factors are variable. This makes sense in that it usually takes much longer to alter capital inputs, in the form of industrial plant and machinery, than it does to alter inputs of labour and raw materials. The short run is not a fixed period of time, and will vary considerably from case to case and industry to industry. At one extreme, if we took the example of the garment industry, a small operation making up garments might be able to increase the number of sewing machines it employs in a matter of weeks. On the other hand, in the electricity generating industry it might take more than a decade to introduce a new nuclear power plant. In the consideration of costs in this chapter we shall concentrate on the analysis of the short run, for which we have assumed that there is a constant state of technology and that one factor input, capital, is fixed. This can be contrasted with the *long run*, in which all inputs are variable, and the *very long run*, in which technology is subject to change; these circumstances will be considered in the next chapter.

Short-run Costs

As the input of the fixed factor is, by definition, unaltered in the short run, its cost is unlikely to alter. Typically *fixed costs* might include rentals on leased machinery, interest on capital, rates and the salaries of those employees who cannot be laid off as output is reduced. *Variable costs* might include raw material costs, the variable part of power and water charges, commissions on sales and some wage costs. The behaviour of total, fixed and variable costs in the short run is shown in figure 4.2.

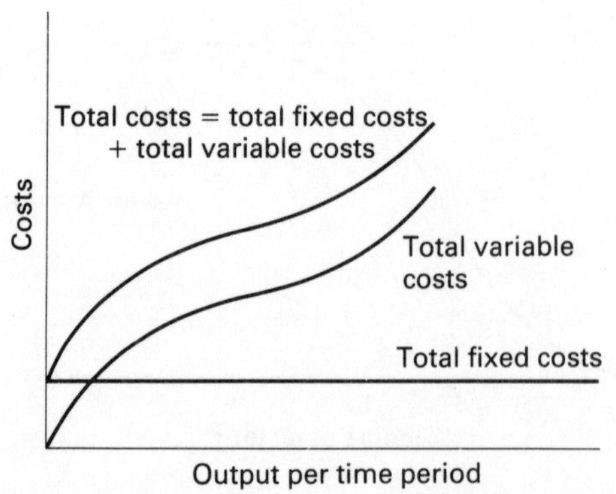

Figure 4.2 *Total costs in the short run*

By definition, fixed costs are constant in the short run, and so they are shown in figure 4.2 as being invariant with output. The behaviour of variable costs reflects the law of diminishing returns. At first, variable costs rise fairly rapidly because too few variable factors are being combined with the fixed factor and the combination is not efficient. As a more effective level of combination is attained, variable costs rise less rapidly as output is increased. Finally, as an ever greater input of variable factors is combined with the fixed factor, diminishing returns set in and variable costs rise rapidly again.

From the basic cost functions shown in figure 4.2 others can be derived which are of considerable analytical use. For example, *average fixed cost* (AFC) is simply the fixed cost per unit of output:

$$\text{average fixed cost (AFC)} = \frac{\text{total fixed cost}}{\text{output}} = \frac{\text{TFC}}{Q}. \tag{4.2}$$

Likewise, *average variable cost* (AVC) is the variable cost per unit of output:

$$\text{average variable cost (AVC)} = \frac{\text{total variable cost}}{\text{output}} = \frac{\text{TVC}}{Q}. \tag{4.3}$$

Similarly, *average total cost* (ATC) is obtained by dividing total cost (TC) by output:

$$\text{average total cost (ATC)} = \frac{\text{total cost}}{\text{output}} = \frac{\text{TC}}{Q} = \frac{\text{TFC} + \text{TVC}}{Q}. \tag{4.4}$$

Marginal cost (MC) is the rate of change of total cost with respect to changes in output. It is measured by the gradient of the total cost curve at any particular point representing a given level of output:

$$\text{marginal cost } (MC) = \frac{\Delta(\text{TC})}{\Delta Q}. \tag{4.5}$$

But, as total fixed cost does not change, it is only affected by changes in variable cost; thus

$$\text{marginal cost (MC)} = \frac{\Delta(\text{TVC})}{\Delta Q}. \tag{4.6}$$

Marginal cost is obtained by deducting the total cost at any given output from the total cost immediately preceding it and dividing by the change in output. The behaviour of cost schedules for a hypothetical firm is shown in table 4.3.

A set of cost curves which behave in a manner consistent with what is implied by the data in table 4.3 is shown in figure 4.3. As fixed costs are constant, total fixed costs at any point on the average fixed cost (AFC) curve must be constant. In terms of figure 4.3, total fixed costs (TFC) =

Table 4.3 *The behaviour of short-run costs*

1	2	3	4	5	6	7	8	9	10
Units of variable input	Units of fixed input	Total output Q	Total fixed costs TEC (£2.50 per unit) (£)	Total variable costs TVC (£1 per unit) (£)	Total costs TC (4 + 5) (£)	Average variable costs AVC (5 ÷ 3) (£)	Average fixed costs AFC (4 ÷ 3) (£)	Average total costs ATC (7 + 8) (£)	Marginal costs MC (from 6 and 3) (£)
0	2	0	5	0	5	–	∞	∞	–
1	2	4	5	1	6	0.25	1.25	1.5	0.25
2	2	9	5	2	7	0.22	0.55	0.77	0.20
3	2	15	5	3	8	0.20	0.33	0.53	0.17
4	2	22	5	4	9	0.18	0.23	0.51	0.14
5	2	26	5	5	10	0.19	0.19	0.38	0.25
6	2	28	5	6	11	0.21	0.18	0.39	0.5
7	2	29	5	7	12	0.24	0.17	0.41	1.0

AFC × Q = (TFC/Q) × Q. In figure 4.3 a perpendicular drawn up to the AFC curve at a given level of output and then across from the curve at right angles to the vertical axis shows the AFC of producing that level of output, and the area enclosed in the resulting rectangle is the TFC. The two rectangles produced by the broken lines in figure 4.3 will always have the same area, as will any other similar rectangle, and this is equal to the value of total fixed costs. The only curve which displays this required property is termed a rectangular hyperbola, and the AFC curve is thus always a rectangular hyperbola.

Marginal cost is equivalent to the slope or gradient (obtained by taking the first derivative) of the total variable cost curve, as was implied in

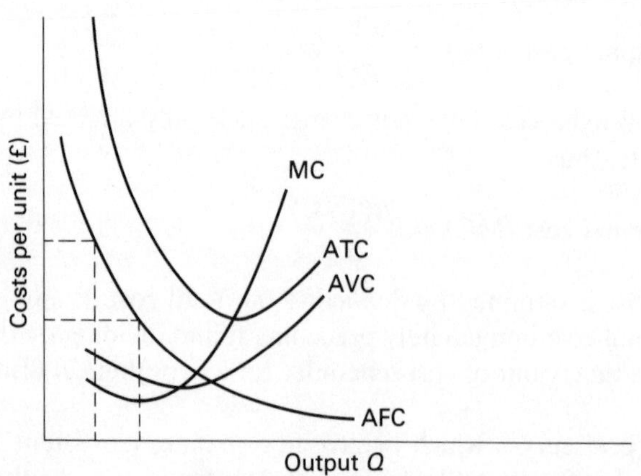

Figure 4.3 *Average and marginal costs in the short run*

expression (4.6). It follows from the behaviour of average and marginal quantities that whenever MC is below AVC, average variable cost must be falling. It reaches a minimum where AVC = MC, and as soon as MC rises above AVC, average variable cost starts to rise. Average total cost is the sum of average variable costs and averaged fixed costs: ATC = AFC + AVC. This can be seen in table 4.3. Similarly, it follows from the nature of the curves that the marginal cost curve always passes through the minimum point of the average total cost curve.

We have now reached a stage where we have a basic tool-kit which can be applied to analyse the factors determining supply and demand; it will be utilized in the next chapter when the theory of the firm is examined more closely. However, in order to develop these basic principles and concepts we have smoothed over and ignored a number of practical difficulties. For example, it has been assumed that information about company costs is readily to hand. Yet it will be seen in chapter 9, when various accounting issues are broached, that the assessment of company costs is by no means a straightforward unequivocal matter.

Similarly, in the development of our treatment of costs it has been assumed that it is possible to switch continuously between the various factor inputs to achieve the most efficient method of producing a given output. In the final section of this chapter we shall move away from this to an examination of the use of linear programming, which provides a very powerful method of analysing the behaviour of costs and output under much more restrictive conditions than previously assumed.

Linear Programming

Linear programming is a powerful analytical technique which can be used to determine the optimal solution to maximization or minimization problems. It is particularly useful in its ability to handle 'constraints', which limit the courses of action available to the decision-taker. These are a common feature of the environment in which businessmen have to operate. The technique can be applied in a great number of decision areas, including the determination of the optimum factor input mix, product distribution analysis (taking in decisions such as plant location or delivery routing), and the design of promotional mix in marketing activities to mention but a few. We shall concentrate on its use in the analysis of the behaviour of production and costs.

Linear programming, as its name suggests, involves a basic assumption that all relationships between variables are linear. It costs are to rise linearly with increases in output, two conditions are required: (a) the firm's *production function* must be linear homogeneous – i.e. factor inputs will be optimally combined only in constant fixed proportions – and furthermore there are *constant returns to scale*, production being equally efficient whatever the level of output; (b) there must be *constant factor input prices*. If all the above conditions are met, total costs will rise linearly with increases in output.

The assumptions may seem unreasonably restrictive, but in practice, over limited output ranges, the treating of factor input prices as constant will frequently be quite justifiable. A further point in favour of linear programming is that the method assumes there are a limited number of processes in which factor inputs can be combined to produce a given output, rather than the continuous substitution of standard economic analysis. The existence of *constraints* on resources is also quite likely in the short term. Examples of this might include shortages of given types of equipment, limitations on warehouse space, shortages of raw materials or even a lack of skilled labour. The technique handles the setting of upper boundary limitations on various inputs with great ease.

To illustrate, suppose that a firm is producing a single product using inputs of two factors L and K. Further assume that there are three alternative production processes A, B and C available to the firm, which use different fixed proportions of inputs K and L to produce the product. Figure 4.4 shows three process rays, drawn through the origin, which link points representing successive units of output and use the two inputs in the appropriate proportions. Thus, A_3, B_3 and C_3 all represent three units of output, but are produced by processes A, B and C respectively, using differing quantities of inputs K and L, as indicated by their positions on the KL plane and measured on the two axes.

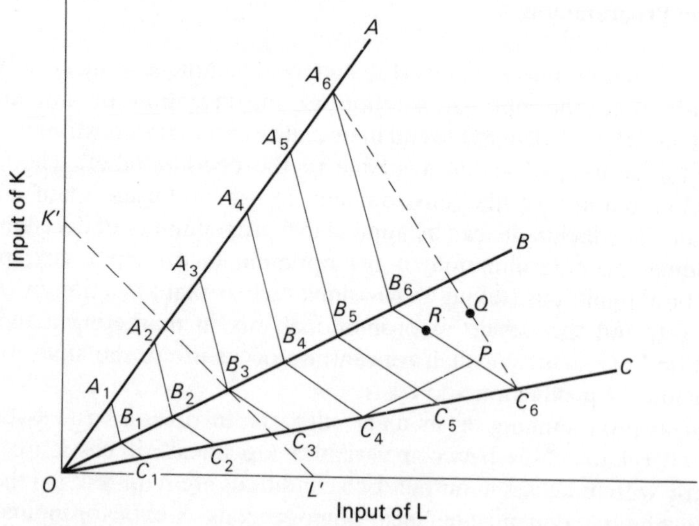

Figure 4.4 *The determination of the least-cost method of production*

Because there are constant returns to scale, OA_1 is equal to A_1A_2, A_2A_3 and so on. Similarly $OB_1 = B_1B_2 = B_2B_3$ etc., and $OC_1 = C_1C_2 = C_2C_3$. This follows since the same proportionate increases in factor input, by definition, produce a constant proportionate addition to output.

If we join up the points of equal output, say A_6, B_6 and C_6, we have mapped out the combinations of inputs which produce an output of six units. This equal product 'curve' is termed an *isoquant.* A similar exercise for outputs of 1, 2, 3, 4 and 5 units produces the set of isoquants shown in figure 4.4.

The argument requires some further clarification. Each point on B_6C_6, for example, represents a combination of processes B and C which produces the same output as OB_6 units of process B or OC_6 units of process C. This is illustrated by taking any point P on line B_6C_6 and drawing a line through P parallel to OB (a similar result would be obtained by drawing a line parallel to OC). With the point P chosen in figure 4.4, this line intersects OC at C_4, indicating that four units should be used using process C and the remaining two using process B. This follows because $C_4P = B_4B_6$ which are opposite sides of the parallelogram $B_4B_6P\ C_4$, and because $B_4B_6 = OB_2$. (The argument also involves the further assumption that using both processes simultaneously will neither enhance nor detract from either's performance.) We are also assuming that the firm is unable to combine K and L in ratios that lie either above production process ray OA or below ray OC. It can further be shown that the isoquants in figure 4.4 represent the most efficient ways of combining production processes to produce a given output.

Suppose we combined processes A and C to produce an output of six units. The broken line in figure 4.4 joining A_6 and C_6 shows the combinations of the two processes that would do this. A point Q on this line shows a combination of the two processes that would produce six units. But there are combinations of B and C on B_6C_6, such as point R, which will also produce six units using fewer inputs since the sum of K and L needed to achieve R is less than to achieve Q. Clearly A_6C_6 is suboptimal and would never be considered. This also demonstrates that linear programming, even though it involves an assumption of constant returns to scale, can handle the type of diminishing returns associated with a diminishing marginal rate of substitution of one input for another.

To demonstrate how the cost of the production process can be minimized using this analysis, we have to consider 'isocost' lines. These link points of equal expenditure on factor inputs, and one such line is represented in figure 4.4 by the broken line joining K' and L'. Given the prices of factors K and L and a certain amount of money expenditure, we could either spend it all on factor K, purchasing K' of it, or on L, as indicated by L', or on combinations of the two which involve the same expenditure and plot along $K'\ L'$; process B is optimal and, given our expenditure level, the best we could achieve would be to produce three units of output using process B as indicated by the intersection of K' L' with point B_3. Any other combination of inputs would involve the same expenditure but would produce less than three units.

We have assumed so far that there are no constraints imposed on the ability of the firm to obtain factor inputs at constant prices. This is unrealistic, and firms are likely to have only limited access to floor space, machinery, labour etc. at any given time. In figure 4.5 it is assumed that constraints limit the maximum amounts of K and L available to K_c and L_c.

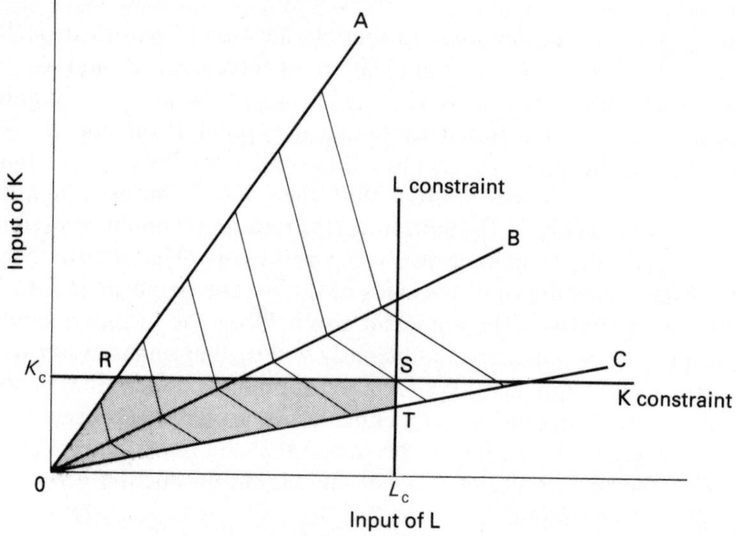

Figure 4.5 *The determination of the least-cost method of production subject to constraints on inputs*

The production possibilities now open to the firm are represented by the shaded area in figure 4.5, which is bounded by the process rays OA and OC and the two constraints. This shaded areas is termed the *feasible space.* Clearly, if the firm wishes to maximize output, it should operate where the feasible space touches the highest attainable isoquant – point S in the diagram. The combination of processes B and C required to achieve this output can be found by constructing the appropriate parallelogram, as illustrated in figure 4.4.

To illustrate further the versatility and practicality of linear programming we shall consider the geometrical solution of another simple problem. Suppose the firm in question produces two products, C and D, which use different combinations of three inputs, K, L and M, in the process of production. The firm is subject to constraints on the availability of all three inputs and, subject to these, wishes to maximize the profitability of the combined output of C and D. The question is: what output mix, given the constraints and differing contributions to profits from the two products, will do this? This type of problem is commonly faced by, for example, oil refiners, food processors, timber processors etc.

This typical linear programming problem involves the following standard elements which will be considered briefly in turn: an objective function, a set of constraints, and non-negativity requirements.

The objective function

The objective function is usually concerned with either cost minimization or, as in this case, profit maximization. As we are in a short-run situation, fixed costs can be ignored, since they will be incurred no matter what decision is made. For this type of problem, therefore, 'profits' are '*contribution profits*' (total revenue minus variable costs). (For further discussion of profits and contribution analysis, see chapter 9.) The unit contribution of each product is its selling price minus the average variable costs of production. Suppose this is £0.5 for C and £1 for D. The objective function can be written as

$$\text{maximize } \Pi_c = £0.5Q_C + £1Q_D \tag{4.7}$$

where Π_c is total contribution profit and Q_C and Q_D are the respective quantities of C and D produced.

The constraints

The constraints will depend on the absolute limitations on the amounts of K, L and M available in each period. Suppose that these are 10, 15 and 12 respectively. Knowledge of these, together with the factor input requirements of the production processes for the two products, are all that we need to develop the constraint equations. Let us suppose that 1, 2 and 0 units of K, L and M respectively are needed to produce C, and similarly 4, 3 and 6 to produce D. We know that the constraints on the availability of inputs are $K \leqslant 10$, $L \leqslant 15$ and $M \leqslant 12$. These can be combined with our knowledge of the production input requirement to produce the following constraint equations:

$$1Q_C + 4Q_D \leqslant 10 \tag{4.8}$$

$$2Q_C + 3Q_D \leqslant 15 \tag{4.9}$$

$$6Q_D \leqslant 12. \tag{4.10}$$

The non-negativity requirements

In the geometric analysis which follows we shall obviously limit ourselves to answers which involve positive outputs. However, linear programming problems are usually much more complex than our simple example; even so, they can be solved rapidly with a computer and the appropriate algorithm.[1] However, a computer would not baulk at providing a mathematical 'solution' which involved, where 'appropriate', negative outputs, even though they make economic nonsense. To avoid these potential embarrassments, positive solutions are specified as part of the system of equations, as shown below:

$$Q_C \geqslant 0 \tag{4.11}$$
$$Q_D \geqslant 0. \tag{4.12}$$

To obtain a geometric solution for our simple problem, the first step is to draw a diagram, on a plane representing outputs of C and D, of our constraint equations (4.8), (4.9) and (4.10). This is done in figure 4.6.

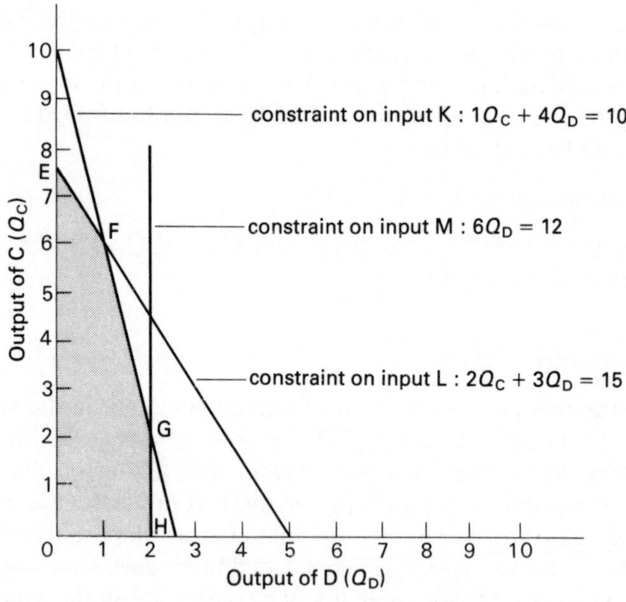

Figure 4.6 *Determining the feasible space*

The constraint equation which results from the limitation of the input of K to a maximum of 10 units per period is given in expression (4.8). We know that this could be used to produce either 10 units of C and no D, as marked by the point of intersection of the line representing the K constraint with the vertical axis; or, at the other extreme, 2 units of D and no C, as marked by the intersection of this line with the horizontal axis; or a combination of C and D which plot along the line joining these two extremes. The lines representing the other constraints are developed on a similar basis, and together they enclose the feasible space – the shaded area EFGH in figure 4.6. It is obvious that the solution of maximum profitability will lie somewhere along the boundary of this area, and the key points to

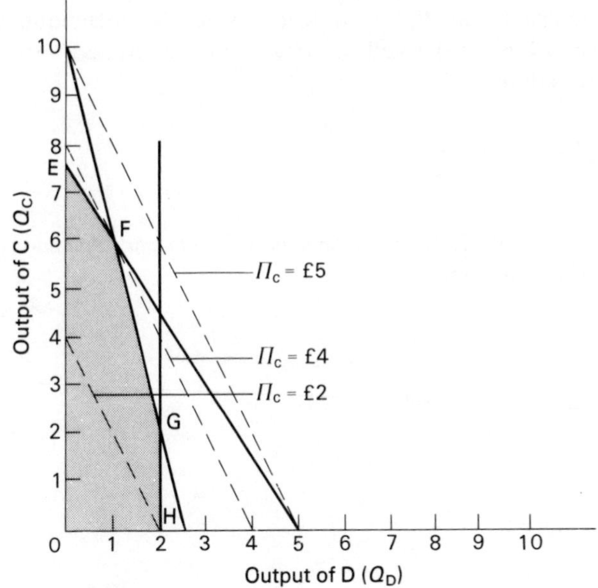

Figure 4.7 *The graphical solution of a linear programming problem*

examine are the corner solutions at E, F, G and H, since combined output is maximized along this boundary.

In figure 4.7 we have taken the previous diagram (figure 4.6) and added a set of iso-profit-contribution (Π_c) lines. These show the particular combinations of outputs of C and D which make the same contribution to profits, and are based on expression (4.7). The point on the boundary of the feasible space which just touches the highest iso-profit-contribution line is the optimum solution. This is point F in figure 4.7. At this point, six units of C and one unit of D are produced, yielding a total contribution to profits of £4 – the maximum attainable under the circumstances.

These simple examples give no more than a hint of the tremendous versatility and potential of linear programming techniques, which are now a well-established part of the decision-maker's tool-kit, since optimization problems subject to inequality constraints are a frequent feature of both business and governmental problems.

The nature of each firm's experience of costs will determine both its and, in aggregate, the industry's response to changes in market conditions. These factors, taken together with the analysis of demand conditions in chapter 3, provide an analysis of how an equilibrium of demand and supply conditions is determined in the market.

In addition, we have now seen how the pure theory of costs can be applied to decisions at the firm level using the technique of linear programming, which is derived directly from a restricted version of the production function.

References

1 See, for example, W. J. Baumol, *Economic Theory and Operations Analysis*, Prentice Hall, 3rd edn, 1972.

5

Market Structure and Business Conduct

Why do firms exist? What is unique about them? What is meant by market structure, and what is its relationship with competition, monopoly, pricing behaviour of firms and other business activities? These are the questions we attempt to answer in this chapter.[1]

The Theory of the Firm

First, firms are collections of people – owners, managers and employees – with (at least in principle) the owners telling the others what to do. Orders are given and received. The people involved do not perpetually make and renew contracts with each other as buyers and sellers do in the outside market. There is, instead, a hierarchy.

Second, firms often have team activities. When groups work together (a) it is often difficult to determine the contribution of each individual and (b) the total output is larger than it would be if each individual acted independently.

Third, owners, unlike employees, are not paid directly for their time or services. Rather they receive the right to the firm's residual surplus, or deficit, of revenues over costs. (Managers often blend the roles of owner and employee if they receive, in addition to a salary, earnings linked in some way to profits.)

So much for the characteristics of the firm as a hierarchy. Why, however, does this replace the outside market? Why would the costs of buying and selling semi-finished goods on a production line, in transactions between independent people renting space on a factory floor, exceed the costs of organizing a firm? Put this way, the question seems trite and the answer obvious. But in fact neither is the case; if the answer was *universally* obvious, then all outside market transactions would cease and all activities would be organized into one giant firm. The question is why in some cases firms exist, and in others they do not.

One reason has already been given. Team activity is often more productive in the aggregate than individual activity. But this itself poses a problem only the firm can solve. Since it is difficult to measure the input of each individual it is easy for an individual to shirk or do less than his part. The loss in output is shared by all team members and cannot be traced to the shirker. He bears less than the full cost of his action; thus each person in a team tends to shirk more than he would if he were self-employed and bearing all such costs. (This is simply an application of demand theory: the lower the cost or price of shirking, the more shirking will take place.)

It is therefore sensible to have a *monitor* to observe the behaviour of the team members, evaluate their contributions and so minimize shirking. The monitor (or manager) must in turn be monitored. The problem of monitoring the monitor is often solved by giving him a reward linked in some way to the residual earnings of the firm. The more successful the monitor, the more his share of firm profits will be. Thus the owner-manager-employee, or firm, relationship comes into being for the purposes of team production and consequential monitoring.

A second reason for the existence of firms is the differing willingness of people to bear risk. Some individuals are more or less *risk-averse* (i.e. wary of risk) than others. Very few people will actually be *risk-preferrers*, i.e. prefer a risky situation to a non-risky one. Since people have different degrees of aversion to risk they must be paid more or less to assume any given risk. Thus, owners can be deduced to be more willing to assume risk than managers or employees. This may be where their comparative advantage lies.

This will be partly a psychological phenomenon and partly one of wealth. If an individual has wealth of £10,000 he will be more willing to risk £1000 than someone whose life savings amount to £1000. In turn, potential owners may not have the skills of management which potential monitors have. They would prefer to hire managers rather than do it themselves. Their asking price for a management salary would reflect this and be relatively high. (This is merely a restatement, for different commodities – risk aversion and management skills – of the arguments put forward in figure 2.2 for Joe and Fred, who had different stocks of, and psychological preferences for, beer and butter.)

This phenomenon, in turn, leads to what is often called the 'divorce of ownership from control'. Managers are frequently not owners of the firms they manage. Entrepreneurs can be presumed to assess the trade-offs of this situation. The cost savings in raising capital must be offset against the less rigorous, but also less expensive, management which will be installed if monitors own little or nothing of the firm they manage.

Pricing and Market Structure

Traditionally, economists divide market structures into three major categories: *perfect competition*, *oligopoly* and *monopoly*. Each has certain

Table 5.1 *Characteristics and results of different market structures*

	Perfect competition	Oligopoly	Monopoly
Characteristics			
Number of sellers	Large	Few	One
Product	Same for all producers	Same or different	One
Rivals' reactions	Each firm acts independently	Interdependance between firms	No rivals
Entry conditions	Free entry and exit	Varies	Barriers to entry exist
Results			
	Lowest cost producers produce the product Consumers pay the lowest price consistent with cost Producers have no discretion in the price which they set	Different results depending on how each reacts to the policies of others	The one firm has monopoly power which permits it to determine price

characteristics and in the first and last cases certain results can be deduced. Table 5.1 summarizes these characteristics and results.

Perfect competition

The demand curve for a perfect competitor can be regarded as a straight line. This may seem at odds with what we discussed in chapters 2 and 3, where it was asserted that demand curves always slope down and to the right. The paradox is resolved by remembering that no individual seller in a price-taking market is large enough, relative to the market's size, to have any significant effect on the good's market price. The point is *not* that the seller believes that the price will never change, but rather that each seller assumes that nothing he can do *individually* can change the price. In fact, even one seller withdrawing or adding his supply to the market will shift the intersection of supply with demand and so raise or lower the market price. But the movement will be so imperceptible that, in reality, the seller can disregard it, and therefore – for exposition purposes – we can legitimately do so as well.

The facility of drawing a horizontal demand curve is useful since it permits us to describe another concept using the same line. This is *marginal revenue* (MR), which is the addition to total revenue that a firm gains when it sells one more unit of output. Clearly if price is unchanged no matter what number of units is sold, marginal revenue is equal to price. With this information, and the cost curves of chapter 4, we can now establish at what level of output a perfect competitor will choose to produce. To do this we assume that the firm is a profit maximizer, i.e. that its profit equals total revenue less total costs, and that costs are correctly calculated to include all opportunity costs (e.g. forgone interest on capital employed is correctly imputed as discussed in chapter 2). Figure 5.1 shows that the firm, if it produces at Q_1 (the level at which marginal revenue equals marginal cost), will earn economic profit (i.e. profit over and above what it could earn elsewhere) of $P - \text{SATC}_1$ per unit, or, in total, that unit profit multiplied by Q_1 (which can be represented by the rectangle of width Q_1 and height $P - \text{SATC}_1$). (SATC refers to *short-run* analysis.)

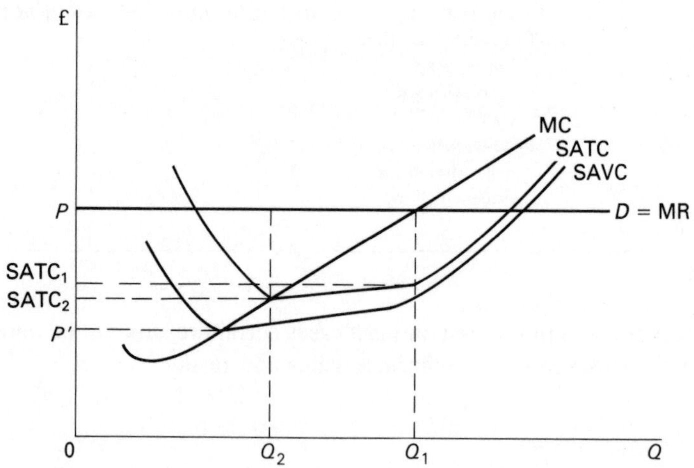

Figure 5.1 *Demand curve, and maximum profit and minimum cost points, for the individual seller in a perfectly competitive market*

Q_1 is, in fact, the output level that gives maximum profit. It might at first be thought that Q_2 (the level at which average total cost equals marginal cost) would be the profit-maximizing output. This is not so. Certainly Q_2 is the level of minimum unit costs and unit profit $P - \text{SATC}_2$ is larger than $P - \text{SATC}_1$. But the volume sold, Q_2, is so much less than Q_1 that total profits are less. The area of the profit rectangle $(P - \text{SATC}_2) \times Q_2$ is less than $(P - \text{SATC}_1) \times Q_1$. We can use logic to prove this. At Q_2, if one unit more is produced, then total revenue TR increases by MR. Simultaneously, total cost TC increases by MC. But total profit is TR − TC and, at one unit more than Q_2, MR is larger than MC, so profit TR − TC becomes greater.

This increase in total profit after Q_2 continues as long as MR >MC, i.e. right up to Q_1, when MC = MR. After Q_1, MC > MR and so TR − TC begins to fall. Q_1 is thus the level of maximum total profit (albeit not the level of minimum unit costs).

Figure 5.1 also indicates at what level of costs and output a firm should close down its operations. Thus a perfect competitor can be seen as having three sequential decisions to take. First, should it or should it not stay in business? If the price is expected to be at $SATC_2$ or above, then it should. All the costs of being and staying in business will be covered. Second, if the answer is positive, should the firm continue to operate or not, i.e. continue not just owning its assets but using them? Since a decision has been taken to continue incurring fixed costs, only variable costs should now be considered. If price is above P' (the level at which average variable cost equals marginal cost) then it should continue operations. If price is below P', it should temporarily discontinue operations. This level of price is known as the 'shut-down point'. If price is expected to be below $SATC_2$ permanently, then the assets should be sold off and owners and employees should put their resources to better alternative uses.

Third, if the owners decide to continue operating, at what level of output should they produce? The answer is at the level where marginal revenue (or price) equals marginal cost.

The answers to these three questions help us to derive the perfect competitor's supply curve, i.e. how much such a firm will be willing to supply at a range of prices. As long as the firm is operating, its supply curve will be the same as its MC curve. (In figure 5.2 this is the thicker portion of MC lying above SAVC.) At price P_1 the firm will take a decision not to operate since the price does not even cover variable costs. AT P_2 it will operate (at least temporarily) producing an output of Q_2 where $MR_2 = MC$.

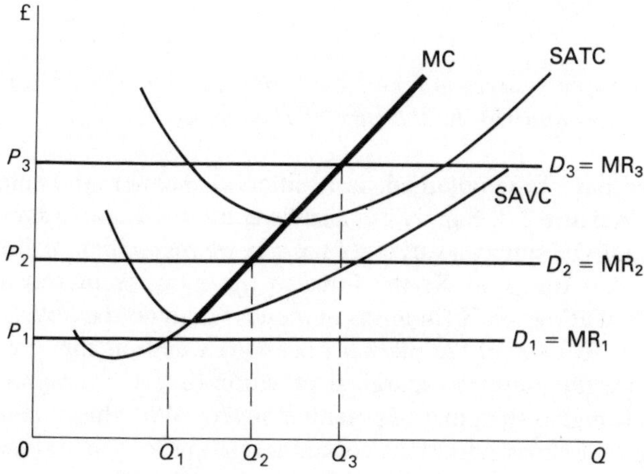

Figure 5.2 *Supply curve and operating decision points for the individual seller in a perfectly competitive market*

Similarly, at P_3 it will happily operate, this time on a continuous basis, at Q_3, where economic profits can be earned.

Figure 5.3(a) shows the supply curve for a typical firm in a perfectly competitive market. If the industry is composed of, say 1000 such firms, then at a price of £20 each firm would be willing to supply 40 units, and so the industry would be willing to supply the sum of all the firms' quantities supplied, namely 40,000 units. A similar aggregation exercise could be performed at all price levels, and so the industry's supply curve (the horizontal sum of all firms' supply curves, ΣMC) would be obtained (figure 5.3(b)). In reality, of course, it is unlikely that all firms would have the identical MC curves assumed for the representative firm. If nothing else, managerial efficiencies would differ and each firm's MC curve would lie at a different level. Nonetheless, the principle of horizontal aggregation would remain unaltered. Only the graphical and numerical neatness and proportion of figure 5.3 would be forfeit.

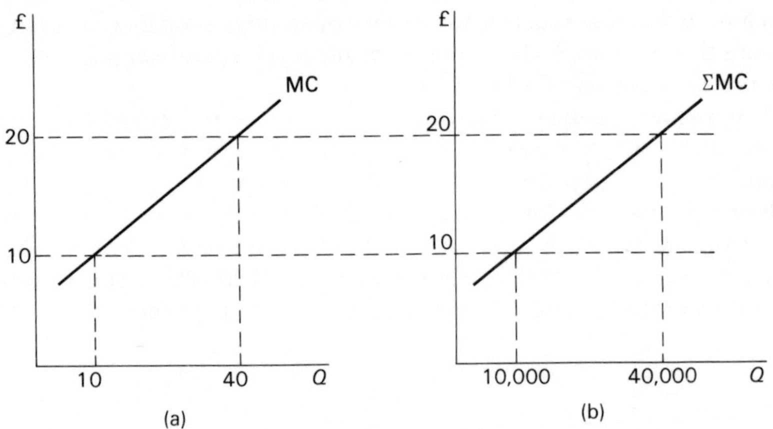

Figure 5.3 *Supply curves in a perfectly competitive market for (a) a typical firm and (b) the industry of 1000 firms*

Thus we have now obtained, in a different manner, the supply curve discussed in figure 2.4. Supply can also be considered, as we saw in figures 2.2 and 2.3, to be simply a variant of the way we regard demand. In a price-taking market for good X, the firms in the industry merely put lower marginal valuations on X (in terms of money) than do the buyers of X and continue to do so until the market price is reached; at this point trading ceases, since the industry's marginal valuation (i.e. its aggregate marginal cost) is now higher than that of potential buyers. With this in mind it is not surprising that three important concepts relating to demand can also be applied to supply.

First, supply has an *elasticity* just like that of demand and it is measured in an analogous manner; namely, the elasticitiy of supply is equal to the relative change in quantity supplied divided by the relative change in price that caused the change in quantity:

$$\text{elasticity of supply} = \frac{\Delta Q_S/Q_S}{\Delta P/P}.$$

Second, as with demand, long-run supply is more elastic than short-run supply. Third, as a demand curve always slopes down and to the left, so a supply curve always slopes up and to the right.

Figure 5.4 shows diagrammatically the difference between long-run and short-run supply elasticity. The causes are similar to those for demand elasticity variations over time. Firms do not make a total response to a price change instantaneously. Existing firms will raise output in response to a price rise but, in the short term, will do so by using existing plant. In the long term they may plan, design and build larger plants, but this takes time. Similarly, a higher price will tempt new firms into the industry, but that also cannot happen instantaneously. So, in the short run, a price rise from P_1 to P_2 may increase the quantity supplied to only Q_2 (from Q_1); in the long term, however, the overall increase would be $Q_2' - Q_1$.

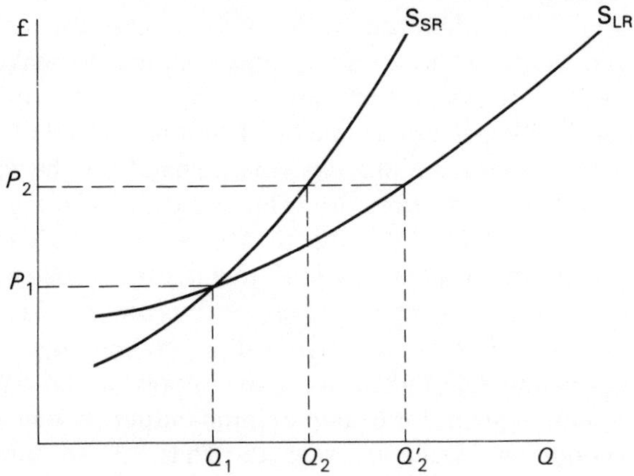

Figure 5.4 *Long-run and short-run supply elasticity*

Figure 5.5 explains these points more fully. First, the price rise does not 'just happen'. Something independent of supply must cause it. Demand in the industry (figure 5.5(b)) increases from D_1 to D_2, causing the equilibrium price to rise from P_1 to P_2. Originally, the representative firm (figure 5.5(a)) was producing q_1 units at P_1 and making only 'normal' (i.e. zero economic) profits. In the short run, the response to the price rise is limited to what existing firms can accomplish in their existing plants. The representative firm consequently increases its output to q_2. The long-run response to this is that new firms enter and existing firms expand in size. As new firms enter, the industry short-run supply curve shifts to the right

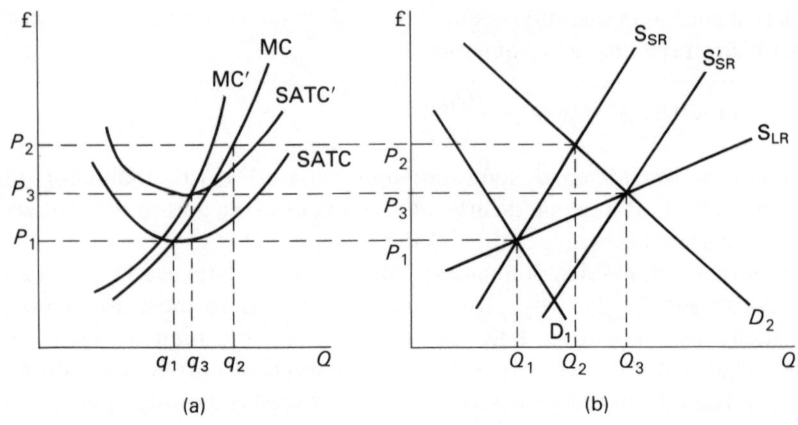

Figure 5.5 *Short-run and long-run effects of a price rise on (a) a typical firm and (b) the industry*

(S'_{SR}). This reduces the price to P_3. If this was all that was happening, entry would continue until, for the representative firm, the price had fallen down to MC to P_1 and quantity had been restored to q_1 (since the intersection of P_3 (= MR) and MC is where existing firms continue to make economic profits because $P_3 > \text{SATC}$ at that output level). But other things are not equal. P_1 is not the long-run price and S_{LR} is not horizontal. The reason is that, as other firms enter the industry, the demand for the *inputs* which firms use rises and so input prices rise. This causes costs to rise and SATC moves upwards to SATC′, and MC to MC′. Now at P_3 there is not incentive for a still further set of new firms to enter the industry and each of the (still increased in number) representative firms now produces q_3 units.

Note that if the expansion of industrial output *lowered* input prices, then the cost curves would fall and the long-run supply would be downward sloping. This could happen, for example, if the output change was so great that other economies could be reaped. Thus, if an industry grew dramatically it might be feasible to organize special training courses for employees. This could improve their efficiency and productivity and so lower the cost of labour per unit, even with a higher wage rate.

Monopoly

For the monopolist price and marginal revenue are not the same; this is because of the downward-sloping demand curve which it faces. As a consequence of this, the addition to total revenue from selling one extra unit is less than the price at which it is sold. This is because the change in total revenue is that received for the last unit (its price) less the revenue forgone on the preceding units due to the lower price that all of them are now sold for. Table 5.2 illustrates this.

Table 5.2 *A monopolist's demand schedule, total revenue and marginal revenue*

P	Q	TR	MR
10	1	10	
9	2	18	8
8	3	24	6
7	4	28	4
6	5	30	2
5	6	30	0
4	7	28	−2
3	8	24	−4
2	9	18	−6
1	10	10	−8

Since the objective is to maximize profit TR − TC, the profit-maximizing output is that where MR = MC (Q, in figure 5.6). To the left of this point an increase in output will increase total revenue more than total costs (because MR exceeds MC) and so will increase profit. To the right of Q, a decrease in output will reduce total costs by more than it reduces total revenue and so will also increase profit. Hence Q, is the output from which no further increases in profit are possible. The corresponding profit-maximizing price is that price which must be set to sell the profit-maximizing output and can be deduced from the demand curve.

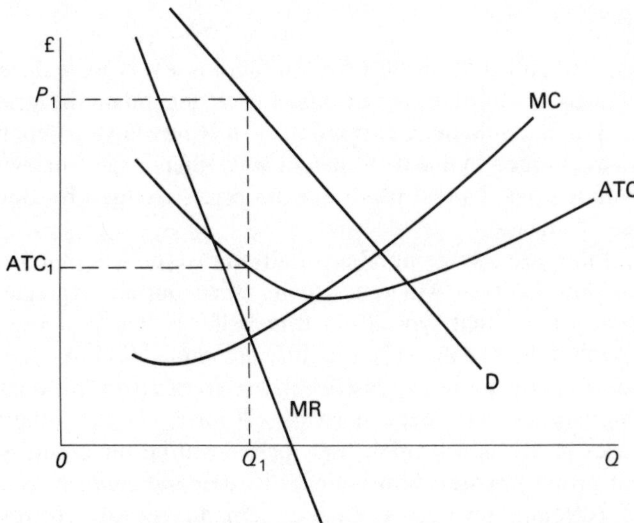

Figure 5.6 *A monopolist's demand and marginal revenue curves*

Several inferences can be drawn from this diagram. First, the firm is making supernormal profits (profits are given by the area $(P_1 - \text{ATC}_1) \times (Q_1 - 0)$). Second the profit-maximizing output may be, but need not necessarily be, producible at minimum ATC. Such a coincidence would be pure chance. Third, the profit of the firm may not be positive – a monopolist may make losses. All that the MR = MC condition results in is profit maximization or loss minimization. Fourth, no matter how low costs are, a monopolist firm will never produce where its demand curve is inelastic (see appendix).

In many markets the individual firm is unable to influence market price and such firms can be called 'price takers'. Price taking (the absence of pricing discretion) is not unique to perfect competition. For example, in real life information is not freely available. Firms do not always know what values consumers place on various products, especially those not yet produced. Competition, then, often takes the form of introducing a new product with the hope that consumers will value it more highly than its costs, and that other firms will not immediately enter, thus allowing the first firm a chance to earn innovational profit.

For example, in the beer industry in the 1970s, the main problem was to decide just how far, if at all, the trend from ale to lager was going to go. In the early 1960s lager made up only a small proportion of all beer produced. By 1973 the figure had risen to 14.8 per cent and by 1978 to 27 per cent. Those brewers who did not correctly forecast this change in consumer taste and so failed to build lager breweries to meet it became relatively less profitable than those who did.

Oligopoly

When there are only a few firms or when there is a very wide difference in the size of firms in a market, the profits of each depend on the strategies of the others. For example the UK retail sales of Rover Group depend partly on the prices charged by Ford, Vauxhall and others. The worldwide sales of Airbus Industries depend partly on the prices charged by Boeing and McDonnell Douglas.

Clearly, there are a large number of alternative beliefs that a firm may hold as to how its rival will react to its price–output strategies. Some writers have argued that typically a firm believes that if it increases its prices its rivals will not follow: so quantity demanded is choked off rapidly as its product is now more expensive relative to its rivals' products. If the firm lowers its price it believes its rivals will lower theirs – otherwise the firm surmises its rivals will think their prices will be undercut. So, given the current price, a typical firm believes its demand curve is as shown in figure 5.7 (often known as a kinked demand curve). However, this approach takes the current price as given; it does not indicate the optimum price.

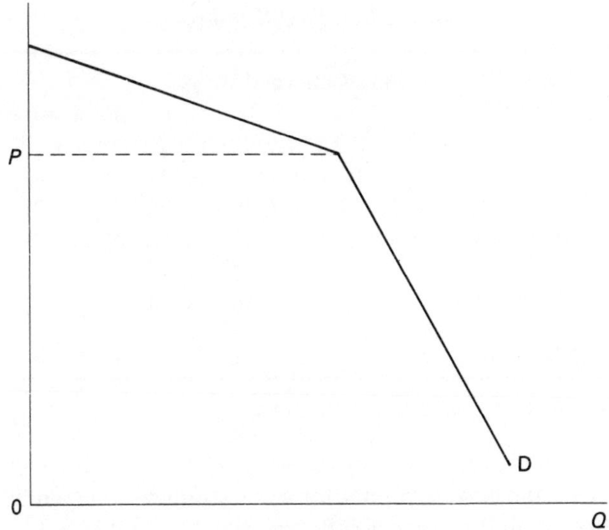

Figure 5.7 *An oligopolist's kinked demand curve*

Others have suggested that firms act strategically, i.e. each firm follows a plan which specifies how it will react to its rivals' decisions no matter what those decisions are. Suppose, for simplicity, that there are only two firms in an industry. One strategy may be for one of them to take its rival's price as given and to choose its profit-maximizing strategy assuming its rival will not reply with a price change.

The outcome can be represented in a table. For example, suppose the profits resulting from the prices of firms A and B are as shown in table 5.3. In the body of the table the profits for A are shown on the left and those for B on the right. Suppose that initially B chooses a price of £1. Since A's strategy is to assume that B will stick to £1, the best A can do is to choose a price of £2 since, along the row corresponding to B's price of £1, A's profits are maximized at £10 when it charges £2 (£10 exceeds the profits from a price of £1 (£9), and £3 (£9) or £4 (£8)). In the next period, B *will* respond because it will take A's price at £2, assume it fixed and choose its profit-maximizing price. This is £4 because at this price B makes more profit than at any other price in the column corresponding to A's price of £2. In the third period A takes B's price as given, looks along the P_B = £4 row and sees that its profits are still maximized at a price of £2. So eventually the two prices which, if there is no change in the table, will hold for ever are P_A = £2, P_B = £4.

Another possibility is that neither firm has any idea as to which strategy its rival will follow but wishes to avoid the lowest profits which it might receive. This would be accomplished by following a *maximin* strategy.

Table 5.3 *Payoff matrix*

		Prices charged by A				
		1	2	3	4	Row minimum
Prices charged by B	1	9, 1	10, 6	9, 9	8, 15	1
	2	8, 2	9, 7	8, 10	7, 20	2
	3	7, 3	8, 8	7, 15	6, 16	3
	4	6, 4	7, 10	6, 12	5, 15	4
	5	5, 5	6, 8	5, 10	4, 14	5
Column minimum		5	6	5	4	

Profits for A are on the left; profits for B are on the right.

Each firm finds the lowest profits for each strategy – shown as the row minimum (for B) and column minimum (for A) in table 5.3 – and then chooses the strategy corresponding to the largest of these. The chosen strategies are $P_A = £2$, $P_B = £5$.

Often the strategies from such a decision rule may not result in the largest combined profits for the two firms together. That is the case in table 5.3. With prices of £2 for A and £5 for B the combined profits are £14 (£6 + £8). But if the two firms could *agree* as to which strategy they would each follow they could choose the strategies which maximize their joint profits. These strategies can be found by adding the two profits in each cell of the table and choosing the strategies which give the largest combined profit: $P_A = £4$, $P_B = £2$, giving a total profit of £27. However, they may then have the problem of deciding how to allocate this between them. B is aware that, if A kept to a price of £4, B could increase its profits by charging a price of £1.

The extent to which the above rather stylized models crudely describe or predict firm behaviour is a hotly debated subject.

Limit pricing and barriers to entry

Earlier in this chapter it was suggested that, in a price takers' market, if price exceeded the minimum of average costs, new firms would enter the industry, supply would increase and price would fall until no supernormal profits were made. But if established firms have advantages which potential entrants do not possess a barrier to entry is said to exist and it may be possible for existing firms to set a price above average cost *without entry occurring*.

The literature considers several types of entry barriers. First, legal provisions may prevent entry absolutely. For example, to operate a taxi in any city in the United Kingdom requires a licence issued only by the local authority. Similarly, most drugs are patented and a licence is required if a firm other than the patent holder wishes to manufacture a drug.

A second type of entry barrier exists if a potential entrant has a higher LRAC curve than established firms. Ignoring economies of scale for simplicity, the two curves may be as shown in figure 5.8. Established firms could set a price at P_L so that an entrant could make only normal profits at best (which it can make elsewhere) and so would not enter. The difference in costs between established firms and potential entrants may be due to the entrant's having to pay higher costs of capital because, for example, it is riskier or may be because the entrant would have to spend more on advertising than established firms since the latter, over time and for a given past expenditure, have gained brand loyalty by consumers' experience of the use of the product or service.

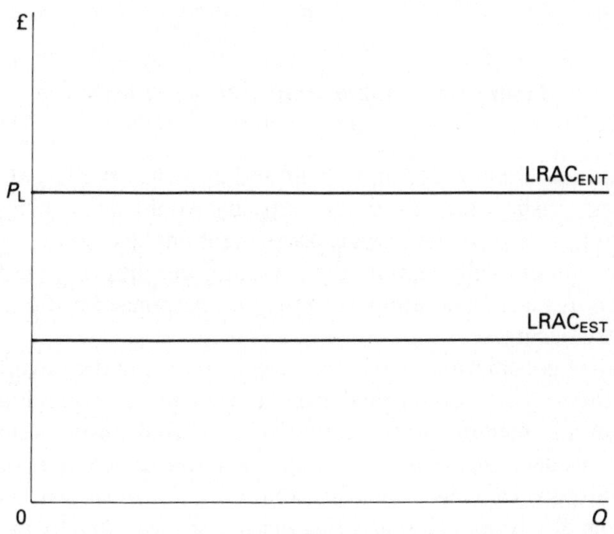

Figure 5.8 *The absolute cost entry barrier*

Economies of scale have been said to provide a third entry barrier. Consider figure 5.9. Suppose for simplicity that there is only one established firm and that both it and all potential entrants face the same LRAC curve. Suppose the established firm would not alter output from Q_L if a new firm entered the industry. The entrant's demand curve would then be the portion AB of the market demand curve. If we move this to the left until it is just tangential to the LRAC – now marked D_{ENT} – it can be seen that the entrant could never make a profit if it entered. At all outputs the entrant's demand curve is below or just touches its average cost curve: average revenue is never greater than average cost.

However, a weakness of this analysis is that, if the entrant did come in,

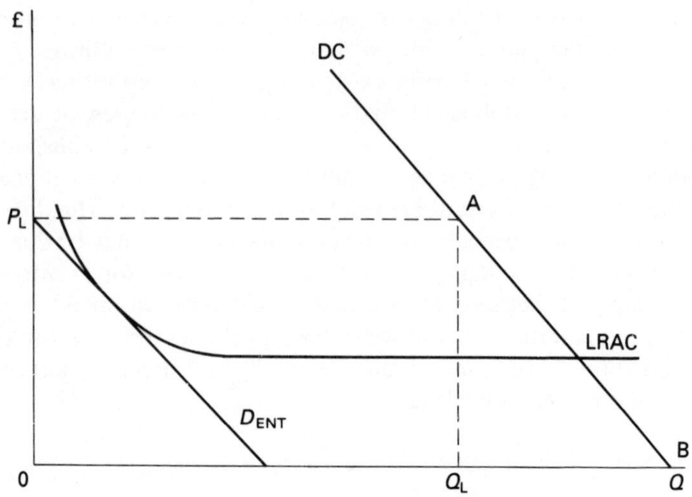

Figure 5.9 *Economies of scale entry barrier*

price would fall along D_{ENT} and might end up below the LRAC curve so that the established firm (and the entrant) would make a loss. If the established firm reduced its output, price might fall less. So the assumption that the incumbent will maintain the pre-entry output is not credible. The analysis ignores a consideration as to the best response for the established firm if entry occurs.

One way of considering such a response is to turn to the payoff matrices of game theory. The established firm may incur an expenditure which would alter his payoffs from alternative actions if entry occurred. For example, consider figure 5.10. The established firm has spent a considerable amount on spare capacity which is useful only if a price war occurs. The resulting payoffs from different strategies are shown: the left-hand figures show the payoffs to the established firm, the right-hand figures those to the entrant. If the entrant stays out of the industry the established firm makes monopoly profits of £10 million, the entrant zero because it is not in the industry. If the entrant enters, the established firm has to decide whether to fight or not – if it does, both firms make a loss of £1 million. If the established firm accommodates the entrant it makes a loss of £2 million and the entrant a profit of £5 million. With this sort of matrix the entrant *can be* credibly deterred from entry. The entrant sees that, if it enters, the best action for the established firm is to fight, making a loss of £1 million and not a loss of £2 million. If the established firm fights the entrant makes a loss. So if the entrant enters it would expect a loss. On the other hand, if it stayed out it would do better – making zero profits. So the entrant stays out. The expenditure by the established firm, which cannot be recouped, has altered the payoffs so that the entrant prefers to stay out.

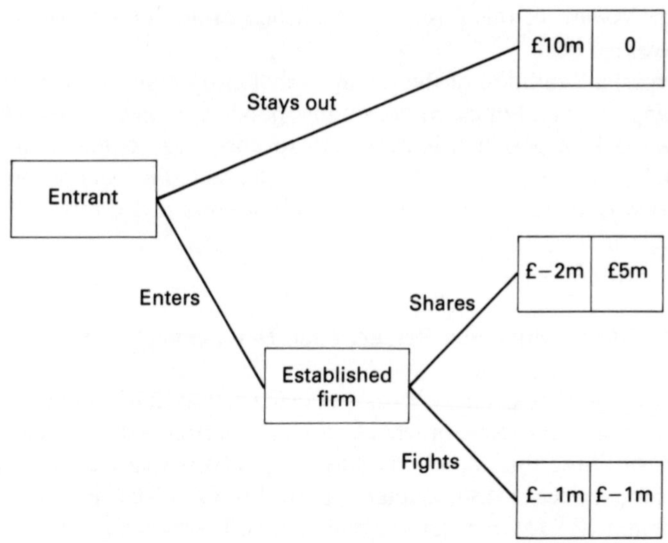

Figure 5.10 *Strategic entry deterrence*

The expenditure must not be recoupable because, if it were, it would not alter the payoffs for the game. The expenditure has altered the payoffs of the game to *commit* the established firm to fight if entry occurs. The fact that the expenditure is not reversible means it is sunk. As an example of a sunk cost suppose a smelter useful only to produce aluminium is built for £100 million. Now suppose that the day after construction is complete the firm decides not to use it but to sell it instead. It is very unlikely that anyone will pay the original cost – even though there is no wear and tear. If the highest price the firm can sell the smelter for is £90 million, then the £10 million (£100 million – £90 million) was sunk when the firm decided to build the plant.

Contestable markets

The level of price which would result in markets where there are no sunk costs has been discussed in recent literature. Baumol, Panzar and Willig[2] argued that, unlike perfect competition where there is a very large number of firms, if producers have no sunk costs then price will always be equal to the lowest level of average costs and so to marginal costs (see chapter 15) regardless of how many firms exist. The reason is that if there are no sunk costs firms can enter freely and also leave the industry selling their assets for what they paid for them less wear and tear. So if the price were set above the minimum of average cost, the supernormal profit would attract entrants who could also earn supernormal profits while they existed and then exit. Aware of this position established firms would never set price above average cost.

However, a limitation of the theory is that entry almost always involves the sinking of costs. For example, simply spending money on advertising to create a stock of goodwill is necessary to encourage demand for a new product, but the stock cannot be resold for the cost of its generation. While the theory is deductively valid, the assumptions are rarely fulfilled in practice.

Product Differentiation and Research and Development

One way to increase profits is to close the market so that competitive entry does not occur; restrictive practices and legal barriers (see chapter 11) are methods of doing this. A second way is by advertising (see chapter 13), which can produce a taste change. A third is to engage in research and development (R&D) in order to obtain a unique product (and so a unique demand curve) or a lower-cost process for a given product and demand curve.

What is R&D? It can be seen as a spectrum stretching from basic research through applied research to development. Basic research is an attempt to increase pure scientific knowledge, and typically occurs in universities or other centrally or charitably funded bodies such as the research councils. An example of basic research was Hertz's experiments with the wireless transmission of sound waves in the nineteenth century, which occurred long before Marconi invented his radio. That was applied research: a deliberate attempt to invent, given the state of knowledge, and begun with a particular application in mind.

Applied research can be divided into two types. First, background applied research is carried out to increase or refine the store of know-how on which future applications can draw (e.g. studies of the causes of the common cold may lead to the discovery of a cure). Again this tends to occur in the universities or the research councils but occasionally in industry also. Second, product- or process-directed applied research is carried out to obtain a product or process within predetermined commercial criteria. This occurs mainly in industry or industrially funded research associations. A new aircraft design or the application of industrial robots for a production line are examples of this.

Development is the adaptation of a newly acquired product or process to the ruling demands of the market-place. Development generally occurs in an industrial environment and examples might be the constructing, testing and refinement of a prototype aircraft, or the test of a chemical to ascertain that it is safe for human consumption.

This R&D spectrum results in technical change – but barriers to the enjoyment of such change can occur at several places. For example:

1 A lack of scientific knowledge can hinder invention. For example, a lack of true understanding of the causes of cancer means that the search for a cure is not well defined and that effort is dispersed and thus less effective than it might be.
2 The hovercraft, conversely, was invented long after the requisite know-how was available; what was lacking was an inventive 'act of insight'.
3 A lack of development can hinder innovation. Penicillin provides a classic example. Fleming discovered its anti-bacterial activity in 1928, but his discovery lay dormant as merely a fact in the scientific literature of the day. It was not until 1939 that Florey and Chain did further development work on it which led to its eventual innovation in 1943 as a marketable product.
4 After innovation occurs, diffusion can be tardy.

(a) For example, there was a failure of horizontal diffusion in the motor industry when firms in the same industry (albeit in America) did not adopt the innovations of disc brakes and radial tyres until long after they had been available in Europe.
(b) Vertical diffusion may be impeded if customers in the industry fail to make use of an innovation. Thus, long after anti-depressant drugs had been made available, the medical profession continued to prescribe tranquillizers. This was because depression was not regarded as a disease or clinical entity in most medical schools at the time. This situation is now rectified in normal medical education after intensive advertising by the pharmaceutical firms involved to overcome the inertia and ignorance of existing prescribers.
(c) Lateral diffusion into apparently unrelated fields may not occur because of a lack of entrepreneurial vision. Thus while Marconi became synonymous with the wireless telegraph, he failed to perceive the potential of radio broadcasting as a news and entertainment medium. It was left to firms such as RCA to exploit this to the full.

As Schumpeter emphasized, however, one way to encourage innovation and diffusion is to conduct R&D formally on a routine basis. This has taken place in industry over the last few decades, and in 1988 expenditure was 1.74 per cent of GDP.

Table 5.4 shows in which sectors of the economy R&D expenditure is incurred. By far the greatest proportion, some 69 per cent, is spent by private industry, public corporations and research associations. The next largest spender is the government sector, at 15 per cent, followed by the academic institutions at over 12 per cent.

Table 5.5 shows the sources of finance for R&D expenditure. A comparison of tables 5.4 and 5.5. illustrates that a high degree of cross-subsidization exists. While the government *performs* 15 per cent of the UK R&D effort, it *finances* 38 per cent. The academic institutions spent over

Table 5.4 *R&D expenditure in the UK: users of finance, 1987*

Sector carrying out the work	R&D expenditure £million	Per cent
Central government		
Defence	820.3	8.9
Civil		
Research councils	378.1	4.1
Other	205.0	2.2
Local government	8.0	0.1
Total (government)	1411.4	15.3
Universities and further education establishments	1119.9	12.2
Public corporations, research associations and private industry	6337.0	68.9
Other	328.5	3.6
Total	9196.8	100.0

Source: *Annual Abstract of Statistics*, HMSO, 1990, table 11.5

Table 5.5 *R&D expenditure in the UK: sources of finance, 1987*

Sector providing the funds		R&D expenditure £million	Per cent
Central government			
Defence		2235.7	19.0
Civil			
Research councils		593.9	5.1
Other		1543.0	13.1
Local government		32.0	0.3
Total (government)	as related by government	4404.6	37.5
	as related by sectors carrying out the work	3445.2	37.5
Universities and further education establishments		41.0	0.4
Public corporations, research associations and private industry		4689.3	51.0
Other		1021.3	11.1
Total		9196.8	100.0

The percentages applying to the government sector were calculated using figures returned by the sectors carrying out the work and these percentages have been apportioned *pro rata* over those subdivisions of the government sector shown here.
Source: *Annual Abstract of Statistics*, HMSO, 1990, table 11.5

£1120 million but provided less than £41 million of this from their own funds: the remainder came from government bodies, industrial grants and contracts, and donations from charitable foundations.

It was conceptually convenient in the R&D spectrum to distinguish between basic research, applied research, and development, but in practice the various stages may be extremely difficult to separate. The dangers of isolating the stages in practice, with a possible resultant blockage in the process of technical progress, are emphasized by the actions of some of the practitioners. Universities establish industrial liaison departments; one of the principal motivating factors is the failure of much university research activity ever to reach the development stage, to say nothing of innovation and production. At the other end of the spectrum, many industrialists show an awareness of the necessity of R&D continuity and allocate a portion of their R&D budget to basic reseach either in-house or by grants to a university.

Table 5.6 shows the distribution of the R&D effort in the United Kingdom across the three stages of the R&D spectrum. The table indicates

Table 5.6 *Distribution of current expenditure on R&D by type of work, 1981*

	Percentage of overall total expenditure				
Sector carrying out the work	Basic research	Applied research	Development	Unallocated	Total
Government					
Defence	0	3.3	6.2	0	9.5
Civil					
Research councils	3.1	0.8	0	0	3.9
Other central government	0.6	3.5	4.7	0.3	9.1
Local authorities	0	0	0	0	0.1
Total (government)	3.7	7.7	11.0	0.3	22.6
Non-government					
Universities and further education establishments	0	0	0	11.2	11.2
Public corporations	0.1	2.5	4.4	0	6.9
Research associations	0.1	0.9	0.5	0	7.5
Private industry	1.5	9.7	45.8	0	56.9
Non-profit making organizations	0.2	0.5	0.1	0	0.9
Total (non-government)	1.9	13.6	50.8	11.2	77.4
Total	5.6	21.3	61.7	11.4	100.0

Totalling discrepancies are due to rounding errors.

Source: calculated from J. R. Bowles, 'Research and development in the UK 1981', *Economic Trends* (August 1984), p. 81, table 4

that 66 per cent of all allocated basic research is performed by certain government establishments. This is similarly the case with applied research, where 36 per cent is performed by private or public industry and the research associations. Development is not the most important activity of the research councils but is a characteristic of research association activity.

Well over 80 per cent of all development expenditure is incurred by industry, private or state owned. In like manner, over 70 per cent of industrial R&D expenditure is allocated to development activities.

Looking at the nation's entire R&D effort, 5.6 per cent is basic research, 21.3 per cent is applied research expenditure and the remaining 61.7 per cent is development (11.4 per cent cannot be allocated between these groups). The table begs two questions. Why should this be the distribution of R&D expenditure? Further, should this be regarded as the optimum for inducing economically desirable technical change?

R&D is an inherently risky activity of uncertain outcome. The nearer to the basic research end of the R&D spectrum is the activity, the greater is the uncertainty of object. The nearer an R&D project approaches development, the more accurately can remaining future costs be assessed, realizable goals defined and the probability of failure reduced. Commercial potential and technical feasibility are almost unknown at the basic end of the spectrum; the predictability of both tends to certainty the nearer is the completion of the development process. This being the case, it is to be expected that profit-motivated industrialists who decide to spend on R&D will tend to incur that expenditure in those portions of the R&D spectrum where a return will be achieved sooner rather than later – at a lower rather than a higher risk – and where the object of the expenditure is definable and of known value rather than vague or uncertain. This is, in fact, the pattern of industrial R&D spending.

Unfortunately the statistics shown in table 5.6 do not allocate expenditure by universities between the three sectors. However, assuming that the distribution is the same as in the 1970s (50 per cent basic, 50 per cent applied) then the predominance of basic research in the universities is also subject to intuitive explanation. Once a major scientific breakthrough has been made in a project in a university the need for profitable exploitation is absent, and other motivating factors, such as scientific interest *per se*, are not as strong in carrying a knowledge increase through to a usable innovation as they are in encouraging further basic research.

The dominance of development expenditure is equally to be expected. Development costs more than basic research. In development, the scale of R&D operations may be approaching full-size factory operation, or a project which has not yet progressed beyond the drawing-board may have to be transferred to a full-scale mock-up model. Crude principles discovered earlier in the spectrum may have to be refined or altered to meet marketing or production constraints which, in turn, may require more sophisticated equipment and more scientific disciplines, represented in larger teams of research workers. In multistage processes, stage efficiencies observed in the laboratory may be completely unacceptable in production itself, particularly with a high-priced raw material or low-priced end product. For example, a three-stage process with a 50 per cent yield at each stage will yield at the end of stage three only 12½ per cent of the original (but now processed) raw materials. In a process with many more stages than three, the development problem of getting a high final stage output can be extremely costly to overcome.

Most industrial R&D activity occurs in what are frequently called the science-based industries such as chemicals, electronics, aerospace and engineering. Table 5.7 indicates that only some of R&D expenditure within manufacturing industry occurs in the more traditional craft-based industries. The inter-industry pattern of R&D effort is determined in part by the vast differences in the amounts and value of equipment required in different fields. For example, while the aerospace industry absorbs 16.9 per

Table 5.7 *Expenditure on R&D in manufacturing industry, 1985*

Product group	Total expenditure £million	Per cent
Chemical industry	941.9	18.9
Mechanical engineering	262.6	5.3
Electronic engineering	1744.7	34.9
Electrical engineering	136.5	2.7
Motor vehicles and parts	371.6	7.4
Aerospace	845.3	16.9
Other manufacturing	394.9	7.9
Metal goods	16.1	0.3
Shipbuilding and repairs	1.8	–
Instrument engineering	57.3	1.1
Food and drink	97.4	1.9
Tobacco	25.8	0.5
Textiles and other man-made fibres	16.0	0.3
Leather, clothing and footwear	5.7	0.1
Timber and wooden furniture	3.3	0.1
Paper and paper products, printing and publishing	21.0	0.4
Processing of rubber and plastics	38.3	0.8
Other manufactured products	15.5	0.3
	4995.7	100.0

Source: *Business Monitor MO14 Industrial Research and Development Expenditure and Employment*, HMSO, 1985, table 4

cent of all industrial R&D expenditure it accounts for only 9.6 per cent of the qualified manpower in industrial R&D. This is largely due to the relatively large sums required for prototype construction and to their relatively early appearance in the R&D process. Chemicals, conversely, employ 15.8 per cent of the qualified manpower in industrial R&D but account for 18.9 per cent of the expenditure incurred. Much chemical research can be performed with relatively inexpensive equipment in the laboratory and the appearance of expensive pilot plants is a relatively late phenomenon in the R&D process.

Differences of this nature, however, do not alter the basic concentration of R&D in the science-based industries as a whole. Table 5.8 shows 80 per cent of all qualified manpower in R&D to be concentrated in such

Table 5.8 *Qualified scientists and engineers within manufacturing industry, 1985*

	Qualified scientists and engineers	
Product group	Full-time equivalents (thousands)	Percentage
Chemical industry	12.3	15.8
Mechanical engineering	4.4	5.6
Electronic engineering	32.4	41.5
Electrical engineering	2.9	3.7
Motor vehicles and parts	4.9	6.3
Aerospace	9.6	12.3
Other manufacturing	6.8	8.7
Metal goods	0.3	0.4
Shipbuilding and repairs	–	–
Instrument engineering	0.7	0.9
Food and drink	1.5	1.9
Tobacco	0.3	0.4
Textiles and other man-made fibres	0.3	0.4
Leather, clothing and footwear	0.1	0.1
Timber and wooden furniture	0.1	0.1
Paper and paper products, printing and publishing	0.4	0.5
Processing of rubber and plastics	0.7	0.9
Other manufactured products	0.3	0.4
	78.0	100.0

Source: *Business Monitor MO14 Industrial Research and Development Expenditure and Employment*, HMSO, 1985, table 14.

Table 5.9 *Expenditure on R&D as a percentage of sales in manufacturing industry, 1985*

Product group	Intramural expenditure as a percentage of sales
Chemical industry	3.5
Mechanical engineering	1.1
Electronic engineering	11.2
Electrical engineering	1.6
Motor vehicles and parts	2.6
Aerospace	12.6
Other manufacturing	0.3
Metal goods	0.2
Shipbuilding and repairs	0.1
Instrument engineering	2.3
Food and drink	0.2
Tobacco	0.4
Textiles and other man-made fibres	0.2
Leather, clothing and footwear	0.1
Timber and wooden furniture	0.0
Paper and paper products, printing and publishing	0.1
Processing of rubber and plastics	0.5
Other manufactured products	0.5

Source: *Business Monitor MO14 Industrial Research and Development Expenditure and Employment*, HMSO, 1985, table 10

industries. Not only do such industries perform more R&D absolutely than the craft industries, they also have an above-average propensity to conduct R&D. Using the ratio of R&D expenditure to sales, table 5.9 indicates that the greatest density of R&D effort occurs in the chemical, electronic, and aerospace industries.

There appear to be two complementary reasons for the absolute concentration of R&D in the science-based industries – profitability and cost differences. A science-based industry is able to utilize more promptly and effectively any change in its related body of technical knowledge. Where an industry's closest related science is relatively far removed, as in the craft-based industries, then discoveries may be initially inapplicable and tardy in providing any net financial return for the outlay required for R&D. For example, chemistry is far removed from the traditional leather goods industry. The chemical discovery of plastics which could be used as leather substitutes was largely ignored by the leather industry. The plastics were initially unattractive and synthetic in appearance and had little capacity for hard wear. To alter this the leather industry would have had to incur large initial outlays on R&D teams (already in existence in chemicals), acquire know-how on plastic manufacture and develop a product with the intention of replacing, rather than supplementing, the raw material already in use. The net profitability gain from such an exercise, at least in the short to medium run, would almost certainly have been negative. Consequently it was a chemical company, Du Pont, which first developed a plastic possessing the necessary pliability, durability and quality of appearance to compete with leather as a material for shoe manufacture.

The costs of R&D performance may be relatively high if an industry does not possess a well-developed scientific base. The possession of a scientific base implies an existing body of well-ordered and verifiable knowledge and information. The approach to an applied research problem can in such circumstances be systematic rather than empirical. That is, a definite goal can be worked towards from this foundation of knowledge by the use of strictly disciplined scientific thought, or deductive 'paper-and-pencil' techniques.

Where no scientific base is present, however, the approach to a research problem will tend to be empirical or random in nature. Solutions to the problem must be sought by trial-and-error experimentation rather than by deductive thought. The empirical approach is therefore relatively more expensive, requiring costly experiments comparatively sooner and more frequently than the systematic approach.

Having said this, one must not play down serendipity, the chance discovery of the highly trained observer. Without serendipity and Fleming's expertise, penicillin would have remained an unwanted mould growing in a glass jar in St Pancras.

If technical progress and R&D are regarded as desirable, is there any particular type of firm or industrial structure which will tend to encourage the activity? This question can be asked independently of the presence or absence of a scientific base in any given industry. It depends also on whether firms are price takers or searchers, on whether there are scale economies or not, on whether the firm is vertically integrated or not, and on whether the industry is or is not highly concentrated. Scale and integration will be discussed in chapter 6. Market concentration will be deferred until chapter 11. In the meantime, table 5.10 summarizes the various (and often conflicting) answers to the question of the relationship between structure and innovation. It is suggested that the reader cross-refers to this table from time to time when studying the relevant parts of the rest of the book.

Table 5.10 *Summary of the case for an association between market structure and innovation*

	Arguments in favour of high concentration	Major reservations
(A)	*Cost of resources.* Market control raises profitability and reduces the demands on management, thus implying a lower opportunity cost of resources devoted to R&D.	There may be financial advantages for enterprising firms, but the opportunities may not be realized if the incentive to innovate is impaired (see (C)–(E) below). Further, the relevance of financial advantages may vary with the scale of the technology.
(B)	*Risk.* Reduced short-run price competition provides greater security and permits a longer time horizon for research	
(C)	*Competitive incentives.* The risk of retaliation discourages oligopolistic price competition. Non-price competition is thereby encouraged, being less readily matched by competitors.	Non-price competition may give way to collusion unless the technology offers large gains from innovation. If one firm can appropriate these gains, the initial market structure may be irrelevant.
(D)	*Market share incentives.* A large market share implies a greater absolute gain from any given proportionate change in costs or revenues. Therefore the costs of R&D are more easily recovered.	(i) Market leaders may gain less if new products replace existing products. (ii) Monopolists may bias the choice of innovations so as to preserve their dominance.
(E)	*Risk of imitation.* Market dominance reduces the risk of imitation by competitors, and enables market leaders to retain the benefits of innovations.	Given that dominant firms may seek to delay innovations competing with established products, they may prefer a 'fast second' strategy, using market dominance to take over the proven innovations of smaller competitors.
(F)	*Size of firm.* (A)–(E) may be reinforced if the monopolists or oligopolists are also large firms. Potential benefits include: (a) Indivisible innovations may require an absolutely large volume of resources. (b) Economies of scale may exist in the R&D process if specialized staff or equipment are required. Large firms are then more able to finance the optimum scale. (c) Economies of scale in marketing or production may enable large firms to exploit innovations more profitably. (d) The risk of failure of an R&D programme may be reduced if the number of independent projects in that programme can be increased. (e) Large firms may have a more diversified product range, giving more scope for the internal exploitation of new discoveries.	The benefits of size may be exaggerated. Reservations include: (i) Large firms may stifle creativity, and restrict invention and discovery. (ii) Advantages of size are more significant for development than for research, and may vary between industries. (iii) If there are no economies of scale in the R&D process, small firms with lower overheads may be more cost-effective and more flexible. (iv) Many small firms do no R&D. The owner-managers of those which do may be more highly motivated and less averse to risk than the salaried managers of large firms. (v) Diversification may encourage basic research, but is less relevant for targeted R&D. If there are economies of scale in R&D, a diversified firm may dissipate its resources over too wide an area.

Source: R. W. Shaw and C. J. Sutton, *Industry and Competition*, Macmillan, 1976, p. 203

Appendix 5.1

To understand intuitively why a monopolist will not produce where its demand curve is inelastic, recall our discussion of elasticity in chapter 3. A demand curve is inelastic if a price reduction results in a total revenue fall (i.e. MR becomes zero and then negative). Graphically, since costs, including MC, can never be negative, MC will never equal MR when MR is negative and so the statement is true. Logically it would be stupid for a profit-maximizing price searcher to increase output (thus increasing total costs) by lowering total revenue (thus reducing profits). This is shown formally in the next few paragraphs.

In our simple example in table 5.3, we used discrete price changes of single units. If we had assumed, as is customary in developing this type of analysis, that both the price and the quantity demanded can be altered by very small amounts, then calculus can be utilized to analyse the behaviour of our demand function. We shall briefly consider how calculus can be applied to the analysis of these functions; those not mathematically inclined should be able to follow the verbal explanations of what follows.

$$\text{total revenue (TR)} = \text{price} \times \text{quantity} = \text{PQ} \tag{A5.1}$$

Marginal revenue is the change in total revenue which results from selling one extra unit of output. This is not the same as the price at which the last unit is sold, since – unless the demand curve is horizontal – the price of all units sold must be reduced in order to sell an extra unit. It is measured by the gradient of the total revenue curve. This can be found by differentiating the expression for total revenue with respect to quantity, i.e.

$$\begin{aligned}\text{marginal revenue (MR)} &= \frac{\text{dTR}}{\text{d}Q} = P\,\frac{\text{d}Q}{\text{d}Q} + Q\,\frac{\text{d}P}{\text{d}Q} \\ &= P + \frac{Q\text{d}P}{\text{d}Q}.\end{aligned} \tag{A5.2}$$

There is a very close link between marginal revenue and price elasticity of demand. Remember that price elasticity measures the proportionate change in quantity demanded in response to a proportionate change in price, and the formula is

$$\eta = \frac{\text{d}Q}{\text{d}P}\;\frac{P}{Q}$$

If we extract P from our expression for marginal revenue in equation (A5.2) we obtain

$$\text{MR} = P\left(1 + \frac{Q}{P}\,\frac{\text{d}P}{\text{d}Q}\right) = P\left(1 + \frac{1}{\eta}\right). \tag{A5.3}$$

Expression (A5.3) shows that marginal revenue is equal to price multiplied by (one plus one over price elasticity of demand). What happens when price elasticity of demand is unity? When $\eta = (-)1$ the expression in parentheses in equation (A5.3) becomes zero and therefore marginal revenue is zero. This is also the point at which total revenue is maximized. This follows since marginal revenue equals the gradient of the total revenue curve, and when the total revenue curve is at a maximum its gradient will be zero. This is because, at that point, the curve is neither increasing nor decreasing. The implication of this is that businessmen, if they are profit maximizers, will behave in setting their prices as if they are operating on the section of the demand curve where elasticities are greater than unity. There is little point in cutting prices if the result will be a drop in revenue.

The last point is particularly interesting since it gives the lie to so many casual denunciations of industrial pricing practices. Consider the petrol industry. People are often heard to say: 'Of course, they can and do raise their prices to maximize their profits. They can do this because petrol is a necessity; there is no price sensitivity (i.e. demand is inelastic).'

Our analysis shows that if the price elasticity for petrol is this low then firms cannot be maximizing profits; or, if they are, then price sensitivity is not so low as the casual gossip suggests. Probably both explanations have some validity. When petrol prices rose in the 1970s short-run usage of cars did drop off, and in the long run car firms have been expending considerable effort in making the increasingly fuel-efficient cars which replacement buyers have been demanding. In short there is some price sensitivity in the petrol market.

Nevertheless studies do show that it is very low. It can only be low (i.e. well below 1.0) if firms are *not* profit maximizing. Since the petrol market is not closed, and as there is not a single seller, this suggests that firms have been continually competing with each other, not of course to raise prices but to lower them. Naturally, they would have liked to act as a single seller in a closed price-searching market and maximize profits by raising prices to the profit-maximizing demand-elastic range, but they have been unable to do so owing to the forces of competition.

What confuses the issues is the problem of rising prices caused by government taxation in the UK, raw material price increases in the oil-producing countries and the general level of inflation itself which makes it difficult to sort out what, in fact, is happening to any one good's real or relative price.

References

1 The first section of this chapter draws on A. Alchian and H. Demsetz, 'Production, information costs and economic organisation', *American Economic Review* 62 (1972), pp. 777–95.

2 W. J. Baumol, J. C. Panzar and R. D. Willig, *Contestable Markets and the Theory of Industrial Structure*, Harcourt Brace Jovanovich, 1982.

Further reading

S. T. Call and W. L. Holohan, *Microeconomics*, McGraw-Hill, 1983.

R. Clarke, *Industrial Economics*, Basil Blackwell, 1985.

F. A. Hayek, 'The use of knowledge in society', *American Economic Review* 35 (1945).

W. D. Reekie and J. N. Crook, *Managerial Economics*, Philip Allan, 3rd edn, 1987.

F. M. Scherer, *Industrial Market Structure and Economic Performance*, Rand McNally, 1980.

6

Scale and Firm Growth

Why do firms grow? What determines the rate and direction of their growth? What is the phenomenon of scale economies to which we referred in chapter 5? We shall now consider the answers to these questions.

Economies of Scale

Economies of scales (or *increasing returns to scale*) is a phrase often used very loosely. A precise definition might relate to a hypothetical plant or firm. If technology is assumed constant, and all inputs (labour, materials, plant size itself) are increased by a given percentage but output per period of time rises by more than that percentage, then scale economies are present. *Decreasing returns to scale* (or diseconomies of scale) arise when all inputs are increased by a certain proportion but output rises by less than that proportion. *Constant returns to scale* are then self-explanatory: output rises or falls in the same proportion as inputs.

Note that, in the definition, all factors are variable – the scale changes – hence the term 'returns to scale'. This contrasts with the law of diminishing returns (or, as it is sometimes known, *returns to factor*) where at least one factor or input is held constant.

Geometrically this is one major distinction between short-run and long-run average cost curves. The short-run curve is composed of a unit fixed cost curve (for a non-varying input) and a unit variable cost curve. It has a U shape for two reasons. First, fixed unit costs are spread more thinly over an increasing output. Second, after a point, diminishing returns set in and the marginal cost curve begins to rise; the rate of decrease of the unit variable cost curve slows, ceases to fall when it equals marginal cost, and then rises.

In the long-run case there is no fixed cost curve because all factors are variable. The long-run average cost (LRAC) is the so-called envelope of the short-run curves. It does *not* show a line joining the bottoms of the Us of each possible short-run curve. Rather it shows, to quote Pratten, 'the

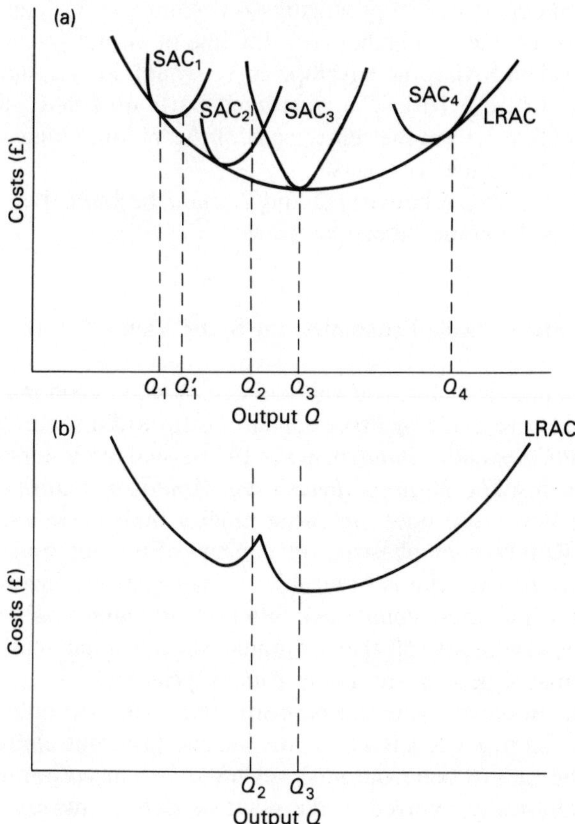

Figure 6.1 *Long-run average cost curve: (a) general form, joining short-run curves for four plants; (b) given that output requirements fall between the points of tangency of short-run cost curves for possible plants*

lowest possible cost of producing at any scale of output after all possible adaptation to that scale has taken place'.[1] To join the bottoms of all the Us by any smooth curve would in fact be a geometric impossibility.

Figure 6.1(a) summarizes our discussion to this point. The figure shows short-run curves for four possible plant sizes and the long-run envelope scale curve. Economies of scale are present as we move from plant size 1 to plant size 3; the LRAC slopes down. At plant size 4 diseconomies set in. Only at Q_3 do the minima of a short-run curve and the long-run curve coincide. Thus in the case of plant 1, with short-run average cost SAC_1, Q_1' is the minimum but Q_1 is the point of tangency.

To return to Pratten's definition: the LRAC shows the lowest cost of producing at any scale after all adaptations have taken place. If for technological reasons it is not possible to build a plant between sizes 2 and

3 then the cheapest way of producing Q_2 is plant size 2. Plant size 3 could also produce Q_2 but at a higher cost; the line of output Q_2 cuts SAC_2 at a lower point than SAC_3; the envelope curve would, in fact, have the tilted-W shape of figure 6.1(b). The right-hand portion of SAC_2 and the left-hand limb of SAC_3 form the centre peak of the W for as long as the former is below the latter and vice versa.

If plant of any size between 2 and 3 *could* be built then the original smooth envelope could indeed be drawn.

Sources of Firms' Scale Economies: the Static View

The first detailed analyses of the sources of scale economies and their implications were made by Professor Sir Austin Robinson in his book *The Structure of Competitive Industry* in the 1930s,[2] and by Professor P. Sargent Florence in his *The Logic of British and American Industry*.[3] Although both these books are now somewhat elderly their basic insights remain unsullied. Robinson emphasized the concept of the optimum size of firm. He analysed the five criteria of technique, management, finance, marketing and risk. Each of these could have different optimum scales of operation and the reconciliation of these optima was essentially an exercise in organizational logic and was a major managerial task.

In brief, Robinson was emphasizing that scale economies and dis-economies can produce LRAC curves for one firm, but the foot of the U need not be at the same output level for different corporate functions. Figure 6.1 basically referred to the plant or factory, not to the firm as a whole. If referred only to technique, not to management, finance, marketing or risk. We shall return to these other criteria below.

Specialization

The larger the output the greater will be the opportunities for, and advantages of, specialization of both men and machinery. Adam Smith noted that the division of labour in a pin factory permitted increased efficiency owing 'first, to the increase of dexterity in every particular workman; secondly, to the saving of time which is commonly lost in passing from one species of work to another; and lastly to the invention of a great number of machines which facilitate and abridge labour and enable one man to do the work of many'.

Increased output may enable firms to employ staff with special skills in engineering, production, marketing, finance or information processing. Smaller firms may have neither the resources to pay for nor the number of tasks fully to occupy and utilize some specialists. They consequently may then have to make do with less well trained personnel whose lower efficiency is not compensated by proportionately lower remuneration.

The principle of multiples

Sargent Florence argued that scale economies could arise from three principles: multiples, bulk transactions and massed reserves. The principle of multiples is also often called the problem of indivisibilities. The economies available from specialization depend upon the specialists being fully utilized in their speciality up to capacity. (It is somewhat inefficient to use a highly qualified accountant or market research specialist for two and a half days out of five, and, because inadequate work is available, to employ them as a bookkeeper or delivery man respectively on the remaining two and a half days.) But the capacity of different specialists is not identical, and they are often indivisible or non-transferable. Thus an accountant can rarely be transferred to a market research man's desk and perform the job with the same competence as a marketing specialist. When capacities vary as well as competences the problem of indivisibilities arises.

Consider the can-making process outlined in table 6.1. The greater the productive capacity of any one indivisible and specialist resource (in this case, the cutter) the greater is the necessary multiple of the others to ensure that the lowest common multiple (LCM) throughout is attained.

Table 6.1 *Can-making process*

	Steel cutters (i.e. cutting rectangles of metal)	Moulders and solderers (i.e. shaping hollow cylinders)	Capping machines (i.e. fixing end onto tin can cylinder)
Capacity in tons of strip steel equivalent per hour	30	5	10
Number of machines required to have each fully utilized	1	6	3

The principle of bulk transactions

This saving can be subdivided into at least three categories. Most obviously, as Sargent Florence pointed out, 'the total monetary, physical or psychological costs of dealing in large quantities are sometimes no greater . . . than the costs of dealing in small quantities; and hence the cost *per unit* becomes smaller with large quantities.' A salesman makes very little, if any, extra effort when he negotiates an order for several thousand units than if the order were for several dozen. The same holds for a firm's purchasing agent and also for the accounting department which maintains records of the transaction.

Second, there is what Austin Robinson called the *integration of processes*. In a sense this is the opposite of specialization and the division of labour. It occurs where output is large enough to justify the cost of one large sophisticated machine (a form of indivisibility) which can carry out a series of formerly consecutive processes simultaneously. This eliminates transfer time from machine to machine of the work in progress. And it eliminates the labour and time required to set up the work on each of a series of successive specialized machines.

Third, there are the *economies of increased dimensions*. For many types of equipment both initial and running costs increase less rapidly than capacity. Tanks, pressure vessels, ships, blast furnaces and other static and mobile containers are examples of this form of economy. Any cubic container whose external dimensions are doubled has its volume increased eight times but the area of its surface walls will only have increased fourfold. This reduces material and construction costs and, where appropriate, heat loss and surface, air or water resistance per unit. Fuel economies are thus gained. Moreover, the labour input required to operate a large machine seldom rises in proportion to that required to operate a small machine with an identical function. For example, a 100-seater plane flying from London to Berlin has a flight deck crew of two: this number is unchanged when the size of plane increases to a 250-seater.

The principle of massed reserves

What Pratten calls the *economies of massed resources* is a scale economy dependent on the law of large numbers or the insurance principle. The economized resource can be any for which demand is uncertain or risky. For example, a firm using several identical machines will have to stock proportionately fewer spare parts than a firm with only one, since the larger firm can assume that all of its machines are unlikely to break down simultaneously for the same reason. Similar economies can exist for raw materials, for finished goods in a central warehouse servicing the fluctuating demands of a chain of retail shops, for labour and for monetary resources.

Sources of Firms' Scale Economies: Dynamic Economies

So far we have assumed that technology is constant – that there is an absence of learning within known technologies – and that no economies of growth are obtainable by firms. We shall now drop the second of these two assumptions. For the first, it is obvious that technology can lower costs, but it is difficult from this alone to conceptualize scale economies, other things being equal. Moreover, there is still no definite consensus among economists as to whether larger or smaller firms are more technologically progressive.

Learning curves

Armen Alchian[4] has argued that 'as the total quantity of units produced increases, the cost of *future* output declines'. This is not the same as saying that unit costs fall as output rises. Rather it is akin to Adam Smith's increasing dexterity due to division of labour; people 'learn by doing'. The whole LRAC is lowered as a consequence of production. It is not simply that the LRAC falls along its length as output rises, but rather that, as output rises, then at any future output the LRAC will have fallen. This phenomenon is known as the learning curve (figure 6.2). Clearly firms will move further and faster down the learning curve the higher is their output in any given period.

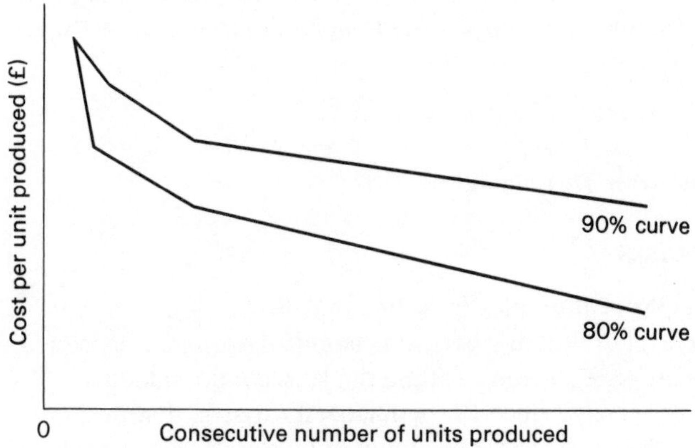

Figure 6.2 *Learning curves*

Since the 1930s the aircraft industry has found the 80 per cent curve (i.e. a 20 per cent reduction in labour costs) to be a fairly exact estimator of its past experience in the construction of aeroplanes. Where machines play a larger part of the production process the 90 per cent curve may be more appropriate. And where machinery is automatic, no learning can be expected. Once a learning curve has been established it is clear that (a) it can be used to forecast labour requirements in the future given assumptions about future production schedules and demand levels, and (b) it will have more impact on a firm with a large rather than a small throughput, all other things including time remaining equal.

Economies of growth

Economies of growth were first described at length by Edith Penrose in *The Theory of the Growth of the Firm.*[5] At first glance they seem easy to understand; but the motives for firms growing are many and varied. The unique aspect of economies of growth as a scale economy is that a given firm, *irrespective of its size*, is able to put additional output on the market at a lower unit cost than any other firm. This is then an economy of scale arising from growth to a size, not an economy of scale arising from a size level. Clearly, to be a valid concept it can only apply to a particular firm which can take advantage of a unique opportunity in supply or demand conditions. It applies to the opportunity rather than the firm, even though it is a firm that perceives and acts on the opportunity. For example a book publisher may suddenly have the opportunity to sign on a best-selling author. If he does, his throughput will increase dramatically and his unit costs will fall, for example via the principle of bulk transactions; but such unit cost reductions through growth are available only to that one publisher, not to each firm in the industry. Other firms may wish to have a best-seller author on their list but this, and therefore growth, is not always possible.

Sources of Scale Diseconomies

Indivisibilities

The principle of multiples indicates that firms should be large enough to achieve a level of output where at least one large and indivisible specialized resource can be used, and so attain the least common multiple (LCM) of all inputs. Conversely, since the specialized input is 'lumpy', if output rises beyond levels which are not common multiples of all input types then some of the indivisible factors may again become under-utilized.

Technical factors

Technical factors are unlikely to produce diseconomies of scale. If inefficiencies arise as a result of over-large plant size then they can be overcome or avoided by replicating units of plant of a smaller optimum size. One example of this is turbine blades. If an over-large turbine is constructed the ends of the blades will travel at a speed near to that of sound. The strains and stresses then imposed on the blades increase more than proportionately with turbine capacity.

In short, technical factors are more likely to limit the sources of scale economies than to act as a source of diseconomies. At worst, constant returns to scale via replication are attainable.

Managerial factors

However, replication of technical inputs leads to problems in other spheres – hence Robinson's stress on the need to reconcile the optima of the critera of technique, finance, risk, marketing and management.

When diseconomies of scale arise they are more likely to be associated with the human and behavioural problems of managing a large enterprise. Consider what Williamson[6] calls the *U-form organization* of figure 6.3. This is a highly simplified organization chart or managerial hierarchy. The functional managers of manufacturing, marketing and finance are all responsible to the chief executive. If any of the three wishes to communicate with the others he must follow the formal chain of command and pass his message through the chief executive, whose function is co-ordination. This will be a time-consuming business wrapped in red tape but, given a large organization with several hundred managers, such indirect co-ordination may be the only practical method of avoiding chaos.

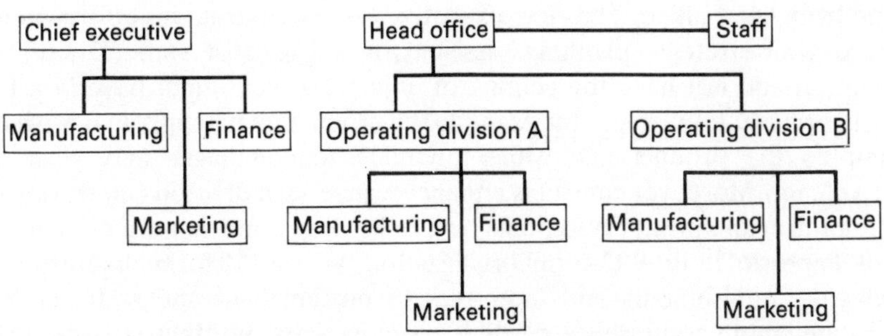

Figure 6.3 *Organizational forms: (a) unitary or U-form; (b) multidivisional or M-form*

The chief executive, however, can only co-ordinate a limited number of subordinates, and if the organization grows too large then another layer of management may have to be inserted. This lengthens the chain of command, and the chief executive, in order to communicate further down the hierarchy, must pass his message through an intermediary. This increases the cost of communication and also introduces the problems of possible message distortion or misinterpretation, with corresponding implications for organizational efficiency.

These arguments are embraced in Williamson's concept of 'control loss'.[7] The decisions taken by a top executive must be based on information passed across a series of hierarchical levels. In turn, the instructions based on this information must be transmitted through these successive stages. This transmission results in a serial reproduction loss, or distortion, of both the information and instructions. This will occur even if those individuals forming the hierarchy have identical objectives. Increases in the scale of the hierarchy result in a reduction in the quality of both the information reaching the top co-ordinator and the instructions passed down by him to lower-level personnel. Moreover, since the capacity of the top administrator for assimilating information and issuing instructions is limited, he can, beyond a certain point, only cope with an expansion of the hierarchy by sacrificing some of the detail provided before the expansion. Thus the quantity of information received and transmitted per unit of output will be less after expansion than before. This is the phenomenon of control loss. As a result it can be argued that functional units will not adhere as closely to the top administrator's objectives of cost minimization as they did before expansion of the firm's output.

To overcome or mitigate such diseconomies the *M-form organization* has been suggested. Responsibility for day-to-day decisions, and even longer-term decisions, is left to the operating divisions (provided only that they do not step outside some predetermined remit such as product groupings or geographical areas). This reduces the information flows to and from head office. The chief executive can concentrate his efforts more on overall strategic planning, assisted by a specialist staff. Divisional managers do not have the conflict of objectives they might have in a U-form organization, where for example the production manager may wish to simplify the product line while the marketing manager may wish to broaden it. Moreover control is enhanced since each division can be run as a mini-firm and profit centre in its own right. This is much more difficult, if not impossible, in a U-form organization. In the M-form organization rewards, punishments and incentives to management and staff can be allocated more accurately according to productivity. For these reasons, M-form firms do not suffer from the same diseconomies as do U-form firms of a similar size.

Finally, there are the problems of morale and motivation of both management and labour force. It is often argued that the *esprit de corps* of a small firm is greater than that of a large. The labour force is more closely identified with the small firm and this results in improved productivity and greater overall loyalty to the organization. Management in the large firm may feel more secure and better insulated from competition than in the small; this may provoke a sluggishness and lack of enterprise which are less likely in managers who see the possibility of being put out of business as a real threat. (We shall discuss this type of inefficiency in more detail in chapter 11.)

Given these economies and diseconomies – the varying optima in technique, risk, marketing, finance and management – how in fact do firms adjust their size to attain optimal scale? Can they do so? Or can they merely attempt to? It is to these factors we now turn.

Reasons for and Methods of Growth

Firms grow for a variety of reasons. Growth may be an objective in itself; managers may like the apparent security that large size brings. On the other hand firms may grow so that they can achieve a size, neither too large nor too small, that reconciles the optima of the five criteria of technique, risk, marketing, finance and management. Sometimes this requires that the firm grows so that it is large enough, say, to reap the scale economies of a large marketing team. On other occasions the firm may simply hive off certain activities, either because they would require the firm's other functions to be inordinately and uneconomically large and costly, or because the firm can never hope to use the function at a frequency that would allow it to minimize costs. In short, some of the criteria may reach the point of decreasing returns to scale before the others achieve such economies to the full. The finance function is a good example of this. Firms have to be large to bear the costs of a Stock Exchange flotation even once in a period of years. Only a specialist finance house performing such an operation regularly and frequently can minimize such costs, and the firm, no matter how large, will generally subcontract the task to such a specialist.

Firms can grow in three main ways. They can expand their existing operations in their current product fields; they can extend their activities into wholly unrelated areas (*diversification*); or they can begin to carry out different but successive stages in the production of their original product (*vertical integration*).

Vertical Integration

Vertical integration can be either backwards or forwards in nature. *Backward integration* is where the firm commences manufacture of products previously purchased from others in order to utilize them in making its original product line. An example of this type of activity would be the acquisition by a tea firm like Typhoo (Cadbury–Schweppes) of a tea plantation. *Forward integration* occurs when the firm moves nearer to the final market for its product and carries out a function previously undertaken by a customer. An example of forward integration is the ownership of many high street shoe shops by the manufacturing British Shoe Corporation.

Causes of vertical integration

Security

Traditionally the most frequently cited reason for vertical integration is a search for security (Austin Robinson). When manufacturers are outbidding each other for supplies because demand conditions are high it may make sound sense to integrate backwards and so have an assured source of materials of a quality and a quantity one can dictate. A major reason for the Shell Transport and Trading Company integrating backwards with the Royal Dutch Petroleum firm to form Royal Dutch/Shell in 1907 was the fact that Royal Dutch was rich in gasoline supplies while Shell Transport's relative strength was that of a bulk transporter and merchandiser. In 1903 Shell had run into difficulties. Its Borneo kerosene was of poor quality and its refinery at Balik Papan was giving trouble, and the (independent) field of Moera Enim was unable to fulfil its contract. The outcome was vertical integration.

Conversely, if demand is slack and manufacturers are competing for business, it can clearly appear to be sensible to integrate forwards and so be assured of 'customer' loyalty. This was one major reason for the ubiquitous takeovers of independent bakery firms by the large flour millers such as Spillers, Rank Hovis McDougall and Associated British Foods in the 1950s and 1960s. Rising affluence in these years was reflected in a declining per caput consumption of bread and flour confectionery, as people began to eat more meat products at their evening meals. To attempt to retain outlets for their flour in this declining market the millers integrated forward by buying large numbers of retail outlets.

Efficiency

Where vertical integration results in cost reductions it is a form of scale economy since, other things being equal, an integrated firm is larger than a non-integrated one. Four main sources of savings are possible. First, there are *engineering economies*. The classic example of these is the combining of iron production with rolling mill operations into a single integrated steel manufacturing process. The need to reheat the iron is removed if the processes are carried out in quick succession.

Second, *marketing economies* are achieved and delivery charges reduced if plants are located in close proximity. Savings are also possible without physical nearness. Advertising and sales promotion expenditure can be pruned when the loyalty of 'customers' is guaranteed. Economies also arise when transactions are continually carried out by the same groups of individuals. Negotiation effort can be reduced when transactions are frequent. Repetition permits the development of routine, reliable and so low-cost information flows. Risk of faulty decisions also falls and decisions in the integrated firm are thus improved.

Third, *financial economies* are achievable in an integrated firm. Capital costs are lower when stocks can be held at lower levels than they would be in separate companies. An integrated firm can co-ordinate production and consumption rates in its various stages and so minimize the need to hold stocks for unforeseen contingencies.

A firm can also find it easier and cheaper to raise capital if it can gain investors' confidence by reducing risk and informing them how this has been achieved. For example, in the 1920s and 1930s film companies in the USA had to raise money to finance the manufacture of films. Loans, however, could generally only be raised against the security of a distribution contract from one or more of the major cinema chains. Given that the film was still unmade and so to some degree an unknown quantity this was no easy task. The situation was a major stimulus to the makers to integrate forwards to owning their own cinema groups.

Finally, *administrative economies* are possible. To the extent that successive stages of production, each with an individual administrative framework, can be combined under a single unit of supervision, there are obvious savings to be made by vertical integration.

Predatory reasons

Predatory causes of vertical integration can be seen as the desire for security writ large. Forward integration can secure a market but it can also foreclose it to competitors. One cannot buy Younger's beer in a pub owned by Watney. Backward integration can guarantee a reliable source of supply, but it can also prevent rivals gaining access to that source; or it can ensure that their costs are raised disadvantageously if the price charged to them is higher than the price set in an intra-firm transfer.

Deterrents to vertical integration

Vertical integration can yield benefits, but like most other activities it also has a cost. The rational businessman who calculates that the costs exceed the benefits will not undertake vertical integration as a means of growth or of reconciling the optima of the five Robinsonian criteria.

Clearly, a firm which is integrated backwards may find itself at a disadvantage in times of low demand. It will have forfeited flexibility in its purchasing policy. Production runs in earlier stages may become too short to achieve minimum unit costs. Relative to outside sources of supply it may also find itself committed to the use of obsolete production techniques.

Conversely a firm which is integrated forwards may find itself, in times of high demand, tied to relatively inefficient and poorly located markets or outlets. The advantage of a 'secure market' may be a disadvantage when demand conditions change.

The administrative costs of co-ordinating successive stages of production may be greater than the savings which result from the integration. Moreover, to the normal difficulties of co-ordination will be added the costs of acquiring skills in a relatively strange technology, be it at a stage of production preceding or succeeding that in which the existing management team have their expertise. Quite apart from the learning costs, which can be overcome in time, the administrative skills required for additional stages could prove to be incompatible with those already possessed.

In addition, a decision to expand by integration diverts corporate resources and funds from alternative courses of action. For example, they can no longer be used to expand a product line and so gain for the firm the advantages of diversification such as risk spreading. Similarly, the opportunities to expand in the same product area (*horizontal integration*), and the gains from scale economies that go with this, are forgone. In short, there are opportunity costs.

Alternatives to vertical integration

Integration is not costless. But some of its advantages in terms of the reconciliation of the optima of the five Robinsonian criteria (and elaborations on these savings) can be obtained without full formal integration. We have already mentioned, as an example, that even giant firms use specialist financial service houses when undertaking a share flotation (or, for that matter, simply use a bank for borrowing rather than directly accepting deposits from the public). There are three alternatives discussed below.

First, in *partial vertical integration*, the firm vertically integrates a sufficiently large proportion of its business to obtain the benefits desired but stops short of total integration. One example of this is provided by the Walls ice cream division of Unilever. Walls is also in the transport business with a large fleet of refrigerated trucks. In order to avoid having large numbers of expensive lorries lying idle in winter (when demand is low), Walls owns only a basic fleet and in times of high demand rents refrigerated vehicles from a hire company such as Avis.

Second, *exclusive franchising* involves the granting of sole rights to resale to a particular customer in a specific trade or locality. It may include the granting of special discount rates to ensure that the outlet, in turn, is exclusively loyal to the supplier. This system provides many of the economies in transportation and promotion which are obtained by ownership of outlets without the associated costs of capital outlay and day-to-day management. Moreover, a poor dealer can probably be dispensed with and replaced more readily than a poorly located but wholly owned retail site. Motor-car distributorships and dealerships are common examples of this type of franchising operation. To protect their own image, car manufacturers tends only to award franchises to garages who guarantee to adhere to certain standards of stock and spare part holding, and who can provide specified engineering and service facilities.

Finally, a firm may be able to exercise considerable buying strength or *countervailing power* if it is large and faced with an unconcentrated supplying industry. It can possibly force prices down to near-competitive levels. Simultaneously, it can ensure that supplies are tailored to its own specification and requirements. This is a relationship not unlike that which Marks and Spencer had for many years with the highly fragmented garment manufacturing industry. Conversely, large specialized firms can charge a relatively high price to diffuse purchasers and so provide much the same profit increase as would formal forward integration. Examples of this occurred in the 1960s when for a short time some large confectionery and tobacco firms refused to deal with certain supermarket chains, preferring to obtain higher prices from and award lower discounts to smaller retailers.

Diversification

Diversification refers to the extent to which a firm produces a variety of different kinds of output. Sometimes it is referred to as *lateral integration* to distinguish it from vertical integration which could (at least semantically) be included in the above definition. Diversification, like other company activity, reflects the firm's desire to achieve certain objectives. For example, the profit-maximizing firm will diversify rather than expand its existing activities if the former course promises the higher rate of return. Another major reason is (again) to attempt to reconcile the optima of the five Robinsonian criteria of risk, management, technique, marketing and finance. For example, in the case of risk, if the probability of loss in market A is 0.2 and in market B is 0.3, then the probability of loss in both simultaneously is 0.2×0.3, namely 0.06. The probability of an extreme occurrence in all markets simultaneously is always very much less than the probability of such an occurrence in any single market. Diversification then can be prompted by the desire to avoid having all the firm's eggs in one basket. It may also be the consequence of the emergence or perception of a previously unavailable profit opening.

What are the *economies of diversification*? The major one is what Penrose called 'the continuing availability of unused productive services'. Briefly this can be subclassified as follows.

First, there is the *balance of processes* (or the reconciliation of the optima of all the Robinsonian criteria except risk). This is the principle generally explained by reference to the size of manufacturing plant required to utilize fully a range of machine types with differing and indivisible throughput capacities (see table 6.1). Overall, throughput must be large enough to equal the least common multiple (LCM) of the various maximum outputs from each machine type. If we take this principle further and consider the whole range of resources in a firm (managers, accountants, market researchers, sales force workers, engineers, research and development staff and so on) it becomes apparent that to utilize fully all of these resources, human and/or physical, the LCM will be very large indeed in terms of output. In the presence of market saturation and the like it is not surprising that diversification may often prove to be the most profitable way to achieve this large LCM.

Second, in addition to avoiding 'idleness in resources' by failing to reach the LCM there is the very similar economy of *fully utilizing specialized services*. For example, if two products have common costs a firm specializing in one product may diversify into the other so that it can achieve economies at the stage of common cost. This need not mean taking up slack as in the previous case; it can do, but it can also include the attainment of any scale economies available at that point of common cost. Thus, a tinned soup manufacturer with his own tin can factory may diversify into tinned fruits in order to achieve further traditional scale economies in the essentially service factory which produces the tin containers.

A third economy of diversification (or *economy of scope* as these savings have recently come to be called) is the *avoidance of risk*, which we have already mentioned. Over time the sales levels of a firm can be affected by seasonal cyclical and irregular factors, and by the direction of the overall market trend itself. If the trend is falling, a specialized firm will clearly wish to diversify so that its total sales will not decline along with those of its primary market. However, this is diversification for the sake of survival rather than diversification in order to minimize risk and uncertainty. Diversification to minimize the impact of seasonal, cyclical and irregular factors on the firm's health would, however, fall into this category.

Firms producing seasonal goods will diversify to keep their plants fully utilized for the whole year; or to avoid having to build up stocks in seasons of lean demand; or to avoid the need to shed and re-engage labour. None of these are costless alternatives. The ideal form of diversification in this instance is obviously to produce goods with a seasonal fluctuation inversely related to that of the original product (e.g. Christmas card firms may diversify into summer postcards, and also attempt to encourage demand for cards at less popular festivals such as fathers' day and St Valentine's day).

In a similar manner, firms in industries typified by a cyclical pattern of demand may diversify into products with a sales pattern the reverse of the original. This may not prove as easy with seasonal fluctuations, given the relative lack of predictability of economic *vis-à-vis* seasonal fluctuations. Another way to obtain a sales cushion is to diversify into a cyclically stable industry. This was one of the motivations behind the merger between Redland (a cement firm subject to the volatility of the cyclical construction industry) and Purle (a firm specializing in the disposal of industrial waste, a stable industry with a rising trend). The fact that Redland also owned derelict quarry sites which were ideal for the dumping of refuse was an added bonus.

Irregular factors, of course, are wholly unpredictable. Diversification to avoid such uncertainty rests on the desire of the firm to avoid having all its commercial eggs in one basket. External market opportunities change and this, coupled possibly with one or more of the other motivating factors, may induce diversification. One obvious example of this two-edged motivation for diversification is the possession of a research and development department. This provides the firm with a built-in engine of diversification which is constantly producing new technological ideas which need not be related to the firm's original market. An illustration of this is how the large Swiss chemical firms, originally founded by Huguenot refugees from France, moved from weaving into dyestuffs. The chemical research required to produce new dyes for woven garments proved also to produce molecules which could be used for human and veterinary medicines, and for animal and plant feedstuffs.

Another example is the possession of marketing expertise. This may be an under-utilized specialist resource merely awaiting an opportunity to arise in order to exploit it by diversification. Thus possession of the financial wherewithal, desire to grow, expertise in the mass marketing of consumer durables plus a respected brand name in the field resulted in Hoover diversifying out of vacuum cleaners into washing machines, refrigerators, dishwashers and other household equipment.

Similarly, production know-how in fermentation techniques coupled with growth of the pharmaceutical market after the discovery of penicillin resulted in the Distillers' Company moving into the large-scale production of fermented antibiotics in their custom-built Liverpool factory.

References

1 C. F. Pratten, *Economies of Scale in Manufacturing Industry*, Cambridge University Press, 1971.

2 E. A. G. Robinson, *The Structure of Competitive Industry*, Cambridge University Press, 1931.

3 P. S. Florence, *The Logic of British and American Industry*, Routledge & Kegan Paul, 1972.

4 A. Alchian, 'Costs and outputs', in *The Allocation of Economic Resources: Essays in Honor of B. F. Haley*, Stanford, 1959.

5 E. Penrose, *The Theory of the Growth of the Firm*, Basil Blackwell, 1959; 2nd edn, 1980.

6 O. E . Williamson, *Corporate Control and Business Behaviour*, Prentice Hall, 1970.

7 O. E. Williamson, 'Hierarchical control and optimum firm size', *Journal of Political Economy* 78 (1967), pp. 359–87.

7

Forecasting

The basic economic tool-kit which has been developed in the first chapters can be applied in the analysis of those interrelated sets of problems concerning production, investment, pricing, financing and marketing, and all the other decisions faced by companies engaged in economic activities, which collectively comprise the corpus of business economics. A central feature of this has been a development of the role of markets and an appreciation of the forces lying behind supply and demand. It will have been readily apparent that a considerable amount of simplification and some quite far-reaching assumptions are required merely to hoist our conceptual apparatus into place before it can be put to any practical use.

One key assumption, previously mentioned yet not fully considered, is the role of information in business decision-making. Most economic models assume the existence of adequate information, yet information is a costly and scarce resource. Businessmen typically have to take decisions in the absence of complete information. Indeed, the bearing of risk and the acceptance of the consequences of decisions taken under risky conditions are key aspects of the role of the business entrepreneur and the normal functioning of the free-enterprise system.

In this chapter we shall begin by looking at some of the ways in which forecasting techniques can help to provide information which will to some extent 'pierce the veil' of the always uncertain future. In particular we shall examine some of the methods available for forecasting demand conditions. Information is rarely likely to be completely adequate. Even in the case of information about the firm's costs, as we shall see in chapter 9, accountants are not in complete agreement about how certain costs should be defined, measured and apportioned. Cost information, too, is hedged around with uncertainties.

We shall then proceed to look at the implications of uncertain information for firms' demand curves and the ways in which this uncertainty can be reduced, in certain cases, by *forward trading*. In chapter 8 we discuss pricing policies and the likely implications of different business objectives for the firm's pricing and output decisions.

Forecasting

In an uncertain world most business and economic decisions rest upon forecasts of future conditions. These will take place at all levels of economic activity, in both the private and the public sectors, and will include both long- and short-range projections. Methods of forecasting may be roughly categorized as follows:

1 Opinion polling
2 Mechanical extrapolations
3 Barometric techniques
4 Statistical and econometric methods.

If a company is about to embark on a forecasting exercise (although in reality this is likely to be a virtually continuous activity), the obvious point of departure is a sales forecast; following this, the economist can move into other contingent areas of corporate forecasting and planning.

Future sales forecasts might be in terms of the short (say three months), medium (one year) or long run (perhaps five years). We have defined the terms along fairly standard lines though definitions will obviously vary between industries and companies.

Figure 7.1 gives a simple illustration of how sales might vary over time. In this figure the long-run trend is upwards, though in the short term seasonal variations produce cyclical sales patterns with pronounced downward swings in the early part of the year. The forecaster must therefore be careful not to be fooled by seasonal variations and not to ignore their timing and implications. Short-run forecasts assist the timing of decisions and can be used as a means of monitoring and controlling decisions based on long-term forecasts.

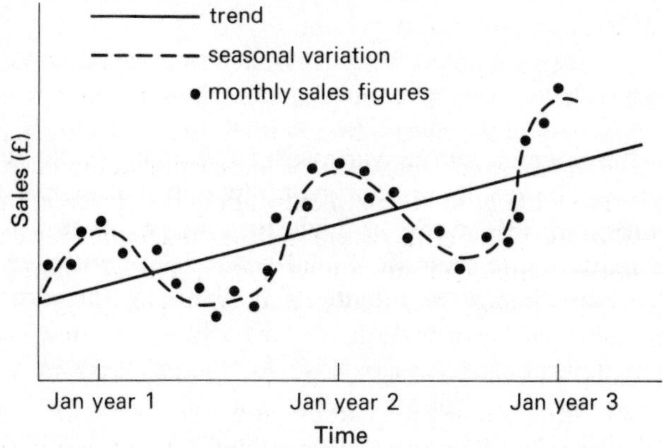

Figure 7.1 *The behaviour of sales figures*

In the case of medium-term forecasts the direction of trend is the most important feature. This could have implications, for example, for the firm's employee recruitment and training policy, and, if confirmed in the long run, for corporate investment plans and the firm's entire long-run strategy.

Forecasts might be further categorized in terms of their scope. Forecasts of the future performance of the entire economy will have implications for individual industries. Market demand forecasts (e.g. for the entire car industry) will give the company an indication of industry prospects. Even if the prospects for the industry are favourable, this is cold comfort if the bulk of trading activity is to be undertaken by rivals. Company demand forecasts (e.g. for the Rover Group) give a guide to the company's likely market share. Given these, the company will wish to make product line forecasts (e.g. Metro or Rover 214), to decide which products should be given relative priority in company production operations.

Forecasting techniques vary widely in their accuracy and sophistication. The most accurate technique is to be preferred, subject to the availability of data, expertise and finance and to the nature of the forecast required. There is little point in engaging in a sophisticated and expensive operation if a simple polling of sales branches would produce the required information.

Opinion polling

The assumption here is that by asking people who are likely to be directly involved, such as consumers or the sales force, attitudes and opinions which affect economic decisions can be assessed and predicted in advance. This is a subjective method of forecasting made up largely of a weighted or unweighted averaging of expectations and attitudes. Survey techniques might include the use of interviews, personal or by telephone, or mailed questionnaires.

Consumer surveys

Surveys of consumer intentions via market research sample surveys are costly exercises. The results are not guaranteed in that people might not wish to divulge their intentions, or might respond in the best of faith and then subsequently revise their views and behave differently. An extreme illustration of the fluidity of intentions is given by the experience of pollsters assessing voting intentions on the run-up to an election. The technique might best be used as a back-up to other methods or in situations where there are no other data available, such as a new product launch. Nevertheless this type of survey is used frequently in a number of areas, including the Confederation of British Industry's (CBI) regular surveys of businessmen's capital expenditure intentions.

Sales force polling

Sales forecasts developed from information provided by the sales force – those closest to the market – are straightforward and cost-effective ways of utilizing professional knowledge. Yet the results may be dependent on 'guesstimates' which may reflect the relative optimism or pessimism of individual staff and be biased by their own preferences with respect to desired sales quotas. The individual's view of the market is likely to be a partial incomplete one, and at best the results of such surveys will need to be carefully revised and monitored in the light of previous experience and future expectations.

Panels of experts

Consulting the views of outside experts or specialists might be appropriate in certain circumstances, perhaps in the case of complex new technological developments where data are not available. For example, at the moment no one is quite sure about the full implications of the advent of cable television and the attendant information revolution for matters such as consumer behaviour, personal communications and the location of the office at home or at work. Telephone or postal contact with a cross-section of expert opinion is cheap and straightforward, and may give either the benefits of a balanced cross-section of opinion or a consensus of ignorance.

Test marketing

Test marketing can be potentially useful in the forecasting of sales in either a new product launch or the introduction of an existing product in a completely new market area. The method involves finding a test area which typifies the planned new market in microcosm; the appropriate socio-economic classes, income and age groupings etc. should be well represented in the test area. Similarly the test launch of the product in terms of the type and scale of advertising must replicate the planned major launch. If the test has been correctly designed and is operated for a period sufficient to reflect not merely novelty purchasing but also regular buying habits, then the response in the test area should give a good guide to the likely success of the launch. However, it is very difficult to model the full launch accurately and there is the further disadvantage of full disclosure to rivals of the company's intentions.

Mechanical extrapolations

This is probably the most frequently adopted method of forecasting. It involves the basic assumption that past patterns of economic behaviour will continue to the extent that past behaviour can be used to predict the future. It has the attraction of also being relatively cheap in that the company is likely to possess most of the relevant historical information.

Trend fitting by eye

At its simplest this might consist of taking a time series of historical sales figures, such as that shown in figure 7.1, and fitting a trend line to it by eye. This can then be used to read off sales predictions for the required future dates.

Ordinary least-squares linear regression

The ordinary least-squares (OLS) technique uses a mathematical formula to produce a line of best fit relating the dependent to the independent variables for data such as those of figure 7.1. When used to fit a line summarizing the relationship between variables the technique also provides a measure of the explanatory power of the relationship on the basis of the relationships observed in the original data. If sales follow a constant growth pattern we might have the following equation, estimated via OLS regression, which could be used to predict in some future year T:

$$\text{sales}\,(Q_T) = a + bT. \tag{7.1}$$

The constants a and b in this equation will have been estimated using *regression analysis* on past data, and to utilize the expression to forecast sales we merely have to insert the year number T for which the forecast is required. (Regression analysis, a set of statistical techniques used to quantify the relationship between two or more variables, is outside the scope of this book. The reader is referred to any standard statistical text for further details.) Although the method can encompass non-linear relations by using the logarithms of appropriate variables, it is perhaps more useful for long-term rather than short-term forecasting. It cannot pick up cyclical turning points or fluctuations, as the underlying assumption is one of constant proportionate change.

Time series analysis

More sophisticated versions of time series analysis than that just considered will allow for the influence of seasonal and cyclical factors as well as the basic trend. For it is usually argued that a time series of movements in a variable over a long period is typically made up of the following elements:

1 trend T
2 seasonal variations S

3 cyclical fluctuations C
4 irregular movements I

The *trend* is a smooth upward or downward movement of the time series over a long period. The *seasonal variations* are, as common sense suggests, cycles within a calendar year which mainly tend to reflect the weather and customs. Thus department stores might expect peaks in sales activity to coincide with certain holiday periods, Christmas in particular. *Cyclical fluctuations* are movements in the business cycle which produce recurrent peaks and troughs in business activity around trend levels; the fluctuations may have a periodicity of varying numbers of years depending on the industry being considered. Finally, *irregular movements* are short erratic movements in the time series resulting from the random shocks produced by non-predictable events. For example, the sudden rise in OPEC oil prices must have led to irregularities in certain time series.

The usual practice adopted in the construction of forecasting models is to assume that the time series can be decomposed into the four previously mentioned components on an additive or, more conveniently, a multiplicative basis. These two constructions are as follows:

$$\text{times series} = T + S + C + I \tag{7.2}$$

$$\text{time series} = TSCI. \tag{7.3}$$

We shall now look at some methods of analysing each of the components in turn.

Seasonal variations can be estimated in a number of ways. One popular method is the *ratio to trend method*. If the trend analysis of sales suggests a June figure of 17,925 units, the estimate can be adjusted for seasonality. Assume that over the previous four years the trend model predicted June sales figures as shown in table 7.1. These show that, on average, June sales figures have been 10 per cent higher than that predicted by trend. Hence the current forecast for June sales should be seasonally adjusted upward by 10 per cent.

Table 7.1 *Ratio to trend seasonal adjustments*

Year (June)	Forecast	Actual	Actual/forecast (%)
1977	15,825	17,249	109
1978	16,350	18,312	112
1979	16,875	18,225	108
1980	17,400	19,314	111
1981	17,925	–	
			Average 110

Cyclical variations can likewise be accounted for by the construction of an index. Annual sales figures will contain the influence of both trend and cycle, designated *TC*. If the original data are divided by trend *T*, a cyclical relative index *C′* is produced. Thus we have

$$\left(\frac{TC}{T}\right) 100 = C'.$$

One method of eliminating the irregular component *I* from the time series is termed *exponential smoothing*. It is also frequently used with raw data as a forecasting technique in its own right. Exponential smoothing methods are basically a refinement of the moving average technique. The basic exponential smoothing forecasting equation for one period ahead is

$$\text{forecast sales}_{t+1} = \alpha \text{ sales}_t + (1 - \alpha) \text{ forecast sales}_t \tag{7.4}$$

where α is a smoothing constant with a value between 0 and 1, i.e. $0 < \alpha < 1$. The expression tells us that forecast sales for time $t + 1$ are made up of two components – the level of sales in the previous period multiplied by α, plus the forecast sales for the previous period multiplied by $1 - \alpha$. The forecast sales for the previous period were made up in a similar fashion, and so we have the recursive relationship shown in the basic equation:

$$\text{forecast sales}_{t+1} = \alpha \,[\text{sales}_t + (1 - \alpha) \text{ sales}_{t-1} + (1 - \alpha)^2 \text{ sales}_{t-2} + \ldots] \tag{7.5}$$

The weights α, $\alpha(1 - \alpha)$, $\alpha(1 - \alpha)^2$, . . . sum to one and decline exponentially since α is a positive constant between 0 and 1. The value of α determines the rapidity with which the system reacts to change. If α is very small then little weight is given to current sales, but the nearer it approaches 1 the greater the weight placed on current sales. If α equals 0.3 the weights attached to the sales of previous periods are calculated as shown in table 7.2.

Table 7.2 *The calculation of weight in an exponential smoothing exercise*

Time period	Calculation of weight	Weight
t	0.3	0.3
$t - 1$	0.3 × 0.7	0.21
$t - 2$	0.3 × 0.7 × 0.7	0.147
$t - 3$	0.3 × 0.7 × 0.7 × 0.7	0.103
All others	etc.	0.240
	Total	1.000

Barometric techniques

The mechanical methods of forecasting rely on future conditions being an extension of past ones. Barometric techniques, on the other hand, assume that present happenings can give an indication of future events. The foundation of the process is based on the observation that there are lagged relationships between many economic time series. This results from the fact that various economic activities are likely to take place at different stages within the business cycle.

Leading indicators are those which tend to herald future changes in the course of business activity. For example, at the start of an upswing of the cycle we might expect to see company order books 'improving', and the resultant improved optimism will lead companies to start adding to their stocks of raw materials, components etc. The behaviour of these variables in aggregate can be used as leading indicators, as shown in figure 7.2.

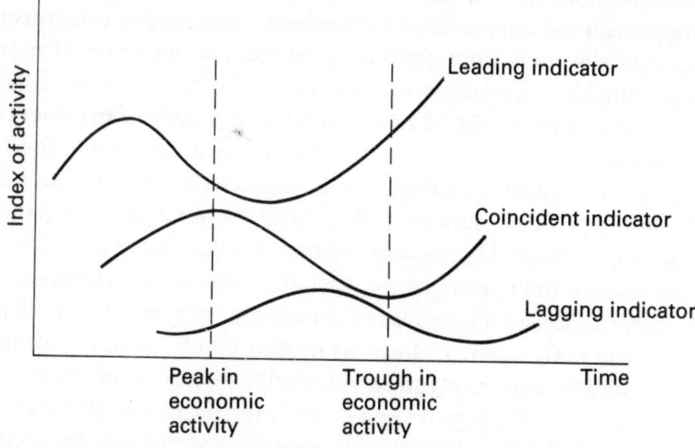

Figure 7.2 *Indicators of economic activity*

Coincident indicators move in step with the cycle; examples of these might include aggregate levels of sales, employment and industrial production. Finally, there are *lagging indicators* which trail behind the level of economic activity; amongst these we might include capital expenditure on new plant and equipment, or the general level of consumer credit outstanding.

Unfortunately, although it is possible to isolate various leading indicators the direction of movements in each does not presage movements in economic activity with complete accuracy. Even if their movement is in the 'right' direction there is the further problem that the lead time between their behaviour and the ensuing change in economic activity is not likely to be constant. Finally, they give little indication of the magnitude of changes in the offing.

One means of meeting some of these deficiencies is to examine the behaviour of a group of leading indicators. *Composite indices* can be formed by taking a weighted average of the behaviour of several leading indicators. Another approach is to form *diffusion indices*, which reflect the percentage of leading indicators that are moving in the same direction at a given time. These approaches at least help to get rid of random fluctuations or *noise*.

Statistical and econometric methods

The behaviour of sales obviously depends on a large number of factors as well as the passage of time. Major influences are likely to include changes in price levels, advertising expenditure, income levels, the age composition and size of the population, and so on. Statistical and econometric methods, similar to those used in time series regression, can be used to analyse the economic relationships between variables.

This approach has a number of advantages. It forces the forecaster to try to build logically consistent prediction models which take into account causal relationships between economic variables. Once a model has been constructed it can be modified and refined in the light of experience. The forecasting process is no longer quite so *ad hoc*. Models built in this fashion should give an indication of both the magnitude and the direction of changes in forecast variables and help to explain the behaviour of economic phenomena. This is very important since the management has a degree of control over some of the variables which, for example, control sales. If they can assess the impact of changes in their pricing or advertising policy they can revise their strategies much more effectively. On the other hand these methods are likely to be relatively costly and time consuming in their development. They provide an extreme contrast with naïve models based on back-of-the-envelope calculations and should only be used if they are cost effective. If conditions are relatively stable it may be possibe to obtain reasonably accurate predictions from 'no change' or 'constant growth' models which make these respective assumptions about the behaviour of the variable concerned. But where changes are frequent and irregular, much more complex models will be required.

Single-equation models

Many of the firm's forecasting problems can be solved with a single-equation econometric model. The first step in the construction of such a model is to specify the hypotheses which purport to explain the relationships between the variables in question. These are set out in an equation of a form suitable for econometric testing. In the construction of a model to be used for forecasting the sales of a good, we might hypothesize that demand Q_D for the good is determined by the price P of the good, the prices S of substitutes, personal disposable income Y, population Pn and company advertising expenditure A. A linear model expressing this relationship could be written as follows:

$$Q_D = a + bP + cS + dY + ePn + fA + g. \tag{7.6}$$

Regression analysis can then be applied to estimate the parameters of the equation – the values of a, b, c, d etc. Once established the model can easily be used for forecasting by substituting the expected values of the independent variables into the equation; these are the values of P, S, Y etc. The result will be a forecast of the value of the dependent variable Q_D. Additionally the model gives the businessman the opportunity of experimenting to test the predicted results of various strategies. He can obtain the model's answers to questions about the likely effects of changing any of the independent variables under his control. For example, he might be interested in the possible results of doubling advertising expenditure.

Simultaneous equation models are resorted to when the interrelationships between variables in the model are so complex as to be beyond the capabilities of single equations.

A number of statistical problems can arise which must be overcome before any confidence can be placed in the predictions of the single-equation model. A brief indication of some of these difficulties follows.

Missing variables

In expression (7.6) the last germ g is an error term included to account for the fact that the model is unlikely to fit the data exactly; there will be discrepancies between the values suggested by the model and actual observed values. The assumption behind the regression techniques applied to estimate the parameters of the model is that successive values of the error term are independent and average out; they thus have an expected value of zero. However, this is not necessarily the case; successive values of the error term might be related, thus showing a pattern of movements. In this case they are described as displaying *autocorrelation*. One possible cause of this is the omission of an important variable from the equation being estimated. If the missing variable behaves as an economic variable and has a regular influence on the data, the error term could behave systematically. This may mean that in reality the model explains the behaviour of the data less convincingly than the standard measurements indicate.

Multicollinearity or intercorrelation of variables

In the use of regression analysis it is assumed that the independent variables P, S, Y etc. in expression (7.6) are truly independent of one another. If this is not the case and two or more of them are correlated, then multicollinearity is said to be present. In this situation it is difficult to ascertain which of the variables has the explanatory power, and the estimated coefficients attached to them are likely to be inaccurate. The easiest way round the problem is to omit all but one of the variables which are linked together.

The identification problem

It is very difficult to be certain in statistical efforts to estimate demand that success has been achieved. Suppose that we are trying to estimate the demand curve for the product shown in figure 7.3. The data available on price charged and quantity purchased at different points in time appear to produce a convincingly downward-sloping demand curve. Yet we cannot be sure of this unless we have additional information. It will be recalled from the discussion in chapter 3 that a demand curve only holds good if all other factors which affect demand are held constant; otherwise it will move about. It may be that our observed points on the line EF are all on the same demand curve and represent various points of market equilibrium attained as supply conditions change. This is shown in figure 7.4. If this is the case, and demand conditions have not changed, EF is a genuine demand curve.

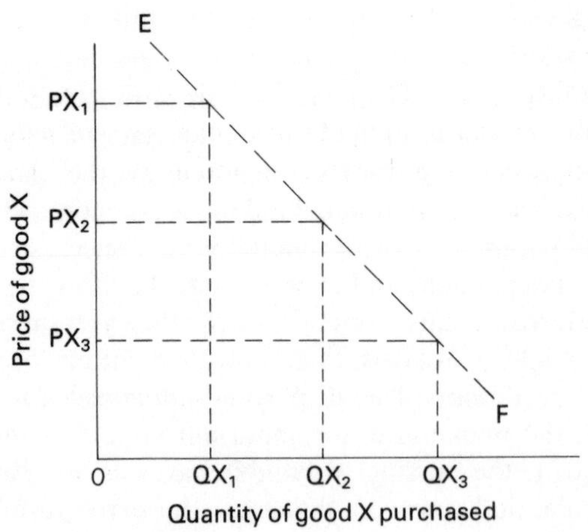

Figure 7.3 *A plot of price–quantity combinations*

On the other hand, non-price variables in both the supply and the demand functions may have changed between the data points. Perhaps new machinery has been installed between observations and the supply curve has moved downwards to the right, reflecting the increased efficiency in production. Perhaps at the same time the prices of substitute goods for X

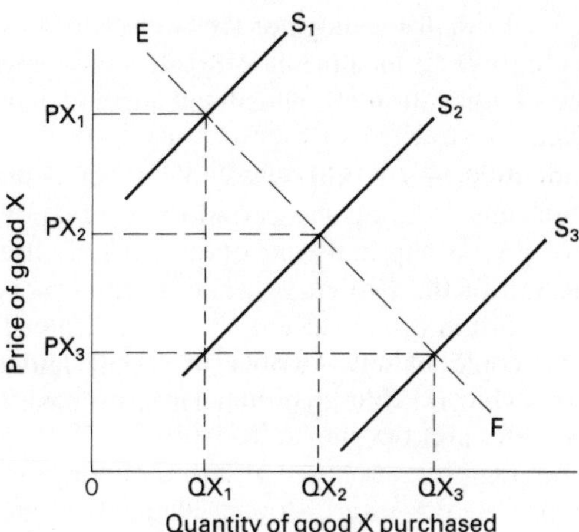

Figure 7.4 *A stable demand curve and shifting supply conditions*

have risen, so that the true demand curves for good X have also shifted downwards to the right. This is shown in figure 7.5. In this case both demand and supply conditions have altered between observations. Our points on EF are a meaningless hybrid of different sets of equilibrium demand and supply conditions.

If it were assumed that EF is the genuine demand curve, wildly inaccurate forecasts could result. Suppose that the current price is PX_1 and the firm is considering lowering its price to PX_2 in the hope of obtaining an increase in sales of $QX_1 - QX_2$. If in fact demand conditions are given by D_1 a much more inelastic demand curve than the one 'estimated', the firm will suffer a very poor response in sales and might be better served leaving the price as it is.

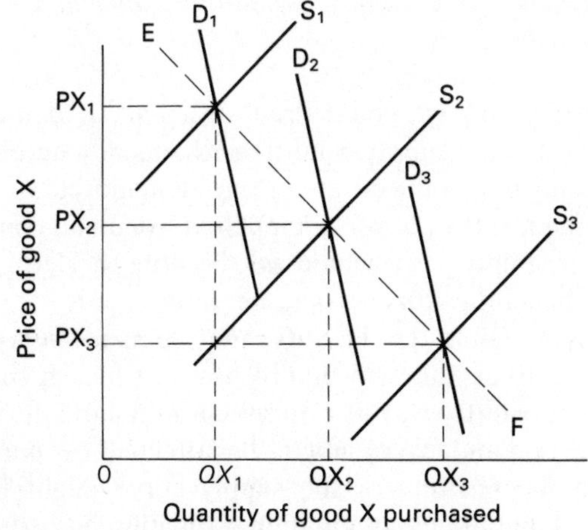

Figure 7.5 *Shifting supply and demand curves*

We are back to Marshall's analogy of the two scissor blades, supply and demand, which jointly determine price. We basically have two simultaneous relationships and identification of the demand curve is only possible under certain conditions.

For a start, identification is impossible if neither demand nor supply conditions have changed during the period of observations. In this case, depicted in figure 7.6, perhaps only one of our pairs of observations lies on the true intersection of the two curves, and all the others merely reflect temporary disequilibrium disturbances. The bar indicates the mean of the observations. We could fit any number of supply and demand curves through the points shown in the diagram. Here we have only one point, with co-ordinates PX_1 and QX_1.

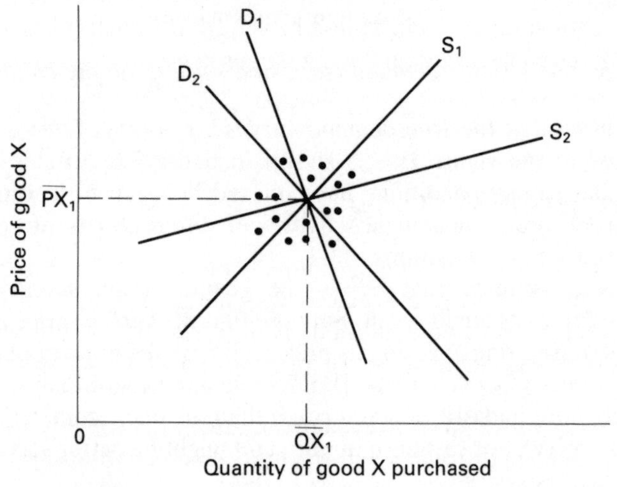

Figure 7.6 *Demand and supply conditions unchanged; identification impossible*

If we had two points we could draw in a line. If demand conditions remained constant and if supply conditions changed, a number of points of equilibrium would be produced along one demand curve and the curve would be identified. If the converse happened – demand conditions altered but not those of supply – we would not be able to identify the demand curve (though the supply curve would be determined).

Finally, it is possible to identify the demand curve if sufficient information exists to explain why and by how much each curve has shifted between observations. By way of example, for an agricultural product the position of the demand curve might be affected by personal disposal income Y, and the position of the supply curve might be affected by temperature T. A simultaneous equation estimation procedure can then be used to estimate the relationships between the four variables – price P, quantity Q, personal disposal income Y and temperature T. It is possible to obtain equations representing both supply and demand functions separately if each simultaneous equation contains a variable that does not appear in the other. In our example we have

$$Q_D = a_1 + a_2P + a_3Y \tag{7.7}$$

$$Q_S = b_1 + b_2P + b_3{}^T \tag{7.8}$$

where a_1, a_2, a_3, b_1, b_2 and b_3 have been calculated from past data relating to the variables as in equation (7.6) above. This pair of simultaneous equations fulfils the requirements and they are duly identified as demand and supply equations respectively. Given forecasted values for P, Y and T, Q_D and Q_S can then be found without the danger that the identification problem will result in inaccurate estimates for either Q value.

If the identifiation problem cannot be solved, the analyst has to fall back on other forecasting techniques such as barometric indicators or opinion polling.

Uncertainty and Demand Curves

The discussion of forecasting techniques and demand curve estimation procedures in the previous section will have suggested that a firm's knowledge of its demand conditions is not quite as straightforward and unequivocal as the demand curve in a typical textbook analysis might imply.

In practice a typical firm that is a price setter will probably be operating in an environment in which information about equilibrium prices and quantities is a scarce costly commodity. Firms are unlikely to possess full information about the quality and price of their rival firms' products. Customers will not be fully informed of the selling prices right across the market.

Suppose that a typical company obtains information about the demand for its product by observing how sales perform at the current price. If it has been in operation for some time, it will have an accumulation of this information plus, presumably, knowledge of its own cost structures. It should eventually be in a position to determine roughly what price is optiminal for its operations. The position of a firm with imperfect knowledge of its demand conditions is shown in figure 7.7.

If the firm knew its costs and demand conditions perfectly, and was a profit maximizer, it would equate its marginal revenue with its marginal costs and sell output Q_0 at price P_0 (figure 7.7(a)). But if the firm was uncertain about its demand conditions, Q_0 could be viewed as the mean of a normal probability distribution (the continuous curve in figure 7.7(b)). The uncertainty is shown by the shaded band drawn around the demand

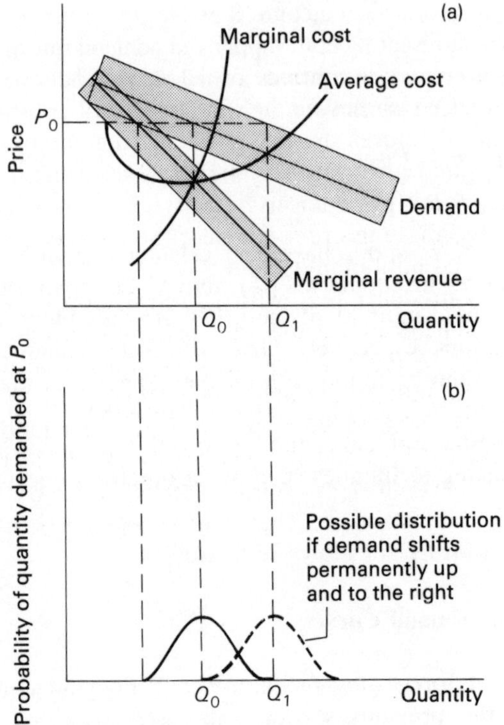

Figure 7.7 *The position of the firm facing uncertain demand*

curve in figure 7.7(a). At a price P_0 the firm would expect sales to vary about an average of Q_0. The extremes of the variation are given by the intersections of a horizontal line drawn through price P_0 and the two edges of the shaded band around the demand curve in figure 7.7(a). These intersections also determine the two extremes of the probability distribution around Q_0 in figure 7.7(b). It follows that the marginal revenue curve is similarly uncertain, and it too is enclosed by a shaded band.

Suppose that in a given period the firm starts to observe sales of Q_1 at price P_0. Does this mean that it will immediately alter its price? It is unlikely to change its price unless it thinks demand conditions have altered and that Q_1 is the centre of a new distribution, marked by the broken curve in figure 7.7(b). It will need to observe steady sales around Q_1 before it is convinced of this. When this happens and it decides that demand conditions have altered it will revise its price accordingly as the new demand and marginal revenue curves suggest.

Although firms typically face uncertainty about demand conditions there are certain strategies that help to diminish these risks. Indeed, in certain cases markets are organized to this end. This leads us to consider futures markets and hedging.

Futures markets and hedging

Many contracts are made in advance of delivery. Whenever something is ordered, rather than purchased on the spot, a forward or futures contract is involved. Organized futures markets exist in commodities of all kinds, foreign currencies and financial instruments. One of the advantages of a futures contract is that price uncertainty is removed, since the price is decided at the time that the order is made, though the 'good' concerned may not be delivered until months later.

For example, a producer may wish to sell a crop of wheat in eight months' time but may be unsure about the price at which he will be able to sell it. A buyer may be looking for a delivery of wheat at the same time. The existence of a futures market with standardized procedures and contracts will enable both to enter into an agreement immediately. The agreement will specify the grade and quantity of wheat, the point at which the producer will deliver in eight months' time (when the contract becomes due), and the guaranteed price. The relative positions of the buyer and seller in such a contract are shown in figure 7.8.

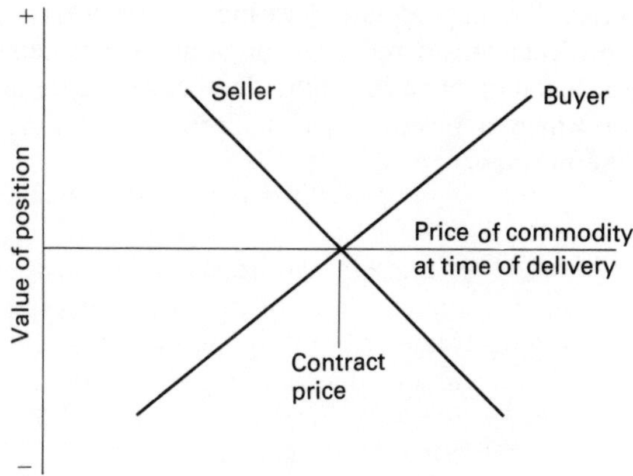

Figure 7.8 *Positions in a futures contract*

The profit of the buyer or seller depends on the actual price of the commodity at the time of delivery. If wheat prices slump following a bumper crop then the seller will profit, but the gains are reversed if the price of wheat exceeds the contract price. By entering into the contract the seller has removed the uncertainty of the price at which he will sell the wheat, but not the risk attached to future price fluctuations.

However, if he already owns a stock of wheat when he enters into the contract he is said to have *hedged* his position. The value of his stock of wheat will increase in step with changes in the price of wheat at the time of delivery. The value of the futures contract will move in step in the same direction but the farmer is 'long' in wheat (he possesses it) and 'short' on the futures contract (he has sold it). Gains on the futures contract will go to the purchasing speculator if prices move up. Thus, from the farmer's point of view, the two movements offset one another and he has hedged away his risk.

His overall position is the same if prices fall. The value of his stock of wheat goes down but he gains on the futures contract and again the two movements cancel out. When he hedges the farmer makes a two-way bet and thus gets rid of risk. The purchaser of the contract makes a one-way bet; if prices rise above the contract price he gains, but if they fall below he loses.

Thus the 'speculator' performs a valuable function in commodities markets – he enables other operators to hedge away risk. However, he does not play this part for nothing and the pattern of futures contract prices in relation to actual commodity prices should be such that on balance he receives a reward for bearing risk. Thus it is argued that typically the futures contract price should be less than the expected spot price (price of the commodity at the time of delivery); this phenomenon is termed *normal backwardation* and generates the speculator's return.

Thus by taking the appropriate positions in futures markets, price uncertainty of the kind considered in the previous section can be removed. In chapter 8 we shall look at various other factors which are likely to affect the manner in which a business sets its prices, including the overall objectives of the business.

8

Pricing Policies

In chapters 3, 4 and 5 we examined the theory of prices and costs. However, the realities of business life often (although not always) make such theories rather less than useful. In this chapter we look at pricing decisions starting from the ground up, as it were, and then refine our discussion in the light of the earlier chapters.

Mark-up Pricing

Whilst the theories of chapter 5 suggest predictions as to how groups of firms behave, when managers are asked how they set prices many studies have suggested that the majority of firms use a 'mark-up' method. That is, to calculate price some form of average costs are calculated to which a mark-up is added. The earliest study with this finding was by Hall and Hitch[1] who found that, of 38 businessmen interviewed, 30 set their price in this way. Subsequent studies by Andrews, Hague, Skinner[2] and others have confirmed this conclusion. In this section we consider how average costs are calculated when mark-up pricing is used, what factors determine the magnitude of the mark-up and whether the practice is consistent with profit maximization.

Calculation of Average Costs

A difficulty is immediately apparent. If the SAC curve is U shaped the value of average costs depends on the output sold. But this depends on the price set, which cannot be set until the average costs are known. To break into this simultaneous relationship in practice, firms often consider the level of average costs at a 'standard output', i.e. a planned or 'normal' proportion of capacity. Other approaches are less precise, using current actual average costs or average costs over a past period. In some cases the mark-up M is added to average variable cost AVC thus:

$$P = \text{AVC} + M,$$

in which case the M must cover average fixed costs. Alternatively the mark-up may be added to short-run average *total* costs, a practice termed 'full cost pricing'.

Determinants of the mark-up

A wide variety of practices may legitimately be called 'average cost pricing' methods. These vary according to the degree to which demand conditions facing the firm affect its choice of price. Following a review of several empirical studies Hay and Morris[3] subjectively estimate that around 25 per cent of firms set a mark-up equal to a fixed proportion of average costs, 25 per cent apply 'demand-based modifications' to this price, for 25 per cent 'demand factors (are) regularly and systematically incorporated' and 25 per cent of firms set prices in ways other than by average cost pricing.

One factor which affects a firm's choice of mark-up is its pricing objectives. Several empirical studies have been carried out to discover the relative popularity of different objectives. Typically these studies do not restrict the respondent only to the practice of mark-up pricing but consider pricing objectives regardless of the way in which prices are arrived at. The results of a recent questionnaire survey of 728 British manufacturing firms by Shipley[4] are shown in table 8.1.

Overwhelmingly the most frequently cited *principal* objective was to achieve a target profit or a target rate of return with, in second place, the

Table 8.1 *Pricing objectives in British manufacturing industry*

Objective	Percentage of firms giving as the objective	Percentage of firms giving as the principal objective
1 Target profit or return on capital employed	87.8	66.8
2 Target sales revenue	47.0	7.4
3 Target market share of sales	17.7	2.2
4 Stable prices	16.5	1.5
5 Stable volume of sales	25.0	5.1
6 Price similarity with competitors	48.1	7.7
7 Prices fair to firm and customers	48.5	12.9
8 Others	5.2	1.4

Source: B. Shipley, 'Pricing Objectives in British Manufacturing Industry', *Journal of Industrial Economics*, 29 (4) (1981), pp. 429–43

objective of setting a 'fair' price. However, Shipley stresses that many firms had multiple objectives, and when the relative frequency of each objective as part of the goal followed is considered, whilst target profit or return on capital employed is still dominant, target sales revenue, price similarity with competitors and 'fair' prices are stated by only half of the respondents. These results are consistent with a frequently referenced study by Kaplan, Dirlam and Lanzillotti[5] of 20 of the largest 200 industrial corporations in the USA. The most frequently stated principal objective was target return on investment with other objectives – such as stabilization of price and margin, pricing to maintain or improve market position, pricing to meet or follow competition and pricing related to product differentiation – each being the principal policy in fewer cases.

Shipley's results suggest that factors other than just costs affect prices charged, including the degree of competition in the market (table 8.1, items 3–8). Few empirical studies have taken a sample of firms which use a mark-up procedure and examined the precise determinants of the margin beyond considering the level of demand. But there is considerable evidence that industries with high entry barriers have higher profit rates[6] which is at least consistent with the view that the degree of potential competition affects firms' choices of prices.

Consistency with Profit Maximization

Many researchers have considered whether mark-up pricing is consistent with profit maximization. Hall and Hitch[7] found that a large percentage of their sample 'do not aim, in their pricing policy, at . . . the maximisation of profit by the equation of marginal revenue and marginal cost'. Hague[8] came to a similar conclusion that managers do not know their marginal cost and revenue equations. In reply to Hall and Hitch Machlup[9] argued that, by reasoning in terms of average cost and margins, managers may be intuitively thinking of marginal revenue and marginal cost since they are intuitively considering changes in total revenue and cost resulting from changed output. But Scherer and Ross[10] have argued that Machlup's defence almost implies that whatever businessmen do is consistent with profit maximization.

In its most rigid form, whereby a fixed proportion or value is added to average costs to arrive at the price and demand is completely ignored, mark-up pricing will clearly not result in maximum profits. Such a rule ignores marginal revenue and marginal costs. It also ignores the reactions of rivals which are in reality likely to occur. Further, if accounting costs are used instead of opportunity costs the firm would not ask itself what is forgone in terms of some alternative use of its funds.

Empirically, some investigators have looked for an effect of demand on prices to see whether they are consistent with profit maximization. It can be shown that if a firm with market power profit maximizes, setting MR equal to MC, then from equation (A5.3) we can derive

$$\frac{P - \text{MC}}{P} = \frac{1}{\eta}.$$

If average cost is constant AC = MC, and so the mark-up as a proportion of price is the inverse of the price elasticity. A change in the price elasticity facing a firm, due, for example, to an increase or decrease in competition, would affect its mark-up. Unfortunately there are no studies which have examined directly the empirical validity of this relationship using data on elasticities and mark-up. Instead many studies have investigated whether, in ways undefined, managers do take into account cost and demand when setting prices, the latter being essential if even an approximation to profit maximization is appropriate. Many studies have found that demand does affect the mark-up set. Dorward[11] surveys six studies to find that, of the 57 firms investigated, 20 took into account both demand and costs when setting price.

Finally many have argued that mark-up pricing is a method of setting a profit-maximizing price when marginal revenue and cost curves are not known.

Pricing and Scale

In certain conditions profits may be higher if the firm lowered its price and replaced its current plant by a larger one. Thus consider a firm which operates at an output level above that corresponding to minimum SATC and which is making supernormal profits. This situation is shown in figure 8.1 where a price of P_3 is charged and output Q_3 produced.

In this case, however, the firm is operating beyond full capacity and it may, in the long run, estimate that it would be more profitable to construct a larger plant to reap the benefits of such economies; this is shown by the larger plant size SATC′, with output and price remaining at Q_3, P_3. If demand is relatively price elastic then price itself could be reduced and still further cost reductions could be achieved; for example, price could be reduced to P_4 and output increased to Q_4 if plant size SATC″ were constructed.

The course of action chosen will, of course, depend on the profitability of each. It will also depend on the elasticity of demand. Thus if demand had been relatively inelastic, such as indicated by D′, then at no point on D′ would it be feasible to consider constructing plant size SATC″. No price reduction, of whatever size, would increase the quantity demanded to a break-even level, let alone a profit level, with such a large plant.

A good example of scale economies being fully exploited by price reduction is given by the airline industry. Although wide-bodied high-

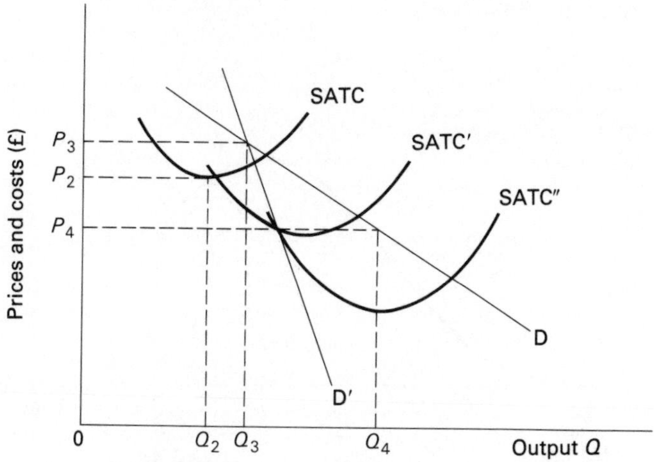

Figure 8.1 *Pricing and scale*

capacity jet aircraft had been in use for several years, no airline was fully tapping the market potential. Planes were crossing the Atlantic often with 40 per cent or fewer of their seats occupied. (In terms of figure 8.1, the position was that of P_3, Q_3 and SATC″.) Laker Airways was the first to realize how price elastic demand was, and although the firm had substantial government opposition to overcome it was eventually permitted to lower prices to a P_4 position. Fears that the demand curve would be like D′ proved groundless.

Pricing and the Product Life Cycle

Most products generally have an S-shaped life cycle of the kind depicted in figure 8.2. The unknown factors are the scales of each axis and the turning-points, rates of growth and decline of the S. These depend on variables such as technological progress, the willingness of the market to accept a new product, and the ease with which imitative products can or cannot be introduced. The strategic pricing decision is whether to adopt what Joel Dean termed a skimming price policy, penetration policy or some other policy between these two extremes.[12]

A *skimming* policy is one of relatively high prices plus heavy promotional expenditures in the early stages of the life cycle. Lower prices are progressively adopted at later stages. This policy is usually adopted for a product which is a major departure from previously available alternatives. Classic examples are ball-point pens, pharmaceuticals and pocket calculators.

Skimming policies will tend to be successful in given circumstances. One such circumstance is when demand is price inelastic early in the life cycle.

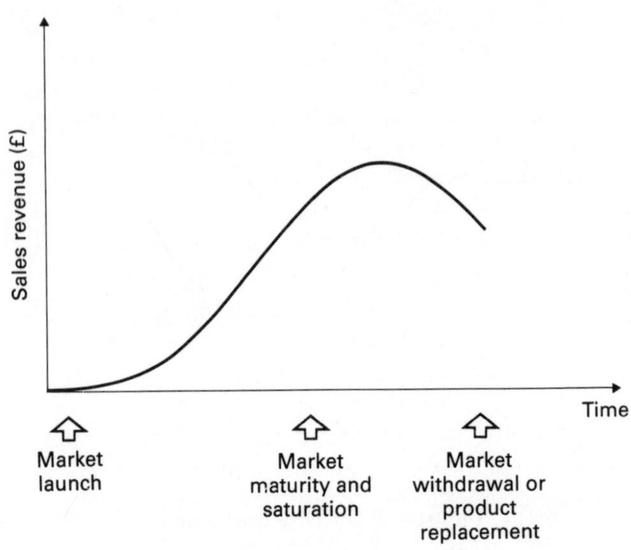

Figure 8.2 *Sales profile over product life cycle*

For example, consumers may be willing to pay relatively highly for a novelty (of whatever kind, be it a life-saving drug or an entertaining Rubik cube), perhaps because the novelty itself makes it difficult to estimate a 'fair' price. Second, sequential skimming over time breaks the market up in ascending order of price sensitivity. Thus the most profitable 'cream' can be skimmed from each successive segment as price is progressively lowered. Third, if elasticities are unknown skimming is a good 'water-testing' approach. Prices can be quickly dropped if they are pitched too high. If they are pitched below the most profitable level, considerable good will may be forfeited if the firm then tries to rectify its error by raising prices. Finally, if the firm requires a high cash flow quickly then skimming may be the optimal alternative (for example, to cover outlays already made on research, retooling or promotion). Certainly this extends the time it will take to commence moving up the S, but if cash is unavailable elsewhere there may be no alternative.

Instead of skimming, firms can pursue *penetration* pricing polices. Here, low prices would be used to maximize instantaneously the penetration of a mass market. Clearly, this should be adopted with a view to long-run rather than short-run profits, since although the lower left limb of the S is truncated it still requires a non-negative length of time to achieve the full volume potential of the market. Moreover, penetration pricing requires that demand elasticity is high. If it is not then a low price will merely result in both a low volume and a low total revenue. In short, penetration pricing does not have the bet-hedging advantages of skimming. Thus penetration pricing is inappropriate when a product will not readily be widely adopted because of consumer caution or unfamiliarity. If these are not present, however, and if demand is elastic, then penetration pricing can be attractive; this is even truer if there are substantial benefits to be obtained from scale economies. In addition, penetration pricing is a useful competitive device to discourage potential competitors. As a 'keep out' warning it can reduce the attractiveness of a market to others, since they too must approach or undershoot the innovator's price (or produce a better product). If the market is very large, of course, then even a low price may not be an effective entry deterrent. Thus Librium and Valium (tranquillizer drugs, and exceptions to the general rule that most new major medicines are priced relatively highly), although priced at or below the level of other tranquillizers, did not discourage continuous further entry into that market.

When market maturity arrives the pricing decision becomes much more closely bound up with market structure and the numbers and types of competitors. These are issues we considered in chapter 5.

Sealed Bid Pricing

When firms tender for contracts under a sealed bid system the main problem is estimating the probable bids of competitors. 'Guesstimates' of these can be obtained from a variety of sources. What sort of level of bids have they submitted in the past? What are their current cost levels? Does trade gossip suggest they are working above or below full capacity? Is their plant and equipment modern and low cost or obsolete and costly to operate? Alternatively, even if their plant is modern and their variable costs low, was the capital cost so great that they must keep the plant in continous operation to recoup their fixed costs? In short, how keen are they to obtain business? With this sort of information a pay-off matrix of the kind shown in table 8.2 can be constructed. Here we have hypothetical data with four price choices and an assumed unit cost of £8.

Table 8.2 *Sealed bid pricing*

Bid (£) (1)	Profit (£) (2)	Probability of our bid winning the contract (3)	Expected pay-off (£) (2) × (3)
10	2	0.9	1.8
11	3	0.7	2.1
12	4	0.5	2.0
13	5	0.3	1.5

Profits, over time, will be maximized with the £11 bid. Over a run of contracts we assume that we will win 70 per cent of them with bids of £11 and lose 30 per cent. This provides an average or expected profit for every contract we bid for (whether we win it or not) of £2.1 per unit. Obviously this type of analysis is only useful if market conditions are fairly repetitious; this need not be the case. In addition, if our firm requires certain or near-certain profits in the short run, then a bid of £10 or less should be made. This will not maximize long-run profits but it will generate near-certain business.

In the final section of the chapter we shall examine how the various alternatives for the firm's ultimate goal might affect pricing decisions.

Alternative Business Objectives

As suggested above it appears to us that there are good reasons why businessmen do attempt to maximize profits (achieved by satisfying consumers). None the less the various alternative theories of business objectives will now be amplified and the reader will be left to judge for himself.

Profit maximization

Figure 8.3 shows the typical accountant's break-even chart, with a fixed cost FC irrespective of output and a variable cost rising as output increases.

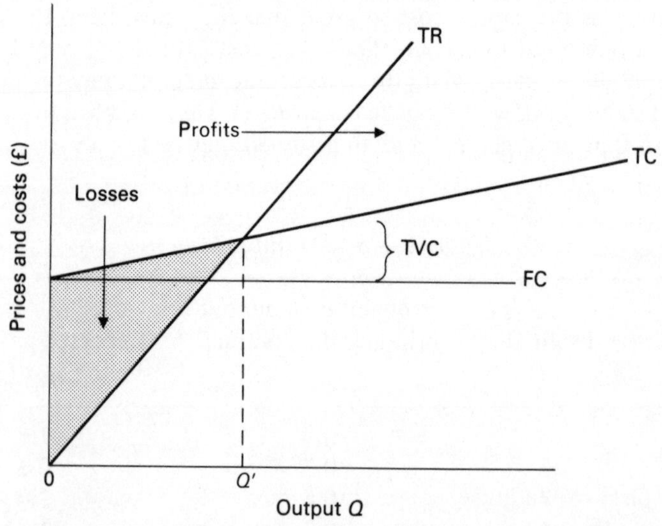

Figure 8.3 *The break-even chart*

Total variable cost TVC is assumed to be uniform and rises in proportion to output, and hence total cost TC is a straight line. Total revenue TR, or sales, is also a straight line and assumes a constant price irrespective of quantity sold. The firm breaks even at output level Q' and the further to the right it can move the higher are its profits.

The economist takes issue with this. Detailed reasons will be provided in later chapters, but a brief discussion follows. In essence, TR is assumed to be curved since to sell even more (other things like advertising held constant) then price must be reduced. After a point price will have to be reduced so far that the volume increase will not compensate for the price reduction and sales value will fall. TVC rises but not uniformly. It rises slowly for a period and then rises more rapidly as the variable inputs (such as labour and materials) begin to cost more owing to diminishing returns (e.g. because, given the same FC, the fixed input, say a factory, must be used more intensively). Overtime rates would be an example of such a disproportionate rise in variable costs.

As a consequence the economist is interested not so much in the break-even point Q' as in the profit-maximization point Q^* (figure 8.4). At Q^* the distance AB (i.e. TR – TC) is maximized (figure 8.4(a)). Figure 8.4(b) shows the profit information only, displayed in the form of a profit 'hill'. The profit-maximizing businessman will produce at output level Q^*.

Sales maximization

Figure 8.5 shows that, for the conditions of figure 8.4, the sales maximizing firm (as opposed to the profit maximizer) will produce at $\bar{Q}$, selling more (at a lower price), earning lower profits (CD) and achieving a higher TR.[13] D is the highest point on curve TR, whereas A was the highest point on the profit hill. Even sales maximizers may produce between A and D, however. If, for example, D is insufficiently high to satisfy shareholders, the firm may be sold and managers may lose their positions if a take-over occurs. Consequently managers may still produce beyond Q^* but below $\bar{Q}$ in order to meet a minimum level of profits, or *profit constraint*, which, while not achieving maximum sales, will accomplish a trade-off between sales maximization and job security. In figure 8.6 this occurs at Q''.

Utility maximization

A more difficult alternative model of managerial behaviour is Oliver Williamson's theory of managers as utility maximizers.[14] He argues that managers attempt to maximize their utility, which has two main components:

1 capital expenditure above that required for economic reasons (this discretionary investment is the firm's reported profits less two amounts: a profit constraint to ensure job security, and corporate

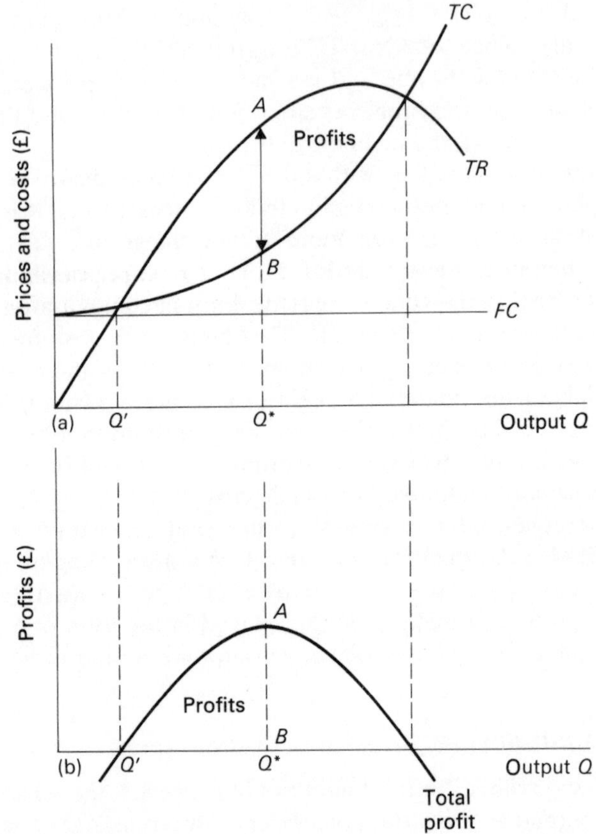

Figure 8.4 *Profit maximization and the profit-maximizing output*

taxation, since by law the government taxes profits before they can be used for purchasing plant, buildings, land or equipment);

2 managerial on-job perquisites (or perks) and the prestige associated with the number of staff the management group has reporting to it.

All these things, it can be argued, provide satisfaction to the management in a way that straightforward profits (which belong to shareholders) do not.

Clearly managers will spend on discretionary investment, staff and perquisites until the profit constraint is attained. That much is similar to figure 8.6. Another similarity is that the output achieved, as in figure 8.6, will be higher than the profit-maximizing output. On this occasion the reason will be due less to a lower price and more to expenditure on staff and perquisites. This is so since staff and perquisites are assumed (in the model) to be equivalent in effect to sales promotion expenditure. That this is not implausible can be seen by considering the effect that high levels of personal staff attention will have on potential customers.

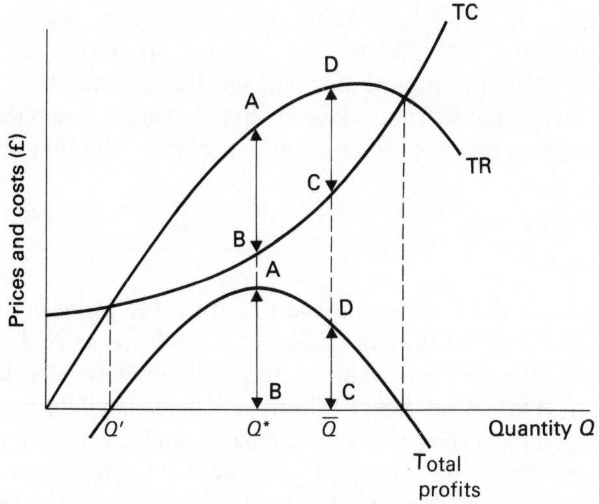

Figure 8.5 *Profit maximization and sales revenue maximization*

How will managers allocate their use of profit above the constraint between the two components of utility? The answer lies in two further assumptions:

(a) capital expenditure is not deductible from profits until after deduction of tax, expenditure on perks and salaries for personnel (this assumption is actually a legal fact);
(b) for each additional pound spent on one or other component the extra or additional satisfaction (not the total satisfaction) obtained diminishes, and vice versa.

Given these assumptions the managers will allocate the surplus to each until the last pound spent on each produces identical additional (or marginal) satisfaction MS, i.e. where

$$MS_P = MS_I\,(1 - t)$$

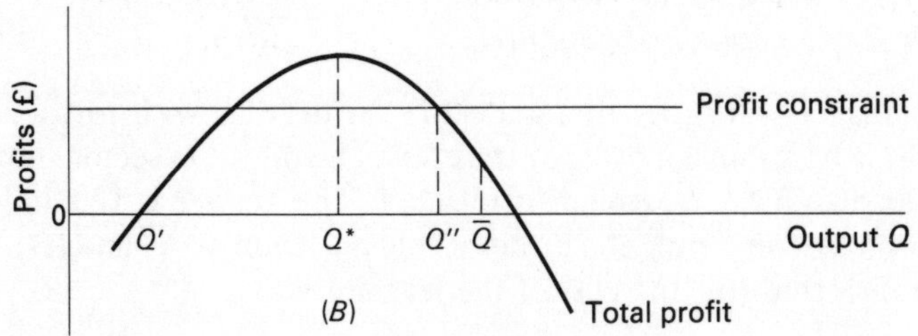

Figure 8.6 *Sales revenue maximization with a profit constraint*

where P and I are perquisites and staff expenditure and discretionary capital expenditure respectively and t is the corporation tax rate. This requires a little amplification. For simplicity, first assume that t is zero and so can be disregarded. Then assume that managers can measure their satisfaction in numbers with some hypothetical unit, and that the following hold:

$$MS_P = 12$$
$$MS_I = 8$$

It would now pay the managers to shift £1 from I to P because this would forfeit 8 units of satisfaction and gain 12, a net increase of 4. Because of assumption (b) this process will not continue indefinitely. MS_P will become less than 12 and MS_I more than 8. Ultimately the two will be equal ($MS_P = MS_I$), management utility will be optimized, and no incursion will have been made into the profit constraint, since all that has occurred is a transfer of supra-constraint resources from I to P.

Now let us reintroduce taxation into the picture. Assume that the corporation tax rate is 25 per cent; then the firm's profit-and-loss account could read as follows under (A):

		(A)	(B)
(A)	Sales	200	200
	less costs (excluding staff and perks)	100	100
	actual profits	100	100
	less staff and perks	40	20
	reported profits	60	80
	less tax @ 25%	15	20
		45	60
	less minimum constraint (assumed)	30	30
	available for discretionary capital expenditure	15	30

If the managers, in order to equate MS_P with MS_I, wish to transfer £15 from P to I, how much must they transfer? The question seems stupid until the difference in tax treatment is recalled. The answer is £20 and can be understood by comparing the profit-and-loss accounts (A) and (B). Thus if £15 is transferred to I the cost of the transfer is

$$\frac{£15}{1-t} \quad \frac{£15}{1-0.25} \quad \frac{£15}{0.75} = £20.$$

So before tax, for every £1 spent on P, £1 must be earned, and for every £1 spent on I, £1/$(1 - t)$ must be earned. Thus to transfer £1 from P to I results in a loss of MS_P per pound earned (Before tax) and a gain of MS_I $(1 - t)$ per pound earned (before tax). Since we are interested in the allocation by managers or reported profits which they must earn (less the constraint), and not the vagaries of the tax system, the required optimum is $MS_P = MS_I\,(1 - t)$.

Maximization and environmental changes

It is interesting to compare the predictions of the three types of theory as to how managers will react to various environmental changes.

If demand falls, a lower price must be accepted at each output level. In figure 8.5, the TR curve pivots clockwise, generally by ever increasing amounts. In figure 8.6, the profit hill consequently falls and shifts to the left. The profit maximizer will reduce output (to remain at the summit of the new hill). The sales maximizer reduces output also as the right-hand slope of the hill now hits the unchanged profit constraint at a lower output level. The utility maximizer will also reduce output. Because the reported profit hill falls, I decreases. Consequently $MS_I(1 - t)$ rises. To restore $MS_I(1 - t) = MS_P$ the available profits are reallocated away from staff and perks towards I, thus raising MS_P relative to $MS_I(1 - t)$. A reduction in P causes a fall in output.

If fixed costs rise the profit hill will fall by the same amount all along its length. The summit will remain unchanged in position. In figure 8.5, the distance AD will be less but Q^* will still be the summit of the hill. In figure 8.6, the sales maximizer will reduce output, however, since the now lower profit hill will hit the profit constraint to the left of Q''. The utility maximizer will also reduce output. The reasons are analogous to the previous case except that the profit hill will fall because TC rises, not because TR falls.

If corporation tax rises, the profit hill will again fall vertically, but will do so proportionately most at its summit and least, in fact not at all, where it cuts the quantity axis and profits are zero. Thus the profit maximizer will remain at Q^* (the position of the lower summit) and the sales maximizer will move to the left of Q'', again to meet the profit constraint. But since the hill is falling less at lower levels (there is less profit to tax) the movement to the left will be less than in the previous case. The utility maximizer will raise output. $MS_I(1 - t)$ has become smaller since t is larger. Perks and staff become relatively cheaper and more attractive. Reallocation away from I towards P occurs until $MS_I(1 - t)$ again equals MS_P. Since P affects output (by assumption) volume sales rise. This is consistent with casual observation. Many firms deliberately try to reduce their tax bills after a tax increase. Raising pre-tax expenses such as P is an easy way to reduce reported profits and so tax.

When variable costs rise TC is pivoted up and to the left by ever greater amounts. The profit hill shifts down and to the left. All three types of firm reduce output in this case, for reasons closely analogous to those given in the case of a rise in fixed costs or a fall in demand.

The reactions of the three types of maximizer to the four changes described are summarized in table 8.3.

Table 8.3 *Reactions of maximizers to environmental changes*

	Profit maximizer	Sales maximizer	Utility maximizer
Demand fall	Output down	Output down	Output down
Fixed cost rise	No change	Output down	Output down
Corporation tax rise	No change	Output down	Output up
Variable cost rise	Output down	Output down	Output down

These varying predictions are of particular value if (a) firms do have different motivations and (b) the government is contemplating the impact of a corporation tax or local rate (fixed cost) change. For example, if firms are mainly profit maximizers a corporation tax change will have no (short-term) effect on, say, employment (it will have an effect on long-term investment). If they are sales or utility maximizers this is just not so, even in the short run.

Clearly the ramifications are enormous. We have already suggested, and will do so again later, that firms probably are, by and large, profit maximizers. To the extent that they are not, our view is that they can be analysed as if they were with little or no loss in comprehension.

References

1 R. L. Hall and C. J. Hitch, 'Price theory and business behaviour', *Oxford Economic Papers* 1–2 (1939), pp. 12–45.

2 P. W. S. Andrews, *Manufacturing Business*, Macmillan, 1949.
D. C. Hague, 'Economic theory and business behaviour', *Review of Economic Studies* 16 (1949).
R. C. Skinner, 'The determination of selling prices', *Journal of Industrial Economics* 18 (1970).

3 D. Hay and D. Morris, *Industrial Economics*, Oxford University Press, 1979.

4 B. Shipley, 'Pricing objectives in British manufacturing industry', *Journal of Industrial Economics* 29 (1981).

5 A. D. H. Kaplan, J. B. Dirlam and R. F. Lanzillotti, *Pricing in Big Business*, Brookings Institution, Washington, DC, 1958.

6 See R. Clarke, *Industrial Economics*, Basil Blackwell, 1985, for a survey.

7 Hall and Hitch, 'Price theory and business behaviour'.

8 Hague, 'Economic theory and business behaviour'.
9 F. Machlup, 'Marginal analysis and empirical research', *American Economic Review* 36 (1946), pp. 519–54.
10 F. M. Scherer and D. Ross, *Industrial Market Structure and Economic Performance*, Houghton Mifflin, 1990.
11 N. Dorward, *The Pricing Decision: Economic Theory and Business Practice*, Harper & Row, 1987.
12 J. Dean, *Managerial Economics*, Prentice Hall, 1952.
13 W. J. Baumol, *Economic Theory and Operations Analysis*, Prentice Hall, 3rd edn, 1972; see also W. J. Baumol, 'On the theory of oligopoly', *Economica* 31 (1958), pp. 75–83.
14 O. Williamson, *The Economics of Discretionary Behaviour: Managerial Objectives in a Theory of the Firm*, Prentice Hall, 1964.

9

Financial Decision-taking and Control

'Annual income twenty pounds, annual expenditure nineteen nineteen six, result happiness. Annual income twenty pounds, annual expenditure twenty pounds ought and six, result misery.' Micawber's words still ring true, but generations of economists and accountants have wrestled with this concept, which is simple but so maddeningly evasive. Profits, loosely defined as the difference between a firm's revenues and costs over a given period, have played a key role in economics since the writings of Adam Smith (1776) at least, yet they still remain the source of controversy. Value theory, the dissection of price into its constituent elements, payments to factors of production, rent, profits etc, lay at the heart of classical economics. The issue of profits – whence they came and where they went – still occupies the foreground of both market and Marxian economics. For present purposes the ideology of profits will be neglected, and we shall concentrate on the problems of how we can measure them.

Consider the problems faced by accountants in the production and audit of a set of company accounts. It is obvious that all business forms, whether companies, partnerships or sole traders, should keep some set of books, if only for the purpose of recording and monitoring their financial position and performance. The legal obligations to maintain these records vary, but we shall defer consideration of the various business forms until the next chapter. Here we concentrate on the large public corporation with shares quoted on the Stock Exchange. In the drawing up of accounts, a major consideration must be the requirements of their users; these include shareholders, investment analysts, the City (the Stock Exchange etc.), creditors and lenders, other companies, employees, management, the government and official bodies, and the general public. Are all their various requirements reconcilable, uniform and reasonably unchanging? If not, a question mark is raised over the utility of one unique set of accounts. Pressure for the production of information will come from various sources – company and tax legislation and Stock Exchange regulations, plus the statements of standard accounting practice issued by professional accountancy bodies, which determine the form and content of accounting statements and which reflect, to varying degrees, the needs of users.

The information produced by the accountant can be used externally to monitor and compare the efficiency with which companies are managed. We shall consider financial accounting, by which we mean that branch of accounting concerned with the assembly and preparation of the financial information required for company shareholders. We shall also consider management accounting, which is concerned with the provision of financial information about the organization to its own managers, to enable them to plan, control, monitor and generally measure the effectiveness of their own operations. Obviously there are close links between the two types of accounting and some of the information generated will be utilized for both.

In recent years a large literature has developed, with its origins in the work of Jensen and Meckling (1976), which views the corporation as a legal entity which serves as a nexus for a set of complex contracts amongst differing owners of factors of production.[1] The typical listed company is operated by professional managers but owned by outside shareholders: a phenomenon termed 'the divorce of ownership from control'. This leads to what is referred to as the principal (outside shareholders) – agent (managers) relationship. The two parties are likely to have different goals or objectives. This causes the generation of agency costs. These result from the managers making suboptimal decisions (from the shareholders' viewpoint) and from actions taken by both parties to limit this potential conflict of interests. These monitoring and bonding costs result from the production of information which enables the shareholders to monitor management's decisions and from contractual bonding arrangements which limit the freedom of management to take actions contrary to the interests of outside parties providing funds. The monitoring process is assisted by the production of annual reports. This has led to the development of a theory which attempts to explain why accounting information is produced and to an explanation of the factors likely to condition the choice of accounting methods adopted.[2]

The development of the principal–agent literature plus the fact that accounting provides information about economic aspects of business activities means that there are links between the two disciplines. Much empirical work in economies has its foundation in accounting data. Yet accountants and economists have been described as 'uncongenial twins'. This is partly because they have had different emphases. Accountants have tended to look backward and report results relating to a historical period, the accounting year. In contrast, economists have concentrated on decision-making at the firm level – a forward-looking process which anticipates future events and the consequences of current actions. The controversy about *inflation accounting* and the move towards *current value accounting* (more of which follows) have moved the two approaches closer. Both are obviously vital processes. If a business is to survive, grow and prosper it must assess past performance, monitor current progress and formulate policies concerning the optimum path(s) to follow in the future. The last is of key concern in company financial management. Decisions must be made about which new venture and/or new production techniques should be adopted, about the scale on which new developments should be made. Related decisions must be made about how to fund these activities. Should it be by debt or equity, or a judicious mix of the two? do shareholders prefer the company to pay them a high proportion of current profits as dividends, or to retain those profits for reinvestment in projects which lead to even greater profits later? What are the objective criteria on which these decisions can be made? These issues will be considered below as we broach the problems of the investment decision, the capital structure problem and financial policy issues.

The Role of the Financial Accountant

Accounting is as old as commercial activity itself. Any delegation of economic responsibilities, if it is to be effective, requires the keeping of records. Early accounting systems, concerned with the management of secular and religious estates, were maintained by the steward to safeguard his position and testify to his honesty, rather than to calculate a 'profit' made. There is evidence that the system of *double-entry bookkeeping* was practised in thirteenth-century Italy.

The system involves a dual classification of all business transactions, applied so that every one appears as a debit on the left-hand side (LHS) and a credit on the right-hand side (RHS) in the ledger records. For example, if a business spends some cash (a RHS entry), either it will receive an asset in exchange, or it will have an expense or profit appropriation to record, or it will have removed a liability (all LHS entries). The system provides a check in that all entries appear twice, and so total debit balances should equal total credit balances. This check does not ensure an absence of errors, as, for example, compensating mistakes can be made. The system is neutral, and therefore unhelpful, with respect to the definitions adopted for classifying items (e.g. capital or revenue expenditure). As it is compatible with numerous systems of classification, and is designed for business generally, it does not ensure that the system meets the requirements of any unique user.

However, it has been universally adopted. A business's resources are termed its *assets*, and the claims of any parties against them are either liabilities or capital claims. *Capital claims* refer to the interests of members; these are the owners of the company, the *shareholders* whose capital claim represents the investment (including profits reinvested) that they have made in the company. *Liabilities* are the claims of external parties who have no direct say in the operation of the company but are its *creditors*;

they have lent it money or provided it with goods or services on credit (the latter group are known as trade creditors). The fact that all assets are claimed by someone, either the shareholders or the creditors, means that certain basic accounting identities follow:

assets = capital + liabilities
capital = contributed capital + retained profits
(capital is known collectively as the *owner's interest*)
capital (net worth) = assets – liabilities.

This identity underlies the structure of the balance sheet, which is a list of components of the above items at a particular time, giving a 'snapshot' view of the financial condition of a company. Comparison of a series of balance sheets may give a better guide to developments within the company over time. The double-entry system applies in the production of all the accounts, but if we take the balance sheet as an example then any entry which affects one side must also affect the other. Suppose that the shareholders have just injected £250,000, which is still held by the company as cash (perhaps before expenditure on an asset). There will be an entry on the debit side (LHS) which will show the value of the cash, and an increase on the credit side (RHS) showing the injection of capital:

cash debits £250,000
capital credits £250,000.

At the time of the passage of the 1948 Companies Act balance sheets tended to conform to this (horizontal) pattern, with liabilities shown on the LHS and assets on the RHS. For many years the form of balance sheets, though not their composition, tended to vary. (For example, in a survey undertaken by the Institute of Chartered Accountants in England and Wales in 1979 of the published accounts of 300 major UK companies, only 13 used the horizontal form of balance sheet presentation.) The appropriate format is now set out by the 1985 Companies Act and virtually all now follow the vertical format, with called-up share capital not paid followed by assets at the top, then liabilities, and finally capital and reserves at the bottom.

The profit-and-loss account purports to show the returns generated from the employment of the company's assets during the accounting year – the period between balance sheets. This account will include an indication of the profit or loss made over the period before the deduction of corporation tax. The gross profit figure is broadly the sales figure minus the cost of sales. From gross profits must be deducted administration and distribution costs, depreciation (the allocation of the original cost of capital equipment), interest payments, hire charges and auditors' and directors' fees. The remaining balance will be the net profit before taxation; this will then be debited with the estimated corporation tax charge for the year. The final section, sometimes called the appropriation account, shows how net profit after taxation has been apportioned between dividend payments to the shareholders and transfer to various reserves.

The Companies Act 1985 specifies the layout of the profit-and-loss account and the costs which have to be disclosed.

In reality for a firm involved in production there are three stages in the calculation of profitability before the final figures emerge in the profit-and-loss account. A manufacturing account will provide a measure of the manufacturing costs over the trading period. In the trading account the various manufacturing costs will be deducted from sales revenue. The resultant gross profit figure will then be utilized in the profit-and-loss account, and together these three accounts lead to the production of the company's income statement. Information from these three accounts is now shown in the shareholder's report in one statement whose format is prescribed by the 1985 Companies Act.

The accounts have been presented separately below for ease of interpretation; they are also of very limited use for management control purposes because they are presented as aggregates. They might make more sense in a single product manufacturing enterprise. For simplicity we have chosen such an enterprise, but this is far from typical.

Accounting example

In tables 9.1, 9.2, 9.3 and 9.4 is presented a hypothetical set of accounts for company XYZ PLC, a manufacturing group. In table 9.1 the manufacturing account gives details of the costs associated with the manufacturing process and includes raw materials' costs; expenditures on wages, rates, heating and power; and the various expenses associated with running the factory and its contents, including depreciation charges, changes in the value of stocks, and work in progress. The result is a costing of the value of goods produced over the year, which is transferred to the trading account (table 9.2). In turn, the gross profits from the trading account are transferred to the profit-and-loss account and used in the calculation of profit before interest and tax (table 9.3). The accounts in tables 9.1 and 9.2 are not normally published, but information of the type presented in those accounts would be vital to the development of the published accounts. A balance sheet for company XYZ is shown in table 9.4.

There has been a movement towards the harmonization of accounting practice as originally envisaged in the European Community (EC) Fourth Directive. This came into force with the 1985 Companies Act. An example of a typical profit-and-loss account and balance sheet conforming to the new requirements is shown in appendix 9.1.

Table 9.1 *XYZ Company PLC: manufacturing account for the year ended 31 December 1990*

	£m	£m
Opening inventory of raw materials as of 1 January 1990		22.3
Purchases		210.0
		232.3
Less closing inventory of raw materials on 31 December 1990		24.8
Cost of materials		207.5
Factory wages		60.5
Prime costs of manufacture		268.0
Factory overheads:		
Repairs	4.0	
Rates	6.0	
Factory gas, water and electricity	11.0	
Depreciation	25.0	
Portion of government grant for purchase of plant and equipment	(1.0)	45.0
		313.0
Less increase in work in progress		1.5
Factory cost of production		311.5
Less stocks of finished goods in factory		10.0
Cost of goods to warehouse: to trading account		301.5

Table 9.2 *XYZ Company PLC: trading account for the year ended 31 December 1990*

	£m
Finished goods:	
Opening inventory 1 January 1990	35.0
Cost of manufactures transferred	301.5
	336.5
Less closing inventory 31 December 1990	30.0
Cost of sales	306.5
Gross profit: to profit-and-loss account	126.5
Sales	433.0

Table 9.3 *Company PLC: consolidated profit-and-loss account for the year ended 31 December 1990*

	£m	1990[a] £m
Group turnover (note 1a)[b]		433.0
Cost of sales		(306.5)
Gross profit (note 2)		126.5
Distribution costs (note 3)	(24.0)	
Administration expenses (note 3)	(27.0)	
		(51.0)
Operating profit		75.5
Interest payable (note 4)		(4.1)
Profit on ordinary activities before taxation (note 1b)		71.4
Taxation (note 5) (see also notes 16 and 17)		(32.3)
Group profit after tax		39.1
Minority interests (note 6)		(0.9)
Profit for the financial year		38.2
Dividends (note 7)		(13.6)
Group retentions (note 8)		24.6
Earnings per ordinary share: 52.22 pence		
Movements in reserves:		
Reserves at the beginning of the year		119.5
Profit retained		24.6
Reserves at end of year		144.1

[a] Comparative figures from the previous year are required by law. These have been omitted for simplicity.
[b] For explanatory notes see text pp. 138–45.

Explanatory notes to accounts in tables 9.3 and 9.4

The Accounting Standards Committee (ASC) has issued various Standard Statements of Accounting Practice (SSAPs) which determine how certain items and issues in company accounts should be treated. In the following explanatory notes the relevant SSAPs will be referenced.

1(a) *Turnover.* Since the passage of the 1967 Companies Act, turnover figures must be provided. The analysis has to be broken down by

(i) different classes of business and
(ii) different geographical markets.

SSAP 5 states that turnover should exclude value-added tax (VAT) on taxable output and, where an enterprise wants to show gross turnover, and the relevant VAT must be disclosed as a deduction from gross turnover.

1(b) *Analysis of profit before tax by different classes of business.*

2 *Gross profit.* This indicates the level of profits before the deduction of expenses.

Table 9.4 *XYZ Company PLC: consolidated balance sheet for the year ended 31 December 1990*

	Note[a]	£m	1990 £m
Fixed assets			
Tangible assets	(18)		92.25
Intangible assets	(19)		58.5
			150.75
Current assets			
Stocks	(14)	82.55	
Debtors		79.9	
Cash at bank and in hand	(15)	46.4	
		208.85	
Creditors			
Amount falling due within one year		(95.25)	
Net current assets			113.6
Total assets less current liabilities			264.35
Creditors			
Amounts falling due after one year	(10)	(81.85)	
Provisions for liabilities and charges			
	(11) and (12)	(16.9)	
			(98.75)
			165.6
Capital and reserves			
Ordinary share capital	(9)		18.25
Profit-and-loss account			144.1
Shareholder's funds			162.35
Minority interest	(6)		3.25
			165.6

[a] For explanatory notes see text pp. 138–45.

3 *Distribution costs and administrative expenses.* Operating profit is calculated after charging

(i) operating lease payments,
(ii) auditor's renumeration,
(iii) depreciation of tangible fixed assets,
(iv) amortization of intangible fixed assets,
(v) directors' emoluments,
(vi) compensation to directors for loss of office,
(vii) pensions to directors/past directors and
(viii) exceptional items.

The fees paid to the chairman, the highest paid director (if not chairman) and other directors will be shown in notes to the accounts. Details will also be provided of aggregate payroll costs, broken down into wages and salaries, social security costs and other pension costs, plus an analysis of categories of employment and high-paid employees.

4 *Interest paid.* The company has a variety of loans with the following interest payments:

	£m
Loans wholly repayable within five years	1.1
Loans not wholly repayable within five years	4.2
Bank loans and short-term borrowings	2.45
Less interest received	(3.65)
Total interest	4.1

5 *Taxation.* Companies are liable for corporation tax at a normal rate of 35 per cent. The small-companies rate applicable on profits up to £150,000 is 25 per cent, and thereafter there is marginal relief available on profits up to £750,000. (These rates applied in the 1989–90 tax year but are liable to change in each successive budget). The figure in table 9.3 is made up as follows:

	£m
Corporation tax	22.7
Deferred tax	5.3
	28.0
Adjustments in respect of prior year	4.3
	32.3

5 For a number of years various types of capital allowances have been available which act as investment incentives (these are considered in detail later in this chapter). Companies can write off approved forms

of industrial investment as charges against their taxable profits. This could mean that periods of intensive investment could be associated with wide swings in company tax bills; most companies therefore create a deferred tax account which can be used to even out charges over a number of years. SSAP 8 provides a standard for the treatment of corporation tax in company accounts.

6 *Minority interests.* It is quite frequent for a holding company to acquire less than 100 per cent of equity of a company taken over. In this situation, as it has control, it is usual to include the full amount of the assets and liabilities of the company taken over in its own accounts and to disclose the interests of the other shareholders as a distinct category in the balance sheet.

The Companies Act 1989 and SSAP 14 set out the procedures to be followed in the preparation of group accounts.

7 *Dividends*

	Pence per share	£m
Interim	8.58	6.26
Final (recommended)	10.05	7.34
	18.65	13.6

8 *Retentions.* It would be unusual practice for directors to distribute all profits as dividends; hence revenue reserves are created from profits to be reinvested in the business. These should be distinguished from capital reserves which are non-distributable. The movements in the reserves are shown as the last section of table 9.3. Companies frequently have reserves under the heading 'share premium account'. This arises when shares are issued at a price above their nominal value. The premium account is itemized separately in the reserves and treated as a part of the company's paid-up capital; it cannot therefore be distributed as revenue. Specific reserves used to be created for this purpose under the title 'dividend equalization reserve', and companies still 'smooth out' dividend payments but do not tend to categorize individual reserves specifically for the purpose.

9 *Ordinary share capital*

	Number of 25p shares	£m
Authorized	108,000,000	27.0
Issued and fully paid	73,000,000	18.25

10 *Loans* (all repayable after one year).

	£m
Loans wholly repayable within five years	8.95

	£m
Loans not wholly repayable within five years	58.4
Short- and medium-term bank loans	12.25
Total loans	79.6

Some of the long-term loans above could be debentures with restrictive covenants to their trust deeds. Companies sometimes render the trust deed null and void by agreement with the trustee through a process known as debt defeasance. This involves the company establishing a collateral portfolio of high-quality debt instruments to be held by the trustee. The nominal amount, interest rate, interest payment dates and maturity dates would be selected to match the profile of the defeased debentures. They would generate the necessary funds for interest and principal repayments.

11 *Deferred liabilities.* Certain funds have been put aside to meet unfunded retirement benefits in the subsidiary. The figure in the example is £4.2m. SSAP 24 provides guidelines for the recognition of the cost of providing pensions on a systematic and rational basis.

12 *Deferred tax.* This account is created to even out the timing effects caused by the systems of capital allowances, advance corporation tax (all considered later in this chapter) and any other factors which affect the timing of tax payments.

	£m
Amount deferred at the beginning of year	10.55
Movements during year	2.15
Amount deferred at end of year	12.7

13 *Capital grants.* The government provides grants towards capital expenditure as part of its industrial and regional development policies. The amounts involved are credited to the profit-and-loss account over the estimated useful life of the asset concerned. The amounts shown in the balance sheet represent the difference between the total grant received and the amount already credited to the profit-and-loss account. The figure in the example is £2.25m. SSAP 4 provides guidelines for this process.

14 *Stocks.*

	£m
Finished and partly processed goods	57.75
Raw materials	24.8
Total	82.55

The problems involved in the valuation of stocks and the different methods available are considered later in this chapter.

15 *Cash and liquid assets.*

	£m
Certificates of tax deposit	6.0
Government securities	2.65
Short-term deposits	28.2
Cash and bank balances	9.55
Total	46.40

16 *Short-term borrowings.* These are made up of bank loans and overdrafts. The figure in the example is £3.9m.

17 *Taxation.* Note 5 was concerned with tax based on profit for the year. This note is concerned with tax planned to be paid this year.

	£m
Current taxation	19.8
Prior years	2.4
Total	22.2

The UK tax liability for the current year includes advance corporation tax (ACT) on the recommended final dividend. This is equivalent to the standard rate of income tax applied to the gross dividend. This rate currently stands at 25 per cent. The dividend after tax, the net final dividend recommended, has to be grossed up as follows:

$$\text{net dividend} = \text{gross dividend } (1 - \text{tax rate})$$
$$= \text{gross dividend} \left(1 - \frac{25}{100}\right)$$

$$\text{net dividend} \left(\frac{100}{75}\right) = \text{gross dividend}$$

$$\text{tax payable as ACT} = \text{net dividend} \left(\frac{25}{75}\right) = £7.35\text{m} \left(\frac{25}{75}\right) = £2.45\text{m}.$$

The above will affect the deferred tax account (note 12), as the whole of this amount can be carried forward to be set off against future corporate tax liabilities. For a fuller discussion of corporate taxation see later in this chapter. SSAP 8 provides a standard and deals specifically with the tax implications of dividends payable and receivable.

18 *Fixed assets.*

	Cost	Aggregate depreciation	Net book value
	£m	£m	£m
Plant, equipment and vehicles	187.95	141.5	46.45
Land and buildings	45.8	–	45.8
Total			92.25

Assets are depreciated in order to ensure that, when they come to the end of their useful lives, sufficient funds wil have been set aside to meet the cost of replacing them. If this were not done the business would be in danger of running itself down and paying profits out of capital. The calculation of depreciation charges is hedged round with difficulties: working life cannot be estimated with a great deal of accuracy since technological change can rapidly make assets redundant, and there is no agreed method of the amount of asset value to be written off in each year (table 9.5).

Table 9.5 *Methods of depreciation*

	Number of companies 1982–3	1978–9	1968–9
Method adopted for all or most assets:			
Straight line	259	260	65
Reducing balance	–	5	3
	259	265	68
Mixture of methods	23	16	16
	282	281	84
Basis not disclosed	18	19	216
	300	300	300

Source: *Survey of Published Accounts 1979*, Institute of Chartered Accountants in England and Wales, 1981; *Financial Reporting 1983–4, Survey of Published Accounts*, Institute of Chartered Accountants in England and Wales, 1984

A popular method is the *stright-line* calculation in which equal amounts are written off in every year of the asset's working life. The *reducing balance* method would write off a constant percentage of the net book value of the asset every year (i.e. the value of the asset after deducting previous depreciation provisions). There are other methods too, and obviously different amounts will be deducted from revenue according to which particular method is chosen. Traditionally the original or 'historic' cost has been the basis of the valuation of the asset. In periods of inflation this cost will no longer be an accurate representation of the cost of replacing the asset concerned, and if historic values are utilized then depreciation provisions will be inadequate, profits will be overstated and businesses will be paying profits out of capital. This problem will be returned to when we consider inflation accounting later in this chapter.

The usual convention used to be to let land and buildings stand at cost rather than depreciate them. Again, in times of inflation they may require revaluation. However, SSAP 12 suggests that freehold land does not require depreciation, but buildings have a limited useful economic life and should be depreciated.

19 *Goodwill.* We shall assume for our example that XYZ PLC, has previously taken over a major distribution chain. The market value of the shares it purchased in the subsidiary was well in excess of the fair value of the net tangible assets of the subsidiary at the time of the take-over. This excess value is termed 'goodwill' and only appears in accounts on consolidation after a take-over or merger. The value of a thriving business is typically greater than the sum of its parts. A number of factors may contribute to the development of goodwill – good relationships with its workforce, its customers, special knowledge, the benefits of advertising, secret processes, franchises, licences etc. This will exist in all sound businesses to a varying degree but is only accounted for in the above case. SSAP 22 provides a standard and suggests that goodwill should be eliminated by amortization on a systematic basis over the useful economic life of the goodwill which must be estimated at the time of acquisition.

Once again this provides an example of a very arbitrary accounting convention. Goodwill is only accounted for in certain circumstances, even though it arises in all businesses (it could conceivably be negative), and when it does arise, why should it be written off? Presumably in a thriving business goodwill will be increasing over time?

Accounting Rules and Conventions

The 1948 Companies Act stated that company accounts should give 'a true and fair view' of the state of a company's affairs. Cynics might suggest that this is a statement of intent rather than an expression of reality. There are a number of reasons why it is difficult to provide an unequivocal statement describing a company's state of affairs. Accounting practices and conventions have evolved in a piecemeal fashion over a very long period. Some changes have been conditioned by successive additions to company law, which to a degree may have reflected the changing but still often conflicting requirements of users. Moreover, there has usually been initial resistance to requirements for greater disclosure of information on the grounds that it might assist competitors. Thus different standards can be in force simultaneously.

Accounting conventions still bear the imprint of times when businesses were owned as well as run by their managers and when the main providers of outside funds were the creditors, who required information about the stewardship of those funds. Traditional *historical cost accounting*, which involves the valuation of assets on the basis of their original costs as shown in our specimen set of accounts, has been built around the following conventions.

1 *Going concern.* This involves the assumption that the business will continue to operate in the foreseeable future. Our accounts did not attempt to represent the 'liquidation value' of the business.
2 *Accruals.* This involves the convention that revenue and costs are recognized or 'accrued' as they are earned and not when the actual payments are made. Accounts therefore do not directly refer to the underlying cash basis of the business. In association with this is the next convention.
3 *Matching costs and revenues.* These are matched as far as their relationship can be established. The revenues and costs shown in the profit-and-loss account should arise out of transactions in the relevant period and any profit shown should be matched with the costs incurred in earning it.
4 *Prudence or conservatism.* This ensures that in cases of doubt profit figures and asset values are always conservatively valued and are recognized when realized, whereas losses or liabilities are given their maximum values. This too can distort the real economic picture.
5 *Consistency.* There should be a consistent treatment of similar accounting transactions both within and across time periods.

Normally, any assets other than money should be valued at the lesser of cost or net realizable value. In traditional historic cost accounts no attempt is made to ensure that the balance sheet gives a realistic statement of value or net worth (and for this reason the method is inadequate in times of inflation). Finally, the monetary unit of measurement, and therefore changes in purchasing power are ignored; the distortions caused by this are fully treated later in this chapter in the section on inflation accounting.

Accounting Problems in the Absence of Inflation

As can be seen from the previous section, there are a number of grey areas in which practice is largely a matter of adopted convention and where individual usage varies. Therefore the comparability of different sets of published accounts is greatly reduced. Some other factors have already been mentioned: the variety of calculations of depreciation provisions (note 18); the rather arbitrary treatment of goodwill (note 19); and the wide latitude available for the calculation of current tax liabilities (notes 5, 12 and 17). A number of other problems can be added to these.

The valuation of stocks

In the drawing up of accounts consideration has to be given to the valuation of current assets in the form of stocks of raw materials, work in progress, finished goods etc. in order to calculate profitability. Various methods are available for the valuation of stocks of raw materials. We shall consider two extreme methods – *last in first out* (LIFO) and *first in first out* (FIFO). In times of changing prices the adoption of either of the two methods can lead to different closing stock valuations (table 9.6) and therefore profit levels (table 9.7). In LIFO, the last additions to the stock (in our example, 10 cwt at £20 per cwt) are considered to be the first issued; in general, stock is issued in the reverse order to receipt. In FIFO, on the other hand, stock is issued in the same order as receipt.

Table 9.6 *Example of stock valuation*

	Receipts			Issues			Balance
	cwt	at £	value(£)	cwt	at	value(£)	(£)
Last in first out (LIFO)							
June	15	10	= 150				150
July	20	15	= 300				450
August	10	20	= 200				650
September				20	(10 at £20)		
					(10 at £15)	=350	300
October				20	(10 at £15)		
					(10 at £10)	= 250	50
First in first out (FIFO)							
June	15	10	= 150				150
July	20	15	= 300				450
August	10	20	= 200				650
September				20	(15 at £10)		
					(5 at £15)	= 225	425
October				20	(15 at £15)		
					(5 at £20)	= 325	100

Table 9.7 *The effects of LIFO and FIFO on the calculation of profit for the example of table 9.6, ignoring production or any other associated costs*

	LIFO		FIFO	
	(£)	(£)	(£)	(£)
Sales		1200		1200
Less:				
Purchases	650		650	
Closing stocks	50		100	
		600		550
'Profit'		600		650

Yet another way of valuing stocks would be to value closing stock on the basis of the *average costs* of raw materials bought in over the accounting period. Further complications arise from the necessity to allocate overhead costs associated with the storage of stocks as well as handling charges, and again methods vary. In practice, LIFO has found acceptance in the USA but in the UK the Inland Revenue requires FIFO for tax purposes. The range of typical practices is shown in table 9.8. SSAP 9 now requires that costs should be valued at the lower of either cost or net realizable value.

Table 9.8 *Disclosure of methods used to calculate the cost of stocks and work in progress*

	Number of instances 1983–4	1978–89
FIFO method	52	41
Average cost	17	21
LIFO method, used by US subsidiaries	3	4
Standard or unit cost	–	8
Retail prices less average sales margin, to derive approximate cost (used by retail stores)	–	5
Other methods using base stock valuation	3	4
Total[a]	75	83

[a] 300 companies were surveyed in 1978 and 276 in 1984 but not all dislosed their method o stock valuation.

Source: *Survey of Published Accounts 1979*, Institute of Chartered Accountants in Englan and Wales, 1981; *Financial Reporting 1984–5, Survey of Published Accounts* Institute of Chartered Accountants in England and Wales, 1985

Extraordinary items

Extraordinary items represent a further adjustment which can have a major effect on the after-tax profit figure. They represent exceptional gains or losses, or those of non-recurring nature not considered part of normal business activity. For example, an asset might be sold which had not been acquired with the original intention of resale, or part of the firm might be closed down with attendant losses, or there might be expropriation of foreign assets and so on. The difficulty arises from the wide grounds for discretion in deciding what exactly is an extraordinary item, and there may be a temptation to hide setbacks under this heading. SSAP 6 seeks to facilitate consistency in the way profits are reported.

Off-balance-sheet Financing Techniques

The variety and use of off-balance-sheet financing techniques has expanded rapidly in recent years. The growth in the popularity of leasing (considered in chapter 10) stimulated the development of SSAP 21, which sets a reporting standard for leasing and hire purchase contracts. Contracts of a financing nature have been brought back onto the balance sheet; the asset is recorded and will be depreciated over its useful life, and the lease obligations are disclosed as a liability.

A brief account follows of other recent developments, which include limited recourse transactions, offsetting assets and liabilities, debt defeasance and swaps. In a limited recourse transaction a borrower borrows money to invest in a specific asset and its attached cash flows. If the borrower defaults on the loan repayments, the lender may take action for recovery only against the particular asset. The lender has no recourse to the borrower's other assets. How should this be accounted for? There is no net liability, since the borrowing is matched by the asset. Yet the asset base of the company has been increased as has its gearing or leverage.

Debt defeasance was discussed previously. The accounting issue is concerned with the exact nature of admissible schemes which may lead to the removal of liabilities from the balance sheet.

Interest rate and currency swaps (discussed in chapter 10), have become popular means of asset and liability management. If existing liabilities are matched by an offsetting swap, can they be removed? How should swaps be accounted for in general?

Another grey area is that of the non-consolidation of 'related' companies or activities. Methods used here include interposed non-corporate entities and special purpose non-subsidiary companies. Typical entity structures used to keep activities off balance sheet in the past have been unit trusts, joint ventures and partnerships. For example, a company and a financier may each hold 50 per cent of the units in a unit trust formed to carry out some major activity. As a non-subsidiary, indeed a non-corporation, the assets and liabilities of that unit trust need not be consolidated in either party's accounts.

Further difficulties arise from the spread in the use of new financial instruments such as options, futures contracts and forward rate agreements (all considered in chapter 10). SSAP 18 addresses accounting for contingencies and SSAP 20 addresses foreign currency transactions, but there are still numerous issues to be resolved relating to the use of these instruments.

The Accountant's and the Economist's Definition of Profits

The foregoing discussion indicates that it is no easy matter to calculate a business's profits exactly, even in the absence of inflation. Professor Stamp was led to declare: 'The "income" of a corporation is an intellectual abstraction even more elusive than the electron. It is represented by nothing that can be seen or touched.'[3] Ideally, accounts should have the following, self-explanatory qualities: relevance, objectivity, reliability, timeliness, comparability, completeness and understandability.[4] This goal has yet to be achieved, but at least Sir John Hicks has provided a clear definition of what we are aiming at when we try to measure a company's profits. He suggested: 'Income . . . must be defined as the maximum amount of money which the individual can spend this week, and still expect to be able to spend the same amount in real terms in each ensuing week.'[5] The crucial idea is that both the individual and the company have to maintain their capital stock. Hicks's maxim could be modified to apply to a company in the following manner: 'A company's profit is the maximum value which the company can distribute during the year, and still expect to be as well off at the end of the year as it was at the beginning.' Yet even if this end is achieved there are still considerable differences between the economist's and the accountant's view of profits.

The economist is not directly interested in past returns or profits; though not 'bunk', they are history, and only relevant to the extent that they aid predictions of their own future values. The economist stresses that the value of any asset, including that bundle of assets which makes up a company, is determined by the value of the stream of net future benefits which accrue from ownership. Thus the economic value of any asset is the sum of the present values of all those future benefits, and estimates of this should determine the values at which assets change hands in markets.

In his consideration of the role of business profits the economist typically forms hypotheses and uses them to build models which can be tested against empirical evidence via the utilization of their predictions. He assumes that the basic factors of production, land, labour and capital require recompense in the form of rent, wages and interest to entice their respective owners to involve them in productive processes. Thus the dividend paid to the owners of a company is not really part of 'profit' but a necessary reward to the owners of capital to entice them to risk their funds in business operations. The picture becomes even more clouded in the case of the single owner-manager. His reward will not be constituted solely by profits. It will consist in part of a wage for his entrepreneurship and labour, and in part of a return on the capital he has risked; only after these factors have been rewarded can the surplus be regarded as profit. In equilibrium, 'normal' profit consists merely of the required return to all factors of production including an appropriate payment to capital providers, and in disequilibrium, or situations of 'imperfect' competition, profits are the surplus above this.

In assessing profits over the historical accounting period, the accountant ignores the opportunity cost of capital provided by shareholders. He also suffers enforced myopia in that he must arbitrarily consider the accounting year, and use (by tradition) historical values when allocating costs and revenues. He is also constrained by the methods considered suitable in company law, which are acceptable to the revenue authorities and promoted by the profession. Yet the problems caused by accounting for inflation have narrowed the ground between the two views, as will be seen in the next section.

Accounting for Inflation

Even in periods where there is zero inflation it could be argued that accounts based upon historical costs do not provide a complete picture of the state of the business. The profit figure in the profit-and-loss account will not necessarily be a good guide to the company's liquidity position; nor is it intended to be. The depreciation charges deducted in arriving at this figure will be unlikely to bear any resemblance to expenditure during the period on fixed and current assets. An extra statement would be required – a statement of sources and uses of funds which would give an accurate indication of the cash position of the business (see the next section).

Apart from this, historical cost accounts are quite adequate given stable prices. However, in periods of a rapidly changing general price level they become woefully inadequate. In the balance sheet the value of assets shown at written-down historical cost will no longer reflect their value to the business, which could be variously defined as the cost of replacing them, or economic value, or net realizable value (see later in this section). The capital employed in the business will be understated, and depreciation provisions based on this original cost (as opposed to replacement cost) will be inadequate. Profit figures will be exaggerated, as will liability to tax.

Similar problems arise in the valuation of stocks. If they are valued on the FIFO basis and their cost has risen rapidly during the course of the year, then the value of stocks consumed in the productive process will be understated. To replace the stocks consumed would cost more than the charges in the profit-and-loss account. If the value of stocks bought in has increased, then there is a 'holding' gain on stock values. This is not truly part of the year's profits, because when the stocks are replaced the business will be put to greater expense to replace the original amount. This element of 'stock appreciation' will once against artificially inflate profits and lead to a greater tax liability.

Similar distortions will take place in the value of other current assets and liabilities. Accounts drawn up in money units cannot directly reflect the decline in purchasing power of money in times of inflation. Yet current assets held in the form of cash will suffer declines in purchasing power, and the real value of liabilities fixed in money terms will decline. Hence there will be holding losses in the value of monetary assets and holding gains on monetary liabilities, but these will not be reflected in the accounts.

The problems seem quite apparent, but what is the best way of dealing with them? This question has occupied accountants for the last decade, and although a solution has emerged its acceptance has been grudging. At best it represents a compromise. A brief historical account is probably the simplest way of introducing the various arguments, and the disagreement and confusion is readily apparent from the number of reports and guidelines referred to in what follows.

Current purchasing power accounting

The most radical change involved in current purchasing power (CPP) accounting[6] was the replacement of the monetary unit by a unit of constant value – the purchasing power unit. Under this system the balance sheet would then reflect the amount of purchasing power represented by the company's net assets, and the profit-and-loss account would show the gain or loss of purchasing power over the accounting year.

Difficulties arose from the choice of the central price index to indicate changes in purchasing power. The use of the retail price index (RPI) would have been controversial, since this index refers to movements in the price of a basket of consumer goods rather than the rate of inflation as experienced by industrial and commercial companies. The suggestion was that CPP accounts should be presented as a supplement to historical cost accounts. Asset values in the CPP balance sheet would be adjusted by movements in the RPI over the accounting period. Depreciation provisions and the cost of stocks consumed would be based upon these revised values. Even more controversial was the inclusion of gains and losses on monetary items as part of CPP profits. This was an inevitable accompaniment of moving away from the use of money units. The value of monetary assets and liabilities would be adjusted for movements in the RPI and these adjustments would show directly in the profit figures. The upshot of this would be that relatively illiquid companies with large monetary liabilities would show a gain in profitability, and companies suffused with cash would show a relative loss of profitability.

The Sandilands Committee[7] decided that the gains in purchasing power should be shown in reserve moments rather than directly in the profits figure, and that the RPI was too crude a measure to reflect a company's experience of inflation accurately. They put forward an alternative recommendation: current cost accounting.

Current cost accounting

The Sandilands Committee recommended that current cost accounting (CCA) should revert to the use of money as the unit of measurement. Accounts drawn up under this system would be adjusted to neutralize the effects of inflation in a manner indicated below. They would replace historical cost accounts, though the net book value of assets on a historical cost basis, and associated depreciation provisions, would be shown in the notes to the accounts.

Under CCA, assets should be shown at their 'value to the business'. This is not necessarily equivalent to *net realizable value*, or what could be raised were the asset to be sold, but should approximate to the amount of loss suffered by the business should the asset be lost or destroyed. This reflects a movement towards the economist's concept of *economic value*. This value would be estimated by adjusting the values of fixed assets and stocks by movements in appropriate price indices – which would reflect changes in the prices of the assets concerned – rather than by the cruder movements of the RPI alone. The value of stocks consumed and depreciation provisions would be based on these revised values. These two adjustments – to reflect cost of sales and the value of assets consumed – were the sole modifications required to the profit-and-loss account to adjust for the effects of inflation. The intention was that the company's profit figure should indicate its *operating gains* (the difference between its sales revenue over the period and the value to the business of the various inputs used in generating its output in that time). *Holding gains*, such as stock appreciation, would not be shown in the profit figure but would be passed through adjustments to reserves in the balance sheet.

It will be noted that no mention has been made of gains and losses on monetary items. The movement back to the use of monetary units meant that such items would disappear from the accounts unless some express move was made to include them, and Sandilands chose to ignore them. This was one of the major causes of the subsequent controversy, but we shall ignore the tedious details of this and move to consideration of the system adopted.

Current cost accounting as represented in SSAP 16

The view in SSAP 16[8] is that three major adjustments are required to ensure that allowance is made for the impact of price changes on the funds required to maintain the value of the net operating assets of a business. These are as follows.

Fixed assets: additional depreciation
Stocks: cost of sales adjustment (COSA)
Monetary working capital: monetary working capital adjustment (MWCA)

The main change is a movement back to the recognition of gains and losses on monetary items. The *depreciation adjustment* is based on the difference between the depreciation due on the current value of the assets and that based upon historical cost values. The Central Statistical Office (CSO) publishes sets of *Price Index Numbers for Current Cost Accounting*, which are used to revalue a company's assets (except in the case of land or buildings, where an independent valuation is required). For example, assume that a company buys an asset worth £10,000 at the beginning of the accounting year in January. If it has an estimated life of ten years and depreciation is calculated on a straight-line basis, then in historical cost accounts £1000 would be written off in the accounts at the end of the year. But now suppose that the relevant price index for this asset has gone up from 120 at the beginning of the year to 144 at the end, a 20 per cent increase. The revised value of the asset will be £10,000 × (144/120) = £12,000 and the relevant depreciation charge in CCA will have risen by a similar factor, to £1200.

The *cost of sales adjustment* (COSA) is made by applying the following formula:

$$\text{COSA} = (C - O) - I_{\text{a}}\left(\frac{C}{I_{\text{c}}} - \frac{O}{I_{\text{o}}}\right) \tag{9.1}$$

where C is the historical cost of closing stock, O is the historical cost of opening stock, I_{a} is the average stock index value for the period, I_{c} is the closing value of the stock index and I_{o} is the opening value of the stock index.

Suppose that the historical cost of closing stock is £10,000 and that of the opening stock £8000. Value is a function of quantity and price, and to disentangle the two effects we apply the formula above. From the overall change in the value of stocks (the first bracketed term) we deduct the difference between the average value of closing and opening stocks. Once this volume effect is deducted we have the cost of stock adjustment COSA. Suppose that the index for stock values in January is 179.6 and in December is 202.4; then the average is 191. Substituting these values in expression (9.1) we have

$$\text{COSA} = £10{,}000 - £8000 - 191\left(\frac{£10{,}000}{202.4} - \frac{£8000}{179.6}\right)$$
$$= £2000 - £930.2$$
$$= £1069.8.$$

In the above example it has been assumed that the historical cost of stocks is calculated on a FIFO basis and that the change in stock levels occurs evenly over the year. The adjustment can then be applied to increase the historic cost of stock to the current cost of stock.

The *monetary working capital adjustment* (MWCA) is made as shown below, where we assume for simplicity that the monetary working capital MWC is made up solely of debtors and creditors. Debtors exceed creditors at both the beginning and the end of the period and the average age of both opening and closing MWC is assumed to be a month. In principle the adjustment is the same as for stocks, but the lag of a month between making payments to creditors and receiving payment from debtors means that the appropriate price index will relate to the previous month. Assume the relevant values for these indices are 178 and 201 for opening and closing MWC, giving an average value of 189.5; then

	Debtors £000		Creditors £000		Balance £000
Opening MWC	10,000	–	6000	=	4000
Closing MWC	11,000	–	6500	=	4500

Applying a formula analogous to expression (9.1) we have

$$\text{MWCA} = 4500 - 4000 - 189.5\left(\frac{4500}{201} - \frac{4000}{178}\right)\ (£000)$$
$$= 500 - 189.5(22.4 - 22.5) = 500 + 18.95\ (£000)$$
$$= £518{,}950.$$

In this case debtors exceed creditors and the MWCA is a charge against profits. Sales on credit are fixed in money terms, and with a positive rate of inflation the real value of those future payments is declining.

Finally, the same principle applies to any long- and short-term liabilities which are fixed in monetary terms. This is the basis of the *gearing adjustment*. Gearing can be defined as the proportion of a company's net operating assets financed by borrowing. (The various methods of measuring gearing will be fully discussed later in this chapter.) For the purposes of adjustment in inflation accounting it is defined as

$$\text{gearing} = \frac{L}{L + S}$$

where L are liabilities (short and long) and S is equity capital plus reserves.

In this case gearing is defined as the proportion of net operating assets financed by borrowing. As a rough guide, averaged over the year, this would be equal to the value of long-term loans, plus deferred liabilities, deferred tax and bank loans, minus any positive cash balances, all divided by the sum of equity capital, reserves and the value of the borrowings used as the numerator.

The resultant gearing ratio will then be applied to the previous inflation adjustments – the revised depreciation charges, COSA and MWCA. The reason for this is that these three adjustments compensate for the impact of inflation on the value of the business as a 'whole' or in 'entity'. Yet in most cases the business as a whole will be financed not by equity alone but by a mixture of equity and debt. All borrowings, fixed in monetary repayment terms, are liabilities which decline in real value, given inflation. These are the holding gains on monetary liabilities which the Sandilands Committee chose to ignore. To reflect these gains, the three previous adjustments, which are additions to costs, are revised down proportionately by the gearing factor. The intention is to maintain the value of that 'portion' of the business which is owned and financed by the equity interest; this could be viewed as the application of the 'proprietorship' concept if it is the value of this interest which has to be protected.

Despite the greater realism provided by the presentation of inflation-adjusted accounts their utilization was relatively short-lived. In 1981 and 1982 70 per cent of those companies whose accounts are regularly analysed by the Bank of England produced supplementary CCA balance sheets. However, by 1984 the proportion had fallen to 15 per cent and it was no more than 1 per cent in 1985.[9]

There were a number of reasons behind this. In 1985 attempts to replace SSAP 16 with new provisions collapsed and, although it remained in force, it subsequently lost its mandatory status. A substantial fall in the rate of inflation meant that it was no longer regarded as a pressing issue. Industrialists disliked the fact that the Inland Revenue refused to accept the (lower) CCA profits as the basis for company taxation. Companies regard the extra effort and cost required to produce CCA accounts as being unwarranted. To an extent, Peasnell, Skerratt and Ward (1987) have confirmed this in a study which provided evidence that CCA disclosure had at most a marginal impact upon share prices.[10] Nevertheless, should inflation increase again, inflation accounting will become an important issue.

Sources and uses of funds' statements

A clearer picture of the way in which funds have been raised and employed during the accounting year can be obtained from a statement of sources and uses of funds. This will distinguish between external and internal sources of funds, and between applications in fixed and working capital. An example of such a statement based on XYZ PLC's historical cost accounts is shown in table 9.9. CCA statements will reflect the revised

Table 9.9 *XYZ Company PLC: statement of sources and uses of group funds for the year ended 31 December 1990*

	£m	£m
Source		
Group profit before tax		71.4
Adjustments for items not involving the use of funds:		
Depreciation		32.0
Deferred liabilities		1.0
Total from operations		104.4
Funds from other sources:		
Capital grants received		0.6
Loans		6.9
		111.9
Application		
Fixed assets	(38.9)	
Taxation	(32.3)	
Dividends	(13.6)	
Repayment of loans	(22.5)	(107.3)
Increase/decrease in working capital:		4.6
Increase in stocks		9.0
Increase in debtors		3.5
Increase in creditors		(6.7)
New liquid funds		(1.2)
		4.6

depreciation charges and the cost of stock and monetary working capital adjustments, but it is debatable whether or not the gearing adjustment should be included, since it is not a cash flow item (see table 10.6 for details of the aggregated sources and uses of funds by industrial and commercial companies in recent years). SSAP 110 provides the standard for funds' statements.

The Role of Management Accounting

Sizer defines management accounting as 'the application of accounting techniques to the provision of information designed to assist all levels of management in planning and controlling the activities of an organization'.[11] Accounting techniques are applied to generate information that will assist managements in their control of company operations, and which can be used as a basis for decision-making and planning. The management accountant will be involved not only in the analysis of historical performance, but also in looking to the future via development plans for investment and funding, the formulation of intermediate targets and budgets with the attainment of long-term objectives in mind, and the monitoring and analysis of current performance. These roles are indicated in table 9.10.

Table 9.10 *The role of management accounting*

Past performance	Current activities	Future objectives
Analysis of past performance	Monitoring current progress	
Measurement of deviations from planned performance, and assessment of likely reasons	Analysis of deviations from planned and budgeted positions	Development plans Investment plans Funding plans
Production of standardized costs – estimates based on past values	Motivation to achieve targets, decisions on corrective action where necessary	
	Pricing and costing decisions aimed at achievement of future objectives	
	Construction of budgets with similar purpose	

In the analysis of past performance and in the production of *standardized costs*, which can be used as a basis for assessing current operating performance, careful attention must be paid to the likely influence of inflation. Likewise, in the compilation of the various budgets for planning the course of the company's production, cash position etc. in the short and medium term, careful consideration must be given to the behavioural implications of the process. If the costs employed as standards are unrealistic and if the budgeted positions are over-ambitious, then the exercise may become dysfunctional and deter performance rather than spur it on.

As in all accounting decisions, there are a number of different ways in which costs can be assessed and overheads allocated. Likewise pricing decisions might be made on a marginal cost or on an average cost-plus mark-up basis, to mention but two possible methods. Neither time nor space permits full consideration of these various areas and we shall concentrate on break-even and contribution analysis. The consideration of long-term investment and funding decisions and the criteria on which these decisions may be made will be considered later in the chapter when attention is switched to financial management.

Break-even and contribution analysis

Break-even analysis (introduced in chapter 8) is concerned with the analysis of changes in the relationship between costs and revenue, and therefore profit, as a function of changes in output. In the break-even chart (figure 8.3 above, repeated here as figure 9.1), it is assumed that fixed costs are invariant and that variable costs are a constant multiple of output, whilst any output can be sold at a constant price. Output $0Q_1$ is the break-even level at which total revenue just covers total cost, and this is associated with a level S_1 of total sales revenue. Beyond this level of sales and output, profits start to appear. The relationships involved are as follows:

total revenue $= PQ$ (price × quantity)
fixed cost $= F$
unit variable cost $= V$
total variable cost $= VQ$
total costs $= F + VQ$.

The break-even point occurs when total cost is equal to total revenue. This is where

$$PQ = F + VQ$$
$$(P - V)Q = F.$$

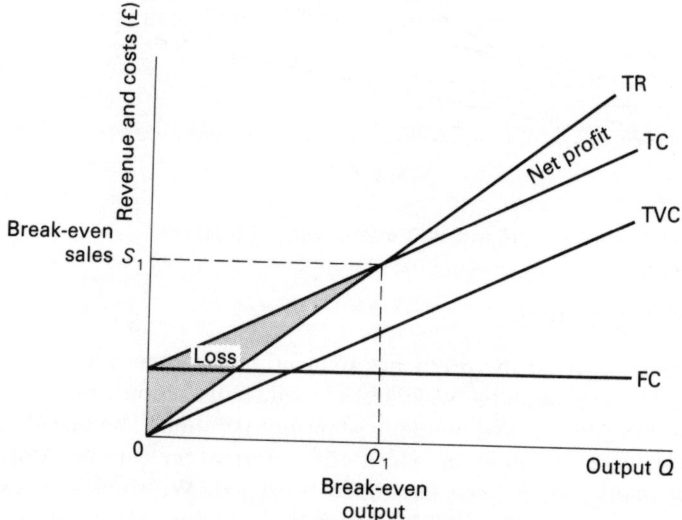

Figure 9.1 *The break-even chart*

The assumptions in the above analysis are not very realistic in that constant unit variable costs imply constant marginal costs and therefore diminishing returns to scale never set in. This means that there is no unique profit-maximizing output and profit continues to rise as a function of output. The reason for this is the neglect of demand conditions in the assumption that any amount can be sold at a constant price. It might be necessary to increase expenditure on advertising and cut price before very large increases in sales can be achieved. Nevertheless, in the short term these assumptions might not be too gross a violation of reality.

In this period when many costs are fixed the contribution that additional sales may make towards fixed costs and profits can be assessed from a variant of the break-even chart which facilitates contribution analysis (figure 9.2). *Total contribution* is defined as the difference between total sales revenue and total variable cost. It is from this contribution that a firm covers its fixed costs and makes a profit. If a firm has a number of product lines and excess productive capacity in each, and at the same time has a shortage of certain required inputs, perhaps raw materials or a particular type of skilled labour, then an analysis of the contribution made on each product line should give an indication of where to concentrate its activities if it wants to maximize its profits in the short run.

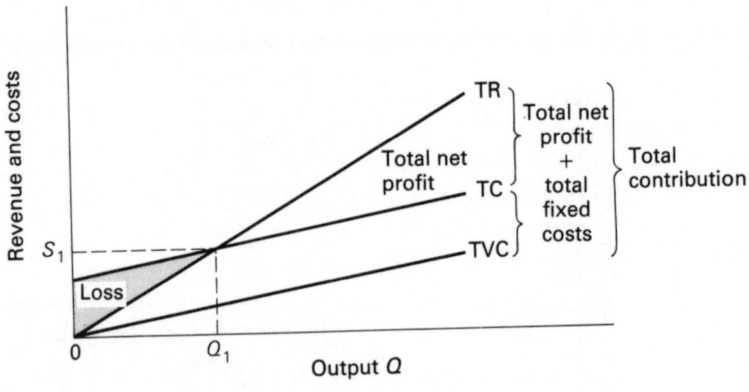

Figure 9.2 *Contribution analysis*

Financial ratio analysis

We have considered the problems involved in the generation of financial information, including the wide areas in which discretion can be exercised and the difficulties posed by the existence of inflation. The broad areas of management accounting in which the information can be utilized by internal management have also been broached. We shall now examine briefly the interpretation and utilization of accounting information via the use of ratio analysis.

We shall begin with the analysis of profitability. If a company is to grow and prosper it must make adequate profits to reward its shareholders and help finance future growth. If the company is not achieving a satisfactory return on the shareholders' equity base, then at worst they may become sufficiently dissatisfied to sell their shares and drive the share price down. If this happens on a large scale the company may be open to a take-over bid by a rival firm whose management are confident that they could make a higher return by managing the assets concerned themselves. At best a depressed share price may make the terms on which new capital can be raised from the market sufficiently unfavourable to deter expansion plans (see later in this chapter for a full discussion of the cost of capital).

The rate of return on the equity interest or shareholders' funds, expressed as a percentage, can be defined as

$$\frac{\text{profit attributable to ordinary shareholders}}{\text{ordinary shareholders' interest}} \times 100.$$

The numerator in the ratio above will have had deducted tax, interest payments and any payments to preference shareholders and minority interests. The denominator is equal to ordinary share capital plus reserves. For simplicity we assume that there are no preference shareholders or minority interests. The rate of return achieved on the company's net operating assets will be a key determinant of the numerator, but this will be modified by the extent of the company's gearing (the proportion of its activities financed by borrowing) and the amount of tax paid as a proportion of pre-tax profits. The shareholders will also be interested in the various external financial ratios considered in chapter 10.

The management will acknowledge the importance of the above financial ratio, but they are more likely to be interested in the rate of return achieved on net operating assets since this gives a measure of how effectively a firm's overall resources are being employed. This ratio stands at the apex of a pyramid of ratios which reflect factors which govern the return on net operating assets and can be used as a basis for control and comparison within and across firms. Great care must be taken when using ratio analysis as a basis for inter-firm comparisons. Accounting ratios are subject to all the previously mentioned caveats concerning accounting processes, and different firms may use different conventions in drawing up their accounts. This problem is recognized by the Centre for Interfirm Comparison which tries to ensure that all firms subscribing to its service conform to a set of instructions concerning definitions of terms, valuation principles etc. so that like is always compared with like.[12] The subscribers can then compare their general company performance with that of similar companies in the same industry and, if required, specific portions of their operations with those of rivals. It is very important that companies which are fairly homogeneous are compared, since the underlying logic behind ratio analysis is the assumption of constant proportionality. There are no

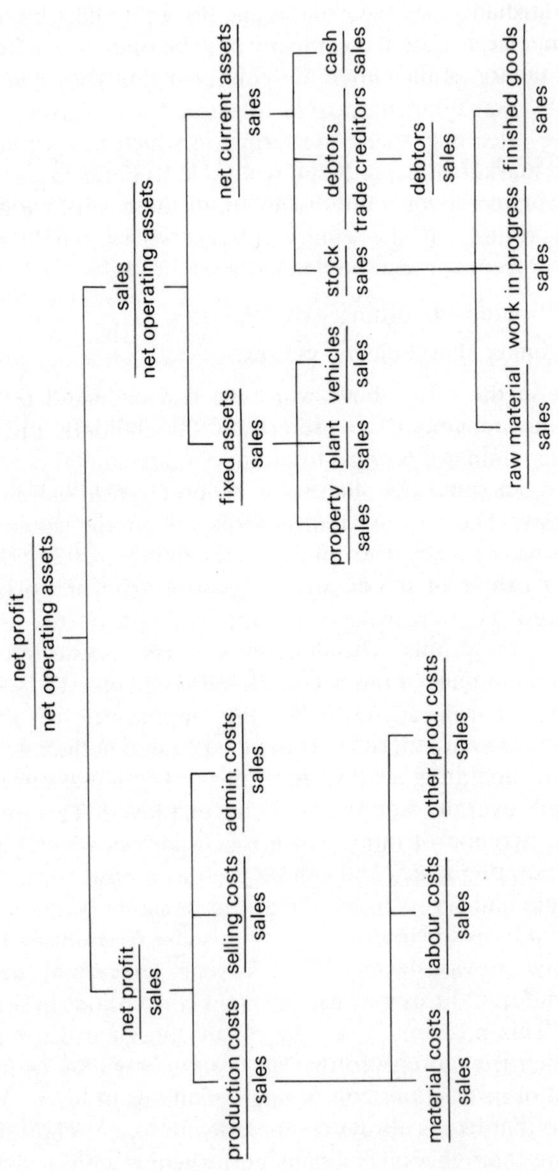

Figure 9.3 *Pyramid of ratios for a manufacturing concern*

underlying economic or logical grounds for assuming the prevalence of this relationship.[13] It may be particularly unrealistic if companies of vastly differing size and activities are compared. Given these reservations, ratio analysis can be a very useful means of analysing the components of a company's performance. Figure 9.3 shows the pyramid of ratios for a manufacturing concern.

If we start at the top of the pyramid, the following relationship emerges:

$$\frac{\text{net profit}}{\text{net operating assets}} = \frac{\text{net profit}}{\text{sales}} \times \frac{\text{sales}}{\text{net operating assets}}.$$

It follows that a relatively high or low rate of return on assets might be due either to a low profit margin, indicated by net profit/sales, or to a low rate of asset turnover, shown by sales/total assets. A low rate of asset turnover might be due either to excessive working capital or to poor use of fixed assets. These factors can be analysed by inspection of the third tier of ratios on the right-hand side of figure 9.3. On the other hand, low profit margins might be due to excessive production, selling or distribution costs, which can be examined via the second tier of ratios on the left-hand side of figure 9.3.

None of the ratios should be analysed in isolation, and there are obvious links between the two sides of the pyramid. A company with relatively old well-depreciated assets will probably have a low ratio of fixed assets/sales and a correspondingly high rate of asset turnover. But old plant will probably mean high production costs/sales and therefore net profit/sales will be correspondingly lower. A company in the same industry with new plant would probably show a lower rate of asset turnover but much higher profits/sales.

The study of a company's trend in ratios over time and appropriate inter-firm comparison should enable the management to pinpoint where things are going wrong, and they can then decide upon the appropriate remedial action. The relative performance between divisions of a firm can be analysed on similar lines so that the management can see where things need to be tightened up.

The Tax System

In the course of this chapter we have already encountered numerous but scattered references to the tax system, and it seems sensible to draw these various threads together. A good starting-point is provided by the recommendations of the Meade Report, which in 1978 recommended a movement to an expenditure-based system of taxation.[14] A tax system could theoretically have an *income base* or an *expenditure base*. The main difference between the two is in the treatment of saving. As income can be used to finance consumption and saving, both are taxed in an income-based system. Under an expenditure-based system tax is only levied on expenditure on final consumption, and saving is therefore exempt. In an income-based system savings are made from taxed income, and are then invested to yield future income in the form of dividends, interest and capital gains, which are liable for more tax. The implications is that savings (or deferred consumption) are taxed twice under an income-based system and once under an expenditure-based system. One of the main aims of the Meade Committee's proposals was the removal of distortions and the encouragement of saving, for at the moment we do not have a purely income-based tax system but a muddled hybrid which contains elements of both income- and expenditure-based tax (as well as VAT, a direct tax on expenditure).

The system of income tax in the UK for the 1989–90 tax year involved a basic rate of 25 per cent with a higher rate of 40 per cent for the upper band of taxable income. The Thatcher administration radically revised and reduced personal tax rates. For example, in the 1981–2 tax year there were six income bands and six different assessment rates for personal income tax ranging from 30 to 60 per cent. The system for the 1989–90 tax year is shown in table 9.11; the rates and bands tend to be adjusted in every government budget.

Table 9.11 *Personal income tax rates* 1989–1990

Rate (%)	Band of taxable income (£)
25	0–20,700
40	Over 20,700

Taxable income is equivalent to gross income minus the various allowances and expenses which can be set against income before tax; the single person's and married man's allowances stood at £2785 and £4375 respectively in the 1989–90 tax year.

Inflation poses an obvious problem. If nominal wages rise roughly in step with inflation, but the bands and allowances are not adjusted in line, then people who previously did not pay tax will begin to pay it and other taxpayers will gradually be pushed into higher bands. This phenomenon is termed fiscal drag.

Another serious anomaly arises from the lack of synchronization of the overlap between the tax system and the welfare benefit system. A wage earner in a low-income family with children may well find that there is little incentive to work overtime or achieve pay increases over a broad range of income. This is because increases in income will lead to loss of income-related benefits, and a liability to tax, with the effect that net income will remain roughly constant.

Further anomalies arise from the hotchpotch of items which can be set off against pre-tax income. Relief is available on interest payments on loans to acquire property and on loans to invest in a partnership or co-operative, and, under the business expansion scheme, on the cost of any 'outside' investor's equity investment in new trading companies, in qualifying trades, up to a maximum of £500,000 in ordinary shares in any one year. This form of saving is thus favourably treated in that it is only taxed once – when the gains from the investment are realized and available for consumption – and is thus equivalent to a tax system based upon expenditure. The same principle applies to the treatment of saving via an approved pension scheme; contributions are deductible from pre-tax income, but the pensions when paid are subject to tax.

Certain types of investment in government stocks receive favourable treatment. Income arising from savings certificates is not liable to tax; this is an incentive to hold the so-called 'granny bonds', which have been made available to all, and in the process to ease the difficulties governments face in raising funds.

Similarly most capital gains above an annual exemption limit are liable to capital gains tax at the recipient's marginal tax rate, but if an investor holds a government gilt-edged stock for more than a year, and the change in interest rates is such that capital gain is produced, he will not be liable for capital gains tax.

Thus it is argued that there are serious distortions in the capital markets which result from the favoured treatment of investment in government stocks and housing, and which therefore inhibit the free flow of capital. The system of company taxation is in even greater confusion.

The corporate tax system

In recent years there have been two major changes in the system of taxation of corporate profits: the introduction of corporation tax in 1965 and the movement to the imputation corporation tax system in 1973. The 'classical system' of corporation tax introduced in 1965 embodies the principle that the tax liability of the company should be completely independent of that of its shareholders. The company has to pay a flat rate of corporation tax on its taxable profits, and the shareholders must pay income tax on their dividends and capital gains tax on any gains made when they sell their shares. If the company chooses to pay dividends from its post-tax profits, then those dividends are taxed at the marginal income tax rate of the recipient; any distributions to shareholders are therefore taxed twice. The system discriminates against dividend payments and favours debt funding, since interest payments are a charge against profits when assessing liability to corporation tax.

The discrimination against dividend payments was removed by the *imputation tax system.* This involves crediting the shareholders for corporation tax paid by the company; if they receive dividend payments, a tax credit equal to the standard rate of income tax due on the dividend is imputed to them and offset against the company's mainstream corporation tax. This means that the shareholders are not liable for income tax at the standard rate on their dividends, although higher-rate taxpayers must pay the appropriate marginal adjustment. From the company's point of view the only difference comes from the timing of some of its tax payments. To the extent that it has to pay ACT at a rate equal to the standard rate of income tax on the gross dividend at the time it makes payments, it is marginally disadvantaged in that the timing of some of its tax payments has been brought forward. Its overall liability to tax remains the same in that any ACT payments are a credit against its mainstream corporation tax payments when they become due. The essentials of the two systems are shown in table 9.12.

Table 9.12 *The classical and imputation corporation tax systems*

	Classical (£)		Imputation (£)
Pre-tax profit	12,000		12,000
Interest payments	(2,000)		(2,000)
Taxable profits	10,000		10,000
Corporation tax (35%)	(3,500)		(3,500)
Available for distribution or retention	6,500		6,500
Ordinary dividend (gross)	2,100		2,800
Income tax (25%)	(525)	ACT (25%)	(700)
Ordinary dividend (net)	1,575		2,100
Retentions	4,402		4,400
Tax due at year end	(3,500)		(2,800)

It can be seen from table 9.12 that the result of the change to the imputation system is that the shareholders have gained at the expense of the Inland Revenue.

Stock appreciation relief

Stock appreciation relief was first introduced in 1974 and went through various modifications until it was abolished in 1984. An example of how it was calculated follows. Relief was given on the opening value of stocks and work in progress minus £2000; the net figure was then multiplied by the increase in the index prices of all stocks to give the relief against taxable profits, as shown in the following example.

Movements in stocks index: December 1980, 180; December 1981, 189.

$$\text{increase} = \frac{189 - 180}{180} = 5\%.$$

	£
Stocks at 1 January 1981	500,000
Stocks at 1 December 1981	800,000
Taxable trading income	1,000,000

$$\begin{aligned}\text{Stock appreciation relief} &= (\text{opening stock} - £2000) \times \text{increase in index}\\ &= £(500{,}000 - 2000)0.05\\ &= £2400.\end{aligned}$$

Taxable trading income becomes:

	£
Original figure	1,000,000
Less stock appreciation	2,400
Taxable trading income	997,600

It has been estimated that in 1978–9 companies' corporation tax payments were reduced by around £1.4 billion as a result of stock appreciation relief.[15]

Capital allowances

Allowances are given on a national basis without any regional discrimination. From 1972 until 1983 up to 100 per cent of any expenditure on industrial plant and machinery could be set off against tax on profits in the year in which it was incurred, and if there were not sufficient taxable profits available it could be carried forward indefinitely. Alternatively the company could claim only part of its allowances in the first year and carry the balance forward, writing it off at 25 per cent on the reducing balance basis. It was estimated that in 1978–9 the first-year investment allowances due on investment in accounts totalled nearly £10 billion.[16]

Similarly, there were allowances on industrial building at an initial rate of 50 per cent of the cost and a subsequent writing-down allowance of 4 per cent per annum (straight line) which became operative once the building was in use. Estimations for the period 1978–9 suggested that roughly £700 million of allowances were due on industrial buildings.[17] However, since 1986 the initial allowances on plant and machinery and on industrial buildings have been removed. The writing-down allowances of 25 per cent and 4 per cent respectively remain in force.

The resultant confusion and the impetus towards reform

The result of these various measures was that many companies were in a situation of tax exhaustion for a number of years. This meant that they did not have sufficient taxable profits to enable them to utilize the various allowances. This was one of the major stimuli to the growth in leasing considered in chapter 10.

From 1970 to 1972, the corporate tax rate stood at 40 per cent; it was raised to 52 per cent in 1973, remaining at this higher level until 1983. Subsequently, it was progressively reduced to 35 per cent in 1986.

Estimates made by the Institute for Fiscal Studies (IFS), from data covering several hundred firms, suggest that during 1975–9 around 30 per cent of their sample were tax exhausted, rising to 35 per cent in 1980–2. The situation has subsequently improved following a sustained increase in company profitability, a fall in the level of interest rates, the reduction in the rate of corporation tax, and a decline in the rate of first-year capital allowances before their subsequent removal. In 1986 the IFS estimated that only a quarter of a large sample of companies that they examined were tax exhausted.[18]

A further wide range of direct taxes have to be considered: social security contributions by individuals and employers; customs and excise duties; VAT; capital transfers tax; stamp duty; etc. The effect of all these measures is that in the UK roughly 42 per cent of taxation is based upon expenditure rather than on income (table 9.13).

Obviously there is a need for further reform, perhaps along the lines suggested by the Meade Committee.[19] If savings were exempt from taxation, most of the previously mentioned distortions would be removed. There are various ways in which an expenditure-based system could be applied – none would be more complicated than the existing system – and it could be planned so that it would be equally progressive.

Financial Management Decisions

Financial management policy and decisions are concerned with seeking answers to the following questions:

1 What projects or investments should the firm undertake?
2 How much should the firm invest?
3 By what methods of funding should the firm finance its investments?
4 How much of the firm's revenue should it distribute and in what form? Alternatively, what should be the firm's policy on retentions?

In seeking an answer to these questions, the management must have a clearly defined set of objectives in mind. Despite the existence of a number of possible objectives of varying plausibility, the custom in the literature

Table 9.13 *Taxation as a proportion of gross national product and the proportion of taxation based upon expenditure (1978 and 1983)*

	Taxation and social security contributions as a percentage of GNP at factor cost		Percentage of total taxation (including social security contributions) derived from indirect taxes	
	1978	1983	1978	1983
Sweden	56	59	28	30
Norway	56	56	37	36
Netherlands	50	53	28	25
Belgium	48	50	28	27
West Germany	46	46	31	31
France	45	51	37	35
UK	38	44	39	42
Italy	36	47	32	28
Canada	35	37	40	39
USA	31	31	28	30
Switzerland	32	32	23	22
Japan	25	30	30	27

Source: Central Statistical Office, *Economic Trends* (May 1986)

has been to assume that the management take decisions on behalf of the owners (the shareholders in the case of a limited company) with the welfare of the owners in mind. It is assumed that maximizing the value of their interest will serve them best. This is not the same as maximizing profitability, though it is closely related to it since profitability is a one-dimensional measure (see chapter 2). It is assumed that investors in capital markets are concerned with three dimensions; returns or profitability, timing and risk. All these factors must be considered.

Time and discounting

Suppose that you have £100 cash. You have the choice of either spending it now or investing it in a risk-free bank account at an interest rate of 10 per cent per annum. If you leave it there for a year you will have the original amount of £100 plus the interest. The interest is £100 × 10 per cent = £10; this could be written as £100$(1 + r)$ where r is equal to 0.10 or 10 per cent in this case. The choice is depicted in figure 9.4.

£100 invested at 10 per cent for a year will be worth £110 in one year's time, as shown above. The line linking the two amounts is a present-value

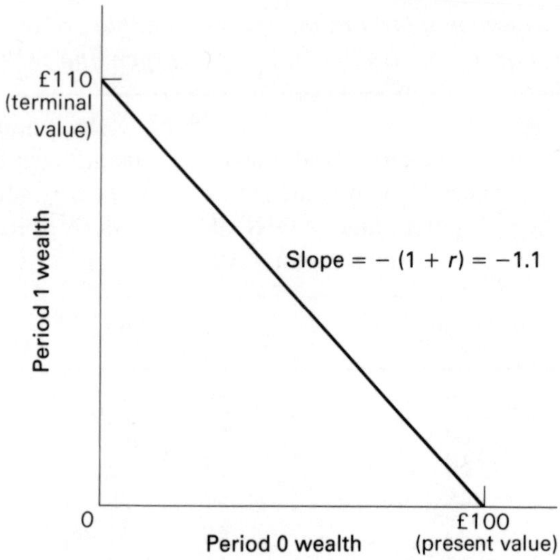

Figure 9.4 *Present value and discounting*

line with a slope equal to the rate of interest. The slope is negative; its magnitude can be seen to be 1.1 since the length of the vertical side of the triangle in the diagram over that of the horizontal is 110/100 = 1.1.

The terminal value of £X invested for a year at a rate of interest r is £$X(1 + r)$. Similarly the present value of £110 in a year's time, given an interest rate of 10 per cent, is £100. This can be calculated generally as £$X/(1 + r)$. Thus as long as the rate of interest is positive we have to adjust amounts received in different periods by an appropriate discount factor to make them equivalent. Even in the complete absence of risk, the discount rate would be positive since people in general prefer to consume now rather than later. If they are to forgo present consumption and channel the value of it into investment, they must be rewarded for so doing.

If the investment in the above example had been at a rate of 10 per cent for three years it would have grown as follows:

present value = £100
value at end of year 1 = £100$(1 + r)$ = £110
value at end of year 2 = £100$(1 + r)^2$ = £121
value at end of year 3 = £100$(1 + r)^3$ = £133

In general a sum £X invested at a rate r for N years will grow in the following fashion:

$$\text{terminal value of £}X = \text{£}X(1 + r)^N. \tag{9.2}$$

On the other hand, the present value of a sum £X received N in the future is given by

$$\text{present value} = \frac{\pounds X}{(1 + r)^N}. \tag{9.3}$$

The present value of a series of different sums $X_1, X_2, \ldots, X_n$ received annually for N years at the end of each year is given by

$$\text{present value} = \frac{X_1}{1 + r} + \frac{X_2}{(1 + r)^2} + \frac{X_3}{(1 + r)^3} + \ldots + \frac{X_N}{(1 + r)^N}$$

$$\text{present value} = \sum_{i=1}^{N} \frac{X_i}{(1 + r)^i}. \tag{9.4}$$

The principle of discounting is of vital importance in any investment decision involving multiperiod returns: different amounts at different times have to be transformed onto a common base before they can be evaluated. This is the rationale behind the use of discounting techniques for determining investment decisions.

Risk

Financial management decisions have to be made on the basis of imperfect information, and their consequences can never be predicted with complete certainty since the future cannot be known. One way of trying to assess uncertainty is to make a *subjective probability estimation* of the possible outcomes. This involves using a 0 to 1 scale to assign probabilities to future events. A zero probability would mean that the event is ruled out of consideration, and a probability of 1 would indicate that it will happen with certainty. Probabilities in between measure degrees of uncertainty. Suppose that you are intending to sell an asset in the near future and that you are not sure about the price you will receive. You estimate that the outcomes in table 9.14 are possible.

If it is assumed that the resultant probability distribution is normal, then it can be completely described by its mean $\bar{b}$ and its standard deviation σ_b. The mean of a probability distribution is calcuated by weighting all the possible outcomes by their probabilities and summing the resultant products, as shown in table 9.14, column 3. The standard deviation, which can be used as a proxy measure of risk, is calculated by taking the deviation of each possible outcome from the mean, squaring it, weighting the product by the probability of the outcome concerned, summing all such products, and then taking the square root of the resultant sum. The calculation of the standard deviation σ_b is shown in the last three columns of table 9.14.

The mean of the distribution is used as a measure of expected value and the standard deviation as a measure of risk. If two investments have the same mean but different standard deviations, then it is assumed that

Table 9.14 *Subjective probability estimations of the sale value of an asset, and the calculation of the mean and the standard deviation*

Subjective probability a	Sale price (£) b	ab	$b-\bar{b}$	$(b-\bar{b})^2$	$a(b-\bar{b})^2$
0.1	70	7	−20	400	40
0.2	80	16	−10	100	20
0.4	90	36	0	0	0
0.2	100	20	10	100	20
0.1	110	11	20	400	40
$\Sigma a = 1.0$		$\bar{b} = \Sigma ab = 90$			$\Sigma a(b-\bar{b})^2 = 120$ $\sigma^2 b = 120$ $\sigma b = 10.95$

investors would prefer the one with the smaller standard deviation or lesser risk. This choice is shown in figure 9.5.

The assumption is that investment *A* would be preferred to investment *B*. Both have the same expected value but there is a much higher probability of extreme deviations from the mean in the case of investment *B*. The level of return could be either much lower or much higher than that of *A*. It is assumed that typical investors are risk averse when risking significant amounts of money. They prefer to avoid risk and will only bear it if they are compensated for doing so. They will put much greater weight on possible deviations below the mean of *B* than on those above it, and will therefore prefer *A*.

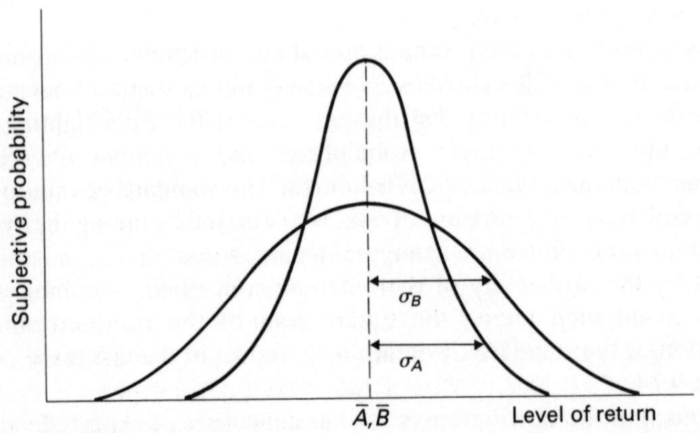

Figure 9.5 *Two investments with the same expected value but different risk*

This means that investments of high risk will have to offer relatively high returns or they will not be undertaken, and that high profits at high levels of risk will not necessarily be preferred to lower profits at lower levels of risk. The key factor will be whether the riskier profits are sufficiently larger to compensate for their risk. This is the idea behind *certainty equivalents*; these equate higher levels of risky wealth with lower levels of certain wealth, and are shown in figure 9.6.

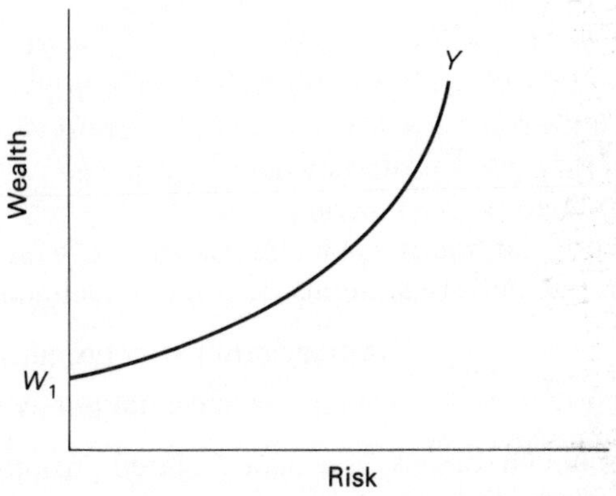

Figure 9.6 *Certainty equivalents*

To an individual investor all points along the line W_1Y in figure 9.6 might be regarded as being equivalent. A high but risky level of potential wealth at point Y is regarded as being equivalent to an absolutely certain but much lower level of wealth at W_1.

The Investment Decision

Investment decisions are obviously of crucial importance to individual companies and to the economy as a whole, playing a key role in determining future growth and productivity. It is vitally important that they are made on a 'correct' basis. There are a number of traditional investment appraisal methods. One of the most popular is the *payback method*; this provides a means of ranking alternative investment projects by the time it takes them to repay their capital cost.

A simple illustration of the method is given in table 9.15. Two projects involve an initial outlay of £200; their year-end receipts are as shown below. Project A recoups its capital cost in three years and has a three-year payback period; project B has a four-year payback period. Project A would be preferred to project B, despite the fact that B nets an undiscounted surplus over costs of £220 ((7 × £60) – £200) whereas A nets only £40. This follows from the fact that only the payback period is

Table 9.15 *The payback method of investment appraisal*

Period (years)	0	1	2	3	4	5	6	7
Project A	−£200	£70	£70	£60	£40	£0	£0	£0
Project B	−£200	£60	£60	£60	£60	£60	£60	£60

considered and not the project's entire working life. The cash flows are undiscounted, so that like is not being compared with like. If the method was used on a universal basis it would lead to serious under-investment since many perfectly good projects would be rejected on the basis of an arbitrarily determined payback period.

Another very popular traditional method is the *return on capital method*, of which there a number of variations. It could be defined as

$$\text{average rate of return} = \frac{\text{average profit after tax and depreciation}}{\text{capital outlay}}$$

This method is popular because the data required are often available in similar form in accounting statements, but it has many defects. It once again ignores the time value of money. It cannot distinguish between projects with different lengths of life. It is also biased by the method of depreciation used.

Table 9.16 *The average rate of return method of investment appraisal*[a]

Period (years)	0	1	2	3	4	5	6	Average profit (after tax and depreciation)	Capital outlay	Average rate of return (%)
Project A	−£100	£50	£40	£30	£30	£20	£10	£30	£100	30
Project B	−£100	£10	£20	£30	£40	£55	–	£31	£100	31

[a] Assume a straight line method of depreciation is used (i.e. project A had £16.66 deducted from profits each year to recoup the capital outlay, while B had £20 deducted annually).

Some of these problems are illustrated by the example of table 9.16. Two projects require an initial outlay of £100, but project A yields returns for six years as opposed to B's five-year life. The method suggests that B is to be preferred since its rate of return is slightly higher. However, A yields much higher returns in early years; these are particularly valuable since they can be reinvested elsewhere at a positive rate of interest. A also offers six years of returns, with an average of £30, rather than five. The method is clearly misleading, and it is because of the distortions mentioned above that *discounted cash flow methods* are to be preferred.

The net present value method

The net present value (NPV) method of investment appraisal involves discounting all the after-tax cash flows from a project at the company's marginal cost of capital. This rate, sometimes termed the required rate of return, is the cost to the company of raising the required funds to finance the project (see later in this chapter). No account is taken of depreciation provisions since the cost of the investment is automatically accounted for in the calculations. The calculation is as follows:

$$\text{NPV} = \text{NCF}_0 \frac{\text{NCF}_1}{1 + r} + \frac{\text{NCF}_2}{(1 + r)^2} + \ldots + \frac{\text{NCF}_N}{(1 + r)^N}$$

$$= \sum_{i=0}^{N} \frac{\text{NCF}_t}{(1 + r)^i}$$

where NCF_i is the net cash flow after tax in period i (in period 0 it will usually have a negative value equal to the cost of the investment, after adjustment for capital allowances) and r is the required rate of return (the firm's marginal cost of capital (MCC).

Table 9.17 *The use of the net present value method*

Period (years)	0	1	2	3	4
Net cash flows	−£100	£70	£80	£60	£50
Discount factors					
$r = 10\%$	1	1.1	1.21	1.331	1.4641
Net discounted					
cash flows	−£100	£63.64	£66.12	£45.08	£34.15

NPV = Σ net discounted cash flows = £109

An example of the use of the NPV method is shown in table 9.17. The decision rule is simple. If the NPV of the sum of the discounted after-tax cash flows is positive, then the project is valuable and should be accepted. To do so will add to the firm's value. This is because it offers a rate of return higher than that required by the providers of the firm's capital – the test discount rate or MCC.

The internal rate of return method

An alternative investment appraisal technique based on the use of discounting is the internal rate of return (IRR) method. The condition for calculating IRR is

$$\mathrm{NCF}_0 + \frac{\mathrm{NCF}_1}{1+r^*} + \frac{\mathrm{NCF}_2}{(1+r^*)^2} + \ldots + \frac{\mathrm{NCF}_N}{(1+r^*)^N} = 0$$

$$\sum_{i=0}^{N} \frac{\mathrm{NCF}_I}{(1+r^*)^i} = 0 \qquad (9.6)$$

where NCF_i is the net cash flow in period i and r^* is the solution discount rate or IRR that satisfies condition (9.6).

The IRR method involves adjusting the discount rate r^* until the net present value of the sum of all the inflows and outflows of cash associated with the project is equal to zero. This solution discount rate is the project's internal rate of return, which can be compared with the firm's MCC. If the IRR is greater than the MCC (IRR> MCC) then the project is profitable and should be undertaken. The calculation of the IRR for the same project as in table 9.17 is given in table 9.18. It can be seen that the project in the example has an IRR of approximately 61 per cent.

Table 9.18 *The use of the internal rate of return method*

Period (years)	0	1	2	3	4
Net cash flows	−£100	£70	£80	£60	£50
Discount factors					
$r = 61\%$	1	1.61	2.89	4.17	6.72
Net discounted					
cash flows	−£100	£43.48	£30.88	£41.39	£11.9

Σ net discounted cash flows ≈ 0

The equivalence of the two methods for the example chosen is shown in figure 9.7. The two methods give the same answers in a straightforward accept/reject investment decision. If the firm's MCC is 10 per cent the project has a positive NPV and should be accepted. Its IRR is much greater than 10 per cent and the project should be accepted according to that decision criterion also. In the use of both NPV and IRR the project becomes marginal with an MCC of 61 per cent. Although both methods are preferable to non-discounting techniques, there are some problems in their application.

Difficulties involved in the application of NPV and IRR

The IRR method is probably more problematic. Some projects may involve negative cash outflows in more than one period over the project's life. If this is the case multiple solution discount rates may emerge and it can be difficult to interpret them. There are adjustments which get round

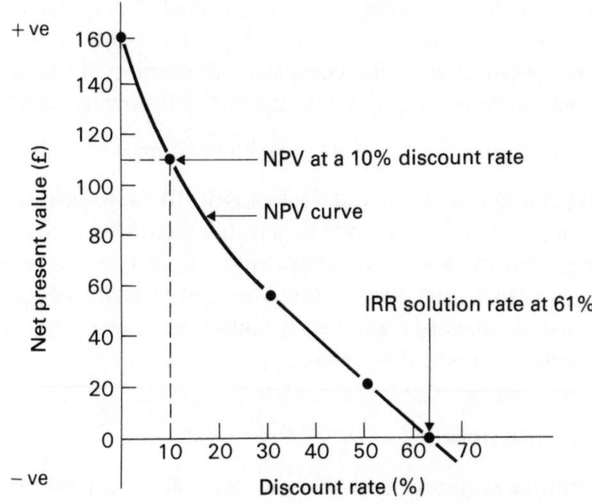

Figure 9.7 *The NPV and IRR methods compared*

the problem but they are rather *ad hoc.* More seriously, as the IRR is a rate of return it cannot distinguish between the relative size and length of life of two different projects (admittedly this criticism applies to some extent to NPV as well). One way round this problem is to use the NPV approach to construct a *profitability index.*

$$\text{profitability index} = \frac{\text{present value of inflows}}{\text{present value of outflows}}.$$

This will give the management an idea of the relative desirability of projects. However, if there exist limited financial resources or some sort of constraint on funds which necessitates choosing some profitable projects at the expense of others, neither NPV nor IRR can cope, and resort has to be made to mathematical programming techniques.

Risk and inflation

Both methods can be adapted quite readily to cope with both risk and inflation. The certainty equivalent method considered earlier suggests that there are two ways in which future cash flows can be adjusted to allow for risk; either the numerator or the denominator in the discount rate can be altered. The adjustment to the numerator is given by αNCF_i, where α is a positive constant and $0 < \alpha < 1$. Future risky cash flow estimates will be revised downwards to reflect risk. (If this is done the discount rate used must be the riskless rate of interest reflecting the time value of money alone, since risk has been accounted for in the numerator.) Alternatively the discount rate can be inflation above the pure interest rate to allow for risk. This is probably the more useful approach since the firm's MCC (considered later in this chapter) usually reflects the capital market's perception of the riskiness of the company's operations. Indeed, the firm's MCC could be viewed as being made up of the following components:

discount rate = pure interest rate + risk premium + inflation premium.

A market-determined cost of capital automatically takes into account both risk and likely inflation. This leads to another potential source of bias. If the MCC has an inflation adjustment built in, care must be taken that estimates of a project's future cash flows are not in terms of today's prices but are adjusted upwards for likely inflation; otherwise a project's profitability will be biased downwards.

Portfolio considerations

The risk premium required by a shareholder will reflect his estimation of the firm's operating risk – the risk associated with its day-to-day operations plus, where appropriate, an additional component for the company's financial risk if it has a lot of borrowings (see the next section for a full treatment of gearing). The shareholder's perception of relevant risk will change if he holds a collection or portfolio of investments in the shares of a number of different companies. In this context an individual share will be important in terms of the marginal contribution it makes, in the form of additional risk and expected return, to his overall portfolio. Following the original contribution by Markowitz, portfolio theory has been extended to the point where it underlies most of the theoretical work on financial markets and provides a means of pricing risky assets.[20] Although the theory involves a considerable amount of mathematics its gist can be conveyed on a common-sense basis.

When an investor purchases a share he cannot be sure of the return he will obtain; dividends are paid out of after-tax profits, and whether or not a company pays a dividend, and how large it is, are at the discretion of the board of directors. The investor could summarize his expectations by drawing up a subjective probability distribution along the lines considered earlier. The mean of the distribution will indicate the return he expects over his investment hold period (made up of dividends and capital gains or losses via changes in the share price). The standard deviation will indicate the risk or uncertainty he attaches to his estimates (assuming the distribution is symmetric and normal).

So far we have not considered the benefits of *diversification*. Investors typically spread their risks by investing in a number of different securities rather than by putting all their money into one. The benefits of diversification can be measured by the extent to which the returns on two securities (i.e. shares) vary together (as measured by their covariance). Let us suppose that one company (A) produces ice-cream and the other (B)

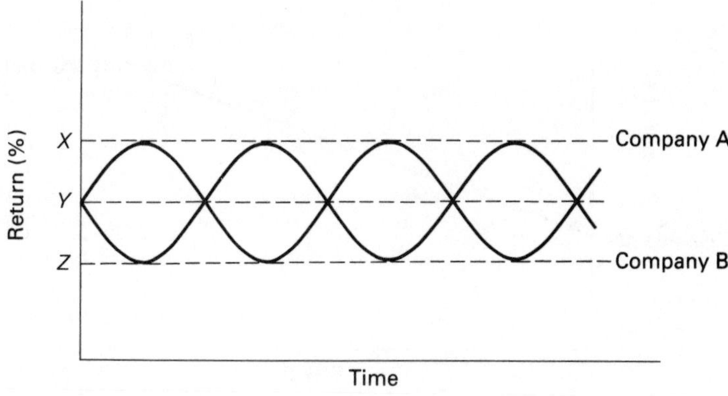

Figure 9.8 *The benefits of diversification*

umbrellas, and therefore bad weather for one means good business for the other. The hypothetical returns on their shares are shown in figure 9.8.

If the investor put all his funds in either company A or company B his return would vary between *X* and *Z*, although over time it would average out at *Y*. By investing in both companies he is guaranteed a return of *Y* at all times; diversification has significantly reduced his exposure to risk. Practical illustration of diversification is given by the investment holdings of the financial institutions shown in tables 10.19–10.22. Investments are spread over a number of different types of security and in home and overseas markets.

The *capital asset pricing model* uses this principle to price risky assets. If it is assumed that all investors hold an effectively diversified 'market' portfolio, then part of a security's risk – the 'unsystematic' component – will have been diversified away. Only the undiversifiable 'systematic' risk will remain, as measured by the covariance between the returns on the security and those on the market portfolio, which by definition cannot be diversified away. Thus securities will be priced, in equilibrium, according to their non-diversifiable systematic risk (normally termed their *beta* (β) *coefficient*). A risk-free security earns a return equal to the risk-free rate, and a risky security earns an additional premium in proportion to its beta coefficient. This may sound rather frightening, but the reader can comprehend what is meant by examining figure 9.9. This shows a simpler linear relationship (equation (9.7)) which can be expressed (as for equation (7.1) in an ordinary least-squares (OLS) equation (equation (9.8)).

The basic linear relationship is

$$\mathrm{E}r_j = \mathrm{RF} + \beta j(\mathrm{ER_M} - \mathrm{RF}) \tag{9.7}$$

where $\mathrm{E}r_j$ is the expected return on security *j*, RF is the risk-free rate, β_j is the covariability of returns on security *j* and those of the market portfolio

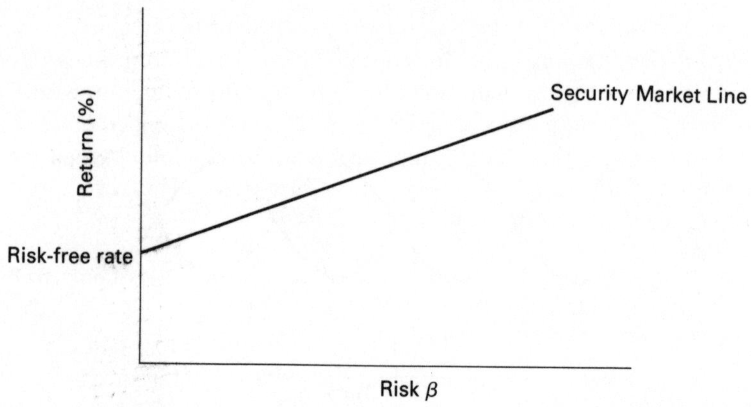

Figure 9.9 *The risk–return relationship according to the capital asset pricing model*

divided by the variance of the market portfolio, and ER_M is the expected return on the market portfolio.

The basic assumptions behind the formal mathematics which lead to the derivation of the above relationship are unrealistic. They run as follows. All investors invest for the same period and have the same expectations about the future returns and the risk of the securities in the market. There are no tax effects. There is only one risk-free borrowing rate. All investors are rational and averse to risk (they dislike risk and will only bear it if compensated by higher returns). All investors hold the fully diversified market portfolio. There is no inflation. Despite its unrealistic assumptions, this model has yielded valuable insights into the market pricing process, and it has some novel implications for capital budgeting. For a start, if a company's shareholders hold its shares as part of a diversified portfolio then, from their point of view, there is no point in the company choosing projects which have offsetting risks or merging with other firms to reduce risk. These risk reduction effects have already been achieved in the portfolios of the shareholders at much lower cost. If the assumptions of the capital asset pricing model are not too gross a violation of reality, an approximate estimation of a company's cost of capital can be obtained by running the following regression:

$$r_j = \alpha_j + B_j\mathrm{RI} + e_j. \tag{9.8}$$

r_j is the return on company j's shares, defined as $(p_t + d_t - p_{t-1})/p_{t-1}$, where p_t and p_{t-1} are the share prices in periods t and $t-1$, and d_t is the dividend received during period t. α_j and B_j are constants estimated by running an ordinary least-squares regression, RI is the return on a stock market index $((\mathrm{RI}_t - \mathrm{RI}_{t-1})/\mathrm{RI}_{t-1})$ used as a proxy for the return on the market portfolio, and e_j is a random error term.

The regression line can be fitted by using the required data over some historical period, and if the project is not going to be financed by a new 'mix' of debt and equity, and does not involve risks different from those of the company's existing operations, then it should provide an estimate of the firm's MCC. In practice it is very difficult to estimate a company's cost of capital, since the above approach requires a number of strong assumptions and financial mix is very important. The difficulties are considered in the next section.

Capital budgeting in practice

During the past couple of decades increasing use has been made of discounting techniques, though traditional non-discounting methods remain popular. Table 9.19 shows the results of a survey of the changing use of investment appraisal techniques in a sample of 100 large UK companies. Many combine the use of a number of different methods.

Table 9.19 *Capital budgeting techniques: trend analysis of usage in 100 UK firms*[a]

	1986 (%)	1981 (%)	1975 (%)
Payback	92	81	73
Average accounting rate of return	56	49	51
Internal rate of return	75	57	44
Net present value	68	39	32

Source: R. H. Pike, 'An empirical study of the adoption of sophisticated capital budgeting practices and decision-making effectiveness', *Accounting and Business Research*, 18 (Autumn 1988)

Capital Structure and Cost of Capital

A company's financial structure is determined by the way in which it is financed; traditionally this is shown on the LHS of its balance sheet. On the other hand, a company's capital structure could be defined as the structure of the permanent financing of the company – in other words, the relative proportions of debt, preference and equity share capital plus reserves. There are various ways in which this relatively simple concept can be defined and measured. Valuations could be on the basis of nominal or market values. The treatment of preference capital is a moot point; should it be placed with debt as a fixed payment commitment, or with equity on the grounds that payment can be waived? Yet another approach would be to measure the proportion of profits accounted for by fixed interest commitments, though this would be a move towards measuring financial structure since short-term liabilities would be included. We shall simply define capital gearing as the ratio of the market value of a company's long-term debt and the market value of its equity capital plus reserves:

$$\text{capital gearing} = \frac{\text{market value of loan capital}}{\text{market value of equity capital plus reserves}}$$

Financial risk

It is obvious that an increase in gearing involves an increase in financial risk, particularly from the shareholder's point of view. Debenture interest payments are prior charges against profits which have to be paid if the company is to avoid being forced into liquidation; therefore the greater the size of these prior commitments, the greater the probability that, in a bad year, profits will not be sufficient to cover them. The moral is that companies with very stable profits and valuable assets against which debenture issues can be secured (hotel and brewery chains are usually highly geared) can risk gearing up. Speculative companies with wildly fluctuating profits should stick to equity finance.

On the other hand, there are positive benefits associated with gearing up. In the absence of inflation, debenture finance is usually cheaper than equity finance in that the yield demanded by investors is not as high (for further consideration of yields see chapter 10). If the interest payment demanded by a debenture holder is not as high as the dividend per share expected by a shareholder, then financing a portion of a company's assets by relatively cheaper debentures will benefit the shareholders of a company; this is further emphasized by the tax deductibility of interest payments. Table 9.20 shows this effect.

Gearing up can benefit the shareholder; in year 1, the shareholder in Hi-gear Corporation receives 10.4 per cent compared with a yield of only 6.5 per cent in Equity Corporation, yet both companies are the same size and making the same return on capital employed. The danger is shown in year 2 when there is a 50 per cent reduction in return on capital employed. This halves the yield to the shareholders in Equity Corporation but reduces that to shareholders in Hi-gear Corporation by 63 per cent. The financial risk involved in high gearing involves increased variability of returns to the shareholders. The crucial question is whether judicial use of gearing can benefit a company's shareholders and lower its cost of capital.

The level of gearing varies both within and across industries in the UK, and on an even greater scale internationally. In part, international variations are a reflection of the lack of developed equity markets on the scale of those of the UK and USA, plus other social, institutional and historical factors. The wide variations are indicated in table 9.21.

Table 9.20 *The return to the equity interest and gearing effects*

Equity Corporation			Hi-gear Corporation		
Capital structure:					
1000 £1 ordinary shares	1000		500 £1 ordinary shares		500
			500 4% debentures		500
Capital employed	1000				1000
	[Year 1]	*[Year 2]*		*[Year 1]*	*[Year 2]*
Gross profits	100	50		100	50
Interest payments	0	0		20	20
	100	50		80	30
Corporation tax (35%)	35	17.5		28	10.5
Net dividend	65	32.5		52	19.5
Net dividend yield	6.5%	3.25%		10.4%	3.9%

Table 9.21 *An international comparison of capital gearing*[a] *(percentages)*

	1970	1975	1980	1982
UK	52	51	49	50
USA	44	37	37	37
France	65	70	70	73
Germany	63	63	64	63
Japan	84	85	84	83

[a] Total debt to total assets ratio. OECD statistics for non-financial companies from each country: USA, estimated total for all non-financial corporations; consolidated accounts; UK, all large (capital employed £4 million) non-financial companies; consolidated accounts; France, 577 industrial and 112 commercial firms from a variety of industries with a minimum turnover of FF25 million in 1977; unconsolidated accounts; Germany, a large random sample of 74,000 corporations, sole proprietorships and partnerships; unconsolidated accounts; Japan, privately owned non-financial corporations; a random sample from each sector of economic activity; unconsolidated accounts.

Gearing and the cost of capital

It was demonstrated previously that the economic value of a project is made up of the sum of the discounted values of the future net benefits that accrue to the owners. The value of a financial asset such as a share or a debenture is determined similarly. The value of a share is made up of the sum of all discounted values of the future dividend payments which are likely to accrue to the owner. To keep things simple assume that these are constant and known with certainty:

$$\text{share price} = \frac{D}{1+r} + \frac{D}{(1+r)^2} + \ldots + \frac{D}{(1+r)^N} \tag{9.9}$$

where D is the constant dividend payment and r is the appropriate discount factor, in his case the risk-free rate. If this is assumed to be a perpetual stream of payments the sum simplifies as follows. First multiply the share value by $1 + r$:

$$\text{share price} \times (1+r) = D + \frac{D}{1+r} + \frac{D}{(1+r)^2} + \ldots + \frac{D}{(1+r)^{N-1}} \tag{9.10}$$

If we subtract equation (9.9) from equation (9.10) we have

$$\text{share price} \times (1+r) - \text{share price} = D - \frac{D}{(1+r)^N}$$

$$\text{share price} \times r = D - \frac{D}{(1+r)^N}.$$

If we then assume that D is a perpetual stream of payments which goes on to infinity the second term will disappear; the result is

$$\text{share price} = \frac{D}{r}. \tag{9.11}$$

This is an important result, but the assumptions of a constant level of risk and a constant dividend payment must be borne in mind. This result can be applied to the valuation of any stream of perpetual payments. Perusal of equation (9.11) will give rise to the following observations. If the company is investing in positive projects which are going to increase the size of future profits and the future size of D, the share value should increase. On the other hand, any increase in the company's risk will increase the discount rate r and therefore reduce the share price. Increases in risk could come either from branching out into risky operations with increased operating risk or from increased financial risk from higher gearing.

We wish to examine the effects of gearing, and so we are concerned purely with the effects of financial risk. Therefore operating risk, investment policy and the possibility of increased future earnings are effects which have to be neutralized by assuming them constant.

As an example, take two companies A and B. Suppose that company A is financed by equity S and debt B. Let Y stand for the income accruing to the shareholders and let I be the interest payments to the debtholders. Assume that two companies of the same size and operating risk make the same rate of return on their assets, which we shall term net operating income; for simplicity assume that this is expected to be constant in perpetuity. Company B is financed entirely by equity. In the example shown in table 9.22 we ignore the influence of taxation.

The example in table 9.22 shows the effects of one extreme of gearing on cost of capital and company value, termed the *net income approach*. This

Table 9.22 *Gearing and the cost of capital*

		Company A (geared)		Company B (no gearing)
Net operating income	Y	£1000	Y	£1000
Interest payments on debt I (pure rate of interest $r \times$ face value of the debt B)	rB	5% of £4000 = £200	0	
Value of debt is perpetual stream of payments to debt holders capitalized at the pure interest rate r	$\frac{rB}{r} = B$	$\frac{£200}{0.05}$ £4000	0	
Net income	$Y - rB$	£1000 – £200	Y	£1000
Value of equity S is the perpetual stream of payments to the equity holders capitalized at the equity capitalization rate k_e	$\frac{Y - rB}{k_e}$	$\frac{£800}{0.10}$	$\frac{Y}{k_e}$	$\frac{£1000}{0.10}$
Value of company	$S_A + B$	£8000 + £4000 = £12,000	S_a	£10,000

suggests that the use of gearing can increase a company's value. The crucial assumption is that the equity capitalization rate does not increase despite the fact that company A has geared up; in the example it remains at 10 per cent. True, the net income payable to the shareholders in A has been reduced by the interest payments on debt ($Y - rB$ is paid to shareholders) but the interest payments to the debtholders have also to be taken into account in that they are capitalized at the pure interest rate r (5 per cent). The value of the geared company is made up of the values of its debt and its equity. But the value of the geared company must be greater if the equity capitalization rate k_e is the same for both, since company A differs from company B by a factor equal to $(-rB/k_e) + (rB/r)$; since $k_e > r$ this must always be positive.

It could be argued that this approach is unrealistic in that gearing up involves increased financial risk to both debtholders and equity holders. A large amount of fixed prior claims against operating earnings increases the probability, in a bad year, of there being insufficient earnings to pay any dividends to the shareholders or, at worst, of bankruptcy. This problem was assumed away in our simplified example, but in practice it suggests that k_e should rise with increases in gearing. The *net operating income approach* to the valuation of geared companies suggests that k_e will rise just sufficiently with increases in gearing to offset any gain from cheaper debt financing, so that the net effect is to leave the value of a geared company unchanged. It can be shown that this will be the case if the equity capitalization rate of the geared company is as follows:

$$k_g = k_e + (k_e - r)\,\frac{B}{S} \tag{9.12}$$

where k_e is the equity capitalization rate of a company with the same operating risk but not gearing, k_g is the equity capitalization rate of the geared company, B is the market value of the debt issued and S is the market value of the equity assuming that gearing has no effect on valuation.

If we apply the figures from the example in table 9.22 to expression (9.12) (S is £6000, the sum that needs to be added to the debt value of company A (£4000) to bring the total to the value of company B where no gearing has taken place (£10,000)) we have

$$k_g = 0.10 + (0.10 - 0.05)\,\frac{£4000}{£6000}$$

$$= 0.133.$$

If the £800 of annual income accruing to shareholders in A were capitalized at this rate the equity in A would be worth £6000 and the combined value of the debt and equity would be equal to £10,000, the same value as company B.

We could define the company's average cost of capital as the rate at which net operating income is capitalized, indicated by the ratio of net operating income to market valuation. In the above example, we would have

$$k_o = \frac{Y}{B+S} = \frac{£1000}{£10{,}000} = 10 \text{ per cent.}$$

In the case of a company using a number of different sources of funds the rate could be viewed as a weighted average of the costs of the sources of funds employed.

$$k_o = W_1 k_e = W_2 k_d \tag{9.13}$$

where W_1 is the proportion of equity in the capital structure ($S/(B + S)$), W_2 is the proportion of debt in the capital structure ($B/(S + B)$), k_e is the cost of equity and k_d is the cost of debt.

It is obvious that the net income and the net operating income approaches to company valuation are extreme views. It is true that Modigliani and Miller have provided theoretical justification for the net operating income approach, but their proof requires perfect market assumptions which do not hold in practice.[21] The 'traditional view' of the effect of gearing upon capital cost is something of a compromise.

The traditional view of the effect of gearing on cost of capital

The 'traditionalists' suggest that judicious use of gearing can lower a company's cost of capital. At relatively low levels of gearing the financing of a portion of the company's assets with relatively cheap debt (assuming no inflation), and the favourable tax treatment of debt interest, mean that the equity capitalization rate does not increase much; therefore the combined effect is to lower the cost of capital and increase the value of the company until the optimum point is reached at a gearing level of G_1 in figure 9.10. At this point the cost of capital is minimized and the value of the company is maximized. Movement beyond this point increases financial risk and the probability of bankruptcy to a degree that motivates both the debtholders and the equity holders to start demanding higher returns to compensate them for higher risk.

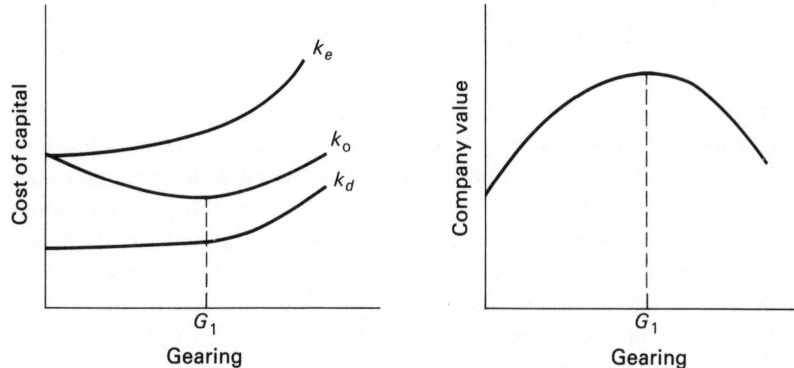

Figure 9.10 *Gearing and cost of capital: the traditional view*

The analysis also implies that if a company is geared up to the optimum level then any new finance must be in those optimal proportions, otherwise the cost of capital will start to rise. There are *spill-over effects* on the costs of existing debt and equity from a new issue of purely debt or equity; such an issue does not maintain the optimal capital mix. For this reason the appropriate hurdle rate or test discount rate for appraising new investment projects is the marginal cost of funding them, which would take into account any spill-over effects, as shown in figure 9.11.

In a given period if X_1 volume of funds is raised in a manner which involves an increase in the average cost of capital, the appropriate discount rate for the projects which the funds are being used to finance is the marginal cost r of raising those funds. The calculation of the cost of capital is far from simple. If equity or retained earnings are to be used the cost is not necessarily the opportunity cost or yield on the company's equity, and likewise the cost of debt issued is not just the tax-adjusted cost of debt. These potential effects on the costs of existing sources must be considered.

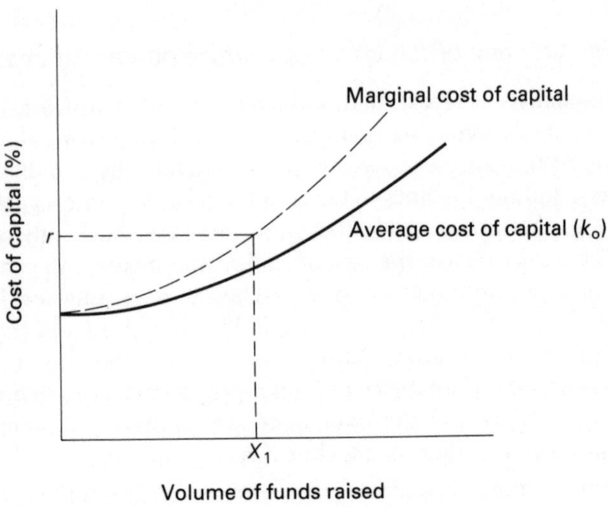

Figure 9.11 *The marginal cost of capital*

The previously mentioned agency costs may be affected by changes in a firm's capital structure. For example the issue of new debt may lower the expected pay-off to existing debtholders. Traditional debenture issues have debt covenants attached which limit the ability of the company's managers to issue further senior debt, raise total borrowings beyond strictly defined limits, or reduce the equity base of the company by paying excessive dividends. A desire to escape these restrictions has led to the growing popularity of the debt defeasance schemes described earlier.

Likewise, investment policies may have implications for security holders; risky corporate strategies tend to favour the interests of equity holders, since they are the ones who reap any benefits. The debtholders do not share in company profits and receive set interest payments.

Donaldson, in an early field study (1961), reported that the US companies in his sample liked to maintain spare debt capacity and operated a 'pecking order' with respect to funds sources. They preferred to fund by retained profits; then, if external sources were required, chose debt, the convertibles and finally equity issues.[22] The maintenance of spare debt capacity meant that they could respond speedily to unplanned changes in circumstances – a major investment opportunity or a take-over bid. What exactly determines companies' capital structures remains a puzzle.

Dividend policy and retentions

A company's dividend policy and its retention policy are two sides of the same coin, since by definition what a company does not distribute is retained. Miller and Modigliani have demonstrated that, in a perfect market, given an investment policy not subject to change, dividend policy does not matter.[23] Shareholders can either enjoy extra dividends now at the expense of the dilution of future returns necessitated by a new issue to finance investment, or forgo dividends now and have offsetting increased returns in the future. Yet markets are not perfect and both companies and governments behave as if dividend policy is important.

In various periods the government has introduced tax measures which discriminate against dividend payments as a means of encouraging reinvestment of profits via retentions, and between 1973 and 1979 dividend increases were restricted as part of counter-inflation policies. The argument was that, if other sources of income were restrained, dividend income should have like treatment.

There are various factors that could make the dividend decision extremely important. Capital gains used to be taxed at a lower rate than dividend income. It is payable on the profit from the disposal of shares for a consideration above the adjusted purchase price. This is the original price inflated by the percentage rise in the RPI over the holding period. In 1989–90, capital gains tax was payable at the investor's marginal personal tax rate on gains above the annual exemption limit of £5000. The liability for the tax is postponed until the shares are actually sold. In circumstances where capital gains are taxed at a lower rate of tax than dividends, higher rate taxpayers could well prefer a policy of low dividends[24] and high retentions so that they can take most of their return via a capital gain. Although the opportunity cost of a new share issue should be the same as financing by rententions, the various transactions and issue expenses make finance by retentions more attractive. On the other hand, uncertainty about future income could lead shareholders to put a premium on dividend payments now rather than uncertain capital gains later. This is popularly termed the 'bird-in-the-hand' argument. Companies seem to be extremely reluctant to change their dividend policy in response to every movement of earnings. Lintner produced evidence of a 'target payout' ratio and a lagged response of dividend policy alterations to changes in earnings.[25] It is argued that there is an 'information content' to dividend policy, and that any change in policy conveys a change in management's expectations of future earnings prospects; they are thus unwilling to alter policy unless they are fairly sure that the company's circumstances have changed.

Financial Management – the Puzzles Remain

Despite considerable advances in our understanding of financial decisions many of the central areas of financial management are puzzles which still await satisfactory resolution. There are many different theories but no clear evidence about how a company should choose its capital structure or dividend policy – or, indeed, about whether the choice really matters.

There is no clear evidence or agreement about the conditions required to make companies invest. These factors, together with the variety of funding methods available to various types of enterprise, the patterns of funding activity in recent years and the financial markets which govern the allocation of savings and investments, are considered in the next chapter.

Appendix 9.1

Pro forma Profit-and-Loss Account

		£
Turnover		*x*
Cost of sales		(*x*)
Gross profit or loss		*x*
Distribution costs		(*x*)
Administrative expenses		(*x*)
Other operating income		*x*
Income from shares in group companies		*x*
Income from shares in related companies		*x*
Income from other fixed asset investments		*x*
Other interest receivable and similar income		*x*
Amounts written off investments		(*x*)
Interest payable and similar charges		(*x*)
Tax on profit or loss on ordinary activities		(*x*)
Profit or loss on ordinary activities after tax		*x*
Extraordinary income	*x*	
Extraordinary charges	(*x*)	
Extraordinary profit or loss		*x*
Tax on extraordinary profit or loss		(*x*)
Other taxes not shown under the above items		(*x*)
Profit or loss for the financial year	£*x*	

Pro forma Balance sheet

	£	£
Called-up share capital not paid		*x*
Fixed assets:		
Intangible assets	*x*	
Tangible assets	*x*	
Investments	*x*	*x*
		x

Current assets:		
Stocks	x	
Debtors	x	
Investments	x	
Cash at bank and in hand	x	
	x	
Less:		
Creditors: amounts becoming due and payable within one year	(x)	
Net current assets/liabilities		x
Total assets less current liabilities		x
Creditors: amounts becoming due and payable after more than one year		(x)
Provisions for liabilities and charges		(x)
Accruals and deferred income		(x)
		£x
Capital and reserves:		
Called-up share capital		x
Share premium account		x
Revaluation reserve		x
Other reserves		x
Profit and loss account		x
		£x

This is an abbreviated version of the new format and full details of the composition of the items listed above would have to be given in notes to the accounts.

References

1 M. C. Jensen and W. H. Meckling, 'Theory of the firm: managerial behaviour, agency costs and ownership structure', *Journal of Financial Economics* (October 1976).

2 See for example R. L. Watts and J. L. Zimmerman, *Positive Accounting Theory*, Prentice Hall, 1986.

3 E. Stamp, 'Accounting standards and the conceptual framework: a plan for their evolution', *Accountants' Magazine* (July 1981), pp. 216–22.

4 Accounting Standards Steering Committee, *The Corporate Report*, July 1975.

5 Sir John Hicks, *Value and Capital*, Oxford University Press, 2nd edn, 1968, p. 174.

6 Accounting Standards Steering Committee, *Provisional Statement of Standard Accounting Practice 7* (PSSAP 7), Institute of Chartered Accountants in England and Wales (ICAEW), 1974, discussed in the text as current purchasing power (CPP) accounting.

7 *Report of the Inflation Accounting Committee* (Sandilands Committee), Cmnd 6225, HMSO, September 1975.

8 Accounting Standards Committee, *Standard Statement of Accounting Practice 16*, ICAEW, 1980, the 'final version' of CCA.

9 'Performance of large companies', *Bank of England Quarterly Bulletin* (September 1986), p. 390.

10 K. V. Peasnell, L. C. L. Sherratt and C. W. R. Ward, 'The share price impact of UK CCA disclosures', *Accounting and Business Research* 18 (Winter 1987), pp. 3–15.

11 J. Sizer, *An Insight into Management Accounting*, Penguin, 2nd edn, 1979, p. 15.

12 H. Ingham and L. Taylor Harrington, *Interfirm Comparison*, Heinemann, 1980.

13 G. Whittington, 'Some basic properties of accounting ratios', *Journal of Business Finance and Accounting* 7 (1980), pp. 219–32.

14 Institute of Fiscal Studies, *The Structure and Reform of Direct Taxation*, Report of a committee chaired by Professor J. E. Meade, Allen & Unwin, 1978.

15 *Report of the Committee to Review the Functioning of the Financial Institutions*, Cmnd 7937, HMSO, 1980, appendix 6.

16 Ibid.

17 Ibid.

18 These are reported by M. Devereux, 'Taxation and the cost of capital', *Oxford Review of Economic Policy* 3 (1987).

19 For further discussion of the Meade Committee findings, see P. W. J. N. Bird, 'An expenditure tax for the United Kingdom', *National Westminster Bank Quarterly Review* (August 1979).

J. A. Kay and M. A. King, *The British Tax System*, Oxford University Press, 1978.

20 H. M. Markowitz, *Portfolio Selection*, Wiley, 1959.

W. F. Sharpe, 'Capital asset prices: a theory of market equilibrium under conditions of risk', *Journal of Finance* (1964), pp. 425–42.

21 F. Modigliani and M. H. Miller, 'The cost of capital, corporation finance, and the theory of investment', *American Economic Review* (1958), pp. 261–97.

22 G. Donaldson, *Corporate Debt Capacity*, Harvard University Press, 1961.

23 M. H. Miller and F. Modigliani, 'Dividend policy, growth, and the valuation of shares', *Journal of Business* (1961), pp. 411–33.

24 See I. R. C. Hirst, *Business Investment Decisions*, Philip Allan, 1988, for a review of alternative policies.

25 J. Linter, 'Distribution of incomes of corporations among dividends, retained earnings and taxes', *American Economic Review*, Papers and Proceedings (1956), pp. 97–113.

10

Financing British Industry

Financial decisions can be analysed in various ways. As a topic finance can be viewed as a question of income and/or risk apportionment and, of course, business control. Alternatively, it has been suggested that financial managers seek an answer to three basic questions:

1 What is the optimum size of an enterprise and how quickly should it grow?
2 What type of assets should it hold?
3 What should be the structure of its liabilities?[1]

We have already encountered questions 1 and 2 and possible answers to them in chapters 6 and 9. This chapter is concerned with reviewing some of the various alternative responses to question 3, which determine the demand for funds, and related issues affecting the supply of funds. To start with, from the point of view of demand, it has to be borne in mind that the range of financing alternatives open to a business are a function of its legal form.

Business Forms and Financing Alternatives

Throughout this book the public company with its shares quoted and traded on the International Stock Exchange is referred to as the 'typical' organization, but other forms of enterprise are more important numerically if not in terms of the value of assets controlled. Indeed, the type of legal entity that an organization assumes is normally a function of its size and the amount of finance required. We consider successively sole traderships, partnerships, private limited liability companies and public limited companies.

The sole trader

The sole trader is the most common business form. It is adopted by most shopkeepers, tradesmen and farmers. There is no distinction between the identity of the business and that of the person who runs it. He trades under his own name and has personal liability for his business debts. This involves considerable risk since personal assets can be put at the disposal of creditors should the business run into debt. Profits from the business are taxed at the owner's marginal rate of income tax. This complete identity of ownership and control means that the owner has total (financial) freedom to run his business as he sees fit. There is a minimum obligation to maintain financial records but not beyond the requirements of income tax, value-added tax (VAT) and social welfare regulations. Small businesses, indeed, do not have to register for VAT until their taxable turnover is in excess of £23,600 per annum (1989–90 tax year).

This relative freedom and simplicity has its disadvantages. The fact that the sole trader is unlikely to produce detailed financial information means that potential external sources of finance will lack sufficient information to judge the business. This means in turn that the equity or risk capital to fund the business is likely to be restricted to the owner's own savings or those of close friends and family. Outsiders would be unwilling to provide risk funds since they have little information and no control regarding the operation of the business. The only other long-term external source of funds will be borrowing. If the owner of the business has sufficient assets to offer as security, perhaps his house, then he will be able to raise funds by a mortgage loan. The asset cover, and the regular interest and capital repayments involved in a loan, guard the interests of the creditors and compensate for the lack of detailed knowledge of the business operations, since the loan is secured against the asset rather than the business. (Such creditors will not, of course, be totally unconcerned with the viability of the business.)

The only financial institution likely to have the requisite knowledge of the sole trader's business soundness will be his bankers. His overdraft facility, and any secured loans he is able to arrange with the bankers, are likely to be his major external sources of finance. He may obtain limited short-term funds by receiving credit from suppliers, and medium-term funds by leasing or hiring equipment, but his financial alternatives remain strictly limited. If he remains a sole trader any continuous expansion of operations is thus likely to be funded from ploughed-back income.

Partnerships

A partnership is an association of two or more people, working together in a profit-oriented business, jointly providing the finance, sharing control and participating in the profits, as required by the 1890 Partnership Act and subject to any overriding clause in the partnership agreement. Partnerships are very common amongst the professions. Indeed, certain professional bodies (e.g. solicitors and accountants) require that their members adopt this business form. The upper limit on the numbers involved in a partnership was 20 but this restriction was removed by the 1967 Companies Act in the cases of accountants, stockbrockers and solicitors. The advantage of the partnership over the sole trader is that there can be a pooling of both funds and personal expertise. But there are still considerable disadvantages.

Partners remain liable for debts. But here exposure to risk is greater than that involved in a sole tradership in that an ill-conceived judgement or breach of faith on the part of one partner could (legally) endanger the personal assets of all the others. The partnership is an unwieldy legal form. It can be dissolved by mutual consent or on the death or bankruptcy of a partner. If one partner owes the business money it is difficult to sue him on behalf of the business since he is part of it. It is difficult to transfer ownership since a partner cannot transfer his interest unless the other existing partners agree to accept the new partner(s). Profits are taxed at the personal income tax rate of the recipient partner, which may mean exposure to high marginal rates.

Sometimes a so-called 'sleeping' partner will put up funds, whilst taking no part in day-to-day business operations; these will be undertaken by other partner(s) with the necessary expertise. There are also provisions for the creation of limited partnerships; these extend the benefits of limited liability to those partners who are prepared to refrain from taking an active part in the business, while the remaining active partners remain fully and personally liable. For this reason limited partnerships are uncommon.

The partnership, therefore, has few advantages over the sole tradership. It facilitates the pooling of capital but can increase the individual exposure to risk. The other external sources of funds available are much the same as those at the disposal of the sole trader.

The limited liability company

The concept of the joint stock company evolved during the seventeenth and eighteenth centuries. These were originally temporary groupings of individuals banding together to finance 'one-off' merchant trading ventures. At the completion of a successful trading voyage each individual financier would share in the proceeds in proportion to his ventured 'stake'. When the idea of permanently subscribing risk capital became established the culmination was the notorious (and fraudulent) episode of the South Sea Company. The 1720 Bubble Act, passed to protect ill-informed share dealing of the type which occurred with South Sea stock, effectively outlawed joint stock companies unless they were set up with parliamentary permission. This hindered the progress of incorporation, but the Industrial Revolution and the development of capital-intensive industries spurred the demand for industrial capital and so for the joint stock company as an appropriate fund-raising vehicle. In 1825 the Bubble Act was repealed. The passage of the Joint Stock Companies Act of 1844 and the Limited

Liability Act of 1856 then paved the way for the development of the modern corporation and industrial capital markets as we know them today.

Types of company

The 1948 Companies Act defines three types of company which can be registered: those limited by shares, those limited by guarantee and unlimited companies. The second and third categories are relatively rare. In *companies limited by guarantee*, in the event of the company being unable to meet its debts, the members are liable for a certain specified sum. This form is usually adopted by companies whose activities are not primarily profit oriented, such as those engaged in promoting charitable causes. *Unlimited companies* are extremely rare and are usually set up to manage family estates.

The normal company is one in which the owners' liability is *limited by shares*. Shareholders participate in ownership by agreeing to purchase shares, and by so doing commit funds up to the nominal or *par value* of the shares concerned. Should the company go bankrupt, through lack of sufficient funds to pay creditors, then the creditors will only receive payment from those funds which can be raised by selling or 'liquidating' those assets (stocks of finished goods, equipment, property etc.) which remain in possession of the company. The shareholders lose (at most) their original stake, but they are not liable for any further money to meet the company's debts, and their personal assets are secure. This is not the case with the sole trader or the normal form of partnership. Clearly 'limited liability' cuts down the risk involved in putting up money to fund business activities enormously. Risk obviously remains, in that any money ventured may be lost, but that is its total extent. The advent of limited liability provided a tremendous stimulus to the growth of industrial capital markets.

Setting up a Private Limited Company

A private company can have between two and 50 members, who have to file the following main documents with the Registrar of Companies.

Memorandum of association

A firm's legal remit is set out within the memorandum of association, which also contains the following details: the name of the company; the situation of its registered office; and the objectives of the company (broadly defined so that they include everything that the company is likely to undertake). These give indications, to both prospective members (i.e. shareholders) and persons dealing with the company, of the nature of its activities, the size of its authorized share capital, information about its division amongst the subscribers plus the subscribers' signatures.

Articles of association

These document the rights of company members and define the manner in which the company shall regulate its activities according to table A of the 1948 Companies Act. Included in the articles are regulations concerning the rights, and variations thereof, to share capital; the provisions for calls on, transfer, transmission and forfeiture of shares, and the alteration of capital; the procedure to be followed at meetings and the voting rights of members; the appointment, powers and process for the retirement of directors; and provisions relating to the annual accounts, profits and dividends, and to the winding-up of the company. The articles can be altered by special resolution at a meeting of the shareholders.

The distinction between a private and a public company

The main distinctions between a private and a public company follow from the restriction on the membership of a private company to a maximum of 50 whereas a public company has a minimum of seven members but no upper limit. There are further restrictions on the right to transfer shares and a prohibition of the offering of its shares or debentures to the general public. This confers the benefit of not having to divulge the information included in a prospectus, which is required when offering shares to the general public.

Private companies controlled by five or fewer 'interests' are defined as 'close companies' following the introduction of Corporation Tax in 1965. They are required to distribute a certain proportion of their profits or are deemed by the authorities to have done so. The intention is to discourage the use of companies as tax avoidance mechanisms, a considerable attraction given the disparity between corporate and personal tax rates.

The advantages of incorporation

Apart from the previously mentioned benefits of limited liability there are a number of other attractions to incorporation. Companies have a separate legal personality, and enjoy perpetual existence until wound up. Company property is distinct from that of the members, and the company can enter into contracts in its own right and sue or be sued. There is not necessarily an identity between the owners and the managers of a company. Should a former owner/manager wish to retire, he could simply do so and maintain his shareholding, or if he wished to realize his interest and use the proceeds to go on a round-the-world cruise, he could arrange for the transfer of his shares. The situation, as we shall see, is even more straightforward for a shareholder in a publicly quoted company.

Sources of finance available to a private company

The private company is better placed to raise finance than the two previously considered business forms. Appropriation of profits to reserves escapes income tax, and hence the company is more likely to be able to finance growth via the retention of profits. The company can issue *debentures* (loan finance) and offer security to the holders by means of a floating charge against the company's assets. Private companies vary enormously in size up to businesses that are very large with turnovers of millions of pounds. For the larger private company a number of financing alternatives will be available.

In the short term (periods up to a year) it will probably take *credit* from suppliers (in the form of delaying payment for consignments of raw materials and components) as well as give it to customers. *Bank overdrafts* will be a major source of short-term funds, as they are for all forms of business. (There is some disagreement about the status of overdrafts in that many companies have persistent overdrafts, but as these facilities can be withdrawn by banks with minimal notice and since the terms can be subject to frequent alteration, they are regarded as being short-term funds.) The company may also be able to arrange medium-term loans (of a period from two to seven years) from its bank.

Table 10.1 shows the total volume of loans and advances to UK enterprises and individuals in November 1988 and August 1989. The

Table 10.1 *Analysis of loans and advances to UK residents in November 1988 and August 1989 (£million) in sterling and foreign currencies*

	November 1988	*August 1989*
Manufacturing	35,416	43,625
Other production	20,353	25,668
Services	79,992	102,892
Financial	75,144	91,348
Persons	78,260	114,666
Total	289,165	378,201
Of which in		
sterling	236,329	304,321
other currencies	52,836	73,880

Source: Central Statistical Office, *Financial Statistics*, No. 331 (November 1989), table 6.7

recipients are classified according to their activities and are placed into five broad groups: manufacturing, other production, services, the financial sector or the personal sector. The figures are aggregated and therefore include loans to all types of businesses, including private and public companies. Traditionally, the London Clearing Banks would provide the lion's share, in the region of 40 per cent of the total. However, foreign banks, initially American ones but more recently Japanese, are providing an increasing share. Originally, the foreign banks were more willing to offer term loans (fixed-term loans of a medium period, two to seven years) than were British banks, who used to prefer lending on overdraft. However, foreign competition and government exhortation have led to an expansion of term lending.

In 1981 the Government introduced a loan guarantee scheme to benefit small companies. This provided insurance to the banks against defaulters on term loans to a value of 80 per cent of the loan. The proportion of the loan guaranteed and the annual premium required for this insurance have since been altered from time to time. The introduction of the scheme ensured that additional funds would be available for loans to small companies. In the first four and a half years of its operation over 1600 small businesses were provided with loans totalling over £500 million.

In evidence submitted to the Wilson Committee the banks were criticized as being too cautious and restrictive in their lending policies to small businesses.[2] Certainly, the terms and conditions are more onerous, but this is largely a reflection of the increased risk and administrative cost of lending relatively small amounts to small businesses. The banks, however, are a major source (in relative and absolute terms) of external funds to small businesses.

Invoice discounting and *factoring* have become increasingly popular methods of raising short-term finance. If a company has sold items and delayed the receipt of payment by extending credit terms, it can approach a finance company engaged in invoice discounting which might offer to advance funds up to 75 per cent of the value of the invoices outstanding. The company benefits from the immediate injection of funds; at a later date, when payment has been received, it repays the finance company together with an interest and service charge.

Alternatively the company can sell its debts to a factor, probably a subsidiary of one of the clearing banks. Factors offer three basic services: debt collection and credit management, insurance against bad debts, and the provision of finance on the security of the debt. As the services are more extensive the cost is proportionately more, but a credit management and debt collection service can be very valuable to a rapidly growing small company, which has neither the time nor resources to expend on this activity.

Deferred tax payments form another useful source of short-term business funds. The extent of the delay depends on the company's accounting dates, but there is typically a year's lag between the generation of profits and the payment of tax on that accounting year's profits. Similarly, any situation in which there is a deferment of expenses due adds to a company's liquidity.

Additions to medium-term funds are likely to come from the *leasing and hiring* of equipment, and from term loans (if available). The availability of long-term funds will be discussed in more detail in the next section, when we consider the transition from private company to public company status.

Table 10.2 gives some indication of the way in which small companies have financed themselves in the recent past. It is derived from a sample survey undertaken by the Wilson Committee of nearly 300 small companies. The companies are categorized according to the size of their capital employed (defined as total capital and reserves and minority shareholders' interests, plus deferred tax, plus bank loans and overdrafts and long-term and short-term loans, plus net amount due to other group members). 'Smaller' companies are defined as those having a capital employed of less than £250,000, and 'medium small' as those having £250,000 to £4 million. (Inevitably the definition of 'small' is somewhat arbitrary. The Bolton[3] and Wilson Committees were considerably exercised by these problems of definition.)

From table 10.2, the prominent features of smaller and medium small companies' balance sheets compared with those of larger companies are as follows.

1 A greater proportion of funds is tied up in short-term assets and liabilities.
2 A large amount of trade credit is both taken and given.
3 The importance of bank overdrafts, as already mentioned, is apparent.
4 There is a slightly smaller shareholder's interest but a marked reliance on loans from directors, perhaps to make up for the deficiency of loans from other sources, which are employed to a greater extent by large companies.
5 There seems to be a more cautious attitude towards liquidity on the part of the smaller companies, who have a higher proportion of assets in the form of cash and short-term deposits.

The small companies are probably wise in the caution indicated in 5. However, some family-controlled businesses have such a fierce desire to maintain their independence, and to avoid any diminution of control or security, that they would prefer to forgo growth opportunities than raise further external finance. This is a matter for the companies concerned, but in recent years there has been a growth of 'half-way houses' which considerably ease the transition from private to public company staus. For even with a membership of 50 the time is likely to arrive when the combined resources of those concerned are not sufficient to meet the financing requirements for expansion.

The transition from private to public company

If a private company wishes to 'go public' then the issuing houses and merchant banks are sometimes willing to place its shares with their own private clients. Private company shares are unattractive in their limited marketability, but the knowledge that a listing is likely in the near future, with the likelihood of an appreciation in value stemming purely from increased marketability, is a considerable sweetener.

For the private company about to go public there are basically three options. First, it can go public but refrain from immediately asking the public to subscribe for its shares. In this circumstance it has to lodge a statement in lieu of a prospectus (issued when making a share issue) with the Registrar of Companies, and by so doing loses most of the privacy of information attached to private status. Second, it can invite the public to subscribe for shares without having them quoted on the International Stock Exchange. Third, it can seek a full listing. The second and third alternatives require the issue of a prospectus, a fairly detailed financial document whose contents will be reviewed later in this chapter.

Companies not yet ready to seek a full quotation can have their shares dealt in the 'over-the-counter' market which has expanded considerably in recent years. The introduction of the Business Expansion Scheme (BES), in 1983, has encouraged the channelling of equity finance to small unquoted firms by offering tax breaks to private investors. (In the 1988–9 tax year a ceiling of £500,000 was placed on the total amount of investment in a company which could qualify for tax relief in any 12 month period under the BES.) In 1983–4, 715 businesses raised £105 million under the scheme, while in the following year 787 businesses raised £140 million.

These tax changes have acted as a stimulus to the venture capital industry. At the end of 1986 there were 110 specialist venture capital groups compared with only 19 in 1979. There are a number of other specialist institutions which also help to fill the gap (these are reviewed in appendix 10.1). In 1931 the Macmillan Committee identified the 'Macmillan Gap',[4] defined as the difficulty encountered by small to medium companies raising external finance up to an amount in the region of £200,000, which would be equivalent to £2 million to £3 million today.

Whether such a problem exists today is a moot point but there have been a number of recent developments (apart from those mentioned above) that must have served to ameliorate this difficulty.

There are now three levels at which companies can have their shares traded on the International Stock Exchange. To achieve a full listing a company must fulfil certain stringent minimum requirements. It must have a market capitalization (number of issued securities × their price) of at least £700,000. In practice this would need to be at least £5 million to £6 million, implying a level of pre-tax profits in excess of £1 million. At least 25 per cent of the company's issued shares should be on the market and the

Table 10.2 *Balance sheet structure, 1975: percentages of total assets/ liabilities*

	Manufacturing			Non-manufacturing			All small companies			
	Smaller	Medium small	Total	Smaller	Medium small	Total	Smaller	Medium small	Total	Large companies
Fixed assets										
Tangible fixed assets, net	29.4	26.6	27.4	33.0	34.0	33.5	32.0	30.3	31.1	36.2
Goodwill	0.4	0.6	0.5	0.1	1.7	0.9	0.2	1.2	0.7	3.2
Investment in unconsolidated subsidiaries	–	1.9	1.3	0.2	0.9	0.5	0.1	1.4	0.8	0.3
Total fixed assets, net	29.8	29.0	29.2	33.3	36.7	34.9	32.4	32.8	32.7	39.7
Current assets										
Stocks and work in progress	21.5	32.6	29.4	26.7	27.9	26.7	24.6	30.2	27.8	27.5
Trade and other debtors etc.	34.8	34.5	34.6	28.7	28.2	28.4	30.3	31.3	30.9	23.3
Investments	3.5	0.8	1.6	1.5	1.9	1.7	2.0	1.4	1.6	4.5
Cash and short-term deposits	10.4	3.1	5.2	10.9	5.4	8.3	10.7	4.2	7.1	5.0
Total current assets and investments	70.2	71.0	70.8	66.7	63.3	65.1	67.6	67.2	67.3	60.3
Total fixed and current assets	100.0	100.0	100.0	100.0	100.0	100.0	100.0	100.0	100.0	100.0
Current liabilities										
Bank overdrafts and loans	6.8	10.4	9.4	12.7	16.5	14.5	11.1	13.4	12.4	9.7
Short-term loans	2.6	0.6	1.2	2.9	2.6	2.8	2.8	1.6	2.1	3.0
Trade and other creditors	35.7	29.5	31.3	34.6	29.7	32.3	34.9	29.6	31.9	25.2

Dividends and interest due	0.5	0.9	0.7	0.8	0.6	0.7	0.7	0.7	0.7	1.0
Current taxation	3.8	3.4	3.5	2.3	3.3	2.8	2.7	3.4	3.1	2.3
Total current liabilities	49.4	44.7	46.1	53.3	52.7	53.0	52.3	48.7	50.3	41.1
Net current assets	20.8	26.2	24.7	13.4	10.6	12.1	15.3	18.4	17.1	19.2
Total net assets	50.6	55.3	53.9	46.7	47.3	47.0	47.7	51.3	49.7	58.9
Capital and reserves										
Shareholder's interest										
Ordinary shares	5.8	10.7	9.3	6.3	9.1	7.6	6.1	9.9	8.3	11.6
Preference etc. shares	0.6	0.9	0.8	0.3	0.4	0.4	0.4	0.7	0.5	0.7
Capital and revenue reserves	28.8	27.6	28.0	20.9	23.5	22.1	23.0	25.5	24.4	26.8
Total shareholders' interest	35.1	39.2	38.0	27.4	33.1	30.1	29.5	36.1	33.3	39.1
Loans from directors	8.3	0.8	3.0	12.3	0.6	6.8	11.2	0.7	5.3	–
Other long-term loans	1.1	6.8	5.1	3.7	6.4	5.0	3.0	6.6	5.0	10.3
Deferred taxation	6.1	8.1	7.5	3.3	7.1	5.1	4.0	7.6	6.0	7.4
Minority interests in subsidiaries	–	0.4	0.3	–	0.1	0.1	–	0.2	0.1	2.1
Total capital and reserves	50.6	55.3	53.9	46.7	47.3	47.0	47.7	51.3	49.7	58.9
Total capital and liabilities	100.0	100.0	100.0	100.0	100.0	100.0	100.0	100.0	100.0	100.0
£ billion	3.0	7.4	10.5	8.4	7.4	15.8	11.4	14.9	26.3	79.2

Source: *The Financing of Small Firms*, Interim Report of the Committee to Review the Functioning of Financial Institutions (Wilson Committee), Cmnd 7503, HMSO, March 1979, appendix 3

company has to show a trading record for five years. An applications for a listing commits the company to meet continuing obligations covering disclosure of information, the directors' code of dealing and compliance with the city code on take-overs and mergers, and other matters.

However, in 1980 the Exchange introduced the Unlisted Securities Market (USM), which has less stringent requirements. At present these companies need only place 10 per cent of their share capital on the market and they need only a three-year trading record. By September 1986, it had enabled some 500 member companies to raise in excess of £1000 million and 71 of these companies subsequently graduated to a full listing.

Finally, at the beginning of 1987, the International Stock Exchange introduced a third market to fulfil the needs of companies which may not meet the requirements for entry to the USM or listing. It requires no trading record and may therefore suit young companies with growth prospects. (Table 10.3 gives details of the number and market shares of securities quoted at 30 June 1986.) Many companies are not in a position to go public. The total number of companies on the Register in Great Britain at 31 December 1986 was 902,273, of which 895,276 were private companies and only 6997 were public ones.

Table 10.3 *The securities market in the United Kingdom (at 30 June 1986)*

	No. of securities	Market value (£m)
Total public sector, UK and Ireland	572	162,171.9
Total Eurobonds	1,189	102,290.0
Company securities		
Loan capital	1,249	17,057.5
Preference capital	1,304	21,504.5
Ordinary and deferred	2,355	1,390,032.9
Sub-total, company securities	4,888	1,428,594.9
Total listed securities	6,649	1,693,056.8
Unlisted Securities Market	402	8,314.1
Third market	16	128.4

Source: *The International Stock Exchange Official Yearbook*, 1987–8

Types of Company Security

The various types of security available to a public company wishing to raise long-term funds are shown in figure 10.1. The share capital is the

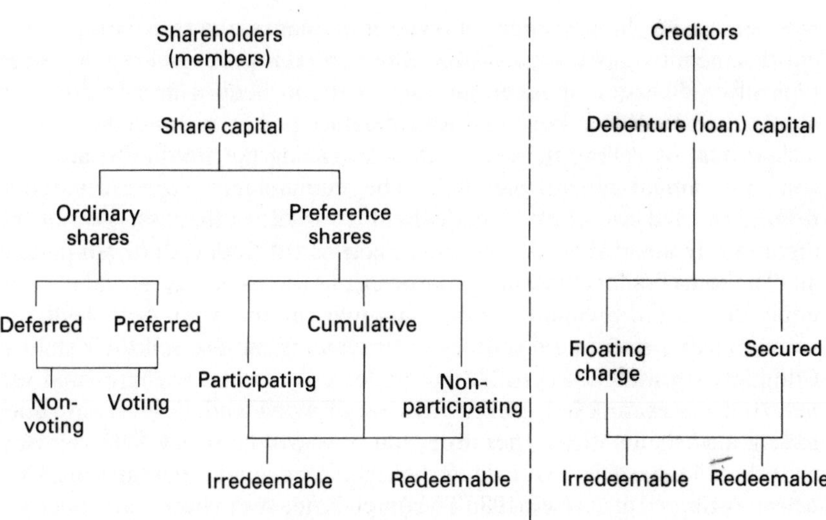

Figure 10.1 *The raising of long-term funds*

company's risk capital and is held by the members of the company. Together with the shareholder's reserves it represents their total interest. As the risk bearers, the shareholders receive payment last, after all interest payments to creditors (the right-hand side of figure 10.1). The payments to creditors are a tax-deductible expense paid out of pre-tax income, whereas the shareholders are paid from after-tax income (i.e. after corporation tax). In the event of the company failing and being put into liquidation the creditors receive capital repayment first.

The basic division in the share capital is between the ordinary and preference shares. The *preference shares* rank first behind creditors for payment of dividends and repayment of capital on liquidation. Usually the dividend is of fixed rate but some preference shares have a right to participate in profits to a further limit extent in good years. In a bad year the dividend may be passed (not paid), but cumulative preference shares have a right to make up for previous passed dividends. Redeemable preferences shares raise funds for a fixed period and the nominal value of the money raised is repaid to the holder at the redemption date. Irredeemable preference shares have no such provisions and if the holder wants to recoup his funds he will sell the shares on the Stock Exchange at the going rate. Since the passage of the Finance Act in 1965, which introduced the tax deductibility of interest payments, very few preference shares have been issued. If a company wants to raise fixed interest finance it makes more sense to issue debentures (the interest on which can be charged against tax payments) than preference shares (whose fixed dividends are paid out of after-tax income).

Ordinary shareholders have security of neither dividend nor capital repayment. The holder's right of ownership, manifest in their voting right, entitles them to appoint and dismiss directors. (However, shareholders are typically a diverse and geographically scattered body with a tradition of apathy, which probably stems from the fact that it is easier to register disapproval by selling the shares than by taking the trouble to attend a company annual general meeting.) The shareholders receive a variable return, and the size of each year's dividend is left to the discretion of the directors. In a bad year the dividend might be cut (reduced) or not paid at all. The shareholders have no recompense, as the risk bearers, and have to hope that trading conditions will improve in the next year, with an accompanying restoration of dividend payments, or else sell their shares. Companies sometimes issue different classes of ordinary shares and the deferred shares rank last for the payment of a dividend. A few companies have issued shares with either restricted or no voting rights. This can be a considerable disadvantage to their holders, particularly in a take-over bid where voting rights are crucial. To compensate, such shares are generally traded at a lower price than voting shares but suffer no dividend reduction.

The holders of a company's loan capital (debentures) remain outside creditors and have an entirely different relationship to the company from that of the shareholders (as indicated by the dotted line dividing figure 10.1). Loan capital represents the company's long-term borrowings and the principal or sum involved is a liability to the company, as are the annual interest payments. These must be paid at the stipulated times in the agreed amounts. If interest payments are not made, the trustees, appointed on behalf of the debenture holders, can force the company into liquidation in order to secure repayments due. Debentures might be secured against a specific piece of property (mortgage debenture) or asset, or by a floating charge against the general assets of the company.

If they are redeemable the company has agreed to repay the principal of the loan at some specified future data, as well as making the regular interest payments (usually biannual) on the loan. An irredeemable debenture holder is in a similar position to an irredeemable preference shareholder, and will liquidate his holding by selling it via the Stock Exchange.

In theory the debenture holders bear less risk than the shareholders, as their interest payments are guaranteed and fixed in amount and the principal of their loan is secured and ranks first in the event of liquidation. In terms of figure 10.1 the shareholders on the left-hand side bear the most risk, followed by the preference shareholders, and then the debenture holders on the right-hand side. It is normally assumed, and the evidence seems to support this, that investors are averse to risk. They do not like bearing risk for the sake of it and will only do so if compensated by the prospect of higher returns. Thus, all other things being equal, the return or yield on a share should be higher than the return on a debenture. The converse of this is the company's position, since the yield on its securities is a cost to the company. The servicing cost of debt should be less than that of equity (the cost of capital was considered in more detail in chapter 9).

Other factors which play a part in the decision to issue debentures are the tax advantage mentioned previously – the tax deductibility of interest payments – and the fact that payments are fixed in nominal terms and will decline in real value with any inflation. If investors have not fully anticipated the likely effect of inflation in setting the desired nominal rate (see expression (10.7)) then there will be an additional bonus to the company. Furthermore debentures do not confer voting rights and do not involve dilution of control. On the other hand, it will be remembered from the discussion in the previous chapter that they do increase financial risk. Thus there are a number of issues to be considered apart from the straight yield or cost of servicing. With regard to this, an understanding of the nature of yields and returns hinges on the concepts of the time value of money and discounting, introduced in chapter 9.

Present values and discounting: yields and returns

It will be recalled from expression (9.2) that the terminal value of a sum S invested for n periods at a rate of interest r is given by

$$\text{terminal value (TV)} = S(1 + r)^n. \tag{10.1}$$

Likewise, the present value of a terminal sum TS received n periods into the future, given an interest rate r, is given by

$$\text{present value} = \frac{\text{TS}}{(1 + r)^n}. \tag{10.2}$$

We can now apply these concepts to the returns on securities. The return on a share held for n periods is made up of the dividend payments over those n periods plus the price for which the share is sold at the end of the n periods, all discounted back to give their present value. In effect we are saying

$$\text{gross return} = d_0 + \frac{d_1}{1+r} + \frac{d_2}{(1 + r)^2} + \dots + \frac{d_n}{(1 + r)^n} + \frac{S_n}{(1 + r)^n}$$

where d_t is the dividend received in each period, $1 + r$ is the appropriate discount factor and S_n is the terminal sale price of the share.

We could write this as

$$\text{gross return} = \sum_{t=0}^{t=n} \frac{d_t}{(1 + r)^t} + \frac{S_n}{(1 + r)^n}. \tag{10.3}$$

To get the net return we would have to deduct the original price paid for the share, S_0, from the gross return. An alternative way of looking at the problem is to view the yield as being the discount rate that will equate the value of future dividend payments plus terminal share value with the current share price:

$$S_o = \sum_{t=0}^{t=n} \frac{d_t}{(1+k)^t} + \frac{S_n}{(1+k)^n} \tag{10.4}$$

where all symbols are as before and k is the yield on the share which equates the value of future payments with the current share price. The yield on a debenture is determined similarly:

$$D_o = \sum_{t=0}^{t=n} \frac{\mathrm{CP}}{(1+R)^t} + \frac{\mathrm{RD}}{(1+R)^n} \tag{10.5}$$

where D_0 is the current market price of the debenture, CP are the fixed 'coupon' or interest payments on the debenture, RD are the redemption provisions equal to the repayment of the nominal or par value of the debenture in period n, and R is the yield on the debenture which equates the value of future payments with the current market price of the debenture.

We have suggested that the yield on an ordinary share (k) would typically be greater than the yield on a debenture (R). This follows from the fact that there is more uncertainty about the value of the future dividend payments (strictly speaking the values in equation (10.4) are expected values since a dividend does not have to be paid) than there is about the coupon payments on debentures, which are fixed in money terms.

Now consider the *effects of inflation*. If there is a persistent and 'high' level of inflation, as previously the case in the UK, then the value of future payments will have to be further discounted to allow for the effects of inflation. If there is inflation the apparent nominal yield will have to be discounted by the rate of inflation given the true yield:

$$1 + r = \frac{1+R}{1+\mathrm{PI}} \tag{10.6}$$

where r is the true real yield, R is the apparent nominal yield and PI is the rate of inflation as measured by a price index.

Cross-multiplying equation (10.6) we obtain

$$\begin{aligned} 1 + R &= (1+r)(1+\mathrm{PI}) \\ &= 1 + r + \mathrm{PI} + r\mathrm{PI}. \end{aligned}$$

We can ignore the small quantity rPI and we then obtain

$$R \approx r + \mathrm{PI}. \tag{10.7}$$

Equation (10.7) shows that the nominal rate is approximately equal to the real rate plus a premium to reflect the rate of inflation. This is known as the *Fisher effect*. The effect of inflationary expectations is likely to be an increase in the discount rate used to value the returns on shares and debentures. This should, on its own, lead to a fall in the present or market values of both. Both the interest payments and the redemption provisions on debentures are fixed, and therefore a debenture is ill placed to deal with inflation. Dividends on a share are not fixed, and if the company can pass on the inflated value of its costs, in its product prices, then profits and dividends could increase in line with inflation. Hence equity (ordinary shares) are a better inflation hedge than debentures and in this sense debentures are more risky. This has been reflected in yields. Since 1959 fixed interest security holders have demanded a higher yield on debentures than the dividend yield on ordinary shares – a phenomenon called the *reverse yield gap*.

A summary of the annual nominal rates of return achieved on portfolios of risk-free securities and 20-year gilts, together with their inflation-adjusted returns, for the period 1919–84 is shown in table 10.4. The picture presented is exactly what we would expect to see if securities markets are populated by risk-averse investors who expect extra compensation for bearing extra risk. The lowest risk securities offer the lowest average returns. (Risk is proxied by the standard deviation of average annual returns, reported in table 10.4.) The risk-free rate of return (the return on treasury bills) averaged 4.71 per cent over the period, compared with 5.72 per cent on 20-year gilts and 14.25 per cent on a portfolio of stocks. The average risk premium – the difference between the return on the portfolio of stocks and that on risk-free securities – was 9.15 per cent. The maturity

Table 10.4 *Summary statistics for historical annual rates of return in Britain (1919–1984)*

	Arithmetic mean (%)	Standard deviation (%)
Risk-free rate of return[a]	4.71	3.93
Return on 20-year government bonds[b]	5.72	13.59
Return on a portfolio of stocks[c]	14.25	27.16
Rate of inflation[d]	4.38	6.21
Risk premium	9.15	25.03
Liquidity premium	1.00	12.43
Real risk-free return	0.56	5.37
Real return on 20-year government bonds	1.63	14.27
Real rate of return on a portfolio of stocks	9.63	24.50

[a]1919–45 return on 3-month bank bills, 1946 onwards return on 3-month treasury bills.
[b]20-year gilt-edged securities returns
[c]1919–62 return on 30-share portfolio, 1962 onwards, Financial Times Actuaries All Share Index returns.
[d]1919–67 De Zoete and Bevan estimates, 1967 onwards retail price index.
Source: D. E. Allen, R. E. Day, J. Kwiatkowski and I. R. C. Hirst, 'Equities, gilts, treasury bills and inflation: historical returns and simulations of the future', *The Investment Analyst*, (January 1987)

premium – the difference between the return on long- and short-dated government borrowings – was 1 per cent on average. This reflects the greater sensitivity of the price of longer-dated borrowings to changes in the level of interest rates. Finally, the inflation-adjusted series show that stocks were a good inflation hedge, offering a real return of 9.63 per cent on average, whilst government borrowings offered returns which barely kept pace with inflation.

The Bond Market

If governments spend more than they collect in taxes then like any private citizen or firm they must make up the deficit by borrowing. This they do by printing IOUs or *government bonds* (*gilts*), which are sold to the general public (households, firms, commercial banks or overseas equivalents) or to the Bank of England (which in effect means selling them to itself). Here our discussion will be restricted to sales to the public.

What is the effect on aggregate demand of financing budgets in this way? Bonds are simply certificates of debt. They have a face or par value which states in pounds what the borrower will pay back on pay-off or maturity day. They also have a coupon interest rate which merely states the amount in pounds that the government will pay each year to the holder of the bond. (When the coupon rate is expressed as a percentage it refers to the interest paid on bonds with a face or par value of £100.)

The actual rate of interest (before adjustment from nominal to real for purposes of inflation) depends on the price the owner had to pay for the bond. This, in turn, is determined in the stock market and is unconnected with the par value. Figures 10.2 and 10.3 are two ways of illustrating these statements.

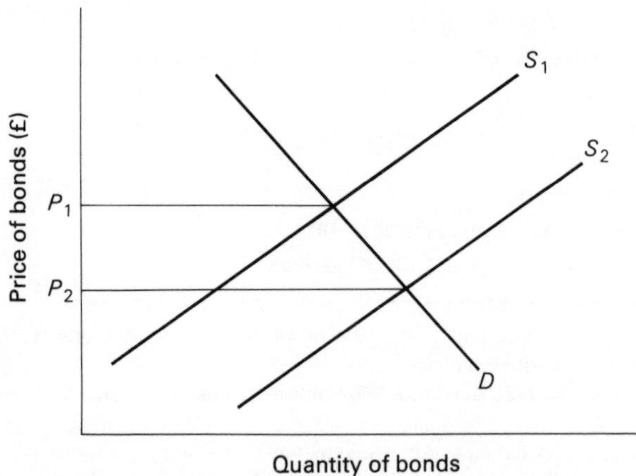

Figure 10.2 *The supply of bonds*

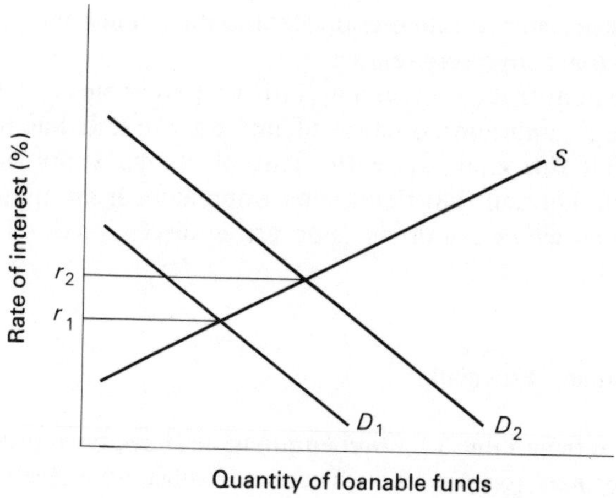

Figure 10.3 *The demand for loanable funds*

In the bond market (figure 10.2) demand slopes down because lenders receive a fixed payment (the coupon) no matter what price they pay for the bond. The lower the price of the bond, the more attractive this fixed payment becomes. Supply slopes up because issuers of bonds will be more willing to make a promise to provide the fixed coupon payment the higher the price they get for the bond in the first place.

Suppose that, on a given trading day in the bond market, supply and demand intersect to provide a market price of P_1. The government now decides to issue additional bonds to finance a deficit. Supply increases from S_1 to S_2 by this new issue of bonds at each and every price, and to clear this increase in supply the bond price must fall to P_2. However, although coupon rates are unchanged, the actual rate of interest earned by bond holders rises. Consider a bond with a face value of £100. Assume that the market price is £50 and that the coupon rate is 5 per cent. The government has an obligation to pay £5 per year to the holder of that bond. £5 as a percentage of £50 is 10 per cent, the actual rate of interest. If the market price now fell to £45, the actual rate would rise to £5 expressed as a percentage of £45, namely 11 per cent. Only when bonds sell for their face values are coupon and actual rates identical.

On the other hand, the bond market can be examined (as in figure 10.3) as the market for loanable funds. Here the government is viewed, not as supplying bonds to the public, but as demanding loans from the public. The public are suppliers of the loans. The higher the actual rate of interest, the more willing are the public to supply loans. The lower the rate of interest, the more willing is the government (and others) to borrow.

If the government wishes to fund its deficit it increases its demand for loanable funds at each interest rate. It issues more bonds. Demand rises from D_1 to D_2 and the previous equilibrium interest rate moves up from r_1

to r_2. The rise in interest rate is equivalent to the fall in bond price in figure 10.2. The two are inversely related.

To some extent then, government borrowing to finance a deficit is likely to affect the equilibrium structure of interest rates. It has been further suggested that this could raise the cost of company borrowing in the debenture market and thus deter some companies from approaching the market – the *crowding-out* thesis. (For further discussion of this see later in this chapter.)

Quoted Company Financing

It can be seen from table 10.5 that equity issues have been predominant in the company new issue market. There are substantial fluctuations from year to year which reflect both the state of company balance sheets and market conditions. The rapid rise in inflation following the OPEC oil price increases and the synchronized movement into recession in 1973–4, plus the depressed state of the stock market, meant that companies had to ease the inflationary pressures on their funding by borrowing at the short end of the market. As soon as the stock market recovered in 1975 there was a flood of equity rights issues (i.e. at the long-term end of the market) to restore balance sheets to a semblance of 'equilibrium' and ease the amount of borrowing.

There were extreme strains on company funding during the 1970s which were the result of a number of factors. Foremost amongst these were persistently high levels of inflation, high levels of interest rates and a continuing decline in real levels of profitability. The corporate debt market was an extremely important source of funds in the 1960s but dwindled in importance in the 1970s before making a recovery in the 1980s (see tables 10.5 and 10.6). High interest rates and uncertainty about the future made companies reluctant to commit themselves to borrowing long term at fixed rates. It made more sense to borrow short or medium term at variable rates.

In contrast, by the end of 1986–7 companies were enjoying the benefits of six years of sustained growth. Long-run interest rates were under 10 per cent and the rate of inflation was close to 4 per cent. In these circumstances companies were much more prepared to make longer-term debt issues. Furthermore, the growth in the use of interest rate swaps and financial futures (considered subsequently in this chapter) has given companies greater flexibility in the management of their interest rate exposure.

A breakdown of the nature of capital issues in recent years is given in table 10.5. Straightforward debt and equity issues make up the bulk of recent new issues. Both have been favoured by some further recent tax changes. Corporate bonds are exempt from capital gains tax if disposed of more than one year after acquisition or on or after 2 July 1986. British

Table 10.5 *New money raised by UK companies by type of security*

	Debt				Preference		Ordinary		
	Convertible debt (£m)	Other debt (£m)	Total debt (£m)	Per cent of total issues	£m	Per cent of total issues	£m	Per cent total issues	Total issues (£m)
1971–5 (average)	71.5	115.4	186.9	26.2	16.5	2.3	510.8	71.5	714.2
1976–80 (average)	52.3	42.4	94.7	9.9	38.3	4.0	819.8	86.0	952.7
1981	373.5	66.9	440.4	16.5	113.1	4.2	2,110.8	79.2	2,664.3
1982	71.3	944.8	1,016.1	45.9	32.5	1.5	1,165.4	52.6	2,214.0
1983	64.4	461.1	525.5	17.7	80.7	2.7	2,370.1	79.6	2,976.3
1984	118.1	1,043.6	1,161.7	36.4	78.4	2.5	1,947.5	61.1	3,187.7
1985	328.5	2,465.9	2,794.3	34.0	455.2	5.5	4,962.3	60.4	8,211.8
1986	140.8	6,415.2	6,555.9	45.0	263.3	1.6	7,763.1	53.3	14,555.3

Source: 'Annual review of the capital markets', *Midland Bank Review*, (Spring 1987)

Table 10.6 *Income and finance of large companies*[1, 2]

	Balance sheet at end of accounting 'year'[3]							
	1977	1978	1979	1980	1981	1982	1983	1984[4]
Balance sheet summary (percentage of total assets)								
Estimated number of companies	1524	1729	1766	1921	2213	2129	1974	1918
FIXED ASSETS								
Net tangible assets	35.6	37.9	37.2	39.6	41.5	42.2	41.8	42.3
Intangible assets	2.2	1.9	1.8	2.8	1.1	1.4	1.8	2.4
Investments in unconsolidated subsidiaries	0.2	0.2	0.3	0.2	0.2	0.5	0.2	0.0
Total net fixed assets	38.0	40.0	39.3	42.6	42.8	44.1	43.8	44.7
CURRENT ASSETS AND INVESTMENTS								
Stocks and work in progress	25.6	24.7	25.7	24.8	22.8	21.6	20.4	19.8
Debtors, pre-payments and government grants received	22.5	22.2	22.6	21.6	22.5	22.5	23.4	22.9
Investments	7.6	6.9	7.0	5.5	5.3	5.6	5.4	6.3
Cash, short-term deposits and tax instruments	6.2	6.1	5.4	5.4	6.4	6.2	7.1	6.3
Total current assets and investments	62.0	59.9	60.7	57.3	57.0	55.9	56.3	55.2
Total assets	100.0	100.0	100.0	100.0	100.0	100.0	100.0	100.0
CURRENT LIABILITIES								
Bank loans, overdrafts and short-term loans[5]	13.5	13.2	13.1	14.0	14.2	14.1	14.0	14.1
Creditors and accounts	24.6	24.3	25.2	24.5	25.7	27.0	28.0	26.7
Dividends and interest due	1.0	1.0	1.1	1.1	1.1	1.0	1.1	1.2

	Balance sheet at end of accounting 'year'[3]							
	1977	1978	1979	1980	1981	1982	1983	1984[4]
Current taxation[6]	2.3	2.7	2.9	3.2	2.9	2.9	2.7	2.6
Total current liabilities	41.5	41.2	42.3	42.8	43.9	45.0	45.8	44.6
Net current assets	20.5	18.8	18.3	14.6	13.3	10.85	10.5	10.5
Total net assets	58.5	58.8	57.6	57.3	56.2	54.9	54.2	55.3
Financed by:								
Shareholders' interest	40.6	42.6	43.8	44.0	43.2	42.4	42.6	43.4
Minority shareholders' interest	2.3	2.6	2.6	3.0	3.3	3.6	3.7	3.7
Deferred taxation[7]	5.9	3.6	2.7	2.5	2.4	2.6	3.3	2.9
Debentures								
Mortgages and long-term loans[8]	9.7	10.0	8.5	7.7	7.3	6.3	4.6	5.3
Gross income[9]	100	100	100	100	100	100	100	100
APPROPRIATION OF GROSS INCOME								
Depreciation and amounts written off	22.0	24.6	22.6	28.8	30.5	29.7	29.1	30.5
Taxation	35.3	30.0	24.0	27.9	29.8	34.8	30.6	25.2
Dividends	10.7	11.9	14.3	14.4	14.2	14.1	17.7	15.2
Interest on long-term loans	5.6	6.4	5.4	6.0	5.0	4.8	4.0	4.0
Minority shareholders' interest	1.5	2.8	3.7	4.1	4.0	3.7	3.8	3.7
Retained income	24.9	24.4	30.0	18.8	16.5	12.9	14.8	21.3
Sources and uses of funds (percentage of total sources and uses)								
Receipts from issue of share and loan capital	6.2	10.1	3.4	4.2	9.7	−0.1	2.0	9.6
Increase in amount owing to								

	Balance sheet at end of accounting 'year'[3]							
	1977	1978	1979	1980	1981	1982	1983	1984[4]
banks, short-term lenders and creditors	17.0	16.4	26.4	17.2	29.4	31.1	30.8	21.6
Gross income	80.6	75.8	73.4	80.9	54.8	62.8	65.0	61.9
Other sources (including exchange differences)	−3.8	−2.3	−3.3	−2.3	6.1	6.2	2.2	6.9
Total sources	100	100	100	100	100	100	100	100
Payments out of income	32.6	29.4	26.6	36.4	24.8	29.0	29.4	21.3
Expenditures on fixed assets etc.	32.3	36.6	34.0	50.0	43.5	47.7	41.9	45.9
Increase in current assets and investments	35.1	34.0	39.4	13.6	31.7	23.3	28.7	32.8
Total uses of funds	100	100	100	100	100	100	100	100

The figures are based on an analysts of company accounts and full details are given in *Business Monitor MA3 Company Finance*, HMSO.

[1] Listed and unlisted limited companies registered in Great Britain with a capital employed in the current year of more than £4.16 million, excluding companies whose main activity is insurance, banking or finance.

[2] There may be a slight discrepancy between a total and the sum of its constituent items due to rounding.

[3] The figures for a particular year relate to companies' accounting years ending between 1 April of the year shown and 31 March of the following year. 75 per cent of the larger companies have accounting periods ending in the fourth quarter of the calendar year or in the first quarter of the following year.

[4] Provisional.

[5] Loans, other than bank loans, which are wholly repayable within five years.

[6] Includes all corporation tax, irrespective of the data on which it is payable, but is net of advance corporation tax recoverable.

[7] Includes tax equalization reserve and amounts charged to deferred tax for such things as capital gains tax and betterment levy.

[8] Loans, other than bank loans, which are not wholly repayable within five years.

[9] Relates to the position after charging directors' fees and emoluments, pensions to past directors, superannuation payments, compensation for loss of office, auditors' fees and any exceptional expenditure (e.g. on reorganization or closure) but excluding any profit or loss on disposal of assets and before allowing for depreciation provisions, all interest on long-term loans but net of short-term interest and hire charges.

Source: Department of Trade and Industry

Government securities and certain other government-guaranteed securities, plus a number of other securities and assets, receive similar favoured treatment.

In January 1987, a further stimulus to equity investment was provided by the introduction of personal equity plans (PEPs). These offer (1989–90 rates) tax incentives for individuals investing up to £4800 a year in UK equities via approved schemes. This amount is allowed to accumulate free from all income tax on dividends and capital gains tax after an initial holding period of up to two years. The scheme is particularly attractive to people in the top income tax band.

The balance sheet structures of large companies in recent years and their methods of financing are shown in table 10.6 which gives a summary of their income and appropriation accounts and their sources and uses of funds.

Companies need finance to function; they need working capital to finance stocks of goods, raw materials and components, work in progress, and trade debtors. The money value of all these increases with inflation and hence additional money is required to replace them as they are used. Furthermore, firms also need to replace (again at higher money prices) plant, equipment, vehicles etc. as they wear out. These extra funds are required merely to maintain the business in inflationary times and even more will be required to finance expansion.

Traditionally, the major source of company funds has been funds which are internally generated. These are composed of trading profits, including depreciation (see below) minus any payments of interest, tax and dividends, plus any capital transfers (investment grants). Since the early 1960s internal funds have usually accounted for about 70 per cent of total funds, but their contribution has declined until recently. External sources have made up the difference, the major component being supplied by bank borrowing, whilst equity and debt issues have remained a sporadic but important source of long-term funds (see table 10.6).

Around 60 per cent of the uses of funds is made up of fixed investment. Other important requirements include additions to stocks and work in progress, the purchase of subsidiaries and trade investments for cash, acquisitions of foreign assets and additions to liquid assets. In 1973 and 1974 the funding of inflationary increases in the value of stocks was a major problem, exacerbated by the fact that companies were taxed on these notional increases in value. Legislation was first introduced in November 1974 to alleviate this problem. From 1976 to 1984 tax relief was granted (see the discussion in chapter 9).

Company funding difficulties until the 1980s had been accentuated by a continuing decline in a real post-tax profitability. Companies should not pay income from capital resources, whose value they should maintain intact. They do this by depreciating or writing off the value of an asset as a charge against profits over its economic life, so that they have sufficient funds set aside to replace it. If there is no inflation, writing off a value equal to the original historic cost is quite sufficient. When measured on this basis, companies' pre-tax returns have appeared quite adequate (see table 10.7). Given the existence of inflation, asset values increase, and depreciation provisions should be inflated to represent replacement cost rather than historic cost. If this is done and the effects of stock appreciation are deducted, then real pre-tax rates of return had declined to around 4–5 per cent by 1979 and post-tax rates of return were lower.[5] However, the 1980s have shown a continuing recovery of the performance of UK companies, as shown in the second half of table 10.7. Confirmation of this improvement on a comparative international basis is given in table 10.8.

The gross operating surplus of an enterprise is equal to its value added (see chapter 4) minus compensation of employees and indirect taxes paid. The share of profits in value added has grown in the UK in recent years

Table 10.7 *Rates of return on trading assets of industrial and commercial companies (percentages)*

Year	Pre-tax historic cost	Pre-tax real
1963	16.1	11.6
1965	16.0	11.4
1967	13.7	10.2
1969	15.0	10.0
1971	15.3	8.9
1973	19.7	8.8
1975	17.7	4.7
1977	18.8	5.8
1979[a]	17.8	4.1
1980	11.4[b]	6.4[c]
1981	11.8[b]	6.2[c]
1982	12.5[b]	7.5[c]
1983	12.7[b]	9.1[c]
1984	14.7[c]	10.7[c]

[a] All figures up to 1979 exclude North Sea oil activities.
[b] Includes North Sea Oil activities, pre-interest rates of return.
[c] Includes North Sea Oil activities.
Sources: [a]'Profitability and company finance: a supplementary note', *Bank of England Quarterly Bulletin* (January 1980); [b]*Business Monitor MA3 Company Finance*, HMSO, 1986, table 13; [c]'Trends in real rate of return', *Bank of England Quarterly Bulletin* (August 1988)

Table 10.8 *Rates of return: gross operating surplus as a percentage of gross capital stock*

	1973	1975	1980	1981	1982	1983	1984	1985	1986	1987
USA	13.3	11.9	11.5	11.4	10.3	11.1	12.6	12.6	12.5	12.5
UK	6.3	5.7	7.5	7.6	8.5	9.6	10.1	10.7	9.7	11.2
Germany	14.2	11.8	11.6	10.7	10.9	11.9	12.1	12.6	13.0	13.0
France	15.7	12.7	12.4	11.6	11.1	11.1	11.3	11.3	11.6	11.7
Canada	11.0	9.6	10.1	9.0	7.8	8.8	9.8	9.8	10.0	10.7

Source: 'Trends in real rates of return', *Bank of England Quarterly Bulletin* (August 1988)

and, until recently, the share of wages had fallen. There has also been a resurgence in investment (see table 10.6) and the trend in capital productivity in the UK during the 1980s has been upward. There are all positive developments.

The decline in company profitability in the 1970s plus the effects of stock appreciation and generous investment allowances meant that many companies were tax exhausted. This was a major incentive to the growth of leasing.

Leasing

In recent years there has been a high and continued rise in the use of leasing. Table 10.9 shows that by 1987 it accounted for about 17.5 per cent of all new capital investment.

Under the pre-1984 tax system many companies did not have sufficient tax liabilities to absorb the capital allowances available on new investment.

Table 10.9 *Leased assets acquired (1978–1987)*

	£million	Percentage of all UK Investment
1978	1214	7.9
1983	2894	12.6
1984	4012	15.2
1985	5757	18.8
1986	5182	16.5
1987	6000	17.5

Source: C. Drury, 'A survey of UK leasing practice', *Management Accounting* (April 1989)

If they find themselves in this situation and they wish to invest, rather than buy the asset themselves they lease it from a leasing company, usually a subsidiary of a bank or financial institution with substantial taxable profits. The leasing company retains the ownership of the asset and can therefore claim the investment allowances. The lessee company, the user, has full use of the asset over its economic life but never actually owns it. The lessor, or owner company, will pass on some of the benefits of being able to claim the investment allowances in the form of reduced lease charges to the lessee. Thus both parties gain from the operation.

Leasing is essentially of two types; financial leasing or operating leasing. A *financial lease* involves a commitment to make obligatory payments over a specified period (usually medium term) sufficient to amortize the capital outlay of the owner company and provide some profit. (Amortization is the process of reducing a debt through a sinking fund.) *Operating leases* are cancellable, do not fully amortize the cost of the asset and often include maintenance clauses. They are very popular in circumstances where equipment might rapidly become obsolete, and computers are often leased under these terms.

Recent changes introduced by the 1984 Finance Act which became fully operational in April 1986 serve to reduce the tax advantages of leasing.

During the period 1984–6 the 100 per cent first-year allowance was phased out and replaced by a 25 per cent annual writing-down allowance to be calculated on a reducing balance basis. This, combined with the reduction in the corporate tax rate to 35 per cent, meant that the tax benefit from capital allowances is now 35 per cent of 25 per cent in the first year (post-1986), compared with 50 per cent of 100 per cent pre-1984. Thus the tax incentive to lease is now greatly reduced.

Financial leasing involves a liability indistinguishable from that of medium-term debt. In the past some firms used leasing because of its off-balance-sheet characteristics. If neither the asset nor the leasing obligation are recorded, the return on capital employed will be overstated and the size of the company's liabilities will be understated. This has led to suggestions that it misleadingly increased a company's creditworthiness for borrowing purposes. It is doubtful that professional analysts would have been misled, but the issue has been resolved by the adoption of SSAP 21 which requires financial leases to be capitalized and brought onto the balance sheet. Nevertheless it remains a very convenient way of arranging for the finance of an asset, which is particularly valued by smaller firms.[6]

Sale and lease-back

If a company owns a valuable asset, usually property, and wants to convert it into an injection of funds and yet retain its use, it can arrange for its sale and lease-back from the new owner. A number of companies owning high street stores have engaged in this operation, and there are ready buyers amongst the financial institutions who are usually keen to add to their property portfolios.

Bills of exchange and the inter-company market

There are a number of additional means by which large companies can raise short-term finance. A bill of exchange could be viewed as a post-dated cheque. When a supplier arranges a sale to a buyer, the buyer might sign an agreement to pay in three months' time. The supplier could then either wait for the full period or sell the bill to a bank or discount house to obtain funds immediately. In the case of a commercial bill the supplier draws up the document and the buyer agrees to pay on the due date. The bills are usually used to finance foreign trade and are secured by documents of title to the goods in transit. Once a bill is accepted by a banking house which thereby accepts responsibility for repayment, the bill can be sold in the discount market at a higher price (thereby obtaining funds on better terms). As a means of providing further security the exporter can insure the credit with the Export Credit Guarantee Department (ECGD) and thereby protect the bank against the possibility of the buyer defaulting.

Another variant on this is buyer credit, which is usually supported by ECGD and involves the finance being provided directly to the foreign buyer by a UK bank. Companies sometimes obtain finance directly from other companies, often with a bank acting as its agent.

In May 1987 the new sterling commercial paper market came into effect. In general issues are allowed by UK and overseas companies which have net assets of at least £50 million and a Stock Exchange listing. The minimum amount which can be issued is £0.5 million and the paper must have a maturity between seven days and under one year.

Project finance

Sometimes a company may be involved in a project, such as North Sea oil exploration, which has a high risk and demands very large funding in relation to the company's resources. In these circumstances, although the company's credit standing is of some importance, the key factor is the commercial viability of the project. Syndicates of banks have been prepared to fund suitable projects. To recompense them for providing medium- to long-term, relatively high-risk, finance, the banks have received higher rates and perhaps royalties as well as interest payments. Various types of non-recourse funding arrangements have become more common in recent years. Table 10.10 summarizes the major forms of financing available to public companies. Since they tend to be larger, can

Table 10.10 *Sources of funds available to public companies*

Long term	Medium term	Short term
Ordinary share capital	Term loans	Bank overdraft
Preference share capital	Hire purchase	Bills of exchange
Debentures	Leasing	Invoice discounting and factoring
Sale and lease-back		Deferred expenses and taxes due
Project finance		Trade credit
Capital grants		Inter-company loans
		Commercial bills

offer better security and provide more detailed information about their activities, their choice of funding is much greater than that available to smaller businesses. Details of capital grants and assistance via regional policy will be covered in chapter 15.

Interest rate and currency swaps

Interest rate and currency swaps became popular in the early 1980s. They have revolutionized debt funding transactions and asset–liability management. They provide tremendous flexibility and act as a bridge between markets in different currencies and different financial instruments.

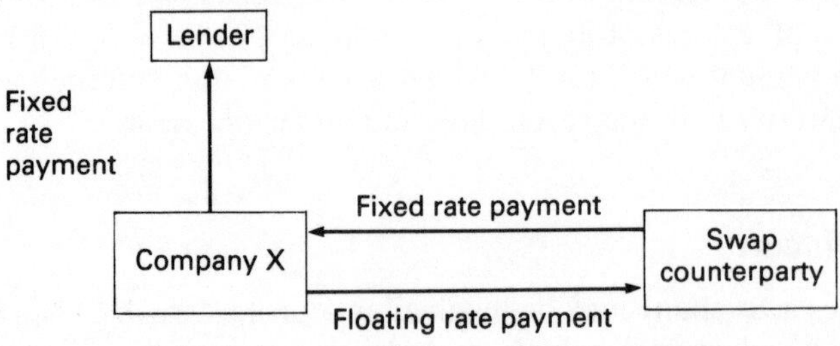

Figure 10.4 *A basic interest rate swap*

An example of an interest rate swap is given in figure 10.4. Company X has borrowed, lets say £25 million, at a fixed rate of interest. Its circumstances change, and it decides it wants to convert this liaibility into floating rate borrowing. (Perhaps it has an asset which is producing a return linked to floating rates and it wants to match the two income streams.) Company X phones a swap broker (a bank or financial institution) and is quoted terms for a swap. If they are acceptable it will agree to pay a floating rate to the swap counterparty (via the broker) and receive a fixed rate payment which it can then pass on to its original lender. The swap counterparty may have borrowed a similar sum for the same term at a floating rate but have decided that it wants to transform the liability into a fixed rate one. Company X has effectively transformed its fixed rate borrowing into floating rate borrowing.

The broker will earn a return by creaming off a few basis points (hundredths of a per cent) from the interest rates quoted in the deal. As both counterparties have separately borrowed identical amounts in the same currency, there is no need for an exchange of principals, and both can repay their respective lenders at maturity.

Currency swaps are similar in structure, but as the borrowing is done in different currencies they usually involve the transfer of principal payments too. Standard indicator rates are used to set the terms in swaps. For floating rate currency swaps the indicator is usually the London Interbank Offer Rate (LIBOR) plus or minus a few basis points. Swaps are driven by the comparative advantages which arise from different credit perceptions, and from institutional and tax arbitrage mechanisms. There is now a massive market in swaps.

Financial futures

In September 1982 the London International Financial Futures Exchange (LIFFE) commenced operation in the Royal Exchange building. It provides facilities for dealing in futures contracts covering interest rates, currencies and the value of quoted ordinary shares – described generally as financial futures.

Financial futures are agreements to buy or sell a standardized quantity of a specific financial instrument on a future date at a price agreed between the parties concerned. The contract will specifically define the type and quality of the financial instrument involved. For example, a 20-year gilt-edged stock with a 12 per cent coupon rate. This degree of standardization permits the operation of a continuous market in financial futures contracts. Indeed, a feature of the recent trend towards the 'globalization' of securities markets is the trading of similar financial futures contracts in London, Australia and the USA, permitting a 24-hour market.

Futures markets can be used for hedging, trading and arbitrage purposes. Hedging (see chapter 7) is used to reduce the risk of loss through adverse price movements in currency rates, share prices or interest rates by taking a position in futures contracts that is equal and opposite to the position in the cash markets. Traders assume price risk by taking positions in one market only, whilst arbitragers take advantage of any pricing discrepancies between the two markets and, by so doing, ensure that prices in the two markets remain 'in line'.

The Euromarkets

One of the most important developments in the late 1950s and the early 1960s was the development of the non-sterling Euromarkets. The internationally syndicated public Eurobond issue was pioneered in 1963 by the late Sir Siegmund Warburg, then chairman of S. G. Warburg & Co. The Stock Exchange's failure to recognize the potential of this market must be regarded as an extraordinary financial oversight. Foreign banks flocked to London to operate in the Eurodollar pool. The syndicated loan market has subsequently diminished in importance and is now overshadowed by fixed and floating rate note facilities and commercial paper programmes. The Eurobond markets have developed to massive proportions. They now dwarf the capital-raising activities of the London markets and had a total primary market volume of US$133 billion equivalent in 1985.

The Stock Exchange

The Stock Exchange developed in response to two major stimuli; the growth of permanent government funding and the growth of company funding. By the late seventeenth and early eighteenth centuries both were fairly well established. If an individual has lent funds for a lengthy period of time to the government, or permanently subscribed to the share capital of a company, then he requires a market where he can liquidate his holding, by selling it to someone else, should he require to do so. Thus, the Stock Exchange and any capital market has a number of functions. It provides a primary market where new money can be raised by the issue of securities – government debt, company debt and equity – plus a secondary market in which existing securities can be bought and sold so that their original holders are not locked in. These two functions are very closely related and the existence of such a market is a major factor in encouraging the channelling of savings into productive investment.

In the channelling of savings the market plays an important allocatory role. The market should be competitive and well informed or 'efficient'. In this context 'efficiency' means that prices should fully reflect all available information, and there is considerable empirical evidence that this is the case.[7] This means that investors should get a fair level of return for the risk of their investment, and that companies should face a realistic cost of capital that can be used as a yardstick in appraising their investment expenditure. The stock market capitalization or valuation of a company's securities is an important indicator of corporate value, based not on historical results but upon investors' expectations of future returns. These expectations can be quite volatile, as economic circumstances and company prospects can change quite rapidly with the unfolding of events. The Stock Exchange seeks to ensure that the interests of investors are safeguarded and that they are well informed. Brokers expend a vast amount of time and effort in analysing company prospects and producing information for the benefit of their clients.

Brief reconsideration of the share and debenture pricing formulae given in expressions (10.4) and (10.5) remind us that a very wide range of factors is likely to influence stock market prices. The appearance of new information at any level – company, industry, or even general economy – might have the effect of causing investors to revise their expectations of a company's future levels of earnings and dividend payments. This would cause revisions to the numerators in expression (10.4). Similarly, such information could change perceptions of the company's risk, causing revisions of the discount factor applied in the denominator in expression (10.4). In the case of fixed interest stocks, changing expectations could also cause revisions in the discount factor. Thus share prices can be very volatile and can change rapidly to reflect alterations in the market's mood, even though the payments on debt are usually fixed, at least in nominal terms. The price of debt will also change in response to changed views of company risk and movements in the general structure of interest rates.

Originally the market was very informal and was conducted in coffee houses (to this day Stock Exchange messengers are termed waiters). The Stock Exchange first published rules in 1812, by which time it had its own premises and operated on lines very similar to those of today.

The Stock Exchange was an independent association of stock-jobbers and stockbrokers, centred on London, and in 1973 amalgamated to include the former regional trading floors. The 'single-capacity' system used to comprise (a) jobbers who acted as principals, making a market by dealing in securities for a profit, and (b) brokers who could not deal directly but acted as agents for their clients who wished to buy or sell securities. In theory the jobbers competed in their activities and earned their living from their 'turn', the difference between the price at which they bought and sold securities and the capital appreciation in the value of their holdings of securities. The brokers charged a fixed commission rate on their dealings which was tapered according to the value of the transaction.

The Stock Exchange rule book, including the fixed commission system, came under attack with the passage of the Restrictive Trade Practices Order of 1976. In October 1979 court proceedings were served on the Stock Exchange.

There was considerable substance to the charge that the Stock Exchange had been insular and uncompetitive. It had failed to make a significant impact in the international capital markets and overseas financial institutions dominated the Euromarkets. The level of dealing costs made the market uncompetitive and a large proportion of the trade in the shares of major British companies was taking place abroad, predominantly in North America. American Depositary Receipts (ADRs) are for investors and traders in the USA holding or dealing in securities of companies located in countries other than their own. They create a substitute instrument for international ownership of shares in a company where use of the original instrument – the share certificate issued by the company – would be less convenient. Their utility depends on the role of the depositary, which must be an internationally recognized institution. The British institutional investors, pension funds and the like, found it cheaper to deal in British companies via ADRs in New York than in London.

Another difficulty was that membership of the Stock Exchange was entirely through personal partnerships. These inevitably had a relatively low capitalization and were not in a position to compete with the large international companies operating in the global capital markets.

In July 1983 Cecil Parkinson, the then Trade Secretary, asked the Stock Exchange to draw up proposals for reform which would enable the Conservative Government to remove the case against them from the Restrictive Practices Court. The proposals led to the reforms known as the Big Bang.

The Big Bang and the Stock Exchange

The Big Bang, which took place on 29 October 1986, had three main commercial features: the abolition of minimum commissions, the abolition of single capacity, and the admission to the Stock Exchange of corporate members. There was also the creation of a semi-separate gilt-edged market within the Stock Exchange.

The introduction of Stock Exchange Automated Quotations (SEAQ), a computerized price information service, in October 1986 has changed the method of trading. It is not dependent on the existence of a physical trading floor, and the abandonment of the floor led to a decision to close the trading floor at the end of 1987 apart from the traded options business.

In March 1986 the membership rules were changed to enable member firms to establish the capital base needed to trade competitively in international securities. They can now be 100 per cent owned by a single outside corporation. Many have been bought by UK and overseas banks, and major overseas securities firms have become direct members of the Exchange for the first time.

Today, all member firms of the International Stock Exchange are broker–dealers. They can act in the capacity both of agent (broker) and of dealer (principal). At the centre of the trading system is a group of broker–dealers who specialize in the dealing function and compete with one another in making markets in securities. They are under an obligation to enter into SEAQ their bid and ask prices – the prices at which they are prepared to buy and sell securities – together with information about how many securities they will trade at this price. When a deal is done, they are obliged to enter details of the deal: the time, price and number of shares involved.

SEAQ securities are divided into four categories:

Alpha securities are the leading securities, which are distinguished by having a large number of market makers dealing in them, widespread investor interest and large capitalizations. In June 1987 there were roughly 100 securities in this category.

Beta securities are slightly less well traded securities. The market makers show firm bid and ask prices up to a stated limit. Details of dealings in these securities are not immediately shown on screen.

Gamma securities are even less frequently traded and screen prices are indications only, not firm quotations.

Delta securities are stocks in which relatively little trading takes place. There are no price quotations but an indication of broker–dealers who are prepared to trade in them.

There is also a market in foreign equities facilitated by the introduction of SEAQ International in June 1985 which provides an electronic price information system. This is open to firms who are not Stock Exchange members and by 1987 had 40 market makers quoting prices on more than 600 foreign stocks from 17 countries. This market is expanding with the advantage of London's geographical location and time zone position between the New York and Tokyo markets.

To allow London to compete further against these two rivals, the government reduced the stamp duty on share transactions from 1 per cent to 0.5 per cent from the date of the Big Bang.

Traded options

The traded options market was introduced in April 1978. Traded options are one of the most flexible risk management tools available to an investor. Call options give the right to buy a fixed amount of an underlying security at a specified price, the exercise price, within a specified period of time. Put options give a right to sell the underlying security at the exercise price. The traded options market offers a continuous market in standardized option contracts.

By June 1986, options were listed on more than 50 companies, the FT-SE 100 share index, two gilt-edged stocks and three currencies.

The market for government stocks

This market, known as the gilt-edged market, has consistently provided the largest proportion of the Stock Exchange's turnover in securities. It is made up of British government and government-guaranteed stocks, plus those issued by local authorities, public boards and Commonwealth governments.

Operations in these markets are part of the government's policy for

Table 10.11 *The public sector borrowing requirement (£million)*

	Central government	Local authorities	Public corporations	Total public sector
1975–6	5493	2381	2379	10,253
1976–7	4156	1996	2152	8,304
1977–8	2750	1420	1203	5,373
1978–9	5796	1311	2126	9,233
1979–80	4279	2969	2772	10,020
1980–1	9080	2120	1486	12,686
1981–2	6380	−225	2477	8,632
1982–3	7247	87	1525	8,859
1983–4	8188	1206	359	9,753
1984–5	6626	2385	1166	10,177
1985–6	4113	1654	58	5,825

Source: *Annual Abstract of Statistics*, 1987, table 16.2

controlling the money supply and managing the national debt. In the past, the need to fund a persistently large public sector borrowing requirement (see table 10.11; see also the section on the bond market earlier in this chapter) led to suggestions that the required movement in yields and general government manipulation of the market led to a 'crowding-out' of the company sector. The high interest rates required to persuade investors to hold government stock arguably forced up company costs, deterred companies from borrowing and inflated their cost of capital.

The Thatcher administration attacked this problem on a number of fronts. Table 10.11 shows that the public sector borrowing requirement has been reigned in during recent years, assisted by asset sales and the privatization programme. The favoured tax treatment formerly reserved for government borrowing has been extended to company debt.

There has also been a radical change in the management of the gilt-edged market, inaugurated by the Big Bang. In the gilt-edged market more than 20 companies are recognized by the Bank of England as primary dealers. The Government sells gilt issues via them and they act as market makers in government stocks. This contrasts with the two jobbers who had previously serviced the entire market pre-Big Bang. Other broker–dealers deal with primary dealers and help distribute stock to investors. Firms of the Inter-Dealers Brokers facilitate the unwinding of market maker's positions on a confidential basis. There are also a group of Stock Exchange money brokers who provide borrowed stock or funds to the market makers to help them finance long or short positions and to support liquidity in the market.

The new market is extremely competitive; some firms have already withdrawn and more are expected to follow. In 1987 the daily turnover of £1.8 billion was an increase of 50 per cent on that in 1986. Commission rates on the larger deals for institutional business had halved to about 0.2 per cent.

The regulatory framework

The passage of the Financial Services Act in 1986 saw the most comprehensive overhaul of investor protection legislation for 40 years. The original structure of the new regulatory system is shown in figure 10.5. The Securities and Investments Board (SIB) will make most of the detailed requirements to rules and regulations for supervising and authorizing the Self-Regulatory Organizations (SROs) outlined in figure 10.5. Practically all parties carrying on investment businesses in the UK are required to be authorized. Most will become members of the practitioner-based SROs.

The Act changed the character of the Stock Exchange by splitting it into two separate functions which comprise a self-regulatory authority supervising its members plus a recognized investment exchange operating a market-place. In November 1986 the Stock Exchange voted to merge with the International Securities Regulatory Organization (ISRO) and for the Exchange to be turned into a limited liability company. From the end of 1986 the Stock Exchange has been owned and run by The International Stock Exchange of the UK and Northern Ireland Limited, with its new self-regularity organization operating under the name of The Securities Association.

Table 10.12 indicates the various areas covered by the different regulatory authorities who supervise company activities and the banking system as well as investment business.

Table 10.12 *The regulatory authorities*

Securities and Investments Board	Bank of England	Department of Trade and Industry	Take-over Panel
Securities markets excluding gilts Unit trusts Insurance broking Fund management Futures markets Corporate finance advice Investment advice	Banking Gilts markets Wholesale money and foreign exchange markets Bullion	Company law compliance covering commercial fraud, insider dealing, prospectuses Insurance companies Partial responsibility for Lloyds, unit trusts	Take-overs and mergers

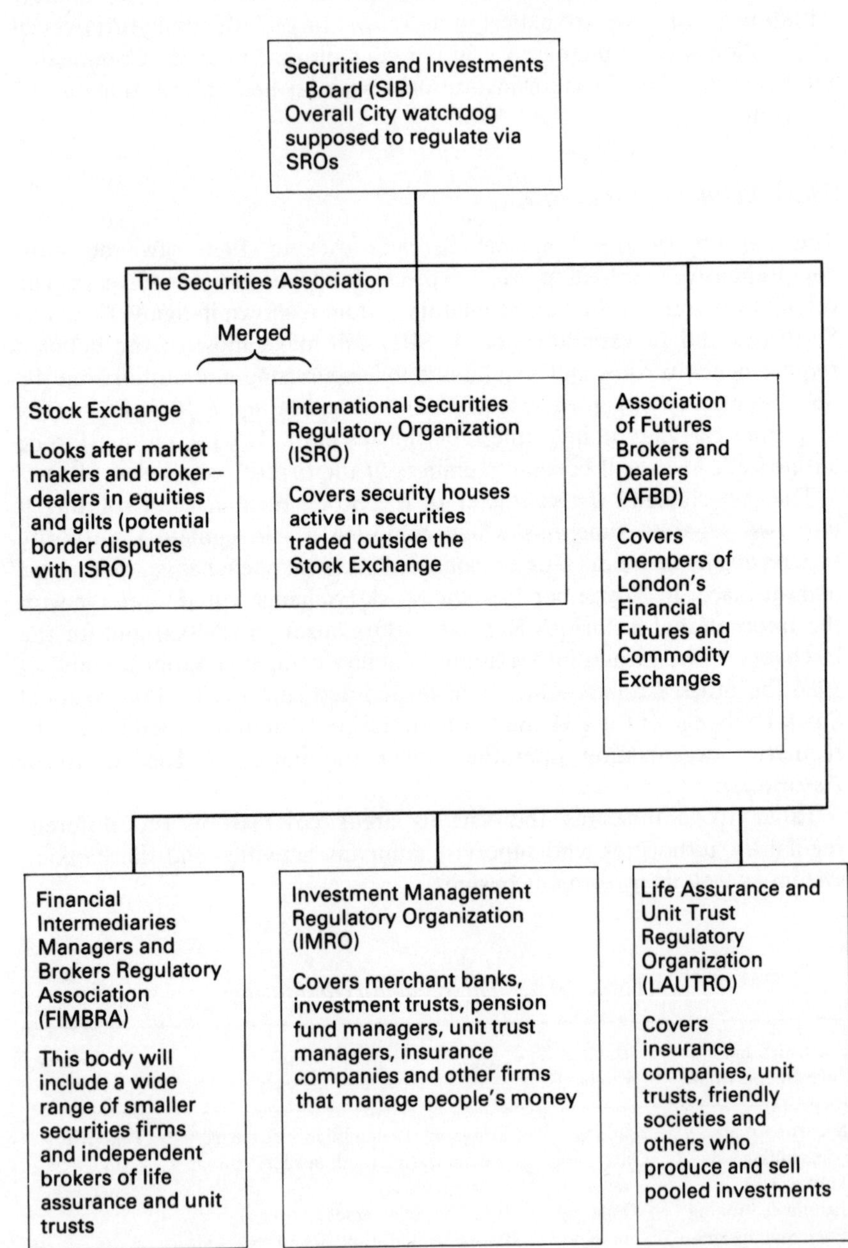

Figure 10.5 *The regulatory framework for financial markets*

The market for company securities

Obtaining a quotation

A company seeking a quotation must agree to conform to the Exchange's regulations, which require the annual disclosure of certain information and additional disclosure when new capital is raised. In the latter circumstance the company must issue a prospectus. This will furnish potential investors with detailed information about the company's recent performance and current standing and will help them make an informed judgement about the attractiveness of the company as an investment proposition. The contents of the prospectus will be fully analysed and reported in the financial press. An indication of the contents, drawn up to conform with the 1948 Companies Act, is given in table 10.13.

Table 10.13 *An outline of the information disclosed in a prospectus*

Details of the names, addresses, and interests and remuneration of the directors
The minimum subscription required in a share issue to purchase property, pay expenses and commissions, repay borrowings and provide for working capital
Details of the timing and amounts payable on allotment of shares
Details of any options (rights to purchase at a prefixed price) held on the company's share or debentures
If property is to be purchased by the issue proceeds, then full details of the purchase consideration, its form (whether shares, cash etc.) and information about the vendors
Full disclosure of the issue expenses and to whom payable
Full disclosure of any contracts made outside the 'normal course' of the company's business during the previous two years
The names and addresses of the company's auditors
The nature and extent of any director's interest in property to be purchased
The voting, dividend and capital rights of all classes of the company's shares
A full report from the auditors giving details of profits and losses for the previous five years and of assets and liabilities at the last accounting date; also an indication of dividends paid on each class of share for the previous five years
If the company has any subsidiaries, then similar disclosure of their accounting details
If the issue's proceeds are to be spent on acquiring another business, then a full auditor's report on that business

In the case of a company obtaining a quotation the Stock Exchange rules also apply. These, in addition, require disclosure of the financial results for the previous ten years and a forecast of trading prospects. A private company going 'public' will have to alter the relevant sections in its articles of association which prevent the public from subscribing for its shares. If it ensures that at least 25 per cent of its share capital is held by the public it can avoid 'close company' status.

Methods of issue

1 *Introduction.* This does not involve the raising of new money but secures a market and a listing for existing shares. The public are not invited to subscribe for shares.
2 *Placing.* This involves the shares being placed by the issuing house with its clients, usually the institutional investors (insurance companies, pension funds). In the case of a public placing at least 25 per cent of the shares must be made available to the public. It is an attractive and inexpensive method of issuing shares but is normally only permitted for the use of smaller companies.
3 *Offer for sale.* The company sells its shares to an issuing house which then advertises a prospectus and resells them to the public. The method can be used either to obtain a quotation for existing shares or to issue new shares. The issuing house could either sell them at the original price and charge a fee, or gain its remuneration by selling them at a higher price.
4 *Issue by tender.* A minimum price is set in the prospectus and the public are invited to submit tenders stating the price and number of shares they would be prepared to take up. The issue is then allocated at a price which will clear it. This method cuts down the profits taken by *stags*. These speculators subscribe to new issues, confident in the knowledge that the issue price (to ensure success) is usually at a discount on the subsequent market price, affording the possibility of a quick profit by subscribing and immediately reselling.
5 *Public issue by prospectus.* The company directly offers the public the right to subscribe for shares at a fixed price, with the full details from the prospectus being advertised. The issuing house acts as an agent for the company and advises on the terms of the issue and arranges the underwriting (see next section) to ensure its success. This method is relatively expensive and only suited to a large well-known company.
6 *Rights issue.* A company which already has a quotation will usually use this method to raise new share capital. It offers the existing shareholders the right to subscribe to new share capital in a fixed proportion to the number of shares they already hold (one for two etc.). The shareholders can either take up the rights or sell them. Either way it ensures that their interests are served, as they can avoid

dilution of control or the penalty of having new shareholders participate in the company on more favourable terms. Rights issues are relatively inexpensive, merely requiring the issue of a circular to existing shareholders rather than the production and advertising of a prospectus, and are consequently the most popular method of raising further capital.

Table 10.14 gives a breakdown of the issue methods used in recent years by companies seeking an initial listing for their equity. The choice of issue method reflects differences in costs plus concern about the performance of the issue in the aftermarket.

Secondary equity issues by companies already listed are usually rights issues. In the period January 1983 to March 1986 £11.6 billion was raised by this method.

Underwriting

The company cannot be sure when offering shares to the public that the issue will be a success. The process of issue takes time and conditions can change very rapidly in financial markets. To guarantee that the required funds will be raised the issuing house will arrange the underwriting of the issue. A number of financial institutions – investment trusts, insurance companies, pension funds etc. – will undertake to take up the issue should it not be fully subscribed by the public. They are paid an underwriting fee (usually 1.25 per cent) whether or not their services are required, and should they have to take up any shares there is the additional attraction that they are usually relatively 'cheap'.

The Stock Exchange indices

The *Financial Times* ordinary index, familiar in the press and news, is a useful indicator of the general state of stock market trends and sentiment. It is an equally weighted index of 30 leading company shares which are representative of their market sector. It is calculated hourly, and the base date is 1935. The *Financial Times* actuaries index is a much more detailed value-weighted index, published daily and broken down into detailed market sectors; it is useful for the purpose of investment analysis, since a company's performance can be seen against that of its market sector.

The FT-SE 100 Share Index was introduced in 1984. It was instituted to provide a reliable index of share prices reflecting market movements so that options and futures contracts written against it could be traded. The largest 100 shares (by capitalization) are included in it, and their capitalization is used as individual weights in the calculation of the index. This is done by computer every minute of the trading day. The base data is Friday 30 December 1983.

Table 10.14 *New issue methods: amount raised by companies seeking a full listing for equity*

Size of issue	1983			1984			1985			Q1 1986			Total		
	Amount raised (£m)	Per cent of total	Number of issues	Amount raised (£m)	Per cent of total	Number of issues	Amount raised (£m)	Per cent of total	Number of issues	Amount raised (£m)	Per cent of total	Number of issues	Amount raised (£m)	Per cent of total	Number of issues
Up to £3 million															
Placings	–	–	–	19.0	100	7	11.3	79.6	4	6.0	100	3	36.3	70.1	14
Offers for sale[a]	7.3	57.9	3	–	–	–	2.9	20.4	1	–	–	–	10.2	19.7	4
Tenders[b]	5.3	42.1	2	–	–	–	–	–	–	–	–	–	5.3	10.2	2
Subscriptions	–	–	–	–	–	–	–	–	–	–	–	–	–	–	–
Total	12.6	100	5	19.0	100	7	14.2	100	5	6.0	100	3	51.8	100	20
£3–5 million															
Placings	–	–	–	–	–	–	–	–	–	3.6[c]	41.9	1	3.6	4.2	1
Offers for sale	3.8	19.9	1	14.7	63.4	4	22.1	63.5	5	5.0	58.1	1	45.6	53.2	11
Tenders	15.3	80.1	4	3.5	15.1	1	12.7	36.5	3	–	–	–	31.5	36.8	8
Subscriptions	–	–	–	5.0	21.5	1	–	–	–	–	–	–	5.0	5.8	1
Total	19.1	100	5	23.2	100	6	34.8	100	8	8.6	100	2	85.7	100	21
£5–10 million															
Placings	–	–	–	–	–	–	–	–	–	–	–	–	–	–	–
Offers for sale	9.7	22.9	1	44.7	87.3	6	105.4	84.2	15	11.0	100	2	170.8	74.3	24
Tenders	32.7	77.1	4	6.5	12.7	1	9.7	7.8	1	–	–	–	48.9	21.3	6
Subscriptions	–	–	–	–	–	–	10.0	8.0	1	–	–	–	10.0	4.4	1
Total	42.4	100	5	51.2	100	7	125.1	100	17	11.0	100	2	229.7	100	31
Over £10 million															
Placings	–	–	–	–	–	–	–	–	–	–	–	–	–	–	–
Offers for sale	79.4	46.0	4	4358.1	87.3	9	539.6	83.4	11	253	93.9	1	5230.1	86.0	25
Tenders	93.2	54.0	5	625.7	12.5	3	80.4	12.4	2	16.5	6.1	1	815.8	13.4	11
Subscriptions	–	–	–	10.8	0.2	1	27.0	4.2	2	–	–	–	37.8	0.6	3
Total	172.6	100	9	4994.6	100	13	647.0	100	15	269.5	100	2	6083.7	100	39
Total issues															
Placings	–	–	–	19.0	0.4	7	11.3	1.4	4	9.6	3.3	4	39.9	0.6	15
Offers for sale	100.2	40.6	9	4417.5	86.8	19	670.0	81.6	32	269.0	91.1	4	5456.7	84.6	64
Tenders	146.5	59.4	15	635.7	12.5	5	102.8	12.5	6	16.5	5.6	1	901.5	14.0	27
Subscriptions	–	–	–	15.8	0.3	2	37.0	4.5	3	–	–	–	52.8	0.8	5
Total	246.7	100	24	5088.0	100	33	821.1	100	45	295.1	100	9	6450.9	100	111

[a] Fixed price offers for sale.
[b] Offers for sale by tender.
[c] An exception to the £3 million limit for placings which was made for technical reasons for an Irish issue.
Source: 'New issue costs and methods in the UK equity market', *Bank of England Quarterly Bulletin* (December 1986), pp. 532–42

External financial ratios

There are a number of financial ratios, published in the financial press, which provide useful tools for the assessment of company performance and the selection of securities. Their use has been complicated by the move to the imputation corporation tax system in 1973, and this will be considered next.

Tax complications

The change in the tax system in 1973 has led to complications in the definitions of what exactly constitute a company's earnings per share. Tax considerations can alter this figure, particularly where a company has substantial foreign earnings, and cannot completely set its advance corporation tax (ACT), paid to the revenue authorities in the UK when it paid dividends to its UK shareholders, against its foreign tax (table 10.15 illustrates this problem). (A fuller account of the tax system was given in chapter 9.)

Table 10.15 *Different definitions of earnings per share*

Profit before tax	100.0	100.0
Less tax (overseas) (35%)	35.0	35.0
Profit after tax	65.0[a]	65.0
Less unrelieved ACT	10.0	21.67
	55.0[b]	43.33[c]
Dividend gross	40.0	86.67
Less tax (25%) ACT	10.0	21.67
Dividend net	30.0	65.0
Retentions	25.0	0.0

[a] Earnings on 'nil' distributions.
[b] Earnings on 'net distribution'.
[c] Earnings on 'maximum distribution'.

The imputation system involves shareholders receiving a net dividend plus a tax credit equal to the standard rate of income tax on the gross (pre-tax) dividend. (If the income tax rate is 25 per cent this can be estimated by 'grossing up' the net dividend by 25/75.) The shareholder does not therefore have to pay any standard rate income tax on the dividend, as the company has already done it for him in the form of ACT; however, he may have to pay the difference required to adjust the tax to his marginal rate if he is in a higher tax band. The company pays part of its corporation tax early when it pays a dividend to shareholders as an ACT payment to the revenue authorities, but it can offset these payments against its mainstream corporation tax when this becomes due. This is where the difficulties arise. If the company cannot completely offset ACT payments against foreign tax, as in table 10.15 (which represents an extreme case where the entire earnings are derived overseas and none of the ACT payments can be offset against foreign tax), or if it is in a situation of tax exhaustion and does not pay sufficient mainstream tax to match ACT payments, then the mere fact that the company has paid dividends, and with them ACT, will alter the earnings per share figures.

It can be seen in table 10.15 that if the company pays no dividends – i.e. there is 'nil' distribution – there is no problem and the earnings are the after-tax profits. However, if the company pays a dividend, and with it ACT, then there may be complications. This is shown in our example where the earnings figure is reduced by the amount of unrelieved ACT to give the 'net' distribution definition of earnings, which takes account of this. If all available earnings are paid out as dividends we have the third definition of earnings, the 'maximum' distribution, which has the greatest effect in altering the earnings figures in our example.

Earnings per share

The earnings per share are simply the earnings available in a given year divided by the number of shares. Earnings figures are usually calculated on a net, nil or maximum distribution basis as shown in table 10.15.

Dividend yield

The dividend yield is given by

$$\text{dividend yield} = \frac{\text{dividend per share}}{\text{market share price}} \times 100.$$

It shows the percentage return received by a shareholder in dividends, and could be calculated net or gross of tax; the gross yield might be regarded as preferable in that it is not distorted by the shareholder's marginal tax positions.

Dividend cover

The dividend cover gives an indication of the extent to which earnings available for distribution exceed or 'cover' the dividends paid:

$$\text{dividend cover} = \frac{\text{earnings available for distribution to ordinary shareholders}}{\text{dividends paid to shareholders}}.$$

It is more realistic if earnings net of taxation and prior charges are compared with net dividends.

Earnings yield

The earnings yield is given by

$$\text{earnings yield} = \frac{\text{earnings per share}}{\text{market share price}} \times 100.$$

The question then arises over which definition of earnings per share is appropriate. The *Financial Times* has adopted the figure based on 'maximum' distribution (as shown in table 10.15).

The price/earnings ratio

The price/earnings (*P*/*E*) ratio indicates how long, given the current figures, the share would take to earn its cost. It is given by

$$\text{price/earnings ratio} = \frac{\text{market share price}}{\text{earnings per share}}.$$

Before the tax complications introduced by the imputation system it used to be the reciprocal of the earnings yield, but different definitions of earnings per share are now adopted. The *Financial Times* calculates this ratio using both the 'net' and 'nil' distribution figures.

The above yields can be used for the relative evaluation of company shares, though they have to be used with caution. Earnings and dividends are 'historic' figures, whereas the share price reflects market expectations about the level of future earnings. Companies with low dividend and earnings yields and high *P*/*E* ratios may well have 'growth' stocks about which the market may be *bullish* (expects the future earnings and price to rise). On the other hand, companies with high yields and low *P*/*E* ratios may well be spent forces of which the market takes a *bearish* view (expects the future earnings and price to fall). These sentiments are already reflected in the current share price.

The Supply of Funds

Up to now we have considered the different types of securities that companies or the government issue and the motives and considerations which may influence the demand for them. However, we have not considered where the funds to purchase them originate, and that is the purpose of this section.

The analysis which follows is best understood when considered in terms of the flow of funds. Any individual, company, institution or even government, when considered over a period of time, will exhibit a financial surplus, deficit or balance. Whichever state pertains will depend on the relationship between the body's savings and investment undertaken, on the one hand, and its purchases or sales of financial assets on the other. If a company is in financial surplus it can either purchase additional financial assets or repay debt. If it is in deficit it must either reduce its holdings of financial assets or borrow more. This means that the following identity holds:

financial surplus = savings – investment
= increase in financial assets – increase in financial liabilities
= net acquisition of financial assets.

This analysis can be applied to individual economic agents or to whole sectors of the economy, as is the case in the national accounts shown in table 10.16. The supply of funds comes from savings made by the personal sector, companies, public corporations and central and local government, plus transfers from overseas. These funds can be channelled into investment, either directly, as tends to happen in every category except personal savings, or indirectly via the acquisition of financial assets. In total, savings and gross investment have remained stable over the last 25 years, accounting for roughly 20 per cent of gross domestic product, but within these overall figures there have been marked sectoral changes. Personal savings had shown a steady growth (see table 10.17), but have recently (1989) shown a marked decline. The other sectors, particularly the

Table 10.16 *Financial surplus or deficit: analysis by sector*[a] *(£million)*

Year	Public	Financial institutions	Industrial and commercial	Personal	Overseas[b]	Residual error[c]
1976	−8,428	−36	−154	5,687	1060	1871
1977	−5,876	130	−755	5,190	206	1105
1978	−8,060	−590	−58	8,731	−707	684
1979	−8,306	−109	−4391	11,599	1630	−423
1980	−11,045	928	−2772	16,605	−2737	−979
1981	−8,179	−2298	2362	18,443	−6159	826
1982	−7,367	−2482	2611	12,937	−3937	−1772
1983	−11,194	−704	5585	10,104	−3134	−957
1984	−13,088	−1141	8552	11,623	−1398	−4734
1985	−9,690	−499	6919	10,148	−3602	−3276

[a] This balance is equal to saving, plus capital transfers, less gross domestic fixed capital formation, less increase in book value of stocks and work in progress. The sum of the sectors for each year is zero.

[b] Equals, apart from the change in sign, the current balance in the balance of payments accounts, plus capital transfers.

[c] The residual error in the national income accounts.

Source: for years to 1980, Central Statistical Office, *Financial Statistics*, April 1981; for 1981 on, Central Statistical Office, *Economic Trends Annual Supplement*, 1987.

Table 10.17 *Personal income and saving (£billion)*

Year	Total personal disposable income[a]	Personal saving[b]	Saving ratio[c] (%)
1970	35.0	3.24	9.3
1974	60.7	8.21	13.5
1980	158.7	24.24	15.3
1985	237.2	27.04	11.4

[a] Equals total personal income before tax, less payment of taxes on income, national insurance etc. contributions and net transfers abroad. Before providing for depreciation, stock appreciation and additions to tax reserves.
[b] Before providing for depreciation, stock appreciation and additions to tax reserves.
[c] Personal saving as a percentage of total personal disposable income.
Sources: Central Statistical Office, *Financial Statistics*, April 1981; 'The financial behaviour of the UK personal sector, 1976–85', *Bank of England Quarterly Bulletin* (May 1987)

public sector, tended to move further into deficit during the 1970s. However, during the 1980s the public sector's financial deficit has been greatly reduced, and industrial and commercial companies have moved into financial surplus.

The exact reasons behind the swings in the personal sector's savings ratio remain obscure, but there are a number of obvious contributory factors. Many of the changes in the personal sector's financial behaviour during the 1980s can be seen as responses to external factors. Persistently high levels of inflation experienced during the 1970s eroded the real value of holdings of financial assets and debt. The increase in the savings ratio could be interpreted as an attempt to maintain liquid balances. Subsequently both inflation and the savings ratio have declined.

The second factor has been the deregulation of financial markets. The resulting intense competition between financial institutions has widened the spectrum of assets available and facilitated new methods of borrowing and making transactions.

Other polices, such as the sale of council houses, have had an impact on personal sector investment, and the privatization programme has been one of the stimuli to wider share ownership. A breakdown of the personal sector's financial portfolio is given in table 10.18.

A positive stimulus to personal savings has been provided by the growth of contractual savings to meet the requirements of pension provisions and life insurance commitments, reinforced by the tax advantages of these forms of savings (Table 10.18 shows that nearly 50 per cent of the personal sector's gross financial wealth is in this form.) Another large portion has gone into savings lodged with the building societies. In theory depositors are given preferential treatment when applying for mortgage loans, and

Table 10.18 *Shares in the personal sectors's financial portfolio (financial assets as a percentage of gross financial wealth)*

	Liquid assets					Illiquid assets						
	Money	National savings	Building society deposits	Other	Total	Shares	Gilts	Life assurance and pension funds	Domestic trade and other credit	Overseas assets	Other	Total
1976	16.9	5.7	16.9	2.3	41.8	16.5	5.6	26.5	5.4	1.4	2.7	58.2
1977	15.1	5.4	16.5	2.2	39.1	17.6	6.5	27.9	5.2	1.2	2.4	60.9
1978	14.5	5.3	16.9	2.3	39.8	16.7	5.2	30.6	5.1	1.2	2.3	61.0
1979	14.7	4.9	16.7	2.4	38.7	15.0	5.0	33.1	5.0	1.0	2.2	61.3
1980	15.3	4.2	16.8	2.9	39.2	14.3	4.9	33.3	5.1	1.0	2.2	60.8
1981	14.8	5.3	16.9	2.3	39.3	13.0	4.6	35.3	4.9	1.0	1.9	60.7
1982	15.5	5.5	16.7	0.4	38.1	12.0	4.7	37.7	4.6	1.1	1.8	61.9
1983	14.0	5.2	16.1	0.4	35.7	12.7	4.2	40.1	4.5	1.2	1.6	64.3
1984	12.7	5.1	16.6	0.4	34.9	12.1	4.1	41.7	4.5	1.1	1.6	65.1
1985	11.9	5.1	16.6	0.4	33.0	12.3	4.0	42.8	4.3	1.1	1.6	66.0
1986	11.1	4.5	15.6	0.3	31.5	13.7	3.4	45.1	3.8	1.0	1.5	68.5

Source: 'The financial behaviour of the UK personal sector, 1976–85', *Bank of England Quarterly Bulletin* (May 1987)

house purchase is a particularly tax-efficient form of investment (interest payments on loans up to £30,000 to finance house purchase are tax deductible and there is no capital gains tax liability on the sale of a 'principal' residence). Deposits with building societies account for about 16 per cent of the personal sector's gross financial wealth (see table 10.18).

The remaining personal sector savings tend to be lodged in liquid assets such as deposits with the banks, other financial institutions, national savings or in government debt of various maturities. Until recently it had not been placed in company securities. Indeed, the personal sector had been a net seller of its direct holdings of company securities since 1956. There had been a number of factors at work behind this trend. The combined effects of income and capital taxes had led to the demise of the 'Aunt Agatha' type of investor. The tax incentive to invest indirectly via pension and life assurance funds has already been noted. The structure of transactions and dealing costs penalize the small investor, and this, plus the benefits of diversification, suggest that it is wiser to invest indirectly via unit trusts of investment trust companies than directly in company securities. However, the trend has been reversed during the last few years (see table 10.18).

The increase in direct personal sector shareholdings in recent years has been stimulated by the success of the privatization programme, the reform of the tax system, and the introduction of direct tax incentives to equity investment such as the Business Expansion Scheme.

The personal sector has traditionally provided the lion's share of the funds coming onto the capital market but this share tends to arrive indirectly, via the financial institutions, who are therefore responsible for deciding where they will be placed.

The Financial Institutions

The financial institutions can be grouped roughly into the banks, discount houses, merchant banks, finance houses, building societies, unit trust and investment trust companies, insurance companies and pension funds. The activities of each and the markets they serve will be briefly reviewed in turn.

Before we proceed, it must be borne in mind that a major 'deregulation' of the financial system has taken place in recent years (Llewellyn suggests that it is more accurately defined as a change in the regulatory matrix[8]). Major elements of this have included the phasing-out of direct monetary controls (1971), the floating of sterling (1972), the abolition of exchange control (1979), the reform of the Stock Exchange (1986) and the deregulation of the building societies (1987). One of the results, combined with the growth of international competition in the financial services industry, is a blurring of the traditional boundaries between the various types of financial institutions. There is an increasing tendency for them to compete directly with one another in the provision of certain ranges of financial services. However, for ease of exposition, they will be considered separately.

The banks

The banks are a heterogeneous group of institutions whose common characteristic is the acceptance of deposits of a short-term nature (table 10.19). They then perform the classic role of the financial intermediary and transform them into advances and loans of longer duration. The Banking Act of 1979 requires deposit-taking institutions to apply to the Bank of England for formal recognition of 'bank' status. The major banks are the London and Scottish clearing banks, plus the Northern Ireland banks, accepting houses and a growing number of branches of overseas banks. They are supervised by the Bank of England, which ensures the observance of certain solvency and liquidity requirements consistent with prudent operation, and also implements the official credit control policy. The banks were required to maintain a 'reserve asset' ratio of 12.5 per cent of 'eligible liabilities' (sterling deposits plus any foreign currency deposits

Table 10.19 *Banks in the United Kingdom: summary of their position at 30 September 1988 (£million (percentages in parentheses))*

Sterling liabilities: total deposits 366,688 (87.00) made up of

Notes outstanding	Sight deposits	Time deposits	Certificates of deposit	Items in suspense and transmission	Capital and other funds
1,230	114,985	215,060	36,642	10,806	42,728
(0.3)	(27.3)	(51.0)	(8.7)	(2.6)	(10.1)

Other currency liabilities: total deposits 592,715 (96.7) made up of

Sight and time deposits	Certificates of deposit etc.	Items in suspense and transmission	Capital and other funds	Total liabilities/ assets
518,343	74,372	7,152	19,668	1,040,989
(83.7)	(12.0)	(1.2)	(3.2)	

Figures in parentheses denote individual sterling liabilities as a percentage of total sterling liabilities, and individual foreign currency liabilities as a percentage of total foreign currency liabilities.

Source: *Bank of England Quarterly Bulletin* (November 1988)

switched into sterling). Reserve assets are largely made up of government stocks with a year or less to maturity, treasury bills, money at call with the discount market, certain other short-term bills, and balances with the Bank of England (excluding special deposits). As a further reinforcement of controls the banks used to be required to lodge 'special deposits' or supplementary 'special deposits' with the Bank of England. The latter 'corset' was abolished in 1980; the special deposits scheme remains in force but has not been activated since December 1979.

In August 1981 a new monetary control regime was implemented which involved the imposition of a 0.5 per cent of 'eligible liabilities' non-operational cash ratio requirement on all monetary sector institutions with liabilities averaging at least £10 million over a selected period. These institutions agreed to maintain at least 6 per cent on average of their 'eligible liabilities' in the form of secured call money with the London Discount Market Association. By so doing they ensured that their acceptance would be eligible for rediscount at the Bank of England – the 'club money' arrangement.

The minimum reserve assets ratio and the 1.5 per cent cash ratio imposed on the clearing banks was also abolished, and the minimum lending rate was suspended.

In July 1982 hire purchase control terms were abolished and in August 1983 the club money arrangements were revised. In future, the restrictions on average and minimum holdings of secured money at call with the London Discount Market Association were to be 5 per cent and 2.5 per cent respectively of eligible liabilities.

There have been major changes in the focus and emphasis of the Bank of England's implementation of monetary policy in recent years. There are now numerous definitions of the money supply including the narrow money aggregate M1, which includes notes and coin and interest- and non-interest-bearing bank sight deposits, and ranging through to M4, which includes bank time deposits and building society shares and deposits. M5 is even broader including other 'near money'. These definitions refer to UK private sector holdings and further definitions include 'public' holdings. A number of developments have made it difficult to define and monitor the behaviour of the money supply. Wholesale deposits are switched between sight and time categories, the use of retail interest-bearing chequing accounts has grown, and the distinction between the activities of the banks and building societies has blurred.

These problems have led the authorities to move away from the setting of explicit targets for the broader monetary aggregates. In 1985, they also stopped overfunding the public sector borrowing requirement as a means of offsetting private-sector-induced growth in the money supply. (This refers to selling more government debt than funding needs require.) Indeed, in 1987 a surplus was achieved and net public sector debt repayment was made for the first time since the 1970s. There is now evidence of 'crowding-in' for maturities of over seven years where negative government issues have been replaced by private sector issues.

The emphasis in monetary policy is now on a more pragmatic approach in which the authorities monitor the growth of broad money and of credit as well as other measures, the most important of which is the exchange rate. Now the short-term interest rate is the key instrument and this is largely linked to management of the exchange rate.

Further, fundamental changes have taken place in the regulation of the banks. These are partly the result of a growing appreciation of the need for an international regulatory framework which recognized the evolution of financial structures and the internationalization of financial business. The ultimate aim is to produce a 'level playing field' that is international in its scope. Banking supervisors' meeting in Basle, have worked since 1975 on a supra-national level at the development of the three 'Cs'. These stand for the concordat, which allocates supervisory responsibility, the consolidation principle, which enhances the effectiveness of parental supervision, and finally the convergence of standards of capital adequacy.

These developments have been further stimulated by the movement towards the creation of a single common market of goods and services in Europe in 1992 involving some 320 million people. The European Community (EC) issued a first Banking Co-ordination Directive in 1977 which cleared away most of the obstacles to the freedom of establishment of banks and other credit institutions, laid down common standards for granting licences and introduced the basic principle of home-country control.

However, the Second Banking Directive, issued in January 1988, rather than requiring a high degree of prior harmonization, established two new principles. The first was that the home country of an institution will be responsible for regulation and supervision, and the second was that there should be a mutual recognition by all member governments of each other's regulatory arrangements.

In the meantime the Bank of England has been examining the nature of banking capital liquidity and developing principles for assessing their adequacy. Indeed, from 1980 it began to apply its own risk–asset ratio system to the supervision of British banks. At the beginning of 1987 there was a joint announcement by the US Federal Reserve System and the Bank of England of their intention to move towards a convergence of supervisory policy.

Two ratios are central to the assessment of capital adequacy: the gearing ratio and the risk–asset ratio. The former relates the total public liabilities of the bank, defined as customer deposits and other creditors, excluding contingent liabilities, less intra-group capital, to the bank's capital. This is roughly defined as equity capital plus reserves. This ratio varies for the various institutions. Typically, the clearing banks have had ratios which have varied in a range between 15:1 and 25:1.

The risk–asset ratio is used as a measure of the adequacy of capital in relation to an institution's exposure to the risk of losses. It takes the asset side of the balance sheet and divides it into categories, each being given a certain weight, e.g. the weight for commercial lending is 1.0 and that for holdings of treasury bills 0.1. The bank's capital is then compared with these re-calculated assets to give the risk–asset ratio. The off-balance-sheet risks are also weighted, and the bank's capital is compared with the sum of the risk-adjusted balance sheet assets and the risk-adjusted off-balance-sheet assets. The intention is to capture the effects of the explosion of off-balance-sheet activities (i.e. arrangements of swaps etc.), which have developed recently as the banks try to increase their generation of fee income.

The liquidity adequacy of each bank is also assessed, using a cash flow approach and a maturity ladder of assets and liabilities which are netted out by maturity. The bank's exchange rate risk exposure is also monitored, as is its exposure to large loans, particularly those which involve borrowers connected with the bank.

A further safeguard is provided by the deposit protection scheme which came into effect in 1982 giving a guarantee of 75 per cent of a depositor's sterling deposits with any one institution.

All together, these constitute an impressive battery of safeguards and controls. The major worry is that these developments, when combined with the passage of the Financial Services Act, may have transformed the regulation of the UK financial system from one of the most liberal to one of the most regulated within the EC. There is an obvious incentive to avoid compliance costs by locating a bank's operations within the most liberal EC territory. This could have implications for London's continued pre-eminence as the banking centre of Europe.

Banking activities can be broadly divided into retail and wholesale banking. The clearing banks' widespread branch network facilitates retail banking and they attract funds via interest-bearing deposit accounts and non-interest-bearing current accounts. Their customers are provided with a broad range of services apart from their money transmission and cash distribution services. Sterling and foreign currency deposits typically make up in excess of 90 per cent of the bank's liabilities, and of the sterling deposits nearly one-third are sight deposits theoretically payable on demand.

Wholesale deposits involve large amounts, usually in excess of £50,000, and bear higher interest rates. These funds are frequently provided by other banks with surplus funds, other financial institutions and large companies. A popular instrument is the certificate of deposit which states that a deposit has been made with a bank which will be repayable to the holder on maturity. These are negotiable instruments and so the bank has the advantage of a fixed-term deposit and the holder can always sell the certificate if he wants immediate liquidity. The foreign and merchant banks (the accepting houses) tend to concentrate their banking activities in the wholesale markets.

Clearing bank lending varies greatly in size and nature, from overdrafts to individual customers up to syndicated multi-million-pound loans to multinational companies. Although traditionally favouring overdraft lending, banks have been increasingly providing term loan facilities to companies as well as their leasing, factoring and instalment credit facilities. The banks also accept bills for customers (traditionally the role of the merchant banks and reviewed with their activities) and maintain their traditional financial advisory role. (A breakdown of bank advances is given in table 10.1).

The discount houses

The discount houses make a market in short-term financial instruments. The banks deposit money at call with them and thereby earn interest on surplus cash. The market includes bank and trade bills – indeed, the houses revived the commercial bill market – plus certificates of deposit, treasury bills, and local authority bills. The discount houses have an agreement to cover the whole of each week's treasury bill issue, which they then pass on to other institutions, in particular the deposit banks. The discount houses are guaranteed that the Bank of England will always accommodate them as a lender of last resort. However, the Bank can intervene in the market when there is a shortage or surplus of cash in a number of ways. Shortages are relieved by its purchasing bills, but if it wishes to create a shortage and raise interest rates it can sell bills to the houses and provide them with the necessary cash by lending them funds at an appropriate lending rate.

Since 1982 the discount houses have been subject to a system of prudential control operated by the Bank of England which parallels that used with respect to the banks. Their capital adequacy is assessed, together with their exposure to various sources of risk including large loan exposures.

Merchant banks

The traditional business of the merchant banks lies in the acceptance of bills. The accepted view was that the 13 members of the Accepting Houses Committee were the major merchant banks. However, although this remains an important part of their business they have an extremely wide and diverse range of activities. On the one hand there are their wholesale banking activities; in these they compete with all the other banks but their advances only account for about 4 per cent of total advances. On the other hand they provide industry and personal clients with the whole gamut of financial services which do not involve them in lending their own funds. Amongst these activities could be included financial counselling, guidance in take-overs and mergers, investment management, and the issuing and acceptance business. They play a major role in facilitating the procurement of funds, both via their acceptance business and through the arrangement of syndicated credit. All are members of the less exclusive Issuing Houses Association and are active in arranging and underwriting UK capital issues and in managing Eurobond issues (bonds denominated in Eurocurrencies). Some of them have a number of other activities, including leasing and factoring, property development, foreign exchange, commodity and bullion dealing etc.

The Big Bang led to a major restructuring and regrouping of the activities of the merchant banks. Many tried to become part of much larger financial services groups. For example, Mercury International, through S. G. Warburg & Co., swallowed up top stockbrokers Rowe and Pitman, gilt-edged jobber Akroyd and Smithers and the former government broker Mullens & Co. Barclay's merchant bank took over jobbers Wedd Durlacher and then bought up the brokers de Zoete and Bevan. This type of comprehensive restructuring of activities is still in the process of unfolding.

Finance houses

The finance houses' traditional business has been instalment credit; most of their activities have been tied up with hire purchase or credit sale. Their main sources of funds are either borrowings, particularly from the banking sector, or deposits from banks and companies. Many are owned by banks or other institutions. Some offer banking facilities with deposit accounts and cheque issue. Their activities have branched out into leasing and factoring, credit granting, and the provision of various types of personal loans. They have branch networks but their facilities are frequently offered directly by the retailer who will have an agreement with a finance house for the provision of credit to his customers.

Building societies

The building societies are mutual organizations (i.e. owned by their members) which attract personal savings on a short-term basis (in the form of share or deposit accounts which are practically withdrawable on demand), and relend them long term in the form of mortgage advances for funding house purchase. These advances account for about 80 per cent of the societies' assets. Their mortgage rate is related to the rate paid to their investors after allowance for expenses. As there are high administrative costs associated with the adjustment of rates they do not follow every movement in short-term interest rates and have more stable 'sticky' rates.

The building societies used to be required to observe a minimum liquidity ratio of 7.5 per cent in the form of cash and liquid investments. Their activities were regulated by the Chief Registrar of Friendly Societies in accordance with the Building Societies Act 1962.

However, at the beginning of 1987, the Building Societies Act 1986 came into effect, providing a new supervisory framework and providing them with a broader range of operating powers. These changes are partly the result of the success of the building societies in recent years. Between 1950 and 1980 they enjoyed massive growth, taking over 50 per cent of the retail savings market and 75 per cent of the growing mortgage market. They benefited from going outside the restrictions experienced by the banks during the 1960s and 1970s.

The 1986 Act introduced the concept of commercial assets, broadly defined as total assets minus fixed and liquid assets. At least 90 per cent of a society's commercial assets must be in the form of first mortgage loans to owner-occupiers. New powers conferred by the Act allow the societies to provide a broad range of financial and house buying services. These include money transmission and foreign exchange services, insurance, the management of personal equity plans plus estate agent and conveyancing services. The 1986 Act also introduced a new supervisory framework overseen by the Building Societies Commission which is chaired by the Chief Registrar of Friendly Societies. In effect, the Commission and the Registry of Friendly Societies now operate as a single government department. The Act sets out criteria for prudent management which are also considered with regard to authorization. These criteria involve the maintenance of adequate reserves and other designated capital sources, an appropriate structure of commercial assets, adequate liquid assets, adequate security for advances secured on land, and appropriate accounting records and control systems. Furthermore, the societies must be managed by officers with adequate skills who are recognized as such.

These changes reflect the fact that the barriers between markets and institutions are being progressively removed. It remains to be seen whether the building societies will continue to thrive against the increased competition offered by the banks.

Unit trusts and investment trust companies

Unit trusts are trusts subject to trust law and are authorized by the Department of Trade according to the Prevention of Fraud (Investments) Act 1958. The interests of unit holders are safeguarded by their trustees and until 1979 the determination of trust management expenses was also governed by the Department of Trade. Their activities are now overseen by both IMRO and LAUTRO (see figure 10.5). They are 'open-ended' funds, through which individuals can invest to obtain the benefits of economies of scale in dealing expenses plus access to professionally managed diversified portfolios. When someone buys a unit he obtains an interest in the trust's assets and investment income. The actual size of the fund will depend on the balance of net purchases and sales of units.

A trust's investment policy is limited both by legislation and by its stated objectives; it may have general, overseas or specialized interests. Authorized trusts can only invest in government securities or shares and debentures. They are limited to holding no more than 5 per cent of their total fund in unlisted securities. They are further limited by the fact that they cannot build up reserves and time their investments but must sell or buy according to the balance unit purchase/sales.

Investment trusts are companies in their own right and are not subject to the same restrictions. They are 'closed-ended' funds with their capital subscribed by their shareholders and debenture holders. Thus they can gear up their investments by fixed interest borrowings, build up reserves and time their entry and exit from the markets. A shareholder who sells thus simply transfers his ownership to another individual. The trust does not redeem in cash as does a unit trust; therefore the managers can be relatively unconcerned about day-to-day fluctuation in demand for shares. Despite these advantages, in recent years there has been a persistent considerable 'discount' or difference between the market value of investment trust company shares and the value of the securities in their portfolios, going well beyond the costs of the interposition of a layer of management expenses. They offer advantages to the small investor similar to those of the unit trusts, and some, like the unit trusts, have general portfolios whereas others concentrate on sectors or geographical areas and seek to maximize either income or capital growth.

The investment holdings of unit and investment trusts are shown in tables 10.21 and 10.22 respectively, where it can be seen that nearly 90 per cent of their holdings are in UK and overseas companies.

Insurance companies

Insurance company business can be conveniently divided into two categories; general (fire, accident, life and marine insurance) and long term (mainly life assurance). Most of the liabilities of general insurance companies are short term and thus a greater proportion of their funds will be placed in short-term securities than is the case with life funds. On the other hand they need to build up reserves and maintain solvency margins, so they also have very substantial long-term investments.

Life assurance involves long-term liabilities and therefore assets tend to be correspondingly long term. The wide variety of policies, including 'with profits' schemes which offer some participation in profits from investments in return for higher premiums, and endowment policies with an emphasis on saving, mean that the companies have to be very conscious of investment returns. An increased awareness of the ravages of inflation has led them to place a greater proportion of their funds in property and equity

Table 10.20 *Investments of unit trusts: amounts outstanding, market values at year end 1985*

	£million	Percentage
Net short-term assets	1,113	5.8
Foreign currency loans	−489	−2.5
British government securities	524	2.7
UK company securities:		
loan and preference	517	2.7
ordinary and deferred	11,151	57.8
Overseas company securities:		
loan and preference	253	1.3
ordinary and deferred	6,104	31.7
Other assets	105	0.5
Total	19,278	100.0

Source: Central Statistical Office, *Annual Abstract of Statistics*, 1987

as possible inflation hedges. They are exceedingly important channellers of funds into the capital markets and the structure of their holdings is indicated in table 10.22.

Pension funds

The pension funds have grown tremendously in scope and importance since 1945 as increased demand and legislation for better pension provision

Table 10.21 *Investments of investment trusts: market values of holdings at year end 1985*

	£million	Percentage
Net short-term assets	360	2.1
British government securities	445	2.5
UK company securities:		
loan and preference	266	1.5
ordinary and deferred	7,662	43.8
Overseas company securities:		
loan and preference	497	2.8
ordinary and deferred	7,429	42.5
Other investments	827	4.7
Total	17,486	100.0

Source: Central Statistical Office, *Annual Abstract of Statistics*, 1989

Table 10.22 *Insurance companies: market values of holdings of assets by long-term and general funds at year end 1984*

	General funds (£m)	General funds (%)	Long-term funds (£m)	Long-term funds (%)
Cash and other short-term assets (gross)	2,499	11.9	4,677	4.0
Agent's balances	2,544	12.2	922	0.8
British government securities	4,709	22.5	27,876	24.1
UK local authority debt	81	0.4	795	0.7
Company securities:				
Debenture and preference	1,604	7.7	4,728	4.1
Ordinary shares	5,509	26.3	45,842	39.6
Authorized unit trust units	17	0.1	5,463	4.7
Loans and mortgages	413	2.0	4,077	3.5
Land, property and ground rents	1,665	8.0	18,902	16.3
Other financial assets	1,897	9.1	2,557	2.2
Total assets	20,938	100.0	115,839	100.0

Source: Central Statistical Office, *Annual Abstract of Statistics*, 1989

has boosted contributions. However, not all schemes involve the building up of investment funds, and some are paid directly out of revenue, as is the case with the state pension scheme. The majority, however, including those operated by the public sector, local authorities and private companies, involve advance funding, in which both employee and employer make contributions over the period of employment, and these funds, together with investment income, are accumulated to meet future pension liabilities.

Funded schemes could be divided between insured schemes, in which the management of funds and actuarial risk is undertaken by a life assurance office, and self-administered schemes, in which the funds are directly invested, although the management of investment funds is usually contracted out to an appropriate specialist financial institution.

The liabilities of the funds are their commitments to present and future pensioners; hence contributors cannot use their pension rights as collateral for raising money, and the liabilities are completely distinct from those of the company or body involved with the scheme on behalf of its employees.

The growth in importance (in terms of the market value of their holdings) of the pension funds continues apace and they are still far from the plateau where accruals will just match liabilities. They therefore have a tremendous influence and significance within the capital market. An indication of the scope and nature of their investment holdings is given in table 10.23. The major change in their holdings in recent years has been a much greater commitment to equity and property, again prompted largely by the influence of inflation.

Controversies and Conclusions

The last four years have witnessed a profound shake-up of British financial markets and the tax system. Corporate and personal tax rates have been radically reduced and there has been a growth in direct share ownership on the part of the personal sector. This marks the reversal of a 30-year trend, though it is still the financial institutions who dominate security holdings within the financial markets. Measures like the Business Expansion Scheme and personal equity plans have stimulated investment in company securities.

The London capital markets have survived both the Big Bang and the stock market crash of October 1987 and have emerged in excellent shape. London is a low cost competitively priced centre for international capital market activity and is unlikely to be undercut by any other centres in the near future.

The next big challenge is likely to be triggered by the moves towards the creation of a Single European Market in 1992 and in the regulatory and commercial responses of the various financial centres to this event.

The 1986 Financial Services Act has established a system of self-regulation under statute. Much depends upon how its provisions are

Table 10.23 *Superannuation funds: holdings in market values at year end 1985*

	£million	Percentage
Short-term assets (net)	3,911	3.9
Long-term borrowing	−251	−0.2
British government securities	17,834	17.7
UK local authority debt	61	0.1
Overseas government securities	611	0.6
Company securities:		
Debentures and preference	1,848	1.8
Ordinary shares	64,596	63.9
Loans and mortgages	172	0.2
Land, property and ground rents	7,925	7.8
Property unit trusts	1,551	1.5
Other assets	2,783	2.8
Total	101,041	100.0

Source: Central Statistical Office, *Annual Abstract of Statistics*, 1987

developed and administered over the next few years. London is undoubtedly a well-regulated financial centre but the compliance costs of enforcing this regulation must be kept to a minimum so that it can remain competitive. At the moment the City seems well placed to remain the premier financial centre within Europe, but competition may intensify after 1992 and the movement towards common standards may reduce any individual regulatory or pricing advantages that it currently possesses.

Appendix 10.1

Special financial institutions

Most of the financial institutions in the UK have evolved from the initiatives of groups of individuals in the private sector. They perceived an opportunity within the financial sector and pursued it for reasons of personal gain or in some cases, as with the friendly societies, for collective benefit.

However, other specialist institutions have been set up by the government to meet specific requirements and to combat perceived inadequacies or weaknesses in certain sections of the markets. The identification of the Macmillan Gap led to the setting up of the Industrial and Commercial Finance Association (ICFA) in 1945; it had the specific function of providing long- and medium-term finance for small- and medium-sized companies. Loans are normally repayable over the period of the loan, typically 15–20 years, at fixed rates determined by ICFC's costs of raising funds. In particularly risky circumstances, equity stakes may be taken as part of a funding package; moreover, the ICFC has the right, rarely exercised, to place a non-executive director on the board of companies in which it invests. Its commitment may vary between £5000 and £2 million. It is jointly owned by the Bank of England and the London and Scottish clearing banks. It is now known as the 3is, Investors in Industry.

Finance Corporation for Industry (FCI) was also set up in 1945 by the same interests to provide longer-term finance for larger companies. Finance for Industry (FFI) was set up in 1973 to act as a holding company for ICFC, FCI and a number of other more specialized subsidiaries. These include Estate Duties Investment Trust (EDITH), which was set up to assist companies with estate duties and has most of its funds in unlisted shares, and Technical Development Capital (TDC) which provides medium-term loan finance for technological innovative businesses.

The British Technology Group was formed in 1982 to take over the roles and functions of two previously separate bodies, the National Research and Development Corporation (NRDC) and the National Enterprise Board (NEB). NRDC was originally established in 1948. It assisted the development or exploitation of inventions and provided finance for industry and trade where adequate finance was not available from other sources. This was done either through joint venture projects or via the provision of equity and loan finance. NEB had been set up in November 1975 under the Industry Act with a view to the provision of equity and loan finance to industry, in particular manufacturing industry. It also provided finance and advisory services to promote industrial restructuring. It acted as a holding company for various companies which have been acquired in the course of its activities or transferred to it by government (British Leyland, for example).

Equity Capital for Industry (ECI) was set up in 1976 with a view to meeting an 'equity gap' in the supply of equity funds to smaller and medium listed companies. It had an initial capital of £46 million provided by a consortium of financial institutions.

There are also a number of government agencies which provide local assistance to industry. For example in 1975 the Scottish and Welsh Development Agencies (SDA, WDA) were set up in their respective areas. They have a brief to further economic activity, safeguard employment, assist in environmental improvement and promote industry in their respective areas. They have a wide range of financial and other powers. They can make loan and equity investments, form companies or enter into partnerships, build and make available factories, and give guarantees. The most recently formed organizations include the Local Enterprise Boards (LEBs) and Local Enterprise Agencies (LEAs). Many of these provide a combination of grants and loans.

References

1 E. Solomon, *The Theory of Financial Management*, Columbia University Press, 1963, p. 9.
2 Committee to Review the Functioning of Financial Institutions (Wilson Committee), *Interim Report – The Financing of Small Firms*, Cmnd 7503, HMSO, March 1979, p. 23.
3 *Report of the Committee of Inquiry on Small Firms* (Bolton Committee), Cmnd 4811, HMSO, November 1971.
4 *Report of the Committee on Finance and Industry* (Macmillan Committee), Cmnd 3897, HMSO, June 1931.
5 See 'Financing British industry', *Bank of England Quarterly Bulletin* (September 1980); 'Profitability and company finance: a supplementary note', *Bank of England Quarterly Bulletin* (January 1980); 'Trends in real rates of return', *Bank of England Quarterly Bulletin* (August 1988).
6 C. Drury, 'A survey of UK leasing practice', *Management Accounting* (April 1989).
7 A. W. Henfrey, B. Albrecht and P. Richards, 'The UK Stock Market and the efficient market model', *Investment Analyst* (September 1977).
8 D. T. Llewellyn, 'Competition and the regulatory mix', *National Westminster Bank Quarterly Review* (August 1987).

11

British Industry and its Changing Pattern

In this chapter the structure of British industry as it is, as it has developed and as it is evolving is examined. Study of industrial structure is interesting, not only for its own sake, but because many economists believe that theoretical linkages between perfect competition and price, and monopoly and price, are reflected in reality in company behaviour. As a consequence public policy recommendations are sometimes made to government, to nationalized industries or to government agencies such as the Monopolies and Mergers Commission which are based on inferences drawn about industrial behaviour, which in turn depend on the view that market structure affects behaviour. Although we noted in chapter 5 that a more meaningful distinction might be made between open and closed markets, and price takers and searchers, than between perfect competition and monopoly, such a distinction is less easy to apply as a generalism (even if more accurate). Consequently here and in chapter 12 we tend to use the more traditional means of measurement and analysis contained in the industrial economist's tool-kit. In the first section of this chapter we examine the organization of British industry. In the second we discuss the validity and meaningfulness of some of the measurement tools used in the descriptive section.

Industrial Structure and Morphology

When considering changes in employment, output and contribution to gross domestic product (GDP) by Standard Industrial Classification (SIC) (see chapter 2) care should be exercised for at least six reasons:

1 The output growth figures are measured by a range of incompatible indices varying largely with data availability (e.g. sales, volume and employment may be used as proxies for net output).
2 The aggregated SIC two-digit indices may disguise contrary movements within the three- and four-digit indices which go to make them up.

3 The growth rate in output between two points in time may conceal different growth rates within sub-periods. Thus while mining has been in almost continuous decline for over three decades, oil has only rapidly risen since 1975.
4 Quality changes are largely, if not totally, ignored by the indices.
5 Employment data do not allow for changes in labour type or in quantity of hours worked.
6 Interdependences between three-digit indices and/or two-digit indices are ignored. Thus if vehicles (SIC 35) change one would expect metal manufacture (SIC 22) to alter in a similar direction since vehicle producers purchase large quantities of inputs from SIC 22.

Table 11.1 summarizes the industrial structure of the UK by net output and by employment in 1988. Again this emphasizes the importance of the secondary and tertiary sectors of the economy. Table 11.2 further subdivides the manufacturing labour force by its sectoral occupation.

Table 11.1 *Relatives importance of sectors of the UK economy 1988*

	SIC	Percentage of GDP[a]	Percentage of employment
Agriculture, forestry, fishing	0	1.42	1.39
Energy and water supply	1	5.53	2.09
Manufacturing	2–4	23.67	23.21
Construction	5	6.52	4.63
Distribution; hotels; catering; repairs	6	13.96	20.50
Transport and communication	7	7.26	6.25
Banking; finance; insurance etc.	8	19.48	11.20
Other services	9	27.72	30.73
		100.0	100.0

[a] After providing for stock appreciation.
Source: *UK National Accounts 1989*, HMSO, tables 2.1 and 17.1

Table 11.3 highlights even more clearly than did the highly aggregated figures of table 2.4 that production growth and decline are not necessarily linked to employment changes. Technology can improve, thus dramatically changing labour productivity for the better. Alternatively, industries may be contracting; firms may wish to avoid declaring workers redundant (itself costly in the short run, given statutory redundancy payments only partially subsidized by government) to minimize the risk that if any trading downturn is temporary then costly labour upheavals, sackings and subsequent recruitment and retraining can be avoided. If this decision is

Table 11.2 *Relative importance of manufacturing sectors by employment: UK 1987*

SIC		Percentage
22	Metal manufacturing	3.23
24	Manufacture of non-metallic mineral products	4.44
25	Chemical industry	6.64
31	Manufacture of metallic goods n.e.s.	5.85
32	Mechanical engineering	13.98
33	Manufacture of office machinery and data processing equipment	1.86
34	Electrical and electronic engineering	10.82
35	Manufacture of motor vehicles and parts thereof	4.74
36	Manufacture of other transport equipment	4.98
37	Instrument engineering	2.02
41/2	Food, drink and tobacco manufacturing	10.77
43	Textile industry	4.40
45	Footwear and clothing industries	5.77
46	Timber and wooden furniture industries	4.08
47	Manufacture of paper and paper products, printing and publishing	9.60
48	Processing of rubber and plastics	4.10
49	Other manufacturing industries	1.69
		100.00

n.e.s., not elsewhere specified.
Source: *Business Monitor Census of Production Summary Tables*, vol. PA1002, 1987

taken then, of course, labour productivity falls and employment declines less rapidly than production. In the period covered by the table, however, factors such as these seem to have been less important than the shedding of labour which, by inference, was surplus to requirements.

Table 11.4, which relates to a much longer time span (1930–89), shows how dramatic has been the broad employment shift in the last 50 years. Manufacturing has remained fairly static as an employer of labour (albeit there have been significant movements within that sector). But the major shift has been from agriculture, mining and other primary industries (9 per cent of the employed labour force in 1930 to 2.5 per cent in 1989) towards the service sector.

This is not necessarily a matter for condemnation. It is a typical pattern in most advanced economies that the tertiary sector should grow in relative importance. Sometimes it is bewailed that this is 'eroding the country's industrial base' but services can be just as important as tangible goods. Without the intangibles of distribution and insurance, many tangible manufactures would never reach the consumer. Without the intangible of advertising, many consumers would never learn of new technologies in consumer hardware such as microwave ovens or video cassette recorders. As material wealth rises people also often tend to prefer the intangible satisfaction of a holiday abroad, a symphony concert, better health care, a football match or even pop music. From the viewpoint of the consumer, social value lies in what the consumer believes the goods or the services are worth. A singer may produce a sound which vanishes the instant it is produced, but if the consumer values it sufficiently highly to pay to listen to that sound then the tertiary sector increases and is valued as productive by those members of society who pay for its use.

Table 11.3 *Relative growth rates of certain sectors of UK manufacturing industry 1980–1986*

		Percentage change 1980–6	
	SIC 1980	Index of production	Employment
Pharmaceutical products	257	+36.6	−6.7
Steel tubes	222	+17.2	−35.9
Computers and office machinery	330	+147.8	−3.9
Telecom equipment etc.	344	+23.8	−14.4
Bread, biscuits and flour confectionery	419	0	−11.2
Footwear	451	−7.5	−22.5
Processing plastics	483	+38.5	−8.9
Woollen and worsted	431	−1.0	−30.0
Motor vehicles and their engines	351	−21.0	−45.0
Soap and toilet preparations	258	+30.9	−11.0
Printing and publishing	475	+6.1	−10.7
Clothing, hats and gloves	453	+12.1	−15.0
Coal extraction and solids fuels manufacturing	111	−21.0	−43.8

Sources: index of production, *Annual Abstracts of Statistics*, HMSO, 1988, p. 144, table 8.2; employment, *Business Monitor Report of the Census of Production Summary Tables*, vol. PA1002, 1982, table 2, and 1987, table 2

Concentration in Manufacturing Industry

Not only has British industry changed significantly in terms of sectoral importance, but so also has its organization and structure. Before considering how the structure has changed, it is important first to understand how concentration is measured.

Table 11.4 *Percentage of employees in employment by industry (mid-year estimates)*

	Primary Agriculture, forestry, fishing, mining and quarrying	Secondary Manufacturing, construction, gas, electricity, water	Tertiary Transport and communications, distribution trades, other services
1930	8.9	41.1	50.3
1941	10.4	43.8	45.8
1950	8.1	49.1	42.8
1960	6.3	47.7	46.0
1970	3.5	46.6	49.9
1980	3.2	37.4	59.3
1989	2.5[a]	28.8	68.7

[a] Including metal manufacturing.

Sources: 1930, 'Analysis of occupation by population', *British Labour Statistics: Historical Abstracts 1886–1968*, HMSO (Great Britain only); 1941, 'Distribution of total manpower', *Annual Abstract of Statistics*, 1935–47, table 128 (Great Britain only); 1950, *British Labour Statistics: Historical Abstracts 1886–1968*, HMSO (Great Britain only); 1960, *Annual Abstract of Statistics*, HMSO, 1963, table 134 Estimated number of employees; 1970, *Annual Abstract of Statistics*, HMSO, 1973, table 141 Employees in employment; 1980, *Annual Abstract of Statistics*, HMSO, 1983, table 6.2 Employees in employment; 1989, *Employment Gazette*, HMSO, November 1989, table 1.4 (Great Britain only)

Measures of concentration

Concentration ratios

There is a wide variety of different methods of measuring concentration. One of the commonest is to measure the percentage of some index of industry size (e.g. sales, assets, employment) which is in the hands of the three (or five) largest firms – the concentration ratio. The larger the ratio the more concentrated is the industry. An alternative is to measure the number of the industry's largest firms which account for a given percentage of industry size. The smaller this number is, the more concentrated is the industry.

Such measures fail to indicate the differences in the remaining number of firms in an industry. They do not indicate whether the tail of firms is composed of a few medium-sized firms or a plethora of small ones. In like manner, they do not indicate whether the top three firms themselves are of a similar size or are composed of one giant and two small firms.

The ratio does not indicate the degree, if any, of collusion or of the intensity of competition, and the number of firms within it is arbitrary. With five firms industry A may be more concentrated than B; with 20 firms the reverse may be true. The last difficulty can be partially overcome with the use of more information, such as concentration curves (figure 11.1). Each curve shows the share of industry (output, employment etc.) possessed by the largest *n* firms. The curves enable comparisons to be made between industries (A, B or C) or between different points in time for one industry (where A, B and C are points in time). They show the concentration ratios firm by firm from one through to the total number of firms in the industry. The firms are ranked along the horizontal axis from the largest to the smallest, cumulatively, until the share of all firms (namely 100 per cent) is reached. Clearly B and C are more highly concentrated than A. C is more concentrated than B only at certain levels of numbers of firms (e.g. at the five- or ten-firm concentration ratios). After 14 firms the situation is reversed; in B the smaller firms have a larger share than in C and there are fewer of them. A would not be regarded as a highly concentrated industry whereas C would; B is moderately concentrated, at least up to the 12-firm level.

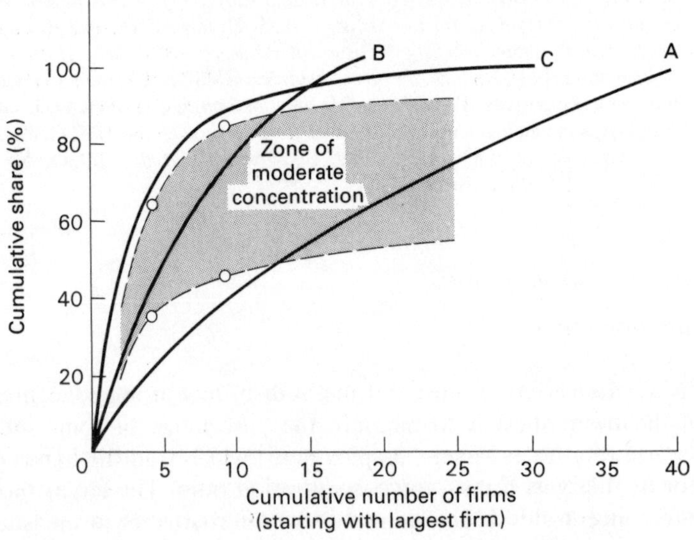

Figure 11.1 *Concentration: cumulative shares*

Table 11.5 shows the approximate standards given by Bain for concentration in manufacturing industries. The zone of moderate concentration is shown in figure 11.1 with three hypothetical cumulative share curves. Again little indication is given as to the intensity of competition.

Table 11.5 *Concentration standards for manufacturing industries*

Percentage of market occupied by the first four firms	Percentage of market occupied by the first eight firms	Degree of concentration
75 or more	90 or more	Very high
65–75	85–90	High
50–65	70–85	Moderately high
35–50	45–70	Moderately low
under 35	under 45	Low

Source: J. S. Bain, *Industrial Organisation*, Wiley, 1967, pp. 137–44.

Alternative measures

An alternative measure of concentration which takes account of the total number of firms in an industry is the Hirschman–Herfindahl index. It focuses on the inequality of firm sizes, or relative concentration, as opposed to the absolute concentration ratios we have looked at so far. It is equal to Σs^2_i where s_i is the share of firm i. This can be shown to be equal to $(c^2 + 1)/n$, where c is the coefficient of variation of firm sizes and n is the number of firms in the industry. When all firms are of equal size the standard deviation of firm sizes is equal to zero and so the index is equal to $1/n$. If there is only one firm in an industry, the standard deviation is again zero and the index reaches a maximum value of unity.

The Hirschman–Herfindahl index, however, although attempting to account for differences in firm size, is still heavily weighted towards larger firms. The square of the market share of a firm with 1 per cent of the market is $0.01^2 = 0.0001$. Adding this to the overall value of the index will make very little difference. In fact, because of this the Hirschman–Herfindahl index is often inverted to obtain the so-called *number equivalent* index: the hypothetical number of firms of equal size which could produce the industry's output and have the same Hirschman–Herfindahl index as the actual number of firms. Thus if a Hirschman–Herfindahl index of 0.2 is calculated, the number equivalent is five, since five firms, with 20 per cent of the market each, would also result in a Hirschman–Herfindahl index of this value ($0.2^2 \times 5 = 0.04 \times 5 = 0.2$).

A more obvious way to obtain a relative measure of concentration (also graphical but less ambiguous than cumulative share curves) is to use a *Lorenz curve* as in figure 11.2. Unlike cumulative share curves the Lorenz curve for one industry will not intersect with that for another. This is because of the difference in method of construction of the two curves. The vertical axis is identical, but the horizontal axis is the cumulative proportion of firms in the industry, not the absolute numbers.

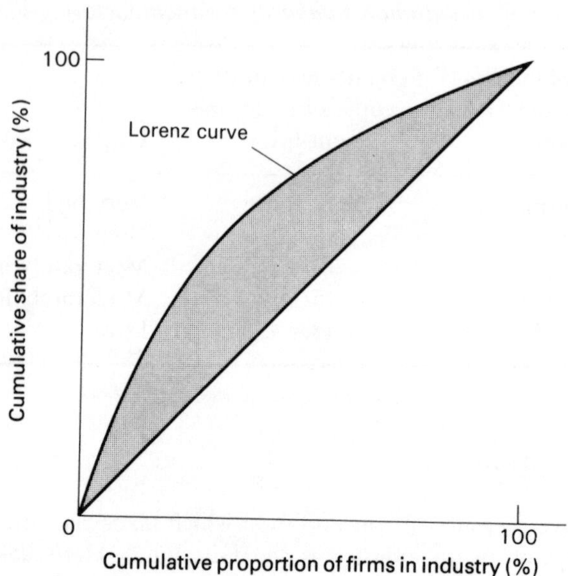

Figure 11.2 *Concentration: Lorenz curve*

Thus curves B and C in figure 11.1 would have common starting and finishing points; their curvature might differ but they would not cross. If all firms are of equal size then the Lorenz curve is the straight diagonal running from bottom left to top right in figure 11.2. The greater the curvature the greater the inequality in firm sizes. The shaded area can be measured by the *Gini coefficient*; this ranges from zero in cases of complete equality to unity when firms are completely unequal in size (i.e. a single-seller monopoly with only one firm plotted in the group in the extreme top left-hand corner). The Gini coefficient is the ratio of the shaded area to the total triangle above the diagonal. Clearly it takes no account of firm numbers. Thus two firms of equal size and 100 firms of equal size could all be plotted on the diagonal and the coefficient in both cases would be zero.

Empirical evidence

Aggregate concentration

Table 11.6 shows the share of the largest 100 non-financial private companies in the UK ranked by worldwide sales and table 11.7 shows the share of the largest 100 private manufacturing firms by net output. These tables indicate a rise in aggregate concentration from the late 1940s until the late 1970s followed by a decline (with the rise occurring in the 1950s).

It appears that the increase in the importance of the top 100 firms was not due to growth in the average size of plant or manufacturing

Table 11.6 *Share of the 100 largest non-financial companies in the UK*

	1968	1975	1980
Domestic sales	26.6	31.4	27.1
Capital employed	65.0	68.4	62.1

Source: A. Hughes and M. S. Kumar, 'Recent trends in aggregate concentration in the UK economy', *Cambridge Journal of Economics* (1984)

Table 11.7 *Share of the 100 largest private manufacturing firms by net output*

Year	Percentage
1949	22
1953	27
1958	32
1963	37
1975	40
1980	39[a]
1987	37

[a] The definition of manufacturing changed in 1980.
Sources: S. J. Prais, *Evolution of Giant Firms in Britain*, Cambridge University Press, 1976, table 1.1; *Business Monitor Report on the Census of Production*, vol. PA1002

establishment, however. Plants, on average, bigger than they were, but this is not the causal feature underlying table 11.6. In table 11.8 the first column, calculated using a method derived by Sargent Florence, shows that the median worker was employed in a plant of 480 people in 1968 (i.e. 50 per cent of all workers were in plants smaller than the 480 employees size, and 50 per cent were in larger plants). The second column, using a measure evolved by S. J. Prais, indicates that 25 per cent of all workers

Table 11.8 *Plant size changes in manufacturing measured by employees*

	Florence median	Prais central range
1948	340	100–1220
1958	440	120–1650
1968	480	130–1600

Source: Prais, *The Evolution of Giant Firms in Britain*, 1976, table 3.2

were employed in plants of under 130 persons in 1968, and 25 per cent in plants of over 1600 employees.

Prais points out that despite this (admittedly non-spectacular plant size increase) the share of the 100 largest plants in net output only rose from 9 per cent in 1948 to 10.8 per cent in 1968. Thus the increase in net output attributed to the largest firms in table 11.7 probably owes far more to an increase in multiplant ownership by individual firms than to an increase in establishment size as such.

Measures of aggregate concentration must, of course, be treated with care. First, they do not necessarily reflect what is happening at the level of the individual industry. Second, the yardstick used may alter the picture somewhat (e.g. net output, employees and capital assets could all be chosen and each could give different implications as to the level of concentration). Third, the number 100 is arbitrary. The top 50 or the top 200 firms, say, may or may not have changed in importance as did the top 100. Further, no indication is given, no matter what the number chosen, about the extent to which the firms examined are the same firms. Some of the top 100 firms in earlier years may now be extinct as a consequence of bankruptcy or take-over; others may have shrunk and so fallen in ranking out of the top 100. Some of today's top 100, however, may not even have been in existence in earlier years; or, if they were, they may have been tiny. The effect that such corporate mobility has for aggregate concentration is concealed, its implications are unclear and the inferences which could or should be drawn are indefinite. And, of course, no attempt is made here to ascertain which industries are or are not subject to overseas import competition or ownership.

Industry level concentration

Table 11.9 shows the five-firm concentration ratios (CR5) for each two-digit manufacturing industry and table 11.10 shows the distribution of CR5 values for three-digit (i.e. more finely disaggregated) industries. The former shows that 12 out of 21 two-digit industries have a CR5 of over 40 per cent when net output is considered and 11 out of 21 when employment is considered. Table 11.10 shows that at three-digit level a greater proportion of manufacturing employment is given by industries with CR5s in the region of 40–49.9 per cent than in any other group, with the proportion in the group with CR5s of 30–39.9 per cent coming second. In terms of net output the greater proportion of output is produced by industries with CR5s in the region of 40–49.9 per cent followed by industries with concentration in the region of 70–79.9 per cent.

Finally table 11.11 shows that UK manufacturing industries are *on average* more concentrated than those of other large European countries. Davies and Caves[1] compared the CR5s of 86 industries to find that the average UK figure was 14 points greater than that for the US. However, in

Table 11.9 *Concentration in UK manufacturing industry 1987*

SIC	Industry	No. of three-digit industries	Unweighted CR5[a] (%) Employment	Net output
11	Coal extraction and manufacture of solid fuels	1	n.a.	n.a.
12	Coke ovens	1	n.a.	n.a.
13	Extraction of mineral oil and natural gas	1	n.a.	n.a.
14	Mineral oil processing	1	49.2	57.8
15	Nucleur fuel production	1	n.a.	n.a.
16	Production and distribution of electricity and gas	2	n.a.	n.a.
17	Water supply industry	1	n.a.	n.a.
21	Extraction and preparation of metalliferous ores	1	n.a.	n.a.
22	Metal manufacture	4	57.6	60.2
23	Extraction of minerals n.e.s.	2	48.5	55.6
24	Manufacture of non-metallic mineral products	8	55.8	58.7
25	Chemical industry	6	37.8	44.1
26	Production of man-made fibres	1	87.1	92.9
31	Manufacture of metal goods n.e.s.	5	17.7	21.1
32	Mechanical engineering	10	29.1	29.1
33	Manufacture of office machinery and data processing	1	31.5	63.2
34	Electrical and electronic engineering	7	45.2	43.3
35	Manufacture of motor vehicles and parts thereof	3	42.9	42.7
36	Manufacture of other transport equipment	5	68.3	68.3
37	Instrument engineering	4	32.5	34.2
41/2	Food, drink and tobacco manufacturing industries	15[b]	55.4	60.7
43	Textile industry	9	42.2	42.3
44	Manufacture of leather and leather goods	2	25.7	27.3
45	Footwear and clothing industries	4	26.2	27.1
46	Timber and wooden furniture industries	7	24.0	27.8
47	Manufacture of paper and paper products, printing and publishing	3	22.5	25.2
48	Processing of rubber and plastics	2	25.4	28.9
49	Other manufacturing industries	5	27.4	30.3

n.a., not available; n.e.s., not elsewhere specified.

[a] Five largest enterprises by size of total employment.

[b] 16 three-digit industries, but in one case figures are not available.

Source: calculated from *Business Monitor Census of Production 1987: Report*, vol. PA1002, table 13

neither study was the correlation between the values for the UK and those for each country in turn very high (0.5–0.8), indicating that if an industry was highly concentrated relative to others in the UK it was not necessarily highly concentrated relative to others in any of the comparator countries.

Table 11.10 *Distribution of concentration ratios in UK manufacturing industry 1987*

Five-firm concentration ratio	No. of industries	No. of employees (thousands)	Percent of employment	No. of industries	Net output (£m)	Percent of net output
0–9.9	5	43.3	2.60	2	260.6	0.58
10–19.9	15	195.0	11.69	13	3,835.3	8.55
20–29.9	14	145.6	8.73	18	3,243.5	7.23
30–39.9	22	247.9	14.86	16	5,439.0	12.13
40–49.9	18	420.0	25.18	17	8,779.0	19.58
50–59.9	10	104.6	6.27	13	5,551.9	12.38
60–69.9	9	128.9	7.73	10	4,980.4	11.11
70–79.9	2	133.3	7.99	8	8,019.9	17.88
80–89.9	6	173.0	10.37	2	802.1	1.79
90–100.0	3	76.1	4.56	5	3,933.2	8.77
	104	1,667.7	100.0	104	44,844.9	100.00

Source: calculated from *Business Monitor Census of Production, Summary Tables*, vol. PA1002, 1987, table 13

Table 11.11 *Four-firm employment concentration ratios in EEC countries*

	Weighted average			
	Italy	UK	West Germany	France
41 industries	30	19	22	19
All manufacturing industries	32	22	24	20

Source: K. D. George and T. S. Ward, *The Structure of Industry in the EEC*, Cambridge University Press, 1975, table 3.2

Explanations of concentration levels

Economists have proposed several theories of concentration. One concerns economies of scale. Consider a price takers' market as explained in chapter 5. If for some reason the market price exceeded the minimum level of long-run average costs, firms would enter the industry and price would be bid down to that minimum level. Since all firms face the same LRAC curve, if it is U shaped (LRAC in figure 6.1) then in the long run all firms will have the same size output, q_0 in figure 11.3. If the total output of the industry is Q_0, then each firm has a market share of q_0/Q_0 and so the five largest firms' share is $5q_0/Q_0$. But if the LRAC curve has a flat bottom as represented by LRAC′ then q_0 is the smallest size that a firm with maximum possible efficiency can be. (This size is known as the minimum efficient firm size

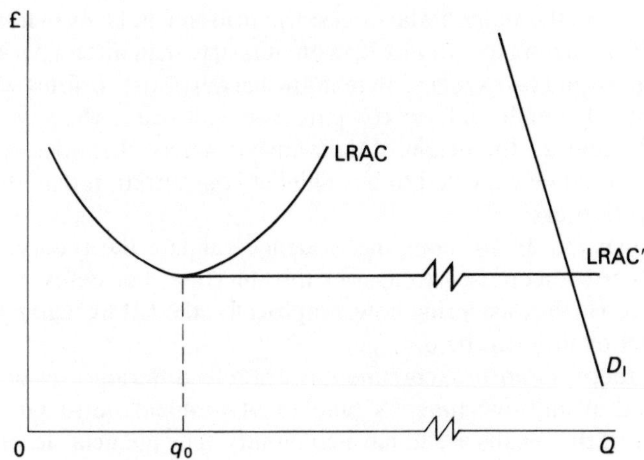

Figure 11.3 *Economies of scale as a determinant of concentration: U-shaped LRAC curve*

(MEF).) Thus the ratio $5q_0/Q_0$ is the lowest share of the largest five firms – their share could be greater if the size of each exceeded q_0.

To explain more fully consider two industries X and Y (shown in figure 11.4) where the same minimum level of LRAC pertains but the size of MEF differs. For industry X, MEF is 5 per cent of industry output, and so if there are no impediments to entry the largest five firms will have at least 25 per cent of total output. Alternatively, for industry Y, MEF is 10 per cent of industry output and so the largest five firms would have at least 50 per cent of the market.

If, in addition, there are barriers to the entry of new firms (see chapter 5) then price would not necessarily be bid down to the minimum level of

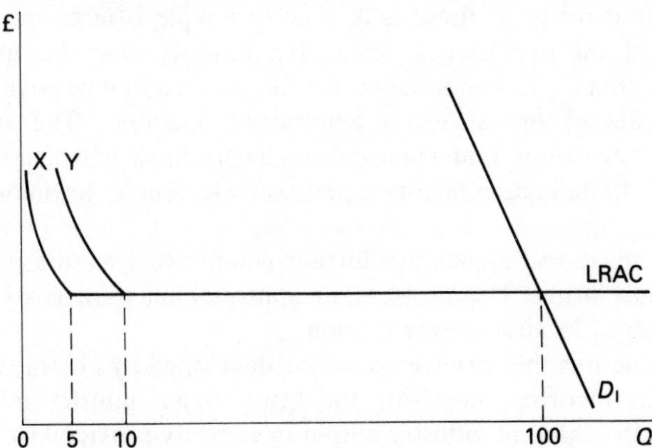

Figure 11.4 *Economies of scale as a determinant of concentration*

LRAC and so the share of the largest five firms might be even less than $5q_0/Q_0$. If high barriers to entry exist in an industry, then after a period of time less entry would be expected than if low barriers exist. If firms which enter are relatively small and we compare two industries, the same in every respect except for the height of their entry barriers, the industry with high barriers would be expected to have higher concentration than the industry with low barriers.

The question arises: does the evidence validate the theory? Different methods have been used to answer this question, but before we describe these it is worth considering how, empirically, the LRAC curve relating to a product or firm can be derived.

First, there is *statistical cost analysis* whereby differing sizes of plants are compared at any one time. A number of problems must be overcome, however, if the results are to have credibility. The financial accounts of the firms to be compared must be uniform. Depreciation policies, for example, must be similar. Factor prices should be identical, a difficult requirement if a plant in Scotland is being compared with one in the southeast. Labour costs in Scotland may be lower but fuel prices may be higher. Each firm should be operating with the most efficient known methods. Perhaps most important of all, each firm should be operating in an equilibrium position on their short-run average cost curves, not on their long-run ones. Short-run costs will be confused with long in the analysis. The statistician cannot even assume that, given a sufficiently large sample, at any one output level short-run costs will be evenly distributed round the long run and so the error will be averaged out. Short-run costs can exceed, but cannot possibly be less than, long-run average costs at any one output level (see figure 6.1).

Second, long-run costs can be estimated by the *engineering technique*. This is based on hypothetial estimations made by those with a knowledge of the production technology involved. Optimal input combinations are estimated for given quantities and the cost curve is found by applying the relevant input prices to these data. The technique is none the worse for being based on hypothetical data. Its accuracy may be questioned, however. Often scale economies or diseconomies cannot be envisaged until a given scale of operations is empirically operated. The subsequent 'scaling-up' problems that chemical engineers have when moving from pilot plant to full-scale factory operation are ample testimony of this assertion.

Both of these techniques are further complicated by the presence of multi-product firms. The problem of apportioning joint costs must too often be solved in an arbitrary fashion.

Finally, there is the *survivor technique* developed by George Stigler. In essence this involves classifying the firms in an industry by size and calculating the share of industry output or capacity provided by each class over time. Size classes whose share increases over time are deemed to be more efficient and to have lower average costs, and vice versa. This technique does not give the precise level of money costs; it shows only the shape of the long-run average cost curve. It presupposes that all size classes of firms face the same economic environment; that they have the same objectives; and, unless technology has been constant over time, that they have been equally adept at introducing and assimilating new techniques. Since the survivor technique is used over time the long-run average cost inferred does comply with the unchanging technology assumption of cost theory.

One method of comparing the evidence with the economies of scale theory is to compare the CR5 with five times the estimated MEF as a percentage of industry output. If the economies of scale theory is a complete explanation, the two values will be identical. Unfortunately, the most comprehensive UK study of manufacturing industries was carried out in 1970. This is shown in table 11.12. Some of the estimates relate to minimum efficient plant size (MEP) and others to MEF; the interpretation of the 'market' is the UK home and export market. The results indicate that in 21 of the 30 industries the MEP was at least 20 per cent of the market and so the largest five plants, if of MEP or above, would supply at least 100 per cent of the market. So the predicted CR5 would exceed the actual CR5 in these cases. Furthermore the cost penalty from operating a plant below MEP was relatively low (under 10 per cent in most cases) so that if firms entered with plants smaller than MEP their comparative disadvantage from the point of view of their costs would not be great.

In contrast, US studies by Bain[2] and Scherer et al.[3] indicate that the level of concentration predicted by considering MEP/market size is much lower than the actual level of concentration for most industries, suggesting that factors other than economies of scale are significant determinants of concentration.

A more comprehensive approach is to examine whether, when factors other than economies of scale (such as size of market, output and barriers to entry) are held constant, there is a significant correlation between the concentration of different industries and MEF or MEP. Only a few of these studies have been carried out for the UK but they do indicate that there is a significant and positive correlation between MEP and concentration. On average the larger MEP is, everything else constant, the more concentrated is the industry. But the evidence also suggests that economies of scale do not explain all of the differences in concentration between industries. Studies relating to the US are more numerous. These show a significant positive correlation between concentration and MEP, and variables intended to represent advertising and the level of capital required for entry, as entry barriers.[4]

Table 11.12 *Minimum efficient size as percentage of UK market, in relation to percentage increase in total cost per unit at 50 per cent minimum efficient size*

Product etc.[a]	MES as per cent of market	Percentage increase in total costs at 50% MES
Aircraft	>100	>20
Diesel engines	>100	>4
Machine tools	>100	5
Newspapers	100	20
Dyes	100	22
Turbogenerators	100	5
Computers etc.	100	8
Steel rolling: plant	80	8
Polymer manufacture	66	5
Electric motors	60	15
Cars	50	6
Refrigerators etc.	50	8
Oil refineries: plant	40	5
Cement: plant[b]	40	9
Bulk steel production: plant	33	5–10
Bread: plant[b]	33	15
Polymer extrusion: plant	33	7
Sulphuric acid: plant	30	1
Cylinder blocks: plant	30	10
Ethylene: plant	25	9
Detergents: plant	20	2.5
Bicycles	10	(small)
Beer: plant[b]	6	9
Bricks: plant[b]	5	25
Warp knitting: plant	3	(small)
Cotton textile: plant	2	(small)
Book printing: plant	2	(small)
Plastics: plant	1	(small)
Engineering castings: plant	0.2	5
Footwear: plant	0.2	2

[a] Unless a plant is specified, 'product' refers to one type, model or range of models.
[b] Serving regional submarket.
Source: A. Silberston, 'Economics of scale in theory and practice', *Economic Journal*, 82 (1972), pp. 369–91

Monopoly power

When governments examine industrial firms they like to know to what extent the firms have monopoly or market power. We shall now examine some common indices of this; none of them is flawless.

Lerner index

Under traditional perfect competition the Lerner index, or price–cost ratio, is equal to zero. It is calculated as $(P - \mathrm{MC})/P$ (P is price, MC is marginal cost). In conditions of monopoly it is positive, and the larger the index, it is presumed, the larger is the firm's degree of monopoly power. However, the index depends partly on price elasticity which, although determined in turn partially by industry structure, is also dependent on the nature of the good sold. Second, the index also depends on the level of costs. High marginal costs could give a low index even if monopoly power was great. Third, the index ignores market size. The index might be low for Sainsbury and high for the corner grocer in a suburban housing estate, yet the market power of each is very different. Fourth, it depends on traditional perfect competition theory yet, as we saw, if entry is free and if demand is downward sloping, price can equal average cost and be well above marginal cost, and no monopoly power need be present.

Cross-elasticity of demand

Cross-elasticity of demand is high in conditions of perfect competition and very low in conditions of monopoly. The more acceptable substitutes are, the higher is the index. Note that this measure depends on the acceptability of substitutes to consumers, not on their numbers. But again it rests on traditional theory. If markets are closed rather than open, even if they are 'near-perfect' by other traditional measures, then monopoly power can be high if all suppliers can take or get a price high relative to costs. Regulation-protected industries such as taxi-drivers or chartered accountants could fall into this category.

Ratio of profit rates to interest rates

This index rests on the assumption that, under perfectly competitive conditions, accounting profits are merely the normal return on interest rate on the capital employed in the business. In such circumstances the ratio would equal zero and would become increasingly large as the firm approached monopoly with larger and larger monopoly profits. It ignores the implications of *X*-inefficiency (i.e. operating at less than lowest technological and managerial costs), and it ignores the possibility that supra-normal profits can arise for reasons, such as risk bearing or innovation, other than monopoly.

Competition

We have already noted that while monopoly and perfect competition are regarded as opposites, the use of the words themselves is misleading.

Moreover, since the measures of monopoly described earlier are imperfect, their use as measures of rivalry (as opposed to perfect competition) will also be misleading, possibly more so. Two measures of firm rivalry are the rank correlation coefficient and the Hymer–Pashigian index. Again both of these have faults, but they do shed further light on industrial structure, particularly inter-firm rivalry from a dynamic viewpoint.

A measure of firm turnover (such as the *rank correlation coefficient*) looks at an industry at two points in time. All the firms in the industry are ranked by size in descending order (something like a sports league table) at the opening of the period and again at the close. They are awarded numbers 1, 2, 3 and so on from the leader downwards. The rank correlation coefficient is then calculated.

If the ranking positions of the firms are unchanged a coefficient of +1.0 is obtained (the implication is that the industry is uncompetitive). The more movement there is in the positioning of the firms the lower is the calculated coefficient and the more competitive the market is deemed to be (the possible values range from −1.0 to +1.0). However, while changes in the rank of a firm can be meaningful in economic terms, they need not be. Certainly if a change in rank implies a substantial change in firm size or market share then it may well have meaning. But if there is any tendency for firms in a market to bunch together in size then rank change measures are meaningless. Alternatively, a market can undergo changes of great economic importance but experience no change in firm ranking. For example, a two-firm industry (a duopoly) composed of firms A and B, where A had 51 per cent of the market and B 49 per cent, would produce a rank correlation coefficient of unity even if A's share rose to 99 per cent and B's fell to 1 per cent. Another defect of the index is that it ignores differences in economic importance between the leading and lagging firms. The 'tail' of small firms may influence the calculated coefficient, but it is what is happening between the large firms (or to them if small ones are growing) that matters.

The *Hymer–Pashigian* or *instability index* takes account of all firms, even the smallest, but is only affected by them if they grow substantially. Equally it is only sensitive to the presence of large firms if they experience significant size changes. It is calculated between two points in time by subtracting each firm's share of the industry from its corresponding share at the later or earlier period (whichever is the larger). The differences are then summed. The higher the value of the index the more unstable and hence the more competitive is the market. To illustrate, consider again a duopoly where A and B exchanged ranking but simply moved from a 51:49 to a 49:51 relationship. The rank correlation coefficient would register unity (negatively), the most 'competitive' value. The instability index would register 4. Conversely, had the market shares changed instead from 51:49 to 99:1 the rank correlation coefficient would be +1.0, implying no ranking change, while the instability index would have a value of 96 (as against 4) implying a very high degree of economic change.

Vertical integration

The degree to which an industry is vertically integrated can be measured in at least three ways.

Ratio of value added to sales

Value added (i.e. sales less expenditures for raw materials, fuel and power) to sales will be higher the greater the number of productive stages carried out by the firm. However, input and output price changes will alter the value of the index. Also, other things being equal, a more profitable firm will have a higher ratio than a less profitable one. The index will also be lower, other things being equal, at later stages of production than at earlier, since sales figures will be higher at each successive stage. It is really only of value when comparing firms in the same industry, at the same stage of the productive process, facing the same input and output prices.

Ratio of inventory values to sales

The rationale for this index is that the greater the number of successive stages performed by a firm the greater will be the value of stocks carried. This assumption is not altogether realistic if vertical integration permits economies on stockholding. Also it is dependent on the levels of both input and output prices.

Degree of dependence on input and output markets

An example of this index as a measure of backward integration is the ratio of inter-firm purchases or transfers at a particular stage to total inputs used at that stage. To gauge forward integration total inter-firm transfers of output at a particular stage would be expressed as a proportion of total output at that stage. These ratios will be invariant with input and output price changes since both numerator and denominator involve the use of the same price. Alternatively, volume rather than value data could be used. The main problems will arise around the definition of a 'stage' in the production process.

Diversification

Here two main methods are in common use.

Ratio of non-primary output to total output

The higher is this ratio the more diversified is the firm. The drawback with it as an index is that no indication is given as to whether non-primary output is divided between several industries or confined to only one.

Straight count of industries in which the firm operates

This overcomes the objection to the previous measure but may give undue weight to many activities which account for only a small proportion of the firm's total business. An alternative or additional measure is to use a composite index, such as the arithmetic product of the non-primary output ratio and the straight count. The danger with composite indices, at least if used in isolation, is that they may conceal more than they reveal. For example, a composite index of 3 would be obtained for a firm with a ratio of non-primary to total output of 1:10 and a straight count of 30 industries, as well as for a firm with a ratio of 1:2 and a straight count of six industries.

Small Firms

There is no single universally accepted definition of a 'small firm'. A frequently quoted description comes from the Bolton Committee[5] which argued that a small firm was one which fulfilled the following: (a) it has 'a relatively small share of its market'; (b) 'it is managed by its owners or part-owners in a personalised way'; and (c) it is managed independently in that its owner-managers can make major decisions without reference to outsiders. To operationalize this characterization, seven different statistical criteria were adopted depending on the industry. For example, a manufacturing firm was classified as 'small' if it employed 200 persons or less, whereas a retailing firm required a turnover of £50,000 updated to £185,000 by the Wilson Committee.[6] However, one should not think that the problems and behaviour of firms just above and below these precise values differ substantially; there is gradual transition.

Table 11.13 shows that the size of the small-firm sector decreased between the mid-1930s and late 1960s but has increased considerably since then. Estimates reported by Mayes,[7] shown in table 11.14, indicate that the employment in very small firms (with under 25 employees) increased in both manufacturing and services, but for small firms in general (in each industry sector under 200 employees) the number employed decreased for manufacturing and rose for services. Storey and Johnson[8] have estimated that in the period 1982–4, whilst the number of net new jobs decreased by 270,000 for UK industry, the number created by firms employing less than 100 persons increased by 680,000.

Table 11.15 shows that, on one criterion, a greater proportion of very

Table 11.13 *The share of small firms in UK manufacturing industry*

	Number (% of total)	Net output (% of total)	Employment (% of total)
1935	97	35	38
1958	94	20	24
1968	94	16	19
1980	96.9	21.5	24.3
1987	98.1	24.5	31.1

The figures above and below the rule are not computed on a comparable basis.
Source: Bolton, *Small Firms*, HMSO, 1971; *Business Monitor Census of Production Summary Tables* vol. PA1002, 1980, table 12, and 1987, table 12

small firms – those with turnover under £500,000 – exist in retailing and construction than in any other industry. In addition, over 90 per cent of firms in the agriculture, forestry and fishing, construction, retailing, catering and other service industries have such a low turnover, whereas less than 70 per cent of firms in mining, quarrying, and public utilities and wholesaling and dealing industries are so small.

Many reasons have been given to explain the increasing employment share of small firms. One has been that (as shown in table 11.14) the proportionate increase in employment in service industries has exceeded that in others and that the average firm size in the service sector is much lower than in the manufacturing sector. Another is that when the demand for labour decreases and unemployment increases, it becomes more difficult for the unemployed to find a job and the relative attractiveness of starting a company increases. Further, when recession leads to company

Table 11.14 *Change in employment (thousands) 1981–1984*

	Size of firm (employees) 1–24	25–99	200+	All
All industries and services	+5840	−790	−7230	−2180
Manufacturing	+590	−1210	−6030	−6650
Services	+5140	+1280	−290	+6130
Distributive trades	+1580	+130	+110	+1820
Banking, finance, insurance	+1720	+940	+180	+2840

Industries classified according to 1980 SIC.
Source: D. Mayes, 'Small firms in the UK economy', *Royal Bank of Scotland Review* (December 1989)

Table 11.15 *Industry distribution of very small firms 1989*

	Number of firms with turnover less than £500,000	Percentage of all industry	Percentage of that industry
Agriculture, forestry, fishing	112,421	7.8	96.2
Mining, quarrying, public utilities	904	0.6	61.5
Manufacturing	112,333	7.8	76.4
Construction	197,613	13.7	90.8
Transport	56,882	3.9	85.9
Postal services and communications	891	0.6	85.5
Wholesaling and dealing	79,729	5.5	68.1
Retailing	238,185	16.5	94.5
Finance, property and professional services	104,614	7.3	88.4
Catering	121,606	8.4	97.0
Motor trades	58,522	4.1	78.3
Business services and central offices	83,923	5.8	87.7
Other services	101,501	7.0	93.8
		100	

Source: calculated from *Business Monitor Size Analysis of UK Businesses*, vol. PA 1003, 1989

rationalization firms may contract out more processes, so increasing the demand for products from outside firms – some of which will be newly formed to meet this demand. In addition, it has been argued that cultural changes in UK society have led people to be more willing to attempt risky ventures, such as starting a new firm, and have meant that company failure is less frowned on socially than before. A further reason is that changes in technology have reduced minimum efficient firm size for some industries and recent technical advances have increased the demand for small equipment installation and training specialists. Greater government assistance for the creation and development of small firms such as the Enterprise Allowance Scheme and Loan Guarantee Scheme have also played a part. Reduced income tax rates may have increased incentives for owner-managers.

However, small firms have had, and still face, a number of difficulties when trying to grow. Several surveys on this topic have been conducted;

Table 11.16 *Problems experienced by small firms in early years*

	Fast growth (%)	Matched (%)
Shortage of suppliers	25	30
Shortage of skilled labour	45	50
High labour turnover	20	10
High wage costs	20	0
Government bureaucracy	25	35
Obtaining payments from large debtors	45	35
Demand shortages	20	35
Shortages of key management skills	60	40
VAT registration	0	5
Obtaining finance	20	10
Time constraints on management team	35	35
Other	15	45

Source: D. Storey, R. Watson and P. Wynarczyk, 'Fast growth of small businesses', Department of Employment Research Paper 67, 1989

the results of one recent investigation are shown in table 11.16. Since new firms are usually small, surveys of new firms are also relevant (table 11.17). In the former survey the owner-managers of 20 fast growing small firms and 20 small firms of the same industrial sector and age were interviewed. The results suggested that the most serious problems facing small firms

Table 11.17 *Difficulties faced by firms new to Cleveland during their first year of operation*

	Percentage of respondents	Percentage of total number of mentions
Shortages of demand	23.2	22.4
Skill shortages	23.9	21.9
Supply shortages	15.1	13.4
High wage costs	13.2	11.4
Industrial disputes	5.7	5.0
Other	15.7	18.4
	100.0	100.0

Number of respondents, 159; number of mentions, 201.
Source: D. J. Storey, 'The problems facing small firms', *Journal of Management Studies*, 22 (3), 1985

were shortages of key management skills followed by shortages of skilled labour, obtaining payments from large debtors, government bureaucracy, demand shortages and time constraints on the management team.

Concerning lack of management skills, Storey et al.[9] discuss three types of problem. First, they argue that sometimes firms are not large enough to justify the hiring of specialist managers, e.g. a production director. Second, the hiring of an unsuitable manager can be more serious in a small firm than in a large one. Finally managers in small firms often lack time to consider the long-term strategy of the firm. Bosworth and Jacobs[10] also note a lack of skills in the areas of finance and long-term market planning in particular and point out that in small firms owner-managers lack time to learn new skills and that several studies[11] have criticized the quality of available training. In January 1988 the Department of Trade and Industry published a White Paper (Command 278) announcing the launch of the enterprise initiatives whereby managers of small and medium-sized firms can gain funding to employ consultants to help them with design, marketing and quality management and with manufacturing systems, business planning and financial and information systems. The difficulties of finding skilled labour refer to both the suitability of labour and the lack of skill amongst job applicants.

Other surveys have found slightly different results. For example, the difficulty of raising finance has been noted by the Macmillan, Bolton and Wilson Committees[12] and various precise descriptions of these difficulties have been proposed as follows. Here we follow the categorization of Hall and Lewis.[13]

(1) Hall and Lewis note that it has been alleged that small firms face difficulties 'in raising small amounts of equity capital'. The Wilson Committee and Binks and Vale[14] found evidence of a decrease in the proportion of long-term capital supplied by people who personally knew the entrepreneur. This has been attributed to the high rates of personal taxation, by greater amount of information available about others sources of finance and lower levels of wealth leading to greater risk aversion. A CBI survey[15] found that small firms had great difficulty in raising funds in the region £50,000–£100,000. Hall[16] argues that venture capitalists will rarely supply less than £200,000 of funds and usually prefer to offer over £250,000.

(2) It has been alleged that some small firms may be viable but are unjustifiably discriminated against by banks. For example, Robson Rhodes[17] have criticized bank managers for lack of skill in appraising business proposals and for relying on an evaluation of the person rather than the business. However, the National Economic Development Council (NEDC)[18] notes that many banks have since introduced schemes to give term loans over five to 20 years, which reduce small firms' reliance on short-term loans, and to give capital holidays. But this, it argues, does not

relieve the fundamental need which is for a higher proportion of start-up equity funding.

In 1983 the Government introduced the Business Expansion Scheme which was designed to increase personal equity investment in unquoted independent companies in certain sectors. Up to £40,000 per annum can be invested but it cannot be removed in less than five years; it is allowed against income tax. Hall,[19] however, criticizes the scheme in that investors have had to wait up to two years for tax rebates, and both Hall and NEDC argue that the overwhelming majority of funds received were £100,000 or more, suggesting that firms needing smaller amounts may not have received them.

(3) The Wilson Committee found that small firms are required to supply a rather high level of security. It found that banks are willing to accept gearing ratios of 100 per cent, whereas ratios of 200 or 300 per cent are common in European countries and in a survey of firms in Nottingham ratios around 25 per cent were observed. Binks and Vale[20] found consistent results. Berry, Hall and Lewis[21] found no evidence to suggest that venture capitalists were less demanding. Wilson argued that the requirement of a high level of security may be a substitute for bank managers spending time evaluating the viability of a small firm in view of the lack of financial expertise on the part of the management but that the level of gearing was not a good guide to such viability or to management commitment.

In response to the Wilson Committee's recommendations, the Small Business Loan Gurantee Scheme was introduced by the government in 1981. This encourages banks to make medium-term loans to small firms where the risks would otherwise have been considered too high. The Government underwrites 70 per cent of the loan and the borrower plays 2½ per cent of the guaranteed loan outstanding. However, Robson Rhodes[22] argues that 47 per cent of the loans made in the early 1980s under the scheme would have been made anyway. Finally, Hall and Lewis[23] found evidence from a series of interviews that regional government agencies (Welsh Development Agency, Scottish Development Agency etc.) were willing to accept less security than banks.

(4) The Wilson Committee[24] also found that small firms were required to pay rates of interest up to 2 per cent above those paid by larger firms and by implication argued that this was too much, notwithstanding the administrative costs of a small loan and the costs of investigation due to inadequate business plans. One possible justification for a higher rate is that smaller firms may be riskier than larger firms because of their lack of track record. Hall and Lewis[25] note that a premium remains and there is currently no evidence to confirm or refute the argument by banks that the

premium is the minimum justified on commercial grounds. They found no evidence to suggest that government regional agencies charged lower interest rates than other debtor suppliers.

(5) Hall[26] notes that venture capitalists appear to prefer investing in London and the southeast. A regional bias was noted in the Business Expansion Scheme too. He argues that over 60 per cent of venture capital companies are created in London and 60 per cent of the companies to which they supplied equity were located in the southeast. However, evidence is as yet unavailable about whether this distribution of funds is unjustified.[27]

References

1 S. W. Davies and R. E. Caves, *Britain's Productivity Lag*, Cambridge University Press, 1987.
2 J. S. Bain, *Barriers to New Competition*, Harvard University Press, 1956.
3 F. M. Scherer, A. Beckstein, E. Kaufer and R. D. Murphy, *The Economics of Multiplant Operations*, Harvard University Press, 1975.
4 B. Curry and K. D. George. 'Industrial concentration: a survey', *Journal of Industrial Economics* 31 (3) (1983).
5 *Report of the Committee of Inquiry on Small Firms* (Bolton Committee), Cmnd 4811, HMSO, November 1971.
6 *The Financing of Small Firms: Interim Report of the Committee to Review the Functioning of the Financial Industry* (Wilson Committee), Cmnd 7503, HMSO, 1979.
7 D. Mayes, 'Small firms in the UK economy', *Royal Bank of Scotland Review* (December 1989).
8 D. J. Storey and S. Johnson, 'Are small firms the answer to unemployment', Employment Institute, London, 1987.
9 D. J. Storey, R. Watson and P. Wynarczyk, 'Fast growth small businesses', Research Paper 67, Department of Employment, 1989.
10 D. Bosworth and C. Jacobs, 'Management attitudes, behaviour and abilities as barriers to growth' in J. Barber, J. S. Metcalfe and M. Porteous (eds) *Barriers to Growth in Small Firms*, London: Routledge, 1989.
11 J. Boswell, *The Rise and Decline of Small Firms*, London: George Allen & Unwin, 1973.
12 *Report of the Committee on Finance and Industry* (Macmillan Committee), Cmnd 3897, HMSO, June 1931.
Bolton Committee.
Wilson Committee.
13 G. Hall and P. Lewis, 'Development agencies and the supply of finance to small firms', *Applied Economics* (1988).
14 M. Binks and P. Vale, 'Finance for the new firm', NUSFU Paper 2, University of Nottingham.
15 CBI, *Finance for Smaller Firms – Local Investment Companies*, 1987.

16 G. Hall, 'Lack of finance as constraint on the expenditure of innovatory small firms', in J. Barber, J. S. Metcalfe and M. Porteous (eds), *Barriers to Growth in Small Firms*, Routledge, 1989.

17 Robson Rhodes, *An Analysis of some Early Claims Under the Small Business Loan Guarantee Scheme*, Department of Trade and Industry, 1984.

18 National Economic Development Council, *External Capital for Small Firms*, 1986.

19 Hall, 'Lack of finance as constraint'.

20 Binks and Vale, 'Finance for the new firm'.

21 A. J. Berry, G. C. Hall and P. Lewis, 'A cost–benefit study of GMEDC', *Report to the Ten NorthWest Districts*, 1986.

22 Rhodes, *An Analysis of some Early Claims.*

23 Hall and Lewis, 'Development agencies'.

24 Wilson Committee.

25 Hall and Lewis 'Development agencies'.

26 Hall, 'Lack of finance as constraint'.

27 Hall and Lewis 'Development agencies'.

Further reading

M. Caw, M. Owen, T. Renier and M. Yaks, 'A study to determine the reasons for the failure of small businesses in the UK', London Business School, First Year Student Project, 1987.

'Small firms', *Midland Bank Review* (Spring 1987).

'Small business: a quiet transformation', *Economic Progress Report* (October 1989).

D. J. Storey, 'The problems facing small firms', *Journal of Management Studies* (1985).

12

Public Enterprise

Introduction

The aim of this chapter is to review the size of the public enterprise sector of the UK economy, the economic theory concerning the pricing objectives of public enterprises, the objectives set for them by past governments and the performance of such enterprises and finally to evaluate arguments for and against their return to private ownership.

Size of the Sector

If the provision of goods and services only by national governments is considered, three main forms of public ownership have been adopted in the UK. The first is the organization of the industry as a government department directly controlled by a minister. The only significant example has been the Post Office until 1969 and no significant example remains in 1990. In the second form the government possesses a majority or sole shareholding in an otherwise normal company. Examples include British Petroleum until the mid-1970s, the British Sugar Corporation until 1981 and British Leyland (now the Rover Group) until 1989. In many cases the shares were held by the government through the National Enterprise Board (renamed the British Technology Group in 1981), a state-owned organization to provide industrial finance and to act as a holding company. The third and most significant form of public ownership is the public corporation. Examples include the National Coal Board, British Railways Board, etc. Yarrow and Vickers[1] list the main distinguishing features as follows:

1 it is a corporate body with its own legal existence;
2 it is not controlled in detail by Parliament;
3 the relevant minister can give general directions concerning certain functions;

4 the minister appoints the board of management;
5 it is financially independent.

Few data are available for the public sector in aggregate, but some idea of the size of public corporations relative to the rest of the economy is given in table 12.1.

Table 12.1 *The importance of public corporations*

Year	No. employed in public corporations/total employment (%)	GDP of public corporations/GDP (%)
1950		8.34
1952		10.19
1954		10.00
1956		9.11
1958		8.71
1960		8.73
1962		10.38
1964		10.21
1966	7.74	9.95
1968	8.33	10.81
1970	8.19	10.36
1972	7.91	10.23
1974	7.83	10.70
1976	7.89	11.79
1978	8.24	11.05
1980	8.05	10.76
1982	7.34	11.25
1984	6.64	9.24
1986	4.84	7.78
1988	3.53	5.44

Source: *National Income and Expenditure* (various issues); *National Accounts*, 1989

The most active period in which activities were taken into public ownership was 1945–51. In this period the Transport Act of 1947 established the British Transport Commission which organized the nationalization of the various private railway companies and road haulage and bus companies. In 1947 the National Coal Board acquired almost every coalmining company in Britain and under the 1948 Gas Act all gas companies were nationalized. The generation of electricity was nationalized in 1948, the distribution of electricity having been in public ownership since 1926. The steel industry was first nationalized in 1951, under a Labour Government, denationalized in 1953 under the Conservative Party and renationalized in 1967 under another Labour Government.

The share in both employment and gross domestic product (GDP) of the public sector increased only slowly during the late 1960s until 1978, but fell considerably thereafter such that in 1988 public corporations employed only 3.53 per cent of the employed UK workforce and produced only 5.44 per cent of the UK GDP. The reduction in the proportion of employment provided by public corporations has been due to two factors: privatization and a greater rate of productivity increase compared with other industries. Both will be discussed later in this chapter.

Table 12.2 lists those corporations still publicly owned at the end of May 1991 together with a list of corporations privatized since 1979. If the two lists are combined it can be seen that in 1979, when public corporations were arguably of greatest aggregate relative size, they predominated in the fuel and power, transport, water and sewage, communications and iron and steel sectors. In 1991 public ownership is no longer the predominant form of ownership in any major sector.

Table 12.2 *(a) Nationalized industries and public corporations as at 31 May 1991; (b) corporations privatized since 1979*

Audit Commission
Bank of England (Banking Department)
British Broadcasting Corporation
British Coal
British Railways Board
British Shipbuilders
British Technology Group
British Waterways Board
Caledonian MacBrayne
Civil Aviation Authority
Commonwealth Development Corporation
Covent Garden Market Authority
Crown Agents
The Crown Suppliers
Development Board for Rural Wales
English Industrial Estates Corporation
Highlands and Islands Enterprise (formerly Highlands and Islands Development Board)
Independent Television Commission
Land Authority for Wales
Local authority airports
Local authority bus companies
London Regional Transport
New Town Development Corporations and Commission
Northern Ireland Electricity Service
Northern Ireland Housing Executive

Northern Ireland Transport Holding Company
Nuclear Electric
Oil and Pipelines Agency
Post Office
Royal Mint
Scottish Enterprise (formerly Scottish Development Agency)
Scottish Nuclear
Scottish Homes
Scottish Bus Group
HMSO
Trust Ports in Northern Ireland
UK Atomic Energy Authority
Urban development corporations
Welsh Development Agency
Welsh Fourth Channel Authority

(b) Major corporations privatized since 1979

Corporation	Date of privatization	
British Petroleum		1979, 1983, 1987
British Aerospace	February	1981
Cable and Wireless	October	1981
Amersham International	February	1982
National Freight Corporation	February	1982
Britoil		1982
Associated British Ports	February	1983
Enterprise Oil	June	1984
Jaguar	July	1984
British Telecom	November	1984
Trust Ports in Great Britain	April	1985
British Gas	December	1986
British Airways	February	1987
Royal Ordnance	April	1987
Rolls Royce		1987
British Airports Authority	July	1987
National Bus Company	April	1988
Rover Group		1988
British Steel	December	1988
Regional Water Authorities in England and Wales	December	1989
Girobank	July	1990
Regional electricity companies in England and Wales	December	1990
National Power and Powergen	March	1991
Scottish Power and Scottish Hydroelectric	May	1991

Source: *National Accounts*, 1990; *Economic Briefing*, December 1990; HM Treasury; *Public Expenditure Analyses to 1993–4*, Cmnd 1520.

The original reasons why certain activities were taken into public ownership were very heterogeneous. The reasons for initiating the nationalization programmes of the late 1940s were first to enable economies of scale to be gained by combining small firms with relatively low outputs into one organization. So, for example, duplicated facilities could be reduced and resources released for other uses. Second, it was thought that government control over basic industries would enable the government to plan the post-war development of the economy more effectively. Third, by nationalizing various industries it was hoped that the working conditions of their employees would be improved. However, in some cases other reasons held. For example Rolls-Royce and British Leyland were nationalized to avoid company failure, British Petroleum was nationalized so that the government could secure oil supplies for the Navy, and the British Sugar Corporation was acquired to promote the UK production of sugar beet in case of war.

The Economic Theory of Public Enterprise Pricing

Economists have argued that under certain circumstances social welfare would be greatest if all industries were in equilibrium (no incentive to adjust price or output) with price equal to marginal cost. To understand this consider a monopoly where the monopolist has lower average costs than any smaller firms could have had. This is called a natural monopoly. It may have been formed by the nationalization of all previously independent suppliers or it may be the result of a competitive process whereby only one firm can survive with the lowest possible average costs. The industry firms' demand curve would be that of the firm and, if it chose the profit-maximizing output, it would produce Q at price P in figure 12.1.

This has two unattractive results. First, in contrast with price takers (but in common with other price searchers) price exceeds marginal cost. When this is so, too little of the good is being produced in the sense that the value consumers place on having one more unit (price) is greater than the additional cost of producing it (marginal cost). Whatever price is set, consumers adjust their purchases so that the marginal value they place on the last unit they buy is just equal to the price they pay for it. When an additional unit of a good is produced, resources are taken from producing something else. Since the marginal cost of producing a good is the marginal value consumers place on the forgone good, and if a monopolist sets price above marginal cost then the marginal value placed on the good by consumers is greater than the marginal values they place on goods they might have bought instead. Resources are not going to their highest-valued uses. If the resources were diverted to the goods and services with the

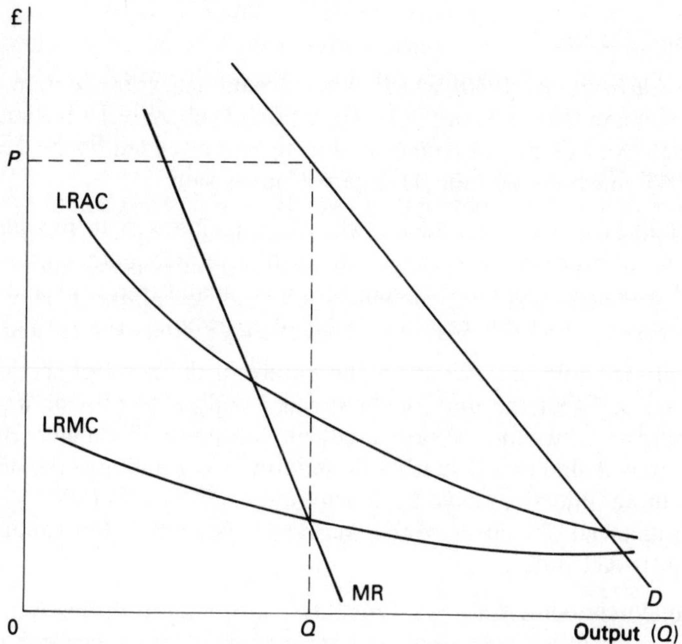

Figure 12.1 *Natural monopoly: profit maximization*

highest marginal value, society would gain because the value placed on the unit forgone would be less than that placed on the unit gained.

If all such readjustments had been made in all activities such that afterwards price equalled marginal cost in every case and any further reallocation would increase the satisfaction of any one person only if that of someone else were reduced, the economy is said to be *allocatively efficient*. This concept of efficiency is based on a value judgement by V. Pareto, a nineteenth-century economist, who believed that social welfare was maximized if all resource reallocations between activities had been made such that any further reallocation would make someone better off only by making someone else worse off.

Objectives

The objectives of public corporations are laid down in their statutes, a series of White Papers and various government requirements placed upon them.

Original Statutes

The statutes of the 1940s which enacted nationalization contain various general statements relating to two types of objectives: technical and financial. An example of technical objectives is provided by the Transport Act 1947 which created the Transport Commission:

> It shall be the general duty of the Commission . . . to provide, or secure or promote the provision of an efficient, adequate, economical and properly integrated system of public inland transport and port facilities . . . with due regard to safety of operation. (section 3(I),p. 8)

Typically the relevant Act states the nature of the good or service to be provided and that the duty of the created body is to provide a good or service in an 'efficient', 'co-ordinated' and 'economical' manner. But none of the Acts define precisely what these terms mean and how the degree to which these objectives have been achieved can be measured.

The financial objectives of the Acts are very similar. For example, the Transport Act states:

> The Commission shall . . . subject to the provisions of this Act, levy such fares, rates, tolls, dues and other charges, as to secure that the revenue of the Commission is not less than sufficient for making provision for the meeting of charges properly chargeable to revenue, taking one year with another. (Section 3(4), p. 9).

Coal Industry Nationalisation Act 1946 states:

> The Policy of the Board shall be . . . that the revenues of the Board shall not be less than sufficient for meeting all their outgoings properly chargeable to revenue account . . . on an average of good and bad years. (Section 4(c), p. 3).

Notice that the items to be subtracted from revenue include interest, depreciation, redemption of capital and provision for reserves. These Acts have been criticized in that they do not state over how many years the revenue may be compared with costs nor describe pricing or investment rules nor define what is meant by 'efficient' or 'economical' provision. The original statutes were sometimes modified by subsequent Acts.

1961 White Paper

In the 1961 White Paper it was argued that over the period 1954–9 the annual rate of return for most public corporations was considerably below that of private sector firms in the manufacturing and distribution industries. It was acknowledged that this may be because the former often faced regulation due to their monopoly power (unlike private companies public corporations had been under public pressure to increase prices by less than general inflation) and that public sector companies face non-commercial obligations which those in the private sector do not. Nevertheless it was argued that

> if the profitability on capital development is assessed on different (and easier) financial criteria from those adopted in industry generally there is a risk that too much of the nation's savings will be diverted into the nationalised industries. (Section 15, p. 6)

and that if prices were too low demand would be artificially stimulated.

It was then argued that the rates of return of most public enterprises *were* too low and, to ensure that the nationalized industry achieved an appropriate balance between financial and non-financial obligations, their performance had to be monitored more closely than before. Therefore nationalized industries were to

1 at least break even over a five-year period and
2 make provision from revenue for
   (a) the difference between historic cost depreciation and replacement cost depreciation
   (b) capital development and premature obsolescence.

The nationalized industries were to be given precise financial objectives usually in terms of an average rate or return. The rate would differ between industries according to their circumstances. Many criticisms have been made of the proposals. Webb[2] argued that the appropriate target rates of return were those expected on new private sector investment and those which had been achieved in the past. Vickers and Yarrow[3] pointed out that the White Paper did not state whether the targets were to be met by reducing costs or by raising prices (when monopoly power was held).

1967 White Paper

The 1967 White Paper defined more precisely the investment and pricing rules which nationalized industries were to follow. The proposals were as follows.

1 Investment projects must give a similar financial rate of return to those in the private sector (unless a lower rate is justifiable when social benefits and costs are considered). Each project must initially be evaluated in terms of its net present value (NPV) (see page 175) using a *test discount rate* (TDR). The TDR 'represents the minimum rate of return to be expected on a marginal low-risk project undertaken for commercial reasons' (Section 9). A TDR of 8 per cent in real terms was set initially for most nationalized industries (and raised to 10 per cent in 1969). While the industry should be concerned with the financial return 'the Government's objective is to secure maximum social return on the capital invested' (Section 14).

2 Some projects which have a negative NPV using benefits and costs private to the industry may be given government approval if it is believed that when values are imputed for social benefits and costs the NPV is positive, i.e. cost–benefit studies would need to be completed.
3 Prices must be set equal to long-run marginal costs except when excess capacity exists, because of a downturn in demand, for example, and then prices should be set equal to short-run marginal costs.
4 Prices must be set so as to attract resources to activities where they most effectively produce goods and services which satisfy the needs of customers. Therefore, except in situations where the fulfilment of social obligations require, cross-subsidization should be avoided.
5 Financial objectives continue to be necessary and will be set taking into account 'return on new investment, soundly based pricing policy, social obligations not covered by a subsidy, efficient operation, national prices and incomes policy'.

The 1967 White Paper was based on economic theory. The TDR was set at a value which represented the real rate of return forgone by society if it invested resources in projects in the public sector rather than in the private sector and so aimed to ensure maximum overall rate of return. The marginal cost pricing rule was based on the required condition for allocative efficiency explained above.

However, the White Paper had a number of limitations. Vickers and Yarrow[4] argue that the White Paper omitted incentive structures to induce managers to act according to the proposals so that where managers had discretion they pursued their own objectives and not those intended for the industries. For example, the new cash inflows forecast in each year to be discounted by the TDR could easily be adjusted to give a positive NPV if managers wished to invest in a particular project. Heald[5] argued that the White Paper did not indicate how the TDR criterion should be modified if the government was unwilling to authorize funds for every project which had a positive NPV. Furthermore, the White Paper did not state which rule – price equal to marginal cost, TDR or financial objective – would have precedence if they were inconsistent. This might arise if the financial target was set at a higher level than could be earned if all projects were appraised using TDR and long-run marginal cost (LRMC) pricing was implemented. In industries with declining long-run average cost (LRAC) curves, LRMC is less than LRAC (see figure 12.1). So setting price at LRMC implies setting price below LRAC which conflicts with any positive financial target and the White Paper's insistence that accounting costs be covered by revenue.

In the event, evidence from four nationalized industries suggests that the LRMC pricing guidelines were rarely implemented.[6] Heald[7] argues that a reason for this was the use of the restraint on nationalized industries price increases as a macroeconomic policy variable to control inflation. Indeed, for this reason, because of the possible conflict between TDR, LRMC pricing and financial targets, the government's use of nationalized industry pricing to redistribute income between sectors of society, and the complexity of setting and monitoring LMRC pricing, Heald argues that the 1967 pricing guidelines were a 'failure'.

1978 White Paper

In the late 1970s the Labour Government believed that the nationalized industries had been mismanaged owing to the government policies requiring them to restrain price increases in the early 1970s and to the suspension of financial targets and of marginal cost pricing policies outlined in the 1967 White Paper. The 1978 White Paper described various government policies as follows to correct the situation.

1 To ensure that funds are allocated to the most productive activities, the return on capital from the best alternative investments must be taken into account. But as the National Economic Development Organization[8] reported, because many nationalized industry projects were regarded as part of an existing system or necessary to maintain safety they were not appraised by applying the TDR. So the White Paper proposed that new investment as a whole which a nationalized industry intends to make should have a positive NPV when discounted by the rate of return which the resources could have earned in an alternative use: the required rate of return (RRR). The RRR was initially set at 5 per cent pre-tax in real terms because this was the forecast rate of return for private sector companies.
2 For those industries with some monopoly power, the government will set financial targets. A separate target will be set for each industry. It will be set after consideration of 'return from effective cost conscious management of existing and new assets; market prospects; the scope for improved productivity and efficiency; the opportunity cost of capital; the implications for the PSBR [public sector borrowing requirement]; counter inflation policy; and social or sectoral objectives for, e.g. the energy and transport industries' (Section 73).
3 Prices are to be set to achieve the financial target; LRMC prices would not be reinstated. Cross-subsidization of, for example, off-peak users by peak users should be avoided.
4 Industries with monopoly power may be able to achieve their financial target by raising prices rather than by increased efficiency. So to give an indication of increases in efficiency each nationalized industry was to publish a series of performance indicators. These have included productivity and unit cost indices.
5 In addition to the above, the 1978 White Paper briefly outlined the 1977 White Paper on cash limits (subsequently known as external financing limits (EFLs)). These proposed annual limits to be set on the annual

change in net indebtedness of public corporations. Nationalized industries raised medium- and long-term external finance by

(a) interest-bearing loans from the National Loan Fund;
(b) the issue of Public Dividend Capital, equivalent to equity sold to the government;
(c) non-interest-bearing government grants;
(d) borrowings from overseas lenders.

Short-term external finance is provided by banks. The EFL relates to all of these (in these calculations private sector loans are treated as if they are from the government). The EFL for an industry is therefore the maximum difference between revenue and current and capital expenditure which it can incur.

According to the 1978 White Paper: 'the Government sees this control over financial requirements as a proper discipline on the industries' financial management and the industries accept it as such. It allows departments to keep in close touch with developments in the industries' short term financial position . . .' (Section 82). But subsequently the EFLs have been set partly with regard to the level of PSBR, since all nationalized industries' external finance is treated as part of the PSBR which in turn is a variable used to effect macroeconomic policy. The PSBR can be reduced by reducing the EFLs of nationalized industries.

A number of criticisms have been made of the 1978 White Paper. For example Heald[9] argued that, like the 1961 TDR criterion, the RRR investment rate does not indicate how investment should be appraised when the amount of capital available to invest is rationed. In addition, for an optimum allocation of resources each investment project must be considered separately whereas the RRR criterion applies to an investment programme as a whole. The value of the RRR to be used was the forecast rate of return on the private sector capital stock as a whole, not on marginal investments. Yet the yield forgone when resources are invested by a nationalized industry is that on a marginal investment. The White Paper did not resolve the difficulty that a financial target may not encourage greater internal efficiency but may instead result in higher prices. The White Paper indicates that the RRR is applied to an industry's investment programme to determine the marginal cost of fixed assets to which are added other marginal costs to arrive at marginal total costs. This may be used to set prices. But the White Paper also states that the RRR is one of many factors which the government considers to set an industry's financial target. This 'will not depend simply on consideration of resource allocation, but also on the weight given to social, sectoral and wider economic policies such as the need to counter inflation' (appendix 1). So not only do these approaches suggest that the RRR, financial targets and pricing rules may be inconsistent but the objectives of the targets are also unclear. Heald lists three possibilities: to increase internal efficiency, to act as a kind of indirect tax to raise government revenue and to reallocate profits from producers to the government.

Turning to the pricing guidelines of the White Paper, while the reasons for the failure of the 1967 proposals are acknowledged, they are not corrected. Instead, LRMC pricing is replaced by a delegation of rules to the industries themselves, with very ambiguous statements as to which should be followed.

Finally, criticisms have been made of the EFL system outlined and implemented. For example, despite the White Paper's statement of the role of the cash limits, they do not necessarily induce or indicate internal efficiency. Instead they could, to some extent, be met by raised prices, lower service quality or reduced capital expenditure. Curwen[10] has noted that there is no satisfactory mechanism to impose sanctions on industries which do not meet their EFLs.

Performance

Economists use the term 'efficiency' in various senses. 'Allocative efficiency' was explained in section 12.2 as being an allocation of resources such that for an additional unit of a good or service the marginal utility which customers obtain (represented by price) equals marginal cost so that the optimum distribution of outputs exists. 'Technical efficiency' occurs when the maximum output is obtained from each quantity of inputs (and so each firm would be optimally located, each worker would be putting in maximum effort to maximize output, the most efficient organizational structure would be used etc.).

Allocative efficiency

Unfortunately, there is insufficient information to be able to tell how allocatively efficient public corporations have been. Table 12.3 compares the financial performance of public corporations with that of industrial and commercial companies. Throughout the period 1970–89 the rate of return to public corporations when subsidies are included has been around one-third that of industrial and commercial companies, and when subsidies to the public corporations are excluded their rate of return is only one-quarter that of the industrial and commercial sector.

These figures can be interpreted in different ways. It can be argued that the public corporations have been more allocatively efficient than industrial and commercial companies. The original statutes intended public corporations to act in a way consistent with maximizing social welfare. Many public corporations of the period have economies of scale, e.g. British Telecom, electricity, water, and in figure 12.1 we showed that LRMCs are less than LRACs when economies of scale exist. So LRMC

Table 12.3 *Financial performance of public corporations and private companies*

Year	Public corporations: Gross trading surplus as a proportion of net assets[a] (%)	Public corporations: Gross trading surplus net of subsidies as a proportion of net assets[b] (%)	Private companies: Gross trading profits as a proportion of net assets[c] (%)
1970	6.3	5.6	18.1
1972	5.7	4.4	18.2
1974	4.9	2.5	16.9
1976	6.2	5.0	15.4
1978	6.5	5.3	17.1
1980	4.7	3.6	15.5
1981	5.6	4.2	15.2
1982	6.6	5.0	16.6
1983	6.7	4.9	18.8
1984	6.2	3.5	19.2
1985	5.2	2.9	20.4
1986	6.2	4.6	16.8
1987	5.1	3.8	18.4
1988	5.2	4.1	18.7
1989	4.2	3.2	17.4

[a] Gross trading surplus for the public corporations before depreciation and including stock appreciation as a proportion of net capital stock at current replacement cost.
[b] Gross trading surplus for the public corporations before depreciation and including stock appreciation after deduction of subsidies as a proportion of net capital stock at current replacment cost.
[c] Gross trading profits for industrial and commercial companies before depreciation and including stock appreciation as a proportion of net capital stock at current replacement cost.
Source: *CSO Macroeconomic Data Bank*, December 1990; Central Statistical Office

pricing – consistent with acting in the public interest – *results in losses*. So the private sector is pricing considerably further above LRMCs than the public corporations are.

Alternatively, Vickers and Yarrow[11] suggest that the rates of return for public corporations have been too far below those of the private sector for the purely allocative efficiency argument to be valid. They support their argument by listing cases where detailed studies of an industry have indicated that LRMC pricing has not been adhered to. For example, domestic coal prices were found by the Monopolies and Mergers Commission to be well above marginal opportunity costs and Hammond et al.[12] found that, before privatization, gas prices were below LRMC and did not reflect the within-year variation in supply costs. Therefore Vickers and Yarrow conclude that the main cause of the relatively low rates of return in the public sector has been overinvestment and internal inefficiency. Molyneaux and Thompson[13] in a review of various individual nationalized industries came to similar conclusions arguing that there had been 'an almost complete failure to implement the principles of marginal cost pricing'. In addition, in most cases (electricity being an exception) cross-subsidization between consumers took place. This was especially true of the National Coal Board and until the mid-1980s of British Telecom also. The deviations from marginal cost pricing were not found to have been socially evaluated in comparison with alternative strategies.

Technical efficiency

In this section we compare the productivity of nationalized industries with that of privately owned firms. Several methods have been followed. One is to compare the productivity of UK nationalized industries with that of public and private companies of the same industry in other countries. Overall these studies suggest that, with some exceptions, UK nationalized industry productivity was lower in the 1970s than that of foreign counterparts. For example, Pryke[14] found that privately owned US electricity generating plants had only 30 per cent of the workers per unit of capital as the British Electricity Boards; the French nationalized industry had 50 per cent of the workers per capital unit. Between 1968 and 1979 the increase in output per man-shift of the National Coal Board was considerably less than that for Poland, France, Belgium and Germany. During the 1970s British Rail's train miles per man-hour was 'only about a third as great as in France, Belgium, Holland, Sweden and Norway'. Pryke found the number of weighted items per worker for the Post Office in 1978 was greater in Holland, the US, Sweden and Australia but lower in Germany, France and Belgium.

However, such comparisons are of limited usefulness. First, the number of foreign comparisons is small in Pryke's study. Second, and more importantly, the degree to which any differences in productivity between UK and foreign firms are due to the public ownership of the former is unclear. As Vickers and Yarrow argue, during the period of many of these studies the productivity of UK firms was generally lower than that of foreign firms, regardless of whether or not they were in public ownership.

One way of evaluating the extent to which maximum output is obtained from given inputs is to derive a relationship between these two variables using data from comparable firms. One such study was conducted by Pryke[15] who compared the performance of each of three public enterprises with three private companies operating in the same industry. In all three cases the publicly owned company was less productive than the private company. For example, privately owned European Ferries were found to have 80 per cent more turnover, considerably higher profit rates and considerably more vehicles per crossing of the English Channel than publicly owned Sealink UK. Similarly, the performance of publicly owned British Airways was inferior to that of British Caledonian, and that of the British Gas Corporation and Electricity Boards at selling appliances was below that of private sector Curry's and Comet. Pryke concluded that the main reason for the differences in performance was that public ownership reduced the incentive for managerial efficiency.

Such data are not usually available, however, because nationalized industries are often monopolists. Faced with this difficulty many researchers have compared productivity trends. The Treasury in *Economic Progress Report*[16] compared the productivity change for nationalized industries as a whole with that for other sectors of the economy. Thus figure 12.2 shows that the output per person employed by nationalized industries grew at about the same rate between 1974–5 and 1980–1 as for manufacturing but grew slightly faster over the period 1980–1 to 1986–7. The *Economic Progress Report* attributes the difference in labour productivity growth to the reduction by the nationalized industries of their previous overmanning and greater managerial efficiency (due to tighter financial targets).

Comparisons of the rate of productivity growth have also been made

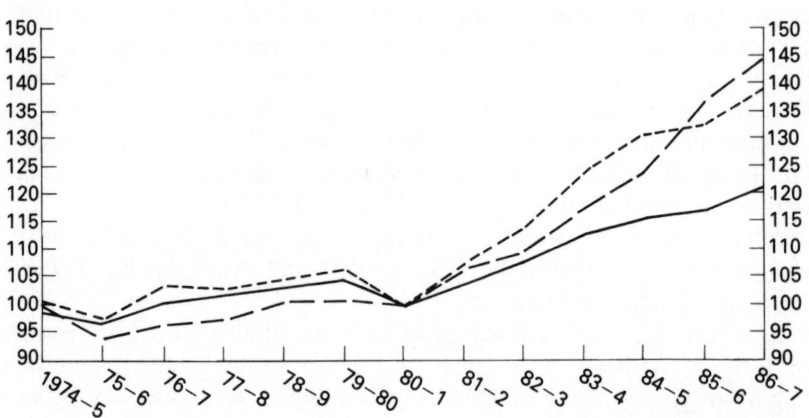

Figure 12.2 *Output per person employed in nationalized and other industries: ——, whole economy (excluding North Sea oil and non-trading public sector; – – –, manufacturing; — —, nationalized industries (public sector at end 1987–8, excluding Girobank and British Shipbuilders (Merchant)); 1980–1 = 100. The 1984–5 and 1985–6 figures for output from nationalized industries and the whole economy have been adjusted to exclude the effect of the coal strike (Source*: HM Treasury, *Economic Progress Report 193*, December 1987)

between individual nationalized industries and the UK manufacturing sector as a whole. A recent study by Molyneaux and Thompson[17] has shown that the growth rate of output per head and of total factor productivity was typically greater in 1978–85 than in 1968–78 and that, in the case of output per head (data are unavailable for total factor productivity), most (seven out of nine) nationalized industries had growth rates above the average for UK manufacturing industry 1978–85. Molyneaux and Thompson attribute the faster productivity growth in the later period to several factors. For example, tighter financial control implemented after the 1978 White Paper forced the nationalized industries to increase productivity, especially those industries which experienced greater competition (British Airways, British Steel Corporation and National Bus). In addition, following the 1978 White Paper performance targets were introduced, efficiency audits by the Monopolies and Mergers Commission were carried out and privatization was suggested – all encouraging greater manager and labour efficiency.

Privatization

This section has two aims: first to outline the meaning of the term 'privatization' and to describe its occurrence; second to review arguments in favour of and against privatization.

Nature of privatization

The term 'privatization' has been used to cover several different changes in the relationship which organizations have with government. These changes include the following.

1 *Transfer of the ownership of assets*: the government offers for sale more than 50 per cent of the shares to the private sector (e.g. British Telecom and British Airways).
2 *Liberalization*: competition is promoted in an industry which was previously a statutory monopoly or into which entry was restricted (e.g. the enabling of private companies to produce services for attachment to the British Telecom network).
3 *Contracting out*: privately financed services are substituted for publicly financed services (e.g. the franchising of a private company to clean schools, hospitals etc. in place of persons employed by the local authority etc.).

The major sales of assets are shown in table 12.2.

Arguments for privatization

Proponents of state ownership have used a number of arguments which they consider to be in its favour. Arguments advanced in the 1920s and 1930s included the view that if very large industries which provided power and transport were state owned then output, employment etc. could be more effectively planned and macroeconomic stability more easily achieved. Another view was that the nationalized industries were to have social objectives rather than the objective of maximizing profits for private owners and employees would share these objectives too. Thus any conflict between employers and workers would be dramatically reduced. Some saw the supply of competing and different firms as wasteful duplication which would be eliminated by the provision by one large (publicly owned) firm. Each of the large number of small firms was seen as producing output of less than minimum efficient firm size (MEF) (see figure 12.3) and so not gaining the full economies of scale which were available by growth, e.g. by nationalization.

More recent arguments have been advanced. First, some industries such as telecommunications, gas supply and electricity distribution have been regarded as natural monopolies. A natural monopoly is an industry where the demand is so limited relative to MEF output that no more than one firm can exist in the industry. This is shown in figure 12.3. If two firms of MEF existed, total output would exceed *S* and so price would be less than average costs; economic losses would be made. If a firm of less than MEF existed, any firm with lowest average costs could undercut the price of the

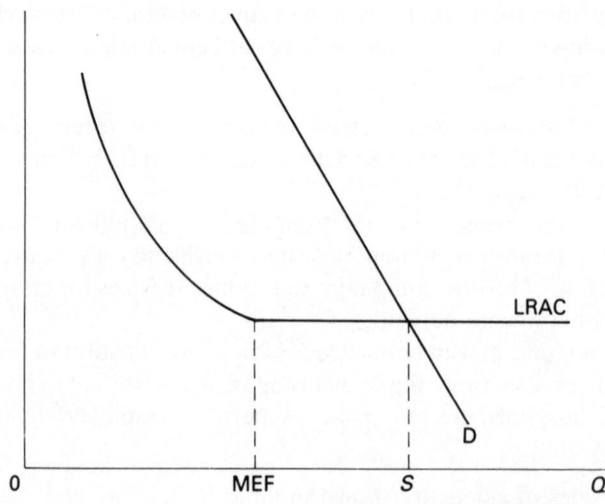

Figure 12.3 *Natural monopoly (definition)*

smaller firm and result in the smaller firm's exit (or growth resulting ultimately in losses).

If only one private firm existed, it would be expected to raise price above marginal costs to maximize profits, so leading to allocative inefficiency as explained earlier in this chapter. This possibility is a genuine concern since British Telecom, British Gas and the Central Electricity Generating Board have been privatized. If such industries had remained in the public sector, they could have been *instructed* to set long-run marginal cost prices.

But an alternative policy to nationalization may be for the government to regulate such an industry, e.g. by legally requiring it to restrict its prices according to a certain formula. Thus, following privatization, British Telecom were required to limit price increases to the rate of increase of the retail price index less 3 per cent – the RPI$-X$ rule. Some, however, believe that regulation is undesirable. For example the Austrian School argue that, if profits are limited, the incentive attracting new entrepreneurs to invent, develop and market new products and processes is reduced. To maintain such an incentive it must be possible for existing firms to be able to maintain super-normal profits for a sufficient period of time. Others[18] disagree.

A second argument in favour of nationalization has been that for a socially optimal resource allocation prices should equal marginal *social* costs. So far in this chapter we have assumed that marginal costs equal marginal social costs. But this may not be so if the production of a good results in a cost or a benefit to someone other than a firm's owners. Such externalities are discussed fully in chapter 15. They may include, for example, the creation of pollution, reduced attractiveness of scenery etc. Proponents of nationalization have argued that if an activity is in public ownership prices can be set equal to marginal *social* cost whereas if the activity is in public hands such externalities will not be included in the prices charged.

A reply to this view is that marginal social costs are in practice extremely difficult to calculate and nationalized industries are unlikely to be able to do so. Also, as outlined in chapter 15, there are alternative ways to public provision for taking externalities into account.

A third argument allegedly in support of public ownership has been that by cross-subsidizing unprofitable services nationalized industries can redistribute income between different social groups. For example, by charging prices below the costs of provision of rail transport to people living in peripheral areas, but prices above costs for other users, income can be redistributed from the latter to the former group. However, income redistribution could be effected directly by cheque or giro, giving recipients free choice as to how to spend the income, rather than by the provision of 'cheap' nationalized industry services which some may not use. Further, regulation might be used to force private firms to cross-subsidize without the service being publicly owned.

The objectives of privatization

We now turn to the objectives of privatization. One argument is that privatization of an organization will result in increased efficiency. When privatized an organization's managers will have greater incentive to maximize the technical efficiency of the organization than if the organization remains nationalized. The managers of a nationalized industry believe that if they make a loss they can borrow this from the government. But managers in the private sector run the risk of being taken over if their share price falls as a result of losses, and if they fail to compete in the product market losses may result in bankruptcy. To avoid these two constraints and to fulfil the wishes of shareholders managers of private enterprises will have a greater incentive to develop new products and provide new services than managers in nationalized firms.

These arguments can be considered further. Following recent literature we shall consider the managers of a private enterprise to be agents acting on behalf of principals, the shareholders. The principals gain the profits resulting from the agent's decisions.

It is often argued that managers wish to pursue their own goals such as growth, a quiet life, high salaries etc. rather than to maximize technical efficiency and profits. Further, managers have the latitude needed to pursue these preferences. First, there are reasons to suppose that the shareholders cannot perfectly constrain the managers to fulfil their wishes to maximize profits. Shareholders are typically very numerous and communicate little with each other. (Institutional shareholders sell their shares rather than issue instructions to managers if they disapprove of their decisions.) Furthermore, managers have more information about the firm than shareholders do and so the latter could not criticize managers for performances which are suboptimal; shareholders do not know what is suboptimal.

Second, empirical evidence by Kuehn, Singh and others[19] suggests that the chance of take-over is only mildly related to profitability. Third, in non-competitive productive markets the threat of bankruptcy is also small. Therefore, given that neither shareholders nor the threat of take-over perfectly constrain managers in non-competitive markets the agents have some scope to pursue their own goals rather than technical efficiency and maximum profits.

In addition, managers in public enterprises are not totally without efficiency incentives. Yarrow[20] notes that recent work by Williamson has suggested that internal monitoring by superiors may be more effective at constraining managers than the threat of take-over. Further, government does not suffer from the problem associated with private enterprises that take-overs may not occur because shareholders wish to gain the benefits of holding shares in the old company, relying on others to sell out. If the government considers that a nationalized industry is not acting efficiently enough it can replace the board directly.

Overall, however, in non-competitive product markets, if the threat of take-over is low there is little reason to believe that private ownership will result in greater technical efficiency than public ownership. Alternatively, in competitive product markets where the scope of the agents to pursue their own objectives is constrained by the threat of bankruptcy and take-over, private ownership is likely to be more technically efficient.

We now turn to allocative efficiency. One would expect that in non-competitive product markets, unless regulated, private sector firms would be less efficient than nationalized industries since the former would be expected to exploit their monopoly power. Alternatively, in competitive product markets we would expect private and public sector firms to be equally efficient since the private firm would have to set price close to the minimum of average cost and hence to marginal cost, while the nationalized industry could be *instructed* to price at marginal cost.

The empirical evidence on the relative technical efficiency of publicly owned firms was described in the previous section. The rate of productivity growth of publicly owned firms since the late 1970s was in most cases at least equal to that of private sector manufacturing. However, Pryke[21] suggested that the lack of bankruptcy or take-over threat reduced the incentives for efficiency in the three cases he studied, but his conclusion has been criticized by many. Thus Kay and Thompson,[22] for example, argued that, since many firms entered the ferry industry but failed and so were *not* included in Pryke's comparison, 'private firms are not necessarily intrinsically more efficient' than public ones. Instead, competition in the capital market threatening take-over and in the product market threatening bankruptcy is more effective at ejecting inefficient private firms than inefficient public firms. When private sector efficiency is observed to exceed that of a public enterprise it is usually in a competitive market. In such cases, they argue, it is the competitive nature of the industry and not the ownership structure of the firms which leads to this observation. When they reviewed studies relating to less competitive industries, no generalizations could be made concerning the relative efficiency of public and private provision. Similar arguments are made by Yarrow.[23]

Finally, there are a number of examples of privatized enterprises – British Telecom, British Gas, and electricity distribution – operating in markets with little effective competition and very little chance of being acquired because of their size; thus, without regulation, they would have little incentive to be allocatively or technically efficient.

We return now to the other objectives of privatization. These have included an anticipated reduction in the PSBR. This may result from the government's receipts of funds from the asset sale net of the loss of the trading surplus which the nationalized industries concerned would have remitted to the Treasury. In fact the PSBR may actually have increased. Purchasers of the shares would be willing to pay up to the present value of the expected future dividends. Therefore if the public enterprise is sold at the maximum price possible the government would not benefit: it would receive a lump sum in return for a stream of earnings with the same present value as the lump sum. However, Kay and Thompson[24] argue that in many cases the issue price set was lower than buyers were willing to pay (the share price rose immediately after sale), and so the government received a lump sum which was less than the present value of dividends expected by shareholders.

A further associated alleged benefit is that if the PSBR were reduced then private sector investment which was 'crowded out' by money being lent to the government sector to finance public sector borrowing would increase. However, Shackleton[25] argues that this effect would only be marginal.

A further objective has been to reduce the power of the trade unions to obtain high wage increases in view of the lack of incentive for managers to maximize technical efficiency. But this result may not occur. A government may have a greater desire than a private company to be strict with trade unions, to avoid a relatively high pay settlement becoming a precedent for nationalized industries as a whole, and so privatization may see the labour force move to more lax employers. The 1984–5 miners' strike is a good example of this since it is unlikely that a private company would have had the financial reserves to allow the strike to continue for so long.

Another objective has been to increase the number of shareholders in the population. However, privatization has been relatively unsuccessful in this regard since in very many cases the majority of shareholders sold their shares to financial institutions within a short time after purchase. For example, Shackleton[26] notes that within one year of flotation the number of shareholders in British Aerospace dropped from 158,000 to 26,000. Furthermore, Yarrow[27] argues that a better method of encouraging wider shareownership is by making fiscal changes that make it more worthwhile for individuals to own shares.

Finally, the objective of income redistribution might be mentioned. There may be a redistribution, following privatization, from those who paid relatively high prices to those who paid relatively low prices. For example, following the privatization of British Telecom the relative prices faced by business and domestic users altered. Second, income may be redistributed from taxpayers to the purchasers of shares if the shares were sold at below the appropriate market price. Yarrow[28] lists the degree of undervaluation on privatization of major firms until 1985. The largest was British Telecom at £1337 million, the lowest Britoil at −£48 million. He continues that it has often been 'large numbers of middle class voters' who received the redistribution. By implication those losing income may be considered as suffering an indirect tax.

Conclusion

In this chapter we have outlined the significance of public enterprise in the UK economy and explained the economic theory of the desirability of marginal cost pricing and allocative efficiency. We have reviewed the objectives laid down in various White Papers for nationalized industries, and arguments concerning the desirability of privatization have been discussed at length. We argued that it is unlikely that privatization would stimulate allocative and technical efficiency unless the privatized firm operated in a competitive environment with a high threat of take-over if its performance were weak. As far as UK privatization is concerned it is debatable whether this has always been the case.

References

1 J. Vickers and G. Yarrow, *Privatization: An Economic Analysis*, MIT Press, 1988.
2 M. G. Webb, *The Economics of Nationalised Industries: a Theoretical Approach*, Nelson, 1973.
3 Vickers and Yarrow, *Privatization*.
4 Ibid.
5 G. Heald, 'The economic and financial control of UK nationalised industries', *Economic Journal* 90 (1980), pp. 243–65.
6 Coopers and Lybrand Associated Limited, 'Review of the pricing polices, investment criteria and financial objectives of four nationalised industries', in National Economic Development Organization, *A Study of UK Nationalised Industries*, 1976.
7 Heald, 'Economic and financial control'.
8 Coopers and Lybrand Associated Limited, 'Review of the pricing policies'.
9 Heald, 'Economic and financial control'.
10 P. Curwen, *Public Enterprise: A Modern Approach*, Harvester Wheatsheaf, 1986.
11 Vickers and Yarrow, *Privatization*.
12 E. M. Hammond, D. R. Helm and D. J. Thompson, 'British Gas: options for privatization', *Fiscal Studies* 6(4) (1985), pp. 1–20.
13 R. Molyneaux and D. Thompson, 'Nationalized industries' performance: still third-rate?', *Fiscal Studies* (1987), pp. 48–82.
14 R. Pryke, 'The comparative performance of public and private enterprise', *Fiscal Studies* 3 (2) (1982), pp. 68–81.
15 Ibid.
16 HM Treasury, 'Nationalised industries' performance', *Economic Progress Report 193* (December 1987).
17 Molyneaux and Thompson, 'Nationalised industries' performance'.
18 G. Yarrow, 'Privatisation', *Economic Policy* 2 (1986), pp. 323–75.
19 D. A. Kuehn, *Takeovers and the Theory of the Firm*, Macmillan, 1975.

A. Singh, 'Takeovers, economic natural selection and the theory of the firm', *Economic Journal* 85 (1975), pp. 497–515.
20 Yarrow, 'Privatisation'.
21 Pryke, 'The comparative performance'.
22 J. Kay and D. J. Thompson, 'Privatisation: a policy in search of a rationale', *Economic Journal* 96 (1986), pp. 18–32.
23 Yarrow, 'Privatisation'.
24 Kay and Thompson, 'Privatisation'.
25 J. Shackleton, 'Privatization: the case examined', *National Westminster Bank Quarterly Review* (1984), pp. 59–73.
26 Ibid.
27 Yarrow, 'Privatisation'.
28 Ibid.

Further reading

HM Treasury, *Nationalised Industries: A Review of Economic and Financial Objectives*, Cmnd 3437, HMSO, 1967.

HM Treasury, *The Nationalised Industries*, Cmnd 7131, HMSO, 1978.

J. Moore, 'Why privatise?', in J. Kay, C. Mayer and D. Thompson (eds), *Privatisation and Regulation – the UK Experience*, Oxford University Press, 1986.

R. Pryke, *The Nationalised Industries: Policies and Performance Since 1968*, Martin Robertson, 1981.

R. Pryke, 'The comparative performance of public and private enterprise', in J. Kay, C. Mayer and D. Thompson, op. cit.

J. Redwood and J. Hatch, *Controlling Public Industries*, Basil Blackwell, 1982.

G. Yarrow, 'Does ownership matter?', in C. Veljanovski (ed.), *Privatisation and Competition: A Market Prospectus*, Institute of Economic Affairs, Hobart Paperback 28, 1989.

13

Markets and Distribution Channels

The Development of the Mass Market

The Industrial Revolution and the techniques of mass production which developed from it reached full flower in the manufacture of Henry Ford's Model T. The Model T was the epitome of the success of the Industrial Revolution. Ford's achievement was due to one main selling point, lowness of price, coupled with a lack of similar inexpensive products in the past. Before the advent of the Model T, the individual seeking a cheap personal transportation system had to invest in a horse and buggy, a product which could hardly be called the most satisfactory of substitutes, and one which, in any event, would be manufactured on a custom-built, one-off, high-cost basis at the local coachbuilders. The poor were thus precluded from owning their own personal transport, and only the very rich could contract out of the disadvantages associated with horse-drawn vehicles by buying the very costly products of Benz and Royce.

Ford's low price depended on standardization of product and uniformity of assembly technique. These are the basic components of mass production technology. Mass production depends in turn on a mass market to absorb the output. In Ford's case the mass market was made possible by mass communication about the product and by its attractively low price. So the circle was completed and marketing's place in its defined.

The Development of the Marketing Concept

Scope for further change in the nature and extent of marketing as we now know it had to wait until later in the twentieth century. The days when lowness of price and uniformity of product were sufficient to sell a product ended. ('You can have any colour you want, so long as it's black', growled Old Henry.) Incomes were rising, people no longer had to buy the cheapest black car as a form of transport. They could afford to exercise their preferences for something different, or defer purchase till a satisfactory product became available. In the automobile trade, General Motors willingly obliged by producing coloured Chevrolets. By 1946, Ford was turning in losses of $10 million each month.

So the marketing concept was born. Firms became aware that to stay in business it was not sufficient to produce a well-engineered product and then try to sell it. The market had to be studied, its varying wants assessed, and then a product, or products, tailored to meet them. Figure 13.1 conceptualizes this change from product orientation to market orientation: the firm's entire way of thinking is reversed.

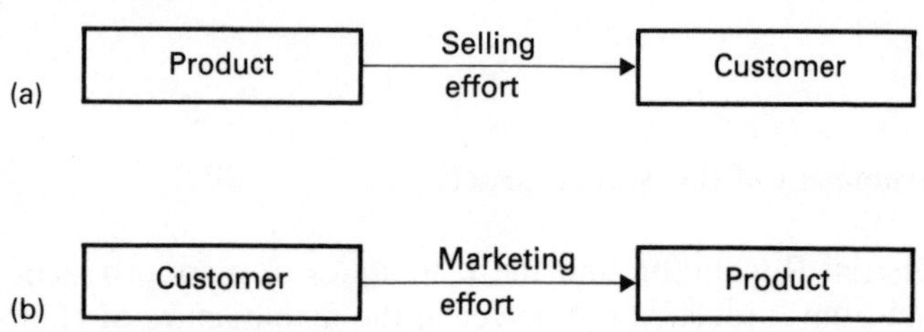

Figure 13.1 *Change in selling from (a) a product-oriented firm to (b) a market-oriented firm*

When firms operate according to the marketing concept they must ask these questions:

1 Who are our potential customers?
2 Where are they?
3 What demographic features do they have (age, sex, marital status etc.)?
4 What other socio-economic features do they possess which will affect their market behaviour?
5 What channel of distribution should we use to reach them?

The first four questions can be quickly answered, at least at the national level. The British population is rising and is forecast to continue to do so. Moreover, it is probable that this growth will continue to be predominantly in the southeast as the population moves from less prosperous areas (table 13.1).

Changes by age grouping in the last decade give guidance as to market trends in the future. Thus, as table 13.2 indicates, the elderly segment is growing more rapidly than the population as a whole; thus 'retirement' goods such as gardening and other leisure-related activities could see an upswing in demand. People born in the post-war baby boom are now about 40 years of age – the point in the life cycle when homes and families are already established, with implications for industries such as toys and infant foods. By inference the early 20s market is also growing relatively fast, with positive implications for firms in leisure-related or electronic

Table 13.1 *UK population*

	UK (millions)	(%)	England (millions)	(%)	Wales (millions)	(%)	Scotland (millions)	(%)	Northern Ireland (millions)	(%)
1951	50.3	100	41.4	82.3	2.6	5.2	5.1	10.2	1.4	2.8
1981	56.3	100	46.8	83.0	2.8	5.0	5.2	9.2	1.5	2.7
2001 (forecast)	59.1	100	49.5	83.4	2.9	4.9	5.1	8.6	1.7	2.9
2021 (forecast)	60.7	100	51.4	84.7	3.0	4.9	4.7	7.7	1.7	1.8

Source: *Annual Abstract of Statistics*, 1989

Table 13.2 *UK population age changes (selected age groups)*

	1979 (million)	1989 (million)	Change (%)
Total	56.2	57.2	+1.8
Under 20 years	16.7	14.9	−10.8
45–64 years	12.6	12.3	−2.4
65 and over	8.3	9.0	+8.4

Source: *Annual Abstract of Statistics*, 1989 and 1991

hardware industries. The middle-aged are declining in number both absolutely and relatively; in turn, this implies a decline in tomorrow's numbers of elderly and, in the nearer future, a weaker demand for replacement furniture, private cars and other durables purchased when children leave home.

All these examples are, of course, subject to the caveat of 'other things being equal'. Other things, however, are rarely equal. One very important demographic change has been the increase in the number of married women who have jobs and who therefore have increased the disposable income of households. The impetus for this has continued through three decades. Table 13.3 provides the figures supporting this statement.

Table 13.3 *Workforce in employment, UK*

	Males (million)	(% change)	Females (million)	(% change)	Total (million)	(% change)
1959[a]	16.2		8.1		24.3	
		−0.1		+12.3		+4.1
1969[a]	16.1		9.1		25.3	
		−5.0		+11.0		+0.0
1979	15.3		10.1		25.4	
		−2.0		+15.8		+5.5
1989	15.0		11.7		26.8	

[a]Data for 1959 and 1969 relate to the employed labour force.
Source: *Annual Abstract of Statistics* 1964, 1972, 1991.

This implies that not only will consumers' expenditure grow as disposable incomes rise but also, as households with two or more incomes grow in number, so consumers' expenditure will be diverted, at least in relative terms, away from necessities towards luxuries. Table 13.4 confirms this hypothesis. In addition, with more and more women at work, the conventional distribution channels have had to adapt to this sociological change.

Table 13.4 *Availability in UK households of certain durable goods, 1975, 1980, 1986*

	1975 (% households)	1980 (% households)	1986 (% households)
Access to one or more cars	57.0	60.3	62.4
Access to two cars	9.6	13.1	14.9
Central heating	46.7	59.1	70.1
Washing machine	71.9	78.7	82.9
Refrigerator	85.3	94.8	96.8
Television	94.8	96.9	97.1
Telephone	51.9	71.6	80.9
Home computer	–	–	15.1
Video recorder	–	–	36.3

Source: *Annual Abstract of Statistics*, 1989

Marketing Channels and Middlemen

The traditional distribution channel is conceptualized in figure 13.2(a). Goods are 'pushed' through from manufacturer to consumer via several intermediaries. The manufacturer's salesmen would approach a wholesaler, whose sales force in turn sold to retailers, who, in their turn, recommended purchase to (often personally known) individual customers. Now, the selling effort is primarily directed at the final consumer (figure 13.2(b)). The mass media are often used for this purpose; face-to-face recommendation has no place in the increasing number of self-service stores, and the goods are 'pulled' by consumers through the channel. The alert retailer must stock the items which consumers have chosen from those listed in advertisements that they, the consumers, have seen.

At first glance the presence of wholesaling intermediaries in distribution channels may appear to be inefficient. This was not and is not necessarily the case. Middlemen perform services to both manufacturers and retailers. Only when this service is either no longer wanted, or is performed by the manufacturer or retailer himself, does the wholesaler become redundant. In short, the wholesaling function always exists, but it need not be performed by an independent entity known as a wholesaler.

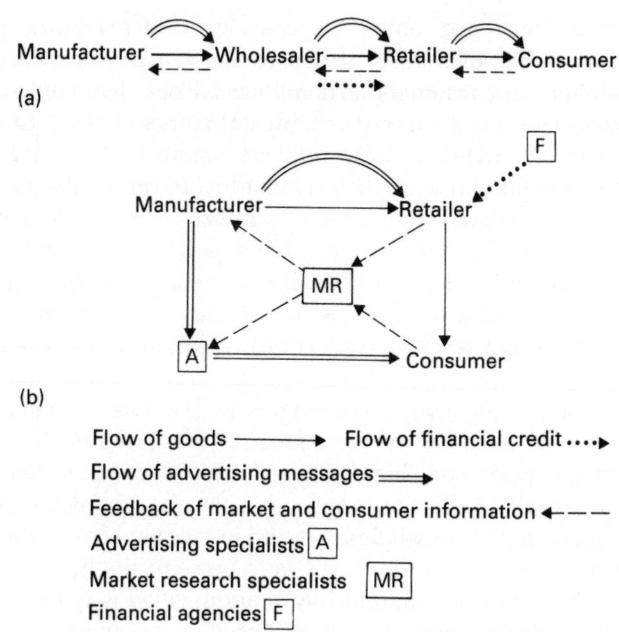

Figure 13.2 *Marketing channels: (a) traditional; (b) modern*

The wholesaler reduces the number of trading relationships between buyers and sellers and by so doing he achieves *economies of intervention*. For example, if three retailers deal independently with three manufacturers there is a total of nine trading relationships. If they deal indirectly through a wholesaler, however, the number of these relationships is reduced to six. Figure 13.3 illustrates this. The number of trading relationships (depicted as lines) is reduced from the product of the number of traders to their sum (from 3 × 3 to 3 + 3). The savings become progressively greater the larger the number of traders.

The wholesaler serves the retailer by assembling goods from a wide variety of suppliers. The retailer now needs to purchase from only one source instead of several. He can rely on the wholesaler's purchasing

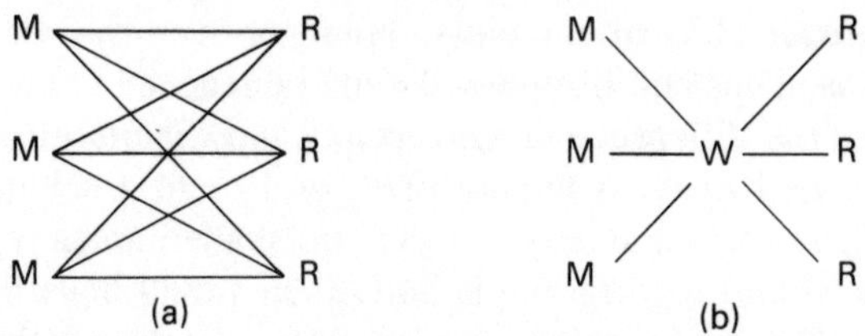

Figure 13.3 *Manufacturers' and retailers' trading: (a) directly; (b) through a wholesaler*

expertise and knowledge, and concentrate his own resources on selling. Similarly, since the wholesaler sorts out the range of goods into each retailer's desired assortment, the retailer need now have only one large drop-off stock instead of many arriving at his warehouse. In addition, wholesalers often extend credit to retailers (figure 13.2(a)) and they also assume a stockholding risk. If each retailer had to carry sufficient stock to guard against the risk of running out of supplies during a busy period then the aggregate stock held would have to be very much greater than that which a central wholesaler would have to carry to meet the variations in demand from the total trade. This has already been referred to as the economies of massed reserves (chapter 6), a variant of the *fire insurance principle.*

The other side of the coin is the wholesaler's service to manufacturers. He eliminates the need for the manufacturer to make a plethora of small drops. Transportation and shipment costs are thus reduced. Similarly the manufacturer's selling costs are reduced in that he now need only visit a relatively small number of wholesalers and not a plethora of retailers. The wholesaler is also closer to the market and presumably therefore can pass back to the manufacturer market information which is more reliable for production scheduling than the manufacturer's own estimates.

The rationale for the existence of a middleman can also be explained in terms of the discussion on trade and exchange in chapter 2. Consider figure 13.4(a) in which the demand and supply curves of figures 2.2 and 2.3 are reproduced. Joe and Fred, it will be recalled, originally had 20 packs of butter each but each could be made better off (in his own eyes) if he traded beer for butter until Joe had 16 packs and Fred had 24. However, for such a trade to occur Fred and Joe must incur transactions costs. They must advertise and inform each other of their wishes. They must transport the exchanged goods and negotiate and seal the bargain.

Assume that the agreed trading price is again 8 pints of beer but that this time there are, in addition, transaction costs of 3 pints of beer per butter unit (irrespective of whether either or both individuals incur that cost). Then Fred will increase his butter holding to 22 packs and Joe will reduce his to 18. (Beer will also change hands.) Assume Fred and Joe incur the costs in a 2:1 ratio. To acquire one unit of butter Fred will willingly part (initially) with 12 pints of beer while Joe will require (initially) 6 pints. From the difference (12 – 6) of 6 pints, 3 pints of beer must be deducted in transaction costs. Thus equilibrium will only be reached in the presence of such costs when the difference in net receipts and expenditure is 3 pints of beer (in figure 13.4(a), at a buying price of 10 and a selling price of 7 respectively). The rectangle between the two shaded areas represents the transaction costs, and less trading is done than would have been done in their absence. The trade point of figure 2.3 is only worth reaching if transaction costs are zero.

Suppose, however, that a specialist wholesaler can undertake the costs

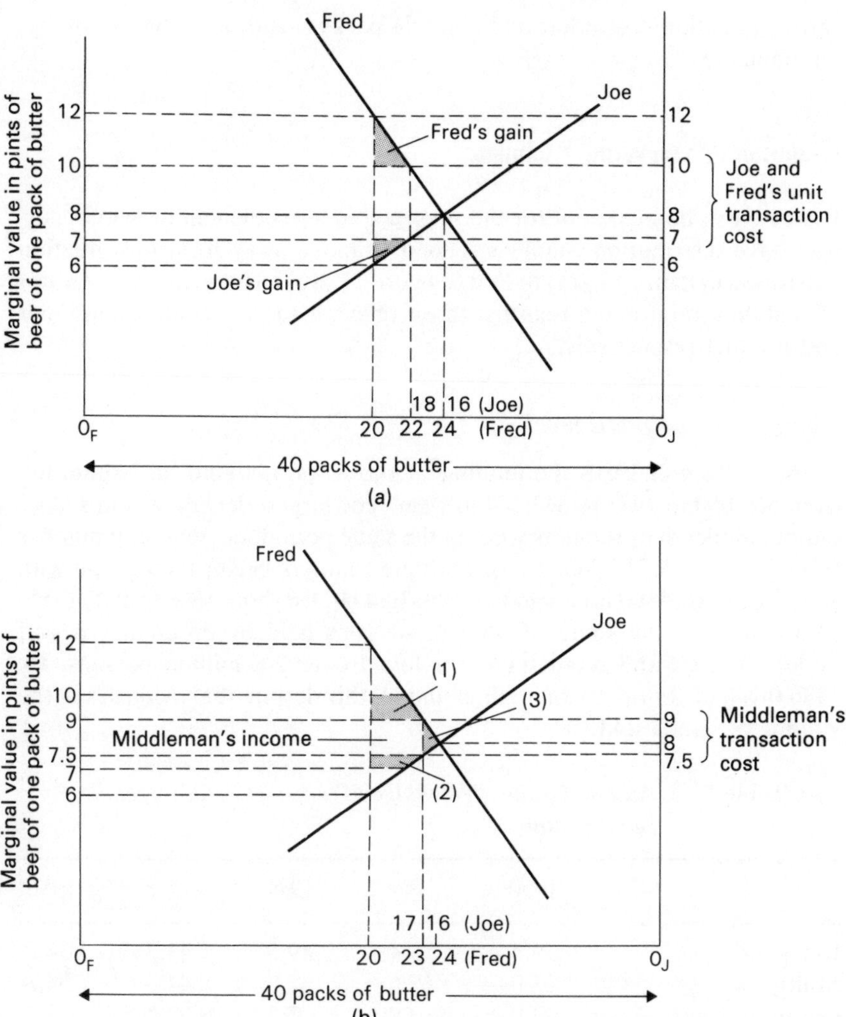

Figure 13.4 *(a) Transaction costs in trade of figure 2.3; (b) middleman costs in same trade. Key to (b): (1) Fred's additional gain from use of wholesaler; (2) Joe's additional gain from use of wholesaler; (3) further gains possible if transaction costs were zero*

of trading more efficiently than Joe or Fred could on their own. Suppose he can do it for half the cost. Then trading will continue until the spread between Joe's and Fred's net transaction costs prices is only 1.5, not 3 (e.g. at 9 and 7.5). Both Fred and Joe are better off as a result of the middleman's intervention (see figure 13.4(b)). The middleman receives an income which covers his normal costs. But again, of course, the original zero transaction cost point of 16 and 24 packs is still, and always will be, unattainable.

Evolution of Marketing Channels

If a case can be made out for the presence of a middleman or wholesaler, why have distribution channels tended to move away from the situation illustrated in figure 13.2(a) to that of figure 13.2(b)? There are three groups of mutually reinforcing reasons; those relevant to the retailer, consumer and product respectively.

Changes at the retail level

In the 1970s and 1980s the number of shops, of any kind, in Britain fell from 510,000 in 1971 to 343,387 in 1986. The largest decline was in single-outlet independent retailers who, in the same period, decreased in number from 338,000 to 217,248. Large multiple retailers began the decade with 88,000 outlets (1386 firms) and by 1986 had 60,356 shops (868 firms). Table 13.5 compares the share of total retail sales held by different types of outlet. In 1971 the retail trade employed over 2.8 million persons. By 1986 this had shrunk to 2.3 million and all this despite real increases in the volume of goods sold.

Table 13.5 *All retail trade: percentage of turnover held, by retailer classificaton*

	1950	1961	1971	1978	1986[a]
Independents	59.4	56.4	49.8	43.2	34.8
Multiples	23.0	27.6	37.9	44.3	54.8
Co-operatives	12.0	10.8	7.2	7.2	4.3
Department stores	5.5	5.3	5.0	5.2	n.a.

n.a., not available

[a] The 1986 data are not directly comparable. Department stores are not distinguished from Independents (from 1986 single outlet retailers) and Multiples (from 1986 retailers with two or more outlets).

Sources: *Board of Trade Journals*; *Annual Abstracts of Statistics*

Independent retailer

The independent retailer is ubiquitous by both location and trade type. One hundred years ago most shops were of this type. They required skilled craftsmen to make shoes, compound medicines, cure bacon or whatever tasks were appropriate to the trade. Breaking bulk and repacking (e.g. for tea and cheese) was common. These functions have now been taken over by the wholesaler and/or manufacturer. The skilled craftsman has been replaced by (often unskilled) salesmen.

The strength of the independents lies in their flexibility of pricing, product range, opening hours, close knowledge of customer requirements and convenient locations. They also often have the apparent advantage of low labour and rent costs if family members are willing to work uncongenial or longer hours, and if the store is part of a domestic residence. These are misleading 'advantages', of course, since the full opportunity costs of the self-employed should be charged against the firm's profits.

The disadvantages of the independents lie in their limited buying power, their limited access to capital to improve premises, and their lack of management skills. The independent retailer has to be his own staff trainer, accountant, buyer, stock controller, salesman, supervisor and window display specialist. Clearly it is impossible for one individual to aspire to such a range of skills.

Department stores

Department stores, unlike the independent retailer, have on the whole retained their market share of all retail sales. Historically (along with the co-operatives) they were the first large-scale retailers. Their basic principles were as follows: entrance was free of any obligation to buy; customer complaints were dealt with by a generous returns policy; merchandise was arranged departmentally; prices were clearly marked; personal service (credit, delivery etc.) was of a high order; and departments existed explicitly to encourage custom (rest rooms, restaurants, generally pleasant environment etc.). This formula was successful towards the end of the last century and early decades of this century as town populations grews; suburban areas were also growing but improved personal transport of all kinds ensured that they were included in the catchment area of the stores; the development of lifts and escalators made the marketing concept of the stores a practical possibility in a multistorey building on one site.

Co-operatives

The co-operative societies have seen their share of total retail turnover drop from 12.0 per cent in 1950 to 4.3 per cent in 1986. Co-operatives are worth examining as an entity distinct from department stores and multiple retailers because they differ not in their trading practices but in their means of ownership and the distribution of their trading surplus. They are owned by their members, some of whom may have provided capital which earns a fixed rate of interest. But any profits are distributed not in proportion to capital provided but in relation to purchases made in the trading period. Members' meetings are run on a one-person, one-vote principle and votes are weighted neither by capital nor by purchases.

Co-operatives have access to many of the advantages of multiples (see next section). However, they have additional and unique disadvantages. Their membership tends to be concentrated in specific geographic areas (generally economically depressed areas with an emphasis on heavy and/or declining industries) and within lower-income groups. Consequently they tend to suffer more than the average of UK retailing in times of economic downturn. In addition they tend to guard their local autonomy and independence jealously which means that several smaller societies fail to achieve the scale economies available to retailers. This situation is compounded by the fact that boards of directors tend to be elected laymen who, as customers in their own right, are often protective of sectional customer interests rather than concerned with the society's overall welfare. (This manifests itself in an unwillingness to close down uneconomic branches or discontinue slow-moving lines, which in turn implies that other parts of the society must cross-subsidize them out of their profits. As a consequence, there is a reduction in the ability of the society to compete in price or other terms with other retail types, particularly multiples.) Lay board members can also fail to see the need to spend heavily on staff training, shop fittings, higher salaries for managerial staff and the like. Internal promotion is also prevalent, thus reducing the pool of managerial talent from which to draw. Certainly some of the above are changing as societies merge and individual board members are less able to influence policy in such short-sighted ways. Table 13.6 shows how the fall in numbers of societies, owing to mergers, has been quite dramatic in the last two decades.

Table 13.6 *Number of co-operative societies*

1960	875	1977	206
1971	313	1979	195
1975	227	1986	98

Sources: *Annual Abstracts of Statistics*; *Nielsen Researcher*

In turn, individual societies have become larger, gained more purchasing muscle, engaged more professional management, and become more loyal to the Co-operative Wholesaling Society (CWS) which they own. The CWS, in turn, has established eight major distribution centres in the UK. These supply 30 per cent of the warehousing and distribution needs of the retail societies for packaged groceries. A further 30 per cent of these products are bought by the societies via the CWS as purchasing agent. The

CWS thus acts as a central buyer and also a national advertiser for retail co-operatives. All of this rationalization activity has halted the relative decline of the co-operative movement. In the process even the previously sacrosanct dividend has been subject to radical alteration. In some outlet types, particularly groceries, it has been abandoned altogether – a somewhat ironical state of affairs since multiples regularly equal or better any price in co-operatives, yet still pay a dividend to their shareholders. In others it has been reduced to minimal level, and elsewhere it has been replaced by trading stamps which can be accumulated by the consumer until sufficient are held to be traded in for either goods or cash. Certainly dividend abandonment had an underlying rationale. When dividends were pitched at a high level, this discouraged the setting of low prices, the ploughing back of profits to improve shops and equipment and the stocking of items with low margins. As an undifferentiated price reduction over a wide range of goods and outlets, it encouraged cross-subsidization and discouraged efficient decision-taking.

Multiples

The story of the multiple retailers since 1950 has been one of major success. They can achieve the economies of large-scale retailing (as can the co-operative and department stores) as well as other benefits. Definitions of multiples vary but a working description is a situation of ten or more shops operating under one management – ownership structure. Because of their scale they can afford to employ (and fully utilize) specialists in accounting, purchasing, advertising, co-ordination and control. Their size enables them to spread overheads such as advertising, rent and staff training over a larger volume of business. Their buying power is large, enabling them to obtain large discounts on list price. In turn this facilitates provision of either a low-service/low-price marketing mix or a high-price/sophisticated service mix, neither of which can an independent compete with on equal terms.

By integrating backwards and carrying out many of the functions of the wholesaler they can capture several economies of integration. Central buying can be practised. Stocks held in a central warehouse can be minimized. Advertising, promotion and pricing policies can be co-ordinated with each other and with the firm's stock position. Test marketing can be undertaken in selected branches. Risks of stock holding such as deterioration and demand changes are also minimized because of the close interaction between the seller and buyer in the multiple organization. Multiples also generally have access to the capital markets, and the cost of finance to the integrated firm may therefore be much less than the use of extended credit by retailers from independent wholesalers. Delivery, order assembly and transport costs are lowered because days of drop-off from the central warehouse can be scheduled smoothly over the week instead of peaking, as with an independent wholesaler, towards the weekend.

These advantages are offset, although only partially, by disadvantages. The multiple may assume overheads that the small independent store never would (e.g. advertising, high-rent sites, elaborate services and the employment of specialists). Moreover, the multiple may well not provide the individual personalized attention to customers that the independent does. In addition, the local management may not have the authority to alter company policy on pricing and selection of stock in order to enable him to adapt to localized consumer preferences and competitors' activities.

All of this has meant that the multiple retailer has in general increased his share of retail sales. Nowhere is this more true than in grocery retailing. One of the first overt consequences of this was the move to self-service selling. Table 13.7 depicts their growth in numbers. The series stops in 1969 when two-thirds of all grocery turnover passed through self-service selling stores; the data collectors felt that although the trend would continue the basic economic interest in it had ceased. Self-service was stimulated in Britain, at least initially, by high labour costs and not by a desire to cut prices (as in the USA). Partly this was due to the existence of resale price maintenance on many goods prior to 1964 and partly to a general staff shortage. Self-service had the major attribute of catering for both traditional shoppers and working wives. Shopping could be a leisurely activity with plenty of time for comparison, or it could be hurried into a compressed period. This, plus bright attractive atmospheres, coupled with well-filled shelves and clearly marked prices, ensured the success of self-service outlets.

Table 13.7 *Number of self-service grocers, UK*

1961	7,700	1967	24,300
1963	12,900	1969	28,062
1965	17,500		

Source: *Nielsen Researcher*

Not only did self-service stores grow in number; they also took an increasing amount of business. In 1965 they accounted for 45 per cent of grocery turnover; by 1969, just four years later, this had risen to 64 per cent. This new method of retailing was more efficient in its use of staff resources; moreover, since the store was in part a warehouse, it resulted in stocks held being minimized. As a consequence, less capital was tied up in stocks and savings were made in working capital. Table 13.8 illustrates the impact of this on the grocery trade as a whole.

Supermarkets, and more recently, hypermarkets also increased in number over the years. (Definitions vary: e.g. a supermarket may be

Table 13.8 *Grocery stocks and sales in UK (1964–1965 = 100, current prices*

	Sales	Stocks
1964–65	100	100
1966–67	107	98
1968–69	122	94

Source: *Nielsen Researcher*

defined as a store with over 4,000 square feet of selling space and a hypermarket or superstore as one with over 25,000 square feet of selling space.) These three developments were particularly suited to the multiple retailer with large capital resources and access to managerial expertise. As a consequence of all these advantages, the multiples have taken an increasingly large share of the retail grocery trade in the country. This is illustrated in table 13.9.

Table 13.9 *Turnover share by types of grocer 1939–1986, UK (%)*

	Co-operatives	Multiples	Independents
1939	23	23	54
1959	22	26	52
1963	19	32	49
1967	15	38	47
1971	15	43	42
1975	14	49	37
1979	15	59	26
1981	14	63	23
1986	11	72	17

Source: *Nielsen Researcher*

The co-operative movement's decline appears to have slowed in the 1960s and 1970s. This is probably due to the process of rationalization referred to earlier. The multiples, however, continue their inexorable advance and the co-operative's decline has now recommenced in the 1980s. Table 13.10 proves one yardstick (sales per square foot) of efficiency. Multiples were more efficient than the co-operatives in 1977 and by 1986 had increased the differential in efficiency by some 63 per cent. All this has considerable implications for manufacturers and wholesalers. Table 13.11 shows how heavily concentrated is the buying power in groceries in Britain.

Table 13.10 *Estimated sales per square foot per week by retailer type (at 1980 prices)*

	1977	1986	Change (%)
Multiples	£3.90	£6.81	+74.6
Co-operatives	£3.16	£3.53	+11.7

Source: Institute of Grocery Distribution Research Services, September 1987

Table 13.11 *Share of all commodity turnover in grocery trade in UK, 1986*

	Per cent of turnover
Top 2% of shops	51
Top 5% of shops	69
Top 10% of shops	79
Top 20% of shops	86

Source: Nielsen Researcher

Changes at the wholesale level

Clearly the futures of the wholesaler and the independent retailer are closely linked. Recognizing this, many wholesalers and retailers clubbed together into voluntary chains or symbol groups such as Spar and VG. In essence the retail members of a *symbol group* retain their independence of ownership but agree to purchase the major part of their merchandise from the wholesaler; to take delivery on specified days; to display prominently given items which may be subject to special promotion by the wholesaler; to pay promptly; and to display the chain symbol. In return supplies are cheaper because of the wholesaler's cost savings; merchandising assistance and large-scale promotion will be provided; and other centralized services such as insurance, shop-fitting advice and market research information may be provided. Table 13.12 shows how the practice of small retailers buying directly from manufacturers has virtually disappeared. Symbol groups have been growing in importance, and although not directly evident from the figures, the traditional wholesaler is becoming more and more of a cash-and-carry outlet for his retail customers.

One interesting feature of table 13.12 is the inferred greater selectivity of the symbol groups. Only significant independents, not 'lost causes', will now be admitted to the groups. An alternative or simultaneous explanation is that cash-and-carry wholesaling has become of more importance and convenience to the retailer. Indeed in 1986, according to the Institute of

Table 13.12 *Trend of purchasing by independent grocers (%)*

	Directly	Symbol groups	Traditional wholesalers and cash-and-carry outlets
1960	32	10	58
1968	9	42	49
1979	0	28	72

Source: *Nielsen Researcher*

Grocery Distribution Research Services, two-thirds of wholesale grocery sales by value passed through cash-and-carry outlets; only one-third was *delivered* to the retailer.

Changes at the consumer level

The changes in distribution channels outlined in figure 13.2 have been due not only to wholesaler and retailer changes but also to consumer changes. Increasing car ownership has increased consumer mobility and choice ability. Rising numbers of working wives have preferred the speed and convenience of shopping epitomized by self-service. Rising levels of ownership of deep freezers and refrigerators have permitted and encouraged large unit purchases.

Changes at the level of the producer

There are two principal reasons for the active entry of the producer and manufacturer into distribution in the last few decades. First, the growth of large-scale production units necessitated long unbroken production runs. This in turn required a steady flow of orders which independent wholesalers and retailers might not be prepared to give (or, if they could be encouraged to give them, the transaction costs of dealing with large numbers of customers might be too great; recall the discussion of figures 13.2 and 13.3). Second, manufacturers realized that sales and profits could probably be increased if they concentrated on promoting their own products to final consumers (pulling goods through the channel), rather than leaving it to a third party or parties to push them through when such wholesalers and retailers were under no obligation to devote special attention to any one manufacturer.

The methods adopted by manufacturers were of three types. First, in formal *forward integration*, as practised by some flour millers, petrol companies and brewers, they own their own retail bakeries, filling stations and public houses.

Second, brewers, car manufacturers and petrol companies have also adopted *tied outlets* as forms of retail control. Here the ownership remains with the original retailer but he is contractually obliged to take a given percentage (often 100 per cent) of his supplies from the manufacturer. Other conditions may also be imposed. For example, a car dealer may have to carry minimum levels of stocks and spares, be able to provide a given level of mechanical servicing to customers and so on. In return the tied outlet will often have exclusive trading rights to a particular geographic region.

Both of these forms of distribution channel control are practised in trades where traditionally the retailer has offered only a restricted range of products. They tend not to be found, for example, in the grocery trade or in the variety chain stores such as Woolworths. The reason is obvious. Only an extremely diversified manufacturer could supply his owned or tied outlets in these fields. Producers are rarely diversified to this extent; their skills lie in the manufacture of a given product, and their knowledge of the retailing problems involved with alien products is slight or non-existent. Hence the cost disadvantages (e.g. errors, learning time) of forward integration would outweigh the benefits. (One exception to this is the Asda hypermarket chain which evolved from the original Associated Dairies. The link with grocery retailing, however, is obvious. Moreover, as the firm has expanded it has become more of a grocery retailer with a self-owned dairy division and less of a dairy producer with a self-owned chain of grocery retailers. Indeed as a hypermarket chain the quantity of non-foods sold by this firm in its stores takes up a large percentage of both turnover and floor space.)

Third, and most common, manufacturers attempt to pull goods through the channel indirectly by *branding and advertising* reinforced with market research.

The Role of Advertising

Implicit control of distribution channels through the use of advertising and market research is outlined in figure 13.2. The intention is to operate primarily through consumer demand, and ideally (from the producer's viewpoint) consumers will refuse to accept another firm's brand and go to another retailer who does stock the advertised product. The original retailer will be encouraged to purchase the product for fear of losing further trade.

Thus although some manufacturers' advertising and promotion is still directed at the retailer (via salesmen, trade journals, trade exhibitions etc.) the bulk of it goes via specialized advertising agents and mass media such as TV and the press to the final consumer. The product-handling middleman is bypassed. The consumer information on which the manufacturer bases his production and promotion decisions comes to him by way of specialized market research agencies. They can obtain data on sales rates by type and location of retailer and on consumption patterns by household and the demographic features of households (family size, income region, education level, newspaper taken etc.). This information is fed at frequent intervals to manufacturers, advertising agents and the advertising media themselves.

When information flows backwards in this way it is both speedier and more accurate than consumer feedback via word of mouth or order level changes in the distribution channel of figure 13.2(a). Traditionally, such backward information flows were either too slow or too distorted to enable the producer to adjust his output quickly to meet consumer demands. Faulty assumptions can distort facts by escalation, quite apart from any distortion caused simply by repeated transmission of a message. For example, consider a retailer with normal monthly stocks and sales of commodity X of 100 cases per month. His policy is to retain stocks at the level of anticipated sales. If sales fall by 20 per cent, 20 cases are left in stock. The retailer then assumes that only 80 cases are going to be sold in future; he thus orders 60, a 40 per cent fall in the normal order to the wholesaler. If the wholesaler services ten retailers, each of whom suffers the same experience, then his sales will drop by 400 cases. If he also works on a policy of stocks equalling anticipated sales then, having 400 cases left in stock, he may assume sales will now only be 600 monthly rather than 1000; he will thus order only 200 cases from the manufacturer. Thus a 20 per cent fall in sales has escalated to an 80 per cent reduction in orders from the manufacturer.

Market research at the level of the retailer, or better still the household, will show far more accurately and quickly what is actually happening in the market-place at consumer level. (For example, *audits* of household consumption on a fortnightly basis, given a sample of households, show what is really being consumed, where products are being bought and by whom. Such audits are often carried out by visual inspection of the sample members' kitchens or even by physical collection of empty containers. The latter may sound rather unhygienic – it is called the 'dustbin audit' – but it does overcome problems of memory default. It highlights frequency of consumption by household types and container size.)

Market research, in short, reinforces the producer's attempt to pull goods through the channel. It enables the producer to tailor his product, his brand image and his advertising to what the consumer wants. In short, he can apply the marketing concept (figure 13.1). He can choose the appropriate media for reaching the customers who do not but might buy the product. He can adjust the product and the packaging according to consumer wants and to the requirements of the retailer that these consumers visit (rather than to the requirements of retailers that are little frequented by the consumers that the manufacturer is primarily interested in).

Advertising itself has two main effects. First, it reduces long-run demand elasticity through its association with branding. Second, it increases short-run price sensitivity. This may sound contradictory; let us examine the statements in turn. Figure 13.5 shows how demand can be made less elastic. D is the long-run demand curve prior to advertising. D′ is the curve after advertising; it is placed up and to the right of D. The original price–quantity combination of P', Q' is thus alterd to P', Q'', or, if the firm wishes to raise price, to P_1, Q_1. Note that the elasticity of D′ is less than that of D. For a similar price rise (P' to P_1) the decreased quantity demanded is less (Q'' to Q_1 as against Q' to Q_2).

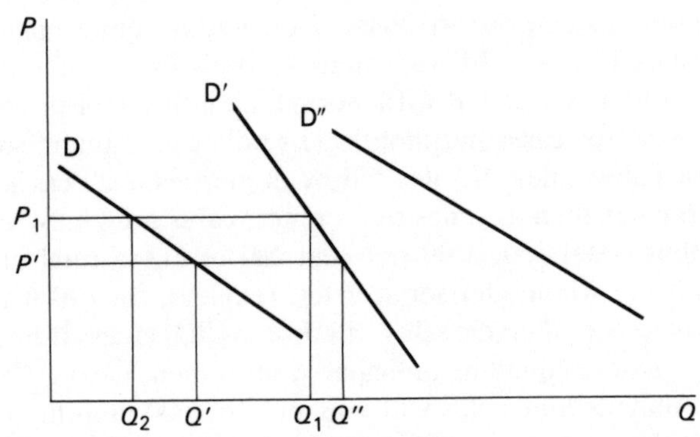

Figure 13.5 *Advertising reduces long-run demand elasticity*

The reason for this is embodied in *brand loyalty.* Branding depends on advertising. As Professor Sir Dennis Robertson put it: 'There is a real spiritual comfort in buying a packet of a known and trusted brand of cocoa rather than a shovelful of brown powder of uncertain origin.' A brand gives the customer assurance that the commodity will be constant in quality, appearance and taste wherever it is purchased. An unidentified commodity may vary from day to day and shop to shop. If the consumer likes it the consumer can continue to buy. Alternatively, if the product is not preferred, the brand identifies it and it can be avoided. A poor brand will go to the wall more quickly than an unidentified low-quality product. There is thus a strong economic motivation for the manufacturer to produce and maintain a product of acceptable and consistent characteristics.

Branding, of course, depends not only on advertising but also on *pre-packaging*, i.e. packaging by the manufacturer rather than the retailer. Modern packaging technology has removed the bulk breaking function away from the 'back shop' to the factory. It permits branding, facilitates stacking on open shelves and encourages self-service retailing. Thus medicines, cheeses, tea, bacon and chickens are now all produced and packaged at a much earlier stage than previously. The large and modern machines which made this possible perform the operations more efficiently and encourage in turn the more productive forms of retailing that we have already examined.

How does branding and advertising increase short-run price sensitivity? In essence, the answer is simple. Long-run price elasticity is always greater than short run because people have time both to learn about and to react to changes in product price (the second law of demand). If it is possible to reduce the learning period by making consumers more aware either of product price itself or of changes in price, then the long-run elasticity moves closer (in time terms) to the current or short-run period. Advertising and branding by making goods more identifiable and by making more information (including price) available about them thus increases short-run demand elasticity. Consumer reaction to price levels and changes is speedier and so price sensitivity is increased. In brief, the demand curve in the short period is shifted (in figure 13.5) from D′ (a possible original position) to D″.

Whether the effect of advertising in both periods together is to raise or lower price elasticity is, of course, an empirical question. Whether price itself is higher or lower is also open to debate. The price that the firm will select will depend not only on the demand curve but also on the cost curve (including advertising). Figure 13.6 illustrates this dilemma.

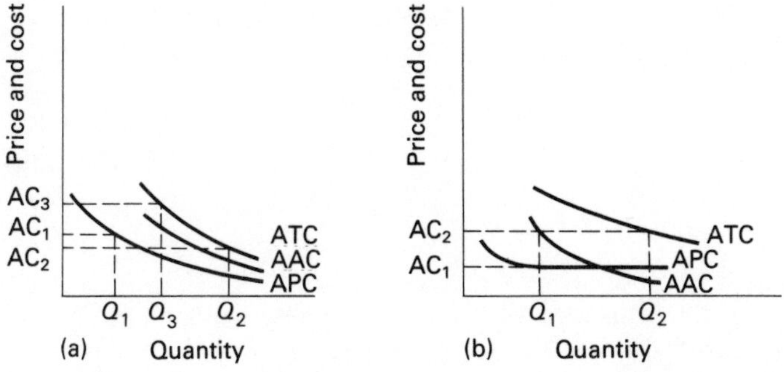

Figure 13.6 *Advertising and overall price selection*

Average total cost (ATC) can only be reduced by advertising where average advertising cost (AAC) is less than the savings per unit obtained in average production cost (APC) when the scale of production is increased. If APC is constant or rising, then any advertising must raise ATC, since advertising itself adds to the costs. The two alternatives are illustrated in figure 13.6. In both diagrams, Q_1 represents output before advertising, Q_2 output after advertising. Even figure 13.6(a) does not give an unambiguous answer, of course. Had output only been raised to Q_3, then ATC would have *risen* from AC_1 to AC_3.

Nothing can be deduced *a priori* about the influence of advertising on total unit costs. Whether cost differences due to advertising will or will not lead to corresponding price differences cannot be determined merely by examining the direction in which costs have moved. If advertising has resulted in lower costs then the new equilibrium price will depend upon what has happened to marginal receipts as well as to marginal costs. The outcome may, but need not necessarily, be a lower price.

14

Industrial Relations and the Market for Labour

In this chapter we shall be concerned with the pricing and allocation of a major factor of production: labour. We can employ the tools of supply and demand to analyse this market, just as we can in any other. Certain major caveats must be borne in mind, however. The market for labour can be segmented on an industrial, geographical and even on a firm-specific basis. Any general principles operate within a complex legal and institutional framework and each individual sector of the market may vary according to the degree of unionization and the relative strengths of sellers and purchasers of labour. Labour mobility and the elasticity of supply of labour might be further governed by local conditions, availability of housing, schools and other factors in the social infrastructure of the locality. In addition the demand and supply of labour are affected by inducements under government policy and by sociological willingness or unwillingness to move from traditional areas of residence. In addition, one major preoccupation of successive administrations has been the containment of inflation and this has on occasion manifested itself in measures aimed at controlling wage increases. The market for labour is thus influenced by a very complicated pot-pourri of factors.

We shall proceed by considering how economic analysis can be applied to the study of the labour market, and then consider in turn some of the other various factors and issues mentioned above.

Economic Analysis and the Labour Market

Adam Smith suggested that: 'The whole of the advantages and disadvantages of the different employments of labour and stock must, in the same neighbourhood, be either perfectly equal or continually tending to equality.'[1] The idea is that factors of production will pursue the most advantageous opportunities of employment, and as long as there are no restrictions on liberty to change occupations the pressure of the pursuit of individual advantage would enforce equality of returns for similar occupations. But the supply of labour is only half the story, and consideration must be given to the demand for labour. This is necessarily a derived demand, since employers demand labour not for its own sake but for the contribution it can make when combined with other factors of production to produce goods and services. In practice it is very difficult to disentangle the contributions made by the different factors of production. Smith was aware of some of the difficulties, but it was Marx who developed them fully, turned them around and argued that the process of production in a capitalist system involved the appropriation by the capitalist interest of surplus value produced by labour.[2] The Marxian approach reaches one of its culminations in the work of Sraffa.[3] A simplistic version of the Marxian view would run as follows: if a man and an oven make a pie the value of that pie belongs to the man only. Smith had pondered the problem and failed to ascertain how much of the pie value belonged to the man and how much to the owners of the oven. The issue is even more complex, however. The man may put as much effort and sweat into producing a mince pie as he would a mud pie. What reward should he and the oven owner receive then? Clearly the mud pie will sell for zero; it has no value, despite the labour input. The meat pie does have a value; this is the price consumers will willingly pay for it. But how is this apportioned? The pie could not be baked without the oven, and the oven could not bake without the man. Let us consider the work of Marshall.

If it is assumed that producers seek to maximize profitability they will apply the familiar marginal conditions developed in chapter 5. They should employ each factor of production up to the point where its marginal contribution to revenue is equal to the marginal cost of employing the last unit of it. Marshall employed the homely analogy of the farmer determining how many shepherds to employ.[4] The demand for labour will be determined by the value of the marginal product of labour in the particular employment concerned. The farmer will be moved to hire another shepherd if he thinks that the man's contribution will be, say, to increase his output of good quality sheep by 20 per annum, and the cost of a shepherd's annual subsistence is less than or equal to the value of 20 sheep. This is shown in table 14.1. It can be seen from the table that the farmer would hire up to 11 shepherds and no more. The value of the marginal product of the eleventh shepherd is equal to 20 sheep and, as a shepherd's wage is the equivalent of 20 sheep, we have marginal equivalency. At this point profits or the surplus are maximized, and to hire any more shepherds would be counter-productive. Marshall went on to argue that in every occupation labour would be hired until its wage was equal to the value of its marginal product; however, he was careful to add that this in itself was not a theory of wages, since to value the marginal product of labour we have to take for granted all the other costs of the productive process. It remains, nevertheless, an important element in a neoclassical theory of wage determination.

Table 14.1 *The farmer's demand for shepherds as determined by the value of their marginal product (all values in terms of the number of sheep produced)*

Number of shepherds	Annual output of sheep	Marginal product due to last shepherd	Average product	Wages bill	Surplus (output − wages)
8	580	–	72½	160	420
9	615	35	68½	180	435
10	640	25	64	200	440
11	660	20	60	220	440
12	676	16	56⅓	240	436

Source: Alfred Marshall, *Principles of Economics* (1890), Macmillan, 9th edn, 1961, book 6, chapter 1

We can extend the analysis further by consideration of the nature of the firm's production function in the short run on the lines introduced in chapter 4. In the short run it is assumed that a factor input, usually capital machinery, is fixed. Given this it follows that the law of diminishing returns will ensure that successively greater labour inputs will add less and less to total output. The total physical product will behave, as a function of labour inputs, in the manner shown in figure 14.1. Marginal physical product will be zero at a labour input of L_1 in the figure; this corresponds to the maximum point on the total physical product curve. We are now in a position to derive the firm's demand curve for labour in the short run.

If it is assumed that the firm's objective is to maximize profits, it will be interested in the marginal revenue product associated with the use of extra units of labour (as shown previously in the example of the farmer hiring shepherds). Furthermore if the firm is operating under conditions of perfect competition, which we shall assume for simplicity of argument, then the marginal revenue associated with selling extra units of output will be a constant equal to the price of the goods sold. In these circumstances, multiplying the previous marginal physical product curve by the good's price (the firm's marginal revenue) will give us a marginal revenue product curve which is the firm's demand curve for labour, as shown in figure 14.2.

If the firm hires labour in a competitive labour market with a wage rate fixed at W_1, it will pay the firm to hire L_1 units of labour so as to maximize profits. The downward-sloping portion of the firm's marginal revenue product curve is its short-run demand curve for labour. By equating this with the marginal cost of labour, in this case the wage rate W_1, the firm maximizes its profits.

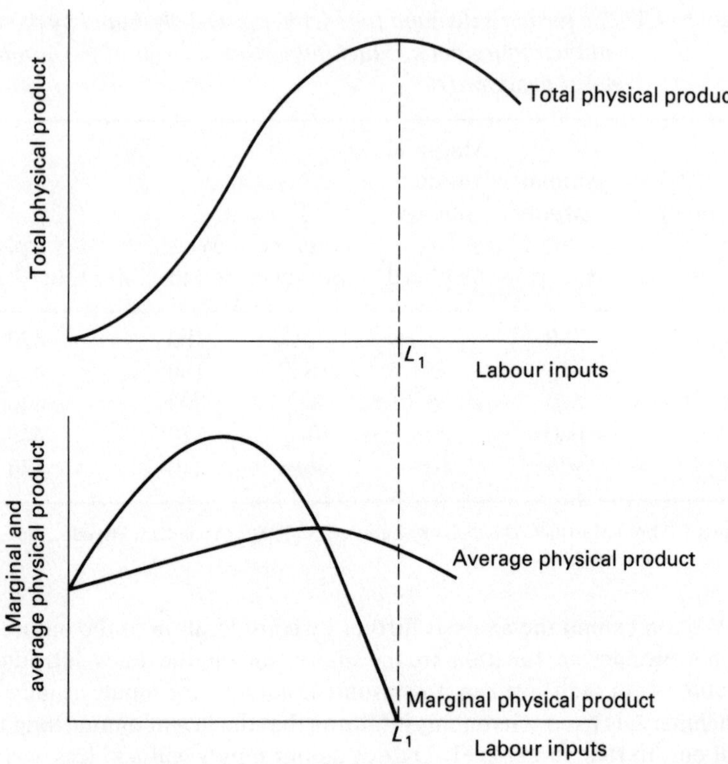

Figure 14.1 *The behaviour of total, average and marginal physical product in the short run, given fixed capital and variable labour inputs*

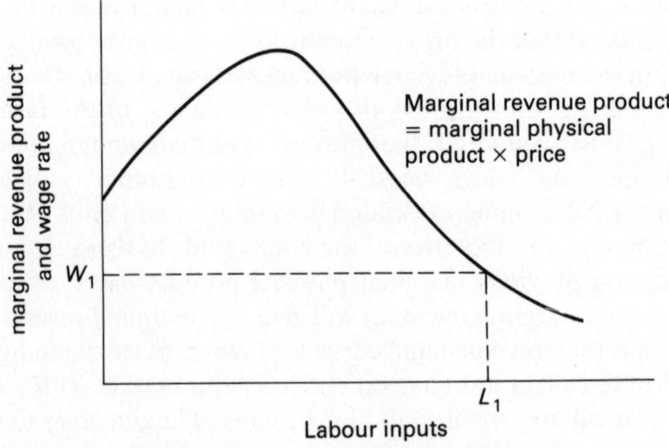

Figure 14.2 *The marginal revenue product curve: the firm's short-run demand for labour*

It can be shown that in the case of a firm selling its product in an imperfect market, which implies a downward-sloping demand curve for its product, the firm will demand less labour than under perfect market conditions. This follows since the marginal revenue curve is below the demand curve, and therefore the marginal revenue product curve is derived by multiplying marginal physical product by the lower figure of marginal revenue rather than price as used in the perfectly competitive case.

The industry demand for labour in terms of marginal productivity theory

The industry demand for labour in the short run under conditions of perfect competition cannot be derived by simply summing the marginal revenue product curves of all its constituent firms. Consider the effect of a lowering of the wage rate. Each firm would react by hiring more labour and by expanding its output. This means that the industry's output as a whole will increase and therefore the equilibrium price will fall. Yet remember that the individual firm's demand curve for labour was derived by multiplying labour's marginal physical product by the constant equilibrium price, which has now changed to a lower value. Thus the marginal revenue product curve must have shifted bodily to the left, and would have shifted in the opposite direction had there been an increase in the wage rate. This is shown in figure 14.3.

In this figure it can be seen that when the wage rate falls from W_1 to W_2 the firm's demand for labour increases from L_1 to L_2, the two points of intersection of the wage rate with the two marginal revenue product curves MRP_1 and MRP_2. The firm's short-run demand curve for labour is

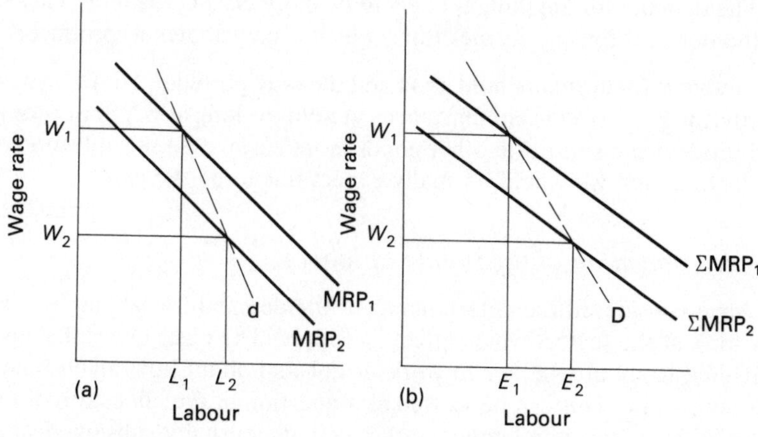

Figure 14.3 *The demand for labour in the short run: (a) the firm; (b) the industry*

therefore the locus of all the points of contact of the various wage rates with the various marginal revenue product curves associated with those differing wage rates. The firm's short-run demand curve is marked d in the diagram. The sum of all the individual firms' demand curves for labour produces the industry demand curve for labour D. If the industry is the sole employer of this type of labour then this would be the market demand curve for that labour, but if more than one industry uses the labour then a similar exercise involving all firms across the relevant industries would produce the overall demand curve for that type of labour.

A similar type of analysis will establish the firm's long-run demand curve for labour. There are additional complications in that changes in the utilization of labour, following a fall in the wage rate, will alter the marginal productivity of capital. It follows that capital inputs will be altered too, but as soon as this happens there are changes in the marginal productivity of labour. The net result of this chain of interactions is that the demand for labour is likely to be more elastic in the long run than in the short run. Marshall enumerated the factors which affect the elasticity of demand for labour but Hicks subsequently modified one of them.[5] We shall also follow Hicks in citing Pigou's more succinct account of Marshall's rules governing the elasticity of derived demand.[6] Pigou's version of the rules are as follows.

1 The demand for anything is likely to be more elastic, the more readily substitutes for that thing can be obtained.
2 The demand for anything is likely to be less elastic, the less important is the part played by the cost of that thing in the total cost of some other thing, in the production of which it is employed.
3 The demand for anything is likely to be more elastic, the more elastic is the supply of co-operant agents of production.
4 The demand for anything is likely to be more elastic, the more elastic is the demand for any further thing which it contributes to produce.[7]

The above rules normally hold good and the only problem, Hicks suggests, is with rule 2 in extreme circumstances. it holds as long as purchasers of the final product can substitute other goods more easily than the entrepreneur can factors, and we would normally expect this to be the case.

The determination of the supply of labour

We have considered the determinants of the demand for labour; we shall now look at the factors which affect its supply. The basic choice facing an individual is about whether to work or not and about how much time to devote to work. This can be viewed as a question of the allocation of time between work and non-labour market activities usually subsumed under the title leisure. The choice is shown in figure 14.4.

This figure is drawn under the assumption that the individual concerned

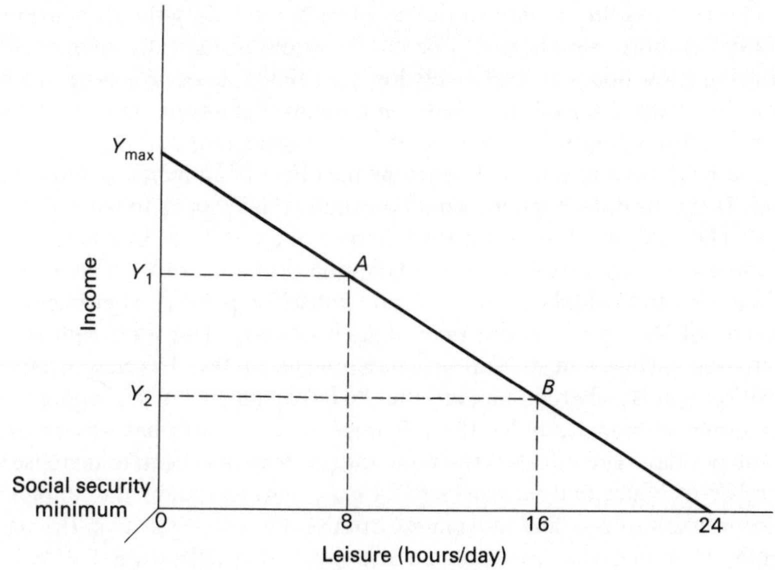

Figure 14.4 *The income–leisure choice*

receives a constant remuneration per number of hours worked. If he chose not to work at all he would draw the state-guaranteed social security minimum and have 24 hours of leisure per day. As soon as he begins to work his income begins to rise and his leisure time falls (ignoring taxation and factors such as the 'poverty trap'). So he starts moving up the line in the diagram, and at its other end, representing a theoretical but impractical extreme, he could work 24 hours per day and have no leisure but an income of Y_{max}. The question is, where on the line will he locate himself? Will it be at point A, which involves having only 8 hours of leisure but an incomes of Y_1, or at point B, where he has 16 hours of leisure but an income of Y_2?

We can approach the problem from the point of view of marginal utility theory considered in chapter 3. The person concerned will work up to the point where the utility of the income derived from the last hour's labour just equals the utility of the hour's leisure sacrificed to earn the income. We have

$$\frac{\text{marginal utility of income}}{\text{hourly wage rate}} = \frac{\text{marginal utility of leisure}}{\text{price of leisure (hourly wage rate)}}$$

It is assumed that successive additions to a person's income will yield smaller increments of satisfaction, and that successive losses of hours of leisure time will lead to progressively greater loss of satisfaction as leisure time becomes ever more scarce. This will determine whether our individual places himself at A or B in figure 14.4.

This conveys the essence of the problem but in reality the circumstances will be far more complicated. The choice would realistically involve either working a few hours at a relatively low part-time rate or switching to a full-time job with a higher rate but a minimum eight-hour day, or, finally, working a few hours' overtime at an even higher rate.

The next obvious question concerns the effect of an increase in the wage rate. If this were to happen, would our individual choose to work more or less? The analysis of this question is shown in figure 14.5. In this figure the original wage rate gives a maximum hypothetical wage of W_1 if no leisure is taken. Our individual chooses to locate himself at point A where he has an income of W_A and a leisure time of L_1 hours/day. The wage rate is then increased giving a maximum attainable wage of W_2. His new preferred position is at B, where it happens that he has an income of W_1, equal to the maximum attainable under the old wage rate, but still has leisure of L_2 hours per day. The effect of the wage rate increase has been to increase the number of hours that he works to $24 - L_2$, and to reduce the amount of leisure taken to L_2. The movement from point A to point B in the figure could be viewed as involving an income and a substitution effect, as considered previously in chapter 3.

An increase in the wage rate means that the relative price of leisure has increased; it is more expensive than previously. The response we would expect via the substitution effect is a reduction in the consumption of

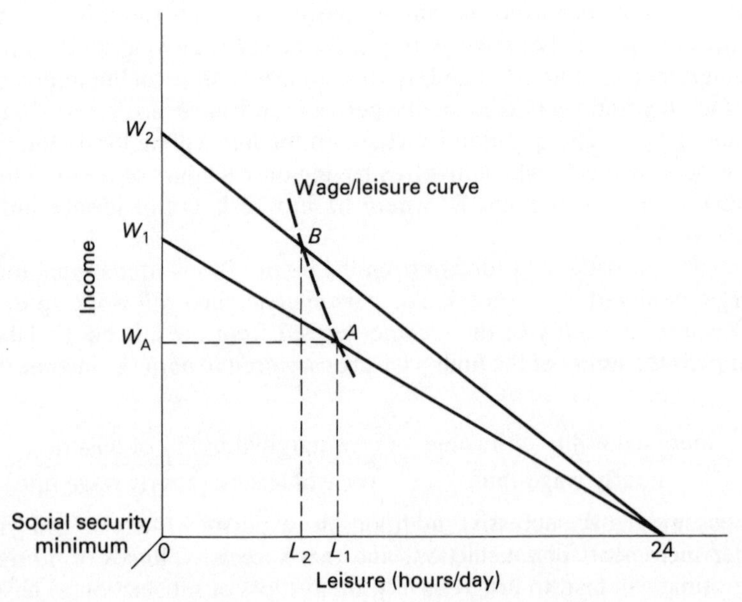

Figure 14.5 *The wage–leisure curve*

leisure as a result of its increased price. But there is also the income effect to consider.

The fact that the wage rate has increased means that at all levels of work the individual will be better off than previously; he has gained an increase in income. The 'normal' effect of an increase in income is to increase expenditure on 'normal' goods. The income effect of the wage increase, if leisure is a normal good, will be to increase the consumption of leisure. The net results will depend upon the balance of these two opposing effects. In the case of the individual in figure 14.5 the substitution effect dominates and the net effect is a reduction in the amount of leisure taken.

The wage–leisure curve in figure 14.5 traces out the relationship between leisure taken (or hours worked) and alterations in the wage rate. It is a short step from this to the derivation of an individual's labour supply curve. which shows the relationship between hours worked and the wage rate. It would probably look something like figure 14.6.

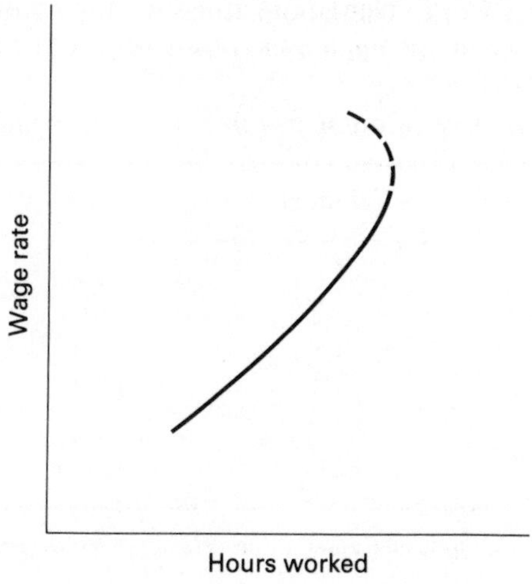

Figure 14.6 *An individual's short-run labour supply curve*

This figure shows that the number of hours an individual is prepared to work is likely to be positively related to the wage rate. There is some controversy about the top section of the curve. Whether an individual chooses to work more or less in response to a wage increase depends on the relative magnitudes of the income and substitution effects. If the income effect outweighs the substitution effect he might well respond by taking more leisure hours. This would produce a backward-bending labour supply curve at high wage rates, as shown in figure 14.6 by the dotted section of the curve. There is not much empirical evidence on this point, and hours actually worked are a function of both supply and demand factors, but it has been traditionally argued that in certain industries absenteeism and 'unofficial' days off might suggest that the labour supply curve behaves in this fashion.

The long-run supply of labour is a function of a number of complex demographic, sociological and educational and other factors. Before we proceed to consider these it might be wise to have a closer look at the labour market in practice. We can begin by looking at the working population.

The Labour Force

The supply of labour will be governed by the overall size of the labour force and by economic activity rates, i.e. by the proportions of the various sex and age groups which make up the population and who are working or actively looking for work. The labour force in Great Britain increased by over 4 million between 1961 and 1990 (see table 14.2).

Table 14.2 *The size of the workforce in Great Britain*[a] *(millions)*

	Females	Males	All persons
1961[b]	7.7	16.1	23.8
1971[b]	9.2	15.9	25.1
1975	9.5	15.8	25.3
1980	10.3	15.9	26.2
1985	10.9	16.1	27.0
1990	12.1	15.9	28.0

[a] Excluding students in full-time education. From 1973, 15 year olds are excluded because the school-leaving age was raised.
[b] Estimates for 1961 and 1971 are taken directly from the Census of Population.
Sources: *Social Trends*, 1983, p. 52; '1990 labour force survey preliminary results', *Employment Gazette* (April 1991), pp. 175–96; *Annual Abstract of Statistics*, 1987, p. 107, and 1991, p. 109

The major changes involve a large increase in the female labour force combined with no change in the male labour force. The increase in the male population has been offset by the raising of the school-leaving age and a decline in activity rates; this decline is most evident amongst older men, who have recently shown a tendency to retire earlier. Details of activity rates are given in table 14.3.

The large increase in the female labour force over the period considered has largely been the result of the growth in the proportion of married women wanting to work plus an increase in demand for part-time workers.

Table 14.3 *Civilian labour force economic activity rates in Great Britain by age and sex (percentages)*

	16–19[a]	20–24	25–44	Females 45–54 Males 45–59	Females 55–59 Males 60–64	Females 60 Males 65 and over	All aged over 16
Females							
1961[b]	71.1	61.8	40.3	41.4		10.0	37.3
1971	65.0	60.2	52.4	62.0	50.9	12.4	43.9
1981	70.4	68.8	61.7	68.0	53.4	8.3	47.6
1989[c]	73.7	75.1	72.0	72.2	54.3	7.6	52.6
Males							
1961[b]	74.6	91.9	98.5	96.8		25.0	86.0
1971	69.4	87.7	95.4	94.8	82.9	19.2	80.5
1981	72.4	85.1	95.7	93.0	69.3	10.3	76.5
1989[c]	75.0	87.1	94.4	88.0	54.6	8.9	74.3

[a] Estimates for 1961 include 15 year olds.
[b] Estimates for 1961 are taken directly from the Census of Population and include those in the armed forces and exclude students.
[c] The civilian labour force includes persons aged 16 and over who are either in employment or unemployed. The definition of unemployment for the 1989 estimates differs slightly from that used in earlier years.
Source: *Social Trends*, 1983, p. 52; *Social Trends*, 1991, p. 68.

The increase in female activity rates is evident from the table. The pattern for males aged from 16 to 60 has shown more stability. However, for the period 1961–89 there has been a significant decrease and this has been especially evident in those aged over 60, reflecting the increase in early retirement for males aged over 55.

There are a number of ways in which the economic analysis developed previously can be applied in the analysis of activity rates. But first and foremost it could be argued that most of the labour force is in households and that it is therefore household rather than individual income which is the most important factor. A distinction is often made between primary workers, such as married men who are likely to be the family breadwinners, and secondary workers, such as their wives, who are more likely to move in and out of the workforce, depending on family circumstances, incidence of childbirth and so on. Indeed, the activity rates for primary workers are much higher. The fact that activity rates have risen in a period in which real incomes have risen, such as between 1984 and 1990 when the activity rate for all persons aged 16 and over rose from 62.1 to 64.0 per cent,[8] suggests that the income effects of increases in income have not outweighed the substitution effects, but this is a complex field in which many factors have altered. There have been alterations in the number of hours worked and in the availability of holidays, as shown in table 14.4.

Table 14.4 *Holidays with pay*

End year	Percentage of manual employees with basic[a] holidays of							Percentage with extra service entitlement
	Two weeks	Between two and three weeks	Three weeks	Between three and four weeks	Four weeks	Between four and five weeks	Five weeks and over	
1972	8	16	39	33	4			12
1973	6	9	36	45	4			14
1974	1	1	30	40	28			20
1975	1	1	17	51	30			26
1976		1	18	47	34			32
1977		1	18	47	34			32
1978		1	17	47	35			36
1979		1	7	42	50[b]			38
1980			2	24	19	55		40
1981			2	11	25	61	1	37[c]
1982			2	5	21	53	19	35[c]
1983				5	17	60	18	36[c]
1984				5	15	61	19	35[c]
1985				1	16	63	20	32[c]
1986					14	63	23	32[c]

[a] Additional to public and customary holidays. There are currently eight days of public holidays.
[b] Includes some employees with entitlement of more than four weeks.
[c] The fall since 1980 is mainly attributable to the deletion from some Wages Council orders and agreements of references to extra service entitlements. This does not necessarily imply that previous arrangements will not continue on a voluntary basis.
Source: Recent changes in hours and holiday entitlements – manual employees', *Employment Gazette* (March 1987), p. 132.

Average normal weekly hours of manual workers in the manufacturing, energy and construction industries were 42.9 at the end of 1990 compared with 40.2 hours at the end of 1970. The labour force is defined as all those in employment: employees, employers, self-employed, Her Majesty's Forces, and those identified by censuses and surveys as seeking work (including those both registered and unregistered as unemployed, but excluding students in full-time education). It is difficult to predict changes in this force with any degree of accuracy. It was estimated that between 1981 and 1986 the total population of working age should have risen by 762,000, but activity rates are affected by, for example, changes in the birth rate and by the level of unemployment, since it is argued that in periods of high unemployment some potential workers are discouraged from seeking work by the difficulty of finding work.[9] (Table 14.2 shows that this estimate was quite accurate and the actual labour force increased by 0.8 million between 1980 and 1985.)

The labour force in terms of type of occupation

The industrial sector of the economy, defined to include manufacturing, gas, electricity, water and construction industries, has been in decline in recent years, with a shrinkage of employees of almost 2 million between 1961 and 1979. This was partly offset by an increase of 0.5 million men working in service industries. Female employees in the industrial sector declined by about 0.75 million against a background of a rise in female employees of 1.5 million between 1961 and 1979. There was also a large increase in part-time working, much of it female and the bulk of it concentrated in service industries. Table 14.5 gives a breakdown of employment by sector.

Notable features of this table are the continuing decline of the manufacturing sector with relative employment down over 11 percentage points since 1973. The other side of the coin is the continuing advance of the service sector; insurance, banking and finance now account for 11.2 per cent and other services now account for 29.5 per cent of total employment. On an international comparative basis with other developed countries, the proportion in the service sector is now relatively large, and the industrial sector is relatively small, as can be seen from table 14.6.

However, the relative advance and decline of the different sectors is symptomatic of major structural changes and dislocations within the UK economy, and is the root of much of the disparity in regional unemployment rates considered in the next section.

Unemployment and the Regional Problem

In an economic sense those members of the workforce who are actively seeking employment and are unable to find it are said to be unemployed.

Table 14.5 *Employees in employment in UK, broken down by industrial sector*[a]

	1973		1977		1981		1985[b]		1989[b]	
Total employees in employment[c]	22,663	(100.0)	22,619	(100.0)	21,205	(100.0)	21,423	(100.0)	22,756	(100.0)
Total, production and construction industries[d]	9,917	(43.8)	9,259	(40.9)	7,847	(37.0)	6,974	(32.6)	6,768	(29.7)
Agriculture, forestry and fishing[e]	432	(1.9)	388	(1.7)	360	(1.7)	341	(1.6)	300	(1.3)
Mining and quarrying	363	(1.6)	350	(1.5)	332	(1.6)				
Manufacturing industries	7,830	(34.5)	7,292	(32.2)	6,041	(28.5)	5,362	(25.0)	5,234	(23.0)
Construction	1,380	(6.1)	1,270	(5.6)	1,134	(5.3)	1,021	(4.8)	1,062	(4.7)
Gas, electricity and water	344	(1.5)	347	(1.5)	340	(1.6)	n.a.		n.a.	
Transport and communication	1,524	(6.7)	1,468	(6.5)	1,440	(6.8)	1,327	(6.2)	1,362	(6.0)
Distributive trades	2,744	(12.1)	2,753	(12.2)	2,636	(12.4)	3,138	(14.6)	3,328	(14.6)
Insurance, banking, finance and business services	1,058	(4.7)	1,145	(5.1)	1,233	(5.8)	1,965	(9.2)	2,555	(11.2)
Professional and scientific services	3,250	(14.3)	3,646	(16.1)	3,695	(17.4)	3,077	(14.4)	3,394	(14.9)
Catering, hotels etc.	794	(3.5)	863	(3.8)	872	(4.1)	1,042	(4.9)	1,124	(4.9)
Miscellaneous services (excluding catering, hotels etc.)	1,359	(6.0)	1,480	(6.5)	1,542	(7.3)	1,972	(9.2)	2,216	(9.7)
National government service[f]	608	(2.7)	650	(2.9)	615	(2.9)				
Local government service	977	(4.3)	964	(4.3)	964	(4.5)	1,587	(7.4)	1,650	(7.3)

[a] All estimates relate to June. Industries analysed according to the SIC 1968 (for 1973, 1977 and 1981) and 1980 (for 1985 and 1989). An attempt has been made to form comparable classes.

[b] For 1985 and 1989 no separate figures were available for mining and quarrying, gas, electricity and water, and national government service.

[c] Excluding private domestic service.

[d] The industries included in the index of production and construction are orders II–XXI of SIC 1968 and SIC codes 1–5 of SIC 1980.

[e] The estimates for agriculture are taken from the census of agriculture and exclude a small number of employees of agricultural machinery manufacturers.

[f] Excluding members of Her Majesty's Forces.

Sources: 1973, 1979, 1981, *Monthly Digest of Statistics*, October 1981; 1985, 1989, *Annual Abstract of Statistics*, 1991

Table 14.6 *An international comparison of civilian employment by sector, 1988 (percentages)*

	Agriculture[a]	Industry[b]	Services[c]	Total[d]
UK	2.3	29.8	66.6	100
Canada	4.5	25.6	69.9	100
France	6.8	30.3	62.9	100
West Germany	4.0	39.8	56.1	100
Italy	9.8	32.4	57.7	100
Japan[e]	7.9	34.1	58.0	100
USA	2.9	26.9	70.2	100

[a] Agriculture, hunting, forestry and fishing.
[b] Mining, quarrying, manufacturing, electricity, gas, water and construction.
[c] Wholesaling, retailing, catering, transportation, storage, communication, finance, insurance, real estate, business services, community, social and personal services.
[d] Totals may not exactly equal the sum of the columns owing to rounding.
[e] Includes the armed forces.
Source: *Employment Gazette* (February 1991), pp. S18 and S19

The distinction is normally made between this type of unemployment, which is involuntary, and voluntary unemployment, which describes those potential members of the workforce who have withdrawn their labour, perhaps because they think the inducement to work at the prevailing rate they command is inadequate. Unemployment is categorized into various types. People changing jobs are unlikely to move between one job and another instantaneously, and so there will always be a certain amount of what is termed *frictional unemployment.* Vacancies will vary with the seasons; hotels, the building industry and agriculture will have varying demands for labour according to the time of year, and so there will be seasonally related unemployment. Both national economies and the collective international economy display cycles of economic activity with periods of boom and slump. If demand is depressed and the authorities are pursuing 'tight' monetary policies with regimes of high interest rates there will by *cyclical unemployment* (the relationship between the rate of unemployment and the rate of inflation will be considered later in this chapter). Finally, and particularly important in the UK context, there is *structural unemployment.* This is caused by changes in the structure and relative importance of different sectors of the economy. The run-down of some of the more traditional industries such as iron and steel, cotton and textiles, shipbuilding etc. means that in the localities where these industries are concentrated – Scotland, northern England and South Wales – there are likely to be higher and more persistent unemployment rates (these problems are considered more fully in chapter 15).

Table 14.7 *UK unemployment rates (seasonally adjusted)*

	Workforce[a] (thousands)	Unemployed[b] (thousands)	Percentage unemployed
1971	25,229	653	2.6
1974	25,676	518	2.0
1978	26,358	1,144	4.3
1982	26,677	2,545	9.5
1984	27,265	2,916	10.7
1986	27,791	3,098	11.1
1988	28,260	2,275	8.1
1990	28,436	1,662	5.8

[a] The workforce consists of the workforce in employment and the unemployed (claimants). Estimates relate to the mid-year.
[b] Estimates of unemployment relate to those aged 18 and over who are claiming unemployment-related benefit at Unemployment Benefit Offices and are average figures over the 12 months of the year.
Sources: J. Lawlor, 'Monthly unemployment Statistics: making a consistent series', *Employment Gazette* (December 1990), pp. 601–8; *Economic Trends Annual Supplement 1991*, HMSO, 1991; *Employment Gazette* (April 1991)

The tight monetary policies pursued in the early 1980s and the industrial 'shake-out' which took place led to record levels of unemployment, as can be seen in table 14.7. The level of unemployment then decreased, and the economy has responded with increases in profitability, productivity and unemployment. However, the level of unemployment was still high by recent historical standards and in the latter half of 1990 began to rise again.

There has been criticism of the unemployment statistics, which are currently based on the number of workers claiming unemployment-related benefit. It is argued that some potential workers, particularly married women, do not bother to claim. On the other hand it is also argued that some people claim without having a real desire to find work. It is difficult to be sure of the numbers involved in these effects, but there can be little disagreement with the view that there are relatively large disparities in regional unemployment rates, as shown in table 14.8.

It can be seen that the north, Scotland, Northern Ireland and Wales have had the highest unemployment rates since 1965 (and for many years before that). The rise in unemployment rates in the early to middle 1980s affected all regions. But if the ratio of the rate in 1986 to that in 1975 is compared it will be seen that the regions which suffered most were Yorkshire, the southeast and the West Midlands, whose rates all rose by a factor of over 4. In the late 1980s the unemployment rates fell in all regions with the north,

Table 14.8 *Regional unemployment rates*[a,b] *analysis by standard regions (seasonally adjusted)*

	North[c]	Yorkshire and Humberside	East Midlands[c]	East Anglia	Southeast[c]	Southwest[c]	West Midlands	Northwest[c]	Wales	Scotland	Northern Ireland
1965	2.4	1.0	0.8	1.2	0.8	1.5	0.6	1.5	2.5	2.8	5.9
1970	4.5	2.8	2.2	2.1	1.6	2.8	1.9	2.7	3.8	4.1	6.6
1975	4.2	2.8	2.5	2.5	2.0	3.3	2.9	3.8	4.0	3.6	5.4
1980	7.7	5.0	4.2	3.6	2.9	4.3	5.2	6.2	6.5	6.8	9.1
1984	15.1	11.6	9.8	7.9	7.7	9.0	12.7	13.5	13.1	12.5	15.9
1986	15.4	12.5	10.0	8.5	8.3	9.5	12.9	13.8	13.6	13.3	17.3
1988	12.1	9.6	7.3	5.4	5.5	6.4	9.1	10.6	10.0	11.3	16.1
1990	8.7	6.7	5.1	3.7	4.0	4.4	6.0	7.7	6.6	8.1	13.4

[a] The number of unemployed as a percentage of the estimated total workforce (the sum of employees in employment, unemployed aged 18 and over, self-employed and HM Forces and participants in work-related government training programmes) at mid-year.

[b] Quarterly averages.

[c] The boundaries of the standard regions were revised in April 1974.

Sources: *Economic Trends Annual Supplement 1991*; *Employment Gazette* (April 1991)

Scotland, Northern Ireland and now the northwest having the highest rates.

It could be argued that the important statistic is not the number of unemployed at any one time but the length of time, i.e. duration, that people are unemployed. Since 1961 unemployment at all durations has increased, but it is particularly marked in the case of those unemployed for a year or more. In 1971 this group accounted for about one-sixth of the unemployed but it had risen to one-quarter by 1979 and in 1990 it was even higher at 32 per cent. The composition of the group varies; the young, the old and the unskilled are particularly at risk. There is a greater demand for skilled labour, and consequently the duration of its unemployment is likely to be less.

We have considered the supply of labour in terms of the composition of the labour force and the distribution of unemployment. We can now look more closely at more detailed aspects of the labour market. We shall begin by looking at pay differentials and then examine some of the factors behind them such as trade union activity, government regulation, strike activity and the like.

Pay Differentials

One of the striking features of changes in pay differentials in both Britain and Western Europe in recent years is the narrowing of pay differentials between manual and non-manual workers. It is also true that the bulk of these changes were concentrated in the early 1970s and that the recent picture has been more static, but pay differentials in Britain widened sharply again by 1989. The broad picture is given in table 14.9.

Table 14.9 *Manual–non-manual differentials in average gross monthly earnings in industry, October 1972 and 1979: men and women combined (non-manual as percentage of manual monthly earnings), plus 1989 Great Britain*[c]

	Great Britain[b]	West Germany	France	Italy
1972	120.7	129.2	167.4	175.3
1979	112.2	137.6	155.9	144.8[c]
1989[a]	147.0			

[a] Average gross weekly earnings.
[b] April to April.
[c] April 1979.

Source: *Employment Gazette* (July 1981); D. Marsden, '*Vive la différence*: pay differentials in Britain, West Germany, France and Italy'; 'Pay in Great Britain', *Employment Gazette* (November 1989), p. 601

Although the relative position of management in Britain has deteriorated there are compensatory factors in the form of the various management perquisites which are not taken into account in the figures, although, admittedly, management make up a small proportion of non-manual workers.

Pay differentials are likely to be influenced by a great many factors, amongst which might be included general economic factors, excess demand or supply of various types of labour in particular industries, union activity and collective bargaining agreements, government policy, and the various 'skill' differentials between occupations. A brief snapshot of the more extreme differentials for manual workers between industries is given in table 14.10. In the other Western European countries similar patterns are displayed, with energy industries and printing being in the top ranks and clothing, footwear, wool and leather being generally well represented at the bottom of the league. Competition with Third World producers is probably a major factor here, but these industries tend to employ a large number of women and younger people. Although differences in occupation 'accounted' for about one-quarter of the dispersion in overall monthly earnings, age, sex and length of service were also important factors. Economic factors are also important; in 1972 the car industry was at the top of the league in the UK, but the combined effects of the oil crisis, the recession and import penetration pushed it well down the league in 1979. By contrast, the West German car industry remains in the top five in that country.

Table 14.10 *The five highest-paid and the five lowest-paid UK industries: manual men, October 1979 (average hourly earnings as a percentage of average for all of industry)*

Five highest-paid industries		Five lowest-paid industries	
Coal mining (deep)	136.9	Knitting mills	90.3
Printing	126.9	Cotton	87.0
Tobacco	126.9	Wool	82.9
Oil refining	122.7	Leather	81.9
Iron and steel	114.4	Clothing	78.2

Sources: *Employment Gazette* (July 1981); Marsden, *'Vive le différence'*

It is no accident, however, that in coal mining and printing in 1979 the unions were particularly strong. This is therefore an appropriate point to consider the role of trade unions and the systems of collective bargaining (a term coined by Beatrice Webb to describe an agreement concerning pay and conditions of work settled between trade unions on the one side and employers or employers' associations on the other) practised in Britain.[10]

The Role of Trade Unions

The Donovan Commission defined a trade union as 'a combination of employees the principal activity of which is the regulation of relations between employees and employers'.[11] The aggregate membership of trade unions in the UK at the end of 1979 was 13,289,000, an increase of approaching 0.4 million more than the previous year's figure. At the same time the number of trade unions was 454 compared with 462 the year previously. Over the previous ten years, trade union membership had increased by 28.8 per cent, while the number of unions, frequently through amalgamations, had declined by 24.4 per cent.[12] However, the subsequent decade has shown a sharp reversal in trade union membership, as shown in table 14.11.

In Britain trade union membership has fallen by about 3 million since

Table 14.11 *Trade union and TUC membership and density in the UK 1970–1988*[a]

Year	Trade union membership (thousands)	TUC membership (thousands)	Trade union[b] density 1 (%)	Trade union[c] density 2 (%)
1970	11,178	10,002	49.9	n.a.
1975	12,026	11,036	53.1	51.1
1979	13,289	12,173	57.1	54.8
1980	12,947	11,601	57.7	54.0
1981	12,106	11,006	56.0	50.6
1982	11,593	10,510	54.8	48.8
1983	11,236	10,082	52.9	46.8
1984	10,994	9,855	51.3	45.2
1985	10,821	9,586	50.3	44.2
1986	10,539	9,243	49.1	43.1
1987	10,475	9,127	47.5	42.6
1988	10,238	8,652	45.3	41.5

n.a., not available.

[a] All figures at 31 December.

[b] Total trade union membership (unadjusted) divided by civilian employees in employment (unadjusted).

[c] Total trade union membership (unadjusted) divided by civilian employees in employment plus the unemployed aged 18 and over (seasonally adjusted).

Sources: 'Membership of trade unions in 1985', *Department of Employment Gazette* (February 1987), pp. 84–6; D. Bird, 'Membership of trade unions in 1988', *Employment Gazette* (May 1990), pp. 259–62; *TUC Report 1989*, Trades Union Congress, 1990

1979, and trade union density has shown parallel dramatic declines (the possible reasons for this are discussed subsequently in this chapter).

The great majority of unions in the UK are affiliated to the Trades Union Congress (TUC), which has its headquarters in London. The craft unions of skilled workers were the first to emerge and in the nineteenth century membership was confined to this small group. Their initial aim was to maintain standards and to control the rate of entry to the craft via the apprentice system. This was the product of the development of an industrial system which required a set of craftsmen who were destined to remain employees for their entire working life rather than own their own workshops.

If we return to the consideration of Marshall's four rules, which determine the elasticity of derived demand for a factor, we see that the craft unions are particularly well placed to make use of rule 2; the demand for their labour is likely to be inelastic, as they normally only account for a small proportion of total production costs. By their control of entry to the craft they were able to control the supply of labour and shift it to the left. This reduction in supply meant that their wages would be high relative to non-craft union labour, with only a slight diminishment in the employment of craft labour. Craft unions will have a membership which spans industries, depending upon where specific skills are required.

In the last decade of the nineteenth and the early decades of the twentieth century, there was a growth of general unions which recruited from a wide variety of workers, mainly unskilled, and from a wide variety of industries. This type of union labour faces a relatively elastic demand, since it is relatively easy to substitute non-union for union labour, and in the earlier years of the century there was usually a substantial pool of unemployed labour. General unions therefore aimed at organizing all sellers of labour so that they could minimize the substitution of non-union labour.

In America and Europe industrial unions which seek to organize all workers in a particular industry, regardless of their level of skill, are quite common, but they have not taken hold in Britain. The nearest parallel was the National Union of Mineworkers which represented the interests of the vast majority of workers in the mining industry, prior to the 1984–5 miners' strike and the formation of the breakaway UDM.

Apart from a continuing tendency to amalgamation, the most notable feature of unionism in the post-war period has been the growth of white-collar unionism – a natural concomitant of the continued growth of the service sector and the relative decline of the manufacturing sector. White-collar unions are now well represented in both the public and private sectors, as evidenced by the growth of the various teaching unions, such as the National Union of Teachers (NUT), and by the representation of local government officers by the National and Local Government Officers' Association (NALGO) and of management in the private sector by unions such as the Association of Scientific, Technical and Managerial Staffs (ASTMS).

Unions in the UK are usually governed by an executive council elected by the membership, and the majority have a full-time staff supervised by a general secretary. The larger unions have full-time officials at local level as well as local and regional organizations of lay members. At the level of the individual plant the workforce usually elects a shop steward who acts as their spokesman and representative in negotiations with management.

The economic analysis of union activities

It is undoubtedly true that both political and economic factors are inextricably linked in the activities of trade unions, but does this mean that economic analysis has to be discarded as a means of analysing their behaviour? This was the basis of the celebrated Ross–Dunlop debate.[13] Ross suggested that union activity could not be analysed along the traditional utility-maximizing lines of economic theory. This followed from the fact that a union is typically made up of a heterogeneous group of people with a heterogeneous set of objectives. At any point in time political compromise within the union would balance these conflicting interests and place greater emphasis on the attainment of certain objectives at the expense of others. Dunlop countered with the view that, although political factors may be important in the short run, in the long run economic forces are of prime importance and the behaviour of wages and conditions of employment will be determined by market forces. The latter is adopted in this text.

However, there are difficulties involved; a major one is concerned with the specification of union objectives. Two obvious ones concern the level of wage rates and the volume of employment within a market, and they cannot be simultaneously pursued, as can be seen in figure 14.7.

D is the demand curve for labour and MS_1 is the supply curve of labour in the absence of union activity. Once the labour market is unionized the union establishes a higher wage for its members than the previous competitive wage OW_1. The new unionized labour supply curve is MS_2 and the equilibrium wage rate is now OW_2, but this is established at the expense of a drop in employment from OL_1 to OL_2. Given a downward-sloping demand curve and an upward-sloping labour supply curve it is inevitable that there must be a trade-off between the level of employment and the wage rate established. The extent of the trade-off depends upon the previously considered elasticity of demand for labour, and hence the craft unions are better placed facing a relatively inelastic demand.

It has been suggested that a compromise between these two objectives can be affected by assuming that unions seek to maximize the wage bill, given by the area of the rectangle $OW_2 \times OL_2$ in figure 14.7 if OW_2 is the equilibrium wage. This can cause difficulties. Suppose a wage rate at OW_2

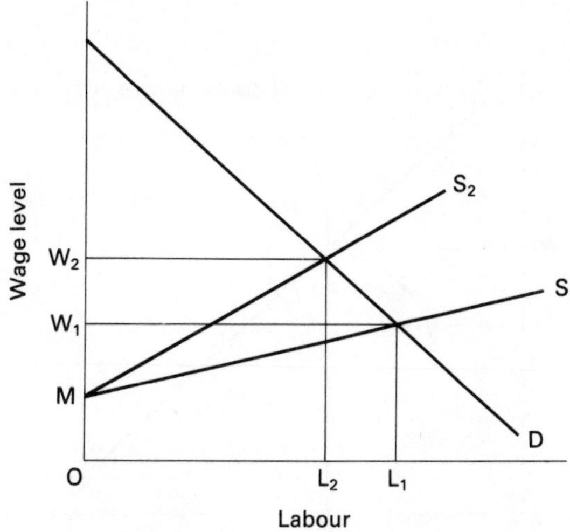

Figure 14.7 *The trade-off between setting the wage level and the volume of employment*

does maximize the wage bill. This implies that if supply conditions had been different and a higher equilibrium wage had been established, then the union would have taken a wage cut. This behaviour is not commonly observed.

It is quite possible that a union will place differing emphasis on the wage rate and the rate of employment depending upon the relative magnitudes of the two. The compromise adopted is revealed in the *wage preference path* shown in figure 14.8. The steeper the slope of this line the greater the emphasis being placed upon increases in the wage rate rather than the level of employment. The kink at the current equilibrium wage rate suggests that the union is loth to accept a cut in wages and is prepared to accept relatively rapid drops in the level of employment in order to maintain its wage levels; however, its response to an increase in demands is to switch to placing greater emphasis upon the wage rate than on the level of employment. The union's preferred response to shifts in the demand for labour is shown by the wage preference path. Downward shifts in demand will cause rapid reductions in employment but upward shifts in demand increase the wage rate.

The term *wage rate* as employed above covers a multitude of aspects of pay bargaining, including overtime and shift rates, sick pay, holiday pay, pensions provision, arrangements to pay laid-off workers and so on. However, it could be argued that the components of this 'package' are regarded by the labour force as being close substitutes, though the emphasis in negotiations will vary with time and circumstance, and from

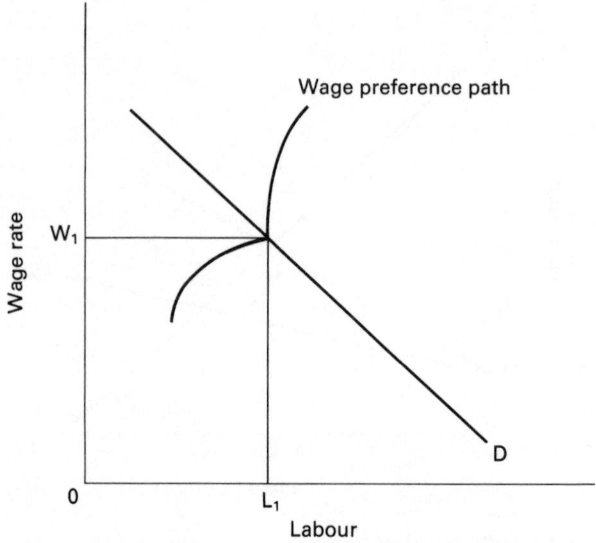

Figure 14.8 *The wage preference path*

the company's viewpoint they are all labour costs. So the analysis holds good.

Theories of Bargaining

We shall begin by considering two models which set limits on the wage rates considered in the bargaining process between employers and unions, but leave the actual solution indeterminate, and then proceed to some more direct theories of the actual bargaining process. In figure 14.9 we utilize the wage preference path again. The initial equilibrium position is at point A with a wage rate set at OW_1 and an employment level of OL_1. Then the demand for labour increases from D to D_1. If the employer could attract all the extra workers he required at the existing wage rate (i.e. there is a perfectly elastic supply of labour), then he would employ OL_3 units of labour in total at a wage rate OW_1. By so doing he is equating the marginal revenue product of labour with its marginal cost, and therefore seeking to maximize his profits. Suppose the union steps in. Its wage preference path indicates that it is prepared to accept lower employment in order to obtain a higher wage rate for its members. Its preferrerd position is at point C with a wage rate of OW_2 and an employment level of OL_2. The points C and B set boundaries to the wage bargaining positions, and the eventual outcome will be somewhere between these two points, depending on the relative bargaining skills and strengths of the two parties.

A similar result is obtained from the neoclassical model of *bilateral*

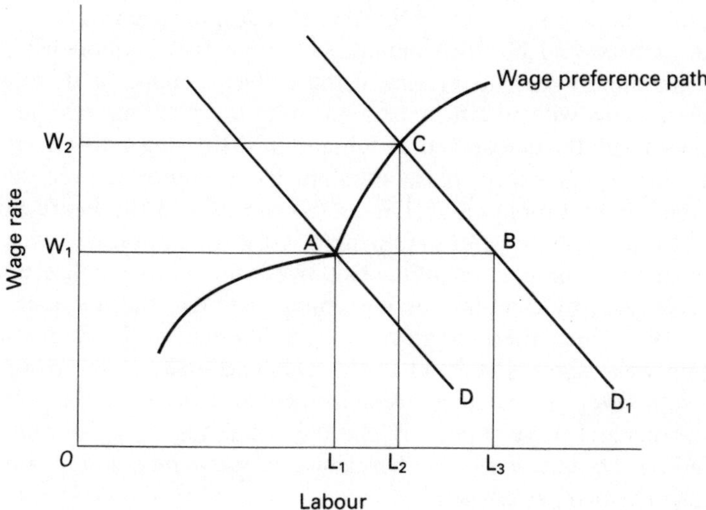

Figure 14.9 *The wage preference path and wage bargaining*

monopoly which assumes that a monopsonistic employer faces a union with a monopoly of the labour supply, as shown in figure 14.10. The employer seeks to maximize his profits by following the familiar marginal conditions; he equates the marginal cost of labour MC LS with his marginal revenue product curve – the demand curve D – as shown at A. He therefore employs OL_1 units of labour and seeks to pay them a wage rate of OW_3,

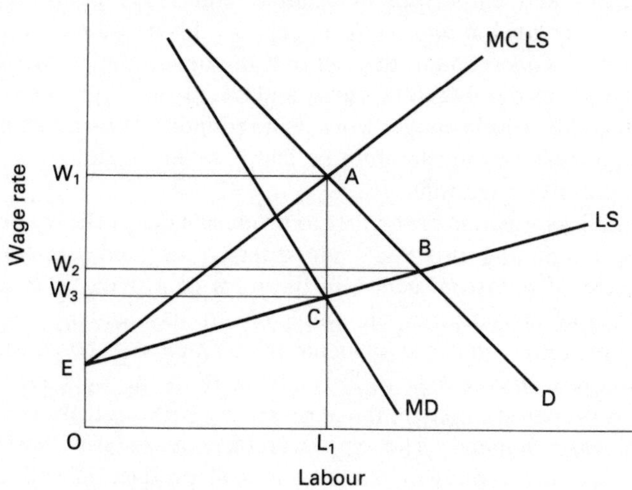

Figure 14.10 *The bilateral monopoly model of employer–trade union bargaining*

since the labour supply curve LS shows that at this wage rate the required labour force would be forthcoming. The union as a monopolist, on the other hand, will seek to maximize the collective rents of its employed members. This will be effected by equating the marginal revenue curve associated with the demand curve for labour, MD (lying below the demand curve, since every unit increase in employment requires a wage rate cut), with the labour supply curve LS, as shown at C. In the figure this also produces the same level of employment OL_1. The union will then try to maximize the economic rent of the employed labour force, indicated by the area EW_1 AC, by charging the maximum wage rate that the market will bear: OW_1. Thus there is an area of indeterminacy between the two extreme wage rates OW_1 and OW_3. This encompasses the competitive wage rate OW_2, indicated by the intersection of the labour supply curve and the demand curve at point B. But the actual wage rate determined will depend on the outcome of the bargaining process and could lie anywhere between the two extremes.

This approach has been criticized on the grounds that the analogy between a monopoly producer and a union is a rather strained one. A company producing goods experiences costs, whereas costs experienced by a union are of a rather different nature and not directly related to changes in the supply of labour. The union is merely an agent which represents its members in the bargaining process, and is unlikely to have an appreciation of the marginal cost or supply price of its members.

This type of approach is implicit in the 'right to manage' models applied in the work of Freeman and Medoff.[14] They assume that it is the firms who decide on the level of employment and the wage-bargaining process between firms and employees determines how much people are paid. Oswald provides further arguments to support this based on the existence of 'seniority'.[15] This refers to the fact that the bulk of union members are likely to have considerable job security and it is the usual practice to lay off the most recently hired younger workers if redundancies are required. The bulk of the members will therefore be happy to let the union concentrate on pushing up the wage rate.

Sir John Hicks was one of the first to produce a direct theory explaining the actual bargaining process.[16] He directly included the threat and potential cost of industrial action in the form of a strike as a means by which a union can compel an employer to pay higher wages. The bargaining process is analysed by means of an employer's concession curve and a union resistance curve. In figure 14.11 W_1 is the wage rate that the employer is prepared to pay in the absence of a strike and W_2 is the union maximum wage demand. The employer faces a trade-off between the expected cost of a strike, in terms of loss of production and customer goodwill, and the cost of conceding a higher wage. If he is faced with the probability of a very long and costly strike he will be prepared to pay a higher rate to buy industrial peace. Hence the employer's curve rises as a

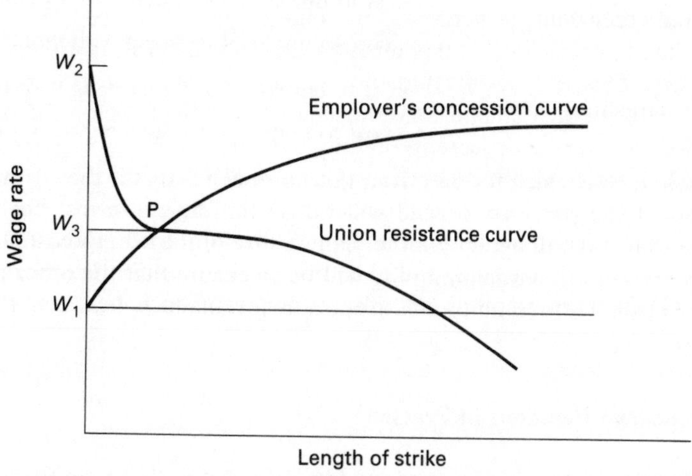

Figure 14.11 *Hicks's analysis of the bargaining process*

function of expected strike length, but it rises at a diminishing rate and there comes a time when he would rather go out of business than pay excessively high wage demands.

The union resistance curve falls as a function of the expected length of strike since there is a limit to both the union's ability to fund a strike and the sacrifices its members are prepared to make. The curve shows the minimum wage that the union will accept rather than strike for a given time. Ultimately it intersects the minimum wage offered by the employer since there is a limit to the period for which the union is prepared to strike. The curve is relatively flat over a portion of its length, since there is a level of wages to which the men think they are entitled; they will hold out for a relatively long time to achieve this, though they will not be very concerned to raise wages above it.

The two curves intersect at P and the corresponding wage rate W_3 represents the highest wage that skilful negotiation can expect to extract from the employer. If the union sets a wage demand below W_3 the employer will be fairly ready to concede but the union negotiators have not done particularly well. It is assumed that in the negotiating process each side has a clear idea of its own, but has to estimate that of the other. If the mutual perceptions are fairly accurate both parties will be fairly ready to settle for wage W_3. But if perceptions are inaccurate, or the curves shift over time, there is a likelihood of a strike.

A similar and straightforward approach resting on the perceptions of relative costs by both sides of the bargaining process was suggested by Chamberlain.[17] If both parties are rational economic agents and wish to produce a solution which minimizes costs, then the following rules hold;

$$\text{employer's bargaining power} = \frac{\text{cost to union of disagreeing with employer}}{\text{cost to union of agreeing with employer}}$$

$$\text{union's bargaining power} = \frac{\text{cost to employer of disagreeing with union}}{\text{cost to employer of agreeing with union}}$$

The simple rule which follows from this approach is that if the cost ratio is less than 1 the party concerned will refuse the other's terms, but if it is greater than 1 it will agree. Neither can be sure of the other's cost position and the successful bargaining ploy will be to ensure that the other party's ratio is pushed above unity whilst one's own remains below.

UK Industrial Relations in Practice

The Donovan Commission suggested in 1968 that at that time Britain had two systems of industrial relations: a formal system embodied in official institutions and an informal one created by the actual behaviours of the parties and individuals involved. The centrepiece of the formal system was the industry-wide collective agreement, which the Royal Commission on Labour of 1891 compared with a 'regular and well thought out treaty'. A broad distinction can be made between 'multi-employer' agreements, which involve a coalition or association of employers acting in common, and 'single-employer' bargaining in which an individual employer independently negotiates agreements with his own labour force. Multi-employer bargaining, spanning industries at a local or national level, developed in Britain in the nineteenth century and advanced further after the First World War. National Joint Industrial Councils fostered negotiations between unions and employers' associations which set pay and conditions of work for individual industries.

For many years successive governments tried to encourage industry-wide bargaining agreements via the creation of wages councils in those industries where trade unionism was weak. The balance of power on these was held by representatives held to be independent of management and unions, and their awards were given statutory force via a wages inspectorate. In Europe industry-wide bargaining has reigned supreme but this has not been the case in Britain. Post-war full employment undermined these agreements and pressure from the labour market led employers to supplement industry-wide wage rates with payments by results, overtime and other supplements.

The trend towards single-employer bargaining was noted by the Donovan Commission, which referred to the remarkable transfer of authority in collective bargaining associated with the market decline, over the previous 30 years, in the extent to which industry-wide agreements determined actual pay. This trend was further confirmed by a major survey of British industrial relations undertaken at Warwick University.[18] This involved a survey of practices at 970 manufacturing establishments during 1977–8. It was found that industry-wide agreements (including wages council awards) were regarded as the most important factor in pay determinations by only 33 per cent of establishments surveyed. Single-employer bargaining was the most important factor for two-thirds of manual workers, and amongst non-manual workers its significance was even greater. The incidence of single-employer bargaining was more strongly associated with large multiplant enterprises. Industry-wide agreements were regarded as providing a 'floor' which affected the earnings of only the lowest-paid workers.

This change has had a major effect on the roles of employers' associations. In the years up to 1914 they were important innovators of industrial relations practice – e.g. in the coal and iron industry they introduced collective regulation of pay before stable unions were formed – but, in the years since, this role has been inherited by the unions and government. Even so, membership of the associations has not declined, though their emphasis has changed from being primarily concerned with negotiating industry-wide agreements to one of operating procedures for the resolution of disputes and providing advisory services. Advising on labour law and government legislation now seems to be a major function.

The Donovan Commission considered that disorder in factory and workshop relations and pay structures was due in no small measure to the conflict between the formal and the informal system of industrial relations. Greater order had to be reintroduced but it could not be done via employers' associations and trade unions working at industry level. It required effective and orderly collective bargaining over issues such as the regulation of hours worked, incentive schemes, work practices, facilities for shop stewards, disciplinary rules etc., and this was likely to be done most effectively at the level of the factory. The desired shift in focus could best be achieved by individual companies' boards of directors.

This view did seem to have been taken on board. The Warwick survey found that there had been a marked increase of specialist industrial relations management at the board of director level and this again appeared to be linked with firm size. In the companies surveyed with more than 5000 employees, 81 per cent had a director with industrial relations as his sole responsibility. There was a further link with establishment practice and the presence of a specialist at board level increased the likelihood of there being a parallel specialist at establishment level.

Following the promptings of the Donovan Commission there was a tightening up of procedural practice and much government legislation during the 1970s was directed to this end. This has included *In Place of Strife* (1979), the *Industrial Relations Code of Practice* (1971) in which employers were encouraged to formalize negotiating procedures, and the setting up of a new branch of the High Court, the National Industrial

Relations Court (NIRC), empowered to sit in judgement over cases of 'unfair industrial practices'. Amongst its powers was the facility to impose a full ballot of union members and to recommend 'cooling off' periods to delay industrial action. Subsequent controversy and opposition led to the abolishment of NIRC and the Commission on Industrial Relations (CIR). In 1971 statutory protection was introduced against unfair dismissal which covered the manner of as well as the reasons for dismissal.

Various other pieces of legislation focused management attention on industrial relations practice. The Equal Pay Act was passed in 1970 and came into force in 1975. The 1975 Sex Discrimination Act outlawed discrimination on grounds of sex or marriage, and the Employment Protection Act of 1975 further extended the rights of employees in cases of unfair dismissal. The Advisory, Conciliation and Arbitration Service (ACAS) was set up in 1974 to provide mediation in industrial disputes on a voluntary basis, although it could offer independent advice to the parties concerned. Its position was confirmed by statute in the following year. Further impetus was given by a series of counter-inflation measures and attempts to control the increase in income by a variety of measures including 'incomes policies' (see later in this chapter).

The trends towards single-employer bargaining, greater professionalism of industrial relations management and the reform of disputes procedures provided a major impetus to the enhancement of the role of the shop steward. The existence of shop stewards is strongly associated with the size of the workforce and a very large proportion are now appointed on a full-time basis.

Another prominent trend in the 1970s was the growth of the closed shop. The Warwick survey estimated that about 46 per cent of manual workers in manufacturing industry were members of a closed shop. In general, company management appeared to be strongly in favour of it, frequently on the grounds that it ensured that unions and shop stewards represented all employees, thereby imparting greater stability to collective bargaining. There has recently been a decline in the closed shop. Multi-unionism, on the other hand, could make collective agreements more difficult to attain and maintain. Management support for union activity was further emphasized by the widespread use of the 'check-off' facility by which the management collected union dues by deducting them at source from wages. Consultative meetings between management and unions are now more prevalent; this was stimulated by Acts such as the Health and Safety at Work Act of 1974 which required joint consultation on these matters. The shop steward frequently plays a key role in the negotiation of factory procedures and agreements.

In summary, the Donovan strategy of the 1970s attempted to develop a more rational and coherent structure of joint regulation between management and unions. It also emphasized co-operation between the state and unions at a national level.

Palmer[19] has suggested that the Donovan approach embodies a shift from liberal collective to corporatist structures for handling British industrial relations. Corporatism can be defined as attempts to regulate the economy, and labour relations, through institutions in which government and the central pressure groups of capital and labour act together. This can be contrasted with liberal policies designed to separate economics and politics. It can be seen in table 14.12 that the Donovan-inspired policies failed to deliver increases in productivity.

The Thatcher administration in the 1980s had moved back to an alternative liberal approach which emphasized market forces, the legislative framework and employee involvement. The 1980s witnessed a tremendous improvement in productivity, as shown in table 14.12. Productivity growth has recently been at record levels, superior to that of most of our competitors, and has succeeded in narrowing the productivity gap possessed by them.

Table 14.12 *An international comparison of changes in output per hour, manufacturing*

	Annual average percentage changes		Labour productivity (Great Britain = 100)	
	1976–9	1979–86	1980	1986
USA	2.1	3.8	273	267
Canada	3.2	2.9	–	–
Japan	6.6	2.6	196	173
Germany	3.2	2.5	225	206
Italy	3.7	2.7	173	153
UK	1.0	3.7	100	100

Source: D. Metcalf, 'Water notes dry up: the impact of the Donovan reform proposals and Thatcherism at work in British manufacturing industry', *British Journal of Industrial Relations*, 27 (March 1989)

There are a number of possible contributory factors to these changes. The circumstances of the labour market have changed dramatically with high levels of redundancy and unemployment. The rules supporting union power have been undermined. The wage councils have been reduced in coverage and constrained in operations. Local authority and National Health Service *de facto* minimum wages have been undercut by the process of contracting out. Strikes have been much less frequent (but will be considered in the next section). Trade Union bargaining power has been eroded by a series of legal measures in the Employment Acts of 1980 and 1982 and the Trade Union Act of 1984 plus the 1988 and 1990 Employment Acts. The 1988 Employment Act gives a statutory right to union members not to be disciplined by their unions for continuing to work during lawful industrial action approved by a majority in a secret ballot. It also removes all legal protection for the closed shop and has made the dismissal of employees on the grounds of non-union membership automatically unfair. The 1990 Act gives further protection to anyone refused a job because that person is, or is not, a trade union member.

Other measures have included the outlawing of various forms of secondary industrial action, the closer regulation of picketing and the narrowing of the definition of a trade dispute. The ballot provisions in the 1984 Trade Union Act mean that the ballot must be undertaken before official strikes if the unions concerned are to retain their immunity. The courts have been ready to grant injunctions against the unions, and various and heavy penalties have been imposed for breaches of the law or contempt of court. Furthermore, employment protection provisions, with regard to, for example, maternity rights and unfair dismissal, have been reduced.

In the private sector there has been a reduction in multi-employer bargaining and collective negotiations are more frequently with a single firm. In the state corporations there have been attempts to decentralize bargaining (e.g. the Post Office), to relate pay and performance more closely (e.g. British Coal) and to circumvent traditional negotiating machinery (e.g. British Rail).

The former corporatist tripartisan approach has been abandoned. Consensus is not regarded as a target and the National Economic Development Council (NEDC) has a peripheral role. In the public corporations union strength is greatly reduced following managements' successful trials of strength in the coal, steel and rail industries. Many individuals and unions have pursued an increasingly independent line. The electricians' union, the EETPU, expelled from the TUC in 1988, have pioneered a package of measures which offer the employer flexibility in production, a no-strike clause in procedure agreements, pendulum arbitration and co-operation in productivity improvements.

Companies have developed a number of practices designed to promote employee involvement in the enterprise. These have included profit-related pay and profit-sharing, joint consultation, quality circles, briefing groups and company newsletters.

Strikes

There are a large number of forms of industrial action including overtime bans, go-slows, working to rules and threatened strikes, as well as strike activity itself. Concentration on strike activity gives only a partial picture; it could be argued that the statistics provided by the Department of Employment understate strike activity in that they exclude stoppages involving fewer than ten workers or those which last for less than a day, unless the total number of days lost in aggregate exceeds 100.

It is frequently suggested that Britain has a poor industrial relations record in terms of the frequency of strike activity, but table 14.13 shows that in terms of other OECD countries our record is not particularly bad, though there is room for improvement.

There are a number of caveats about the comparability of the statistics shown in this table. Definitions of stoppages vary; some countries include only those directly involved, whereas others include indirect involvement (i.e. workers laid off because of a dispute elsewhere in the plant); and finally the method of compilation and source of statistical returns varies. The figures are shown in relative rather than absolute terms to adjust for differences in the size of the labour force of the countries shown. In terms of the average number of working days lost per 1000 employees, the UK is ranked fifteenth out of 20 for the period 1979–88. Our record is better than that of Italy, Canada, Greece, Ireland and Spain, though we fare worse than Japan, France, Germany, Switzerland and Austria by a large margin.

Not surprisingly, the industrial relations systems in these various countries vary considerably. In Canada and the USA collective agreements are legally binding, and so contravention is illegal. Hence disputes tend to arise over new agreements and can be protracted, as the terms are binding once agreed. In Sweden and West Germany agreements are also legally binding and yet there are far fewer strikes, perhaps because of the existence of more comprehensive grievance procedures. However, before we consider the various possible causes of strike activity we shall look in more detail at the British record.

In 1980 in the UK there were 12.0 million working days lost through stoppages compared with 29.5 million in 1979. Disputes over pay caused 48 per cent of the stoppages in 1980 and 89 per cent of working days lost. In 1990 there were only 1.9 million working days lost through stoppages. The causes which led to the greatest number of stoppages were disputes over pay (34 per cent), manning and work allocation (24 per cent) and dismissal and disciplinary proceedings (13 per cent). The causes which led to the greatest number of working days lost were pay (55 per cent), duration and patterns of hours worked (24 per cent) and dismissal etc. (9.2 per cent).[20] The annual average of working days lost over the periods 1970–9 and 1980–9 were 12.9 million and 7.2 million respectively. The pattern varies markedly from year to year as can be seen in table 14.14, but has shown a recent marked decline.

The major cause of the considerable fluctuations shown in this table is the change in the incidence of large strikes, which we shall arbitrarily define as those which involve the loss of 200,000 working days or more.[21] Over the period 1960–79 there have only been 64 such strikes, but they accounted for 46 per cent of the total number of working days lost.

The more notable of the large strikes in the 1960s included three one-day

Table 14.13 *Industrial disputes: working days lost per thousand employees*[a] *in all industries and services 1979–1988*

	1979	1980	1981	1982	1983	1984	1985	1986	1987	1988	Average[b] 1979–83	1984–8	1979–88
UK	1270	520	190	250	180	1280	300	90	160	170	500	400	450
Denmark	80	90	320	50	40	60	1060	40	60	40	120	250	180
France[c]	210	90	80	130	80	80	50	60	50	70	120	60	90
FRG	20	10	–	–	–	260	–	–	–	–	10	50	30
Greece	1040	1740	480	830	320	320	620	710	970	3610	880	1270	1080
Ireland	1750	480	500	500	380	470	520	380	320	180	720	370	550
Italy	1910	1140	730	1280	980	610	270	390	320	220	1210	360	780
Netherlands	70	10	10	50	30	10	20	10	10	–	30	10	20
Portugal	200	200	280	170	230	100	100	140	40	n.a.	220	(90)	(160)
Spain	2290	770	670	360	580	870	440	300	630	1400	950	740	850
Japan	20	30	10	10	10	10	10	10	10	–	20	10	10
USA[c]	230	230	190	100	190	90	70	120	40	40	190	70	130
Canada[c]	840	930	890	610	460	400	130	540	220	310	750	320	530
Austria	–	10	–	–	–	–	10	–	–	–	–	–	–
Finland	130	840	340	100	360	750	80	1350	60	90	350	470	410
Norway	–	60	20	170	–	60	40	570	10	50	50	150	100
Sweden	10	1150	50	–	10	10	130	170	–	200	250	100	170
Switzerland	–	–	–	–	–	–	–	–	–	–	–	–	–
Australia	780	630	780	370	310	240	230	240	220	260	570	240	400
New Zealand	370	360	360	300	340	380	660	1060	290	310	340	540	450

(), averages based on incomplete data; n.a., not available; –, less than five days lost per thousand.

[a] Employees in employment: some figures have been estimated.

[b] Annual averages for those years within each period for which data are available, weighted for employment.

[c] Significant coverage differences

Source: D. Bird, 'International comparisons of industrial disputes in 1988 and 1989', *Employment Gazette* (December 1990), pp. 609–13.

Table 14.14 *Stoppages of work in the UK 1960–1990*

Year	Number of stoppages[a]	Working days lost (thousands)
1960	2,849	3,024
1964	2,535	2,277
1968	2,390	4,690
1972	2,530	23,909
1976	2,034	3,284
1980	1,348	11,964
1984	1,221	27,135
1986	1,074	1,920
1988	781	3,702
1990	598	1,890

Data relate only to disputs connected with terms and conditions of employement and relate to stoppages in progress.
Stoppages involving fewer than ten workers or lasting less than one day are excluded except where the aggregate working days lost exceeded 100.
Sources: *Department of Employment Gazette* (August 1972); *Employment Gazette* (January 1986), (April 1991)

stoppages in the engineering industries, five in 1962 and one in 1968; the seamen's strike in 1966; the car workers' strike in 1969; and the miners' strike for a 40-hour week in the same year. In the 1970s the miners struck three times, in 1970, 1972 and 1974; the dockworkers twice in 1970 and 1972; the postal workers in 1971; the local government workers, health workers, firemen and other public service staff in 1970, 1978 and 1979; the construction industry struck in 1972; the car workers and print workers in 1978; the lorry drivers in 1979; and – the largest in terms of working days lost up to the time – the engineering workers in 1979.

Of the 64 large strikes in that period, 40 were known to be official. Large disputes occur over most sectors of the economy, though strike activity is concentrated in certain sectors. In the 20-year period up to 1979, 80 per cent of the working days lost in large stoppages were accounted for by strike activity in four industrial sectors: engineering and shipbuilding, mining, transport and communications, and vehicle manufacture.

The frequency of strike activity does appear to have declined during the 1980s. In the 1970s the annual strike frequency was about 2000 disputes per year for the whole period, whereas during the 1980s it was never above 2000 and fell below 600 in 1990 (see table 14.14). The decline after 1984 may reflect the impact of the ballot provisions introduced in the Trade Union Act 1984, which were effective from September 1984. Another factor may have been the defeat of the miners in 1984–5. This bitter struggle accounted for 22.5 million days lost from the annual total for 1984 of 27.1 million. A series of unions have failed to achieve their objectives after prolonged industrial action. These include the civil servants (1981), health workers and train drivers (1982), telecommunications workers and printers (1983), the previously mentioned miners (1984–5), teachers (1985–7) and the printers once more (1986–7).

The attitudes of union members to strike activity appears to have changed. There seemed to be support for the introduction of secret ballot provisions and there has been a greater readiness to cross other worker's picket lines. For example, most Nottinghamshire miners refused to join the 1984–5 strike and even went so far as to form an independent union. Similarly, many journalists refused to boycott the new plant set up by Rupert Murdoch at Wapping.

What are the contributory causes of strike activity? Clegg has put forward a theory of strikes which suggests that plant bargaining leads to a relatively large number of official strikes whereas industry or regional bargaining leads to a smaller number of larger official strikes.[22] Comprehensive and efficient disputes procedures cut down the number of unofficial strikes, whereas disputes are more likely where the distinction between official and unofficial action is ill defined. Yet Clegg concedes that this theory does not explain the incidence of major strikes, which he suggests are due to changing economic circumstances and relationships between unions and government.

In a pioneering paper, Prais has shown that the frequency of strikes in manufacturing industry plants is closely correlated with plant size and that the burden of strikes on larger plants is greater in three respects: the chance of having a strike-free year is lower, the expected number of strikes per year is greater, and the number of days lost per employee is greater.[23] Further corroboratory evidence has been provided by Edwards, in work emanating from the Warwick survey, in which plant size appeared as the most significant determining factor in strike activity, though the nature of union organization had a slight influence too.[24] Obviously these are not the only contributory causes of strike activity, which will vary according to circumstances, but these are the factors which show up in statistical analysis. The conclusion to be drawn from this is not evident. Is it that we need a more rigidly enforced system of binding labour contracts which might serve to inhibit strike activity? Have the recent changes in the law caused the reduction of strike activity during the 1980s, or is it merely the impact of unemployment and part of a short-term cyclical trend, as Kelly suggests?[25]

Counter-inflation Policies

The experience of a persistent and ever-increasing upward trend in the rate of price inflation during the 1960s and 1970s has led to a preoccupation on the part of successive British governments with measures aimed at controlling inflation. These have taken various forms, but could be categorized under the following headings: monetary policy, fiscal policy, and wages and price controls. We shall be concentrating on the policies, but before we turn to them we shall briefly consider the various hypotheses about the causes of inflation.

Theories about the causes of inflation may be roughly divided into two groups; demand-pull and cost-push. *Demand-pull theories of inflation* are based on the argument that the causes of inflation originate on the demand side of the market. If the aggregate demand for goods and services exceeds their supply this can cause a rise in the general price level as frustrated consumers bid up prices by competing for scarce supplies of goods and services. This will in turn lead to an increase in the derived demand for factors of production, including labour, and therefore money wages will tend to increase.

Under the *cost-push hypothesis* a variety of factors on the supply side might be the cause of inflation. Firms might decide to demand higher profit margins or monopolistic trade unions might force up money wage rates. Producers, faced with increased costs, pass them on by marking up their prices and so the price level is forced up. The resultant increase in prices could lead to a fall in demand and a rise in unemployment if the supply of money is unchanged, or the authorities might seek to maintain demand by increasing the supply of money.

The picture is confused by the fact that an excess in the supply of money might be the root cause of demand-pull inflation – 'too much money chasing too few goods'. Thus the money supply features in both analyses of the causes of inflation, but the suggested policy measures differ. If demand-pull is the basis of the problem, fiscal and monetary measures can be used to reduce excess demand without having too disastrous an effect on the level of activity in the economy, whereas if cost-push factors are the cause – perhaps trade union aggressiveness in pushing up wages – then monetary and fiscal measures might be a very blunt weapon to use against this, in that it might require very high levels of unemployment and reduced activity levels before the unions temper their claims. For this reason successive administrations have been tempted into trying to control wage increases directly by a variety of incomes policies; however, there has been argument about the efficacy of these policies, and we shall consider some of the empirical evidence before considering them in detail.

In 1958 Phillips published an empirical investigation of the relationship between employment and the rate of change of money wage rates in the UK over the period 1861–1957.[26] The famous *Phillips curve* depicted a stable and inverse relationship between the level of employment and the rate of change of money wages, as shown in figure 14.12. Other things being equal, this seemed to show that, according to the remarkably consistent evidence from the data over this long period, if demand were

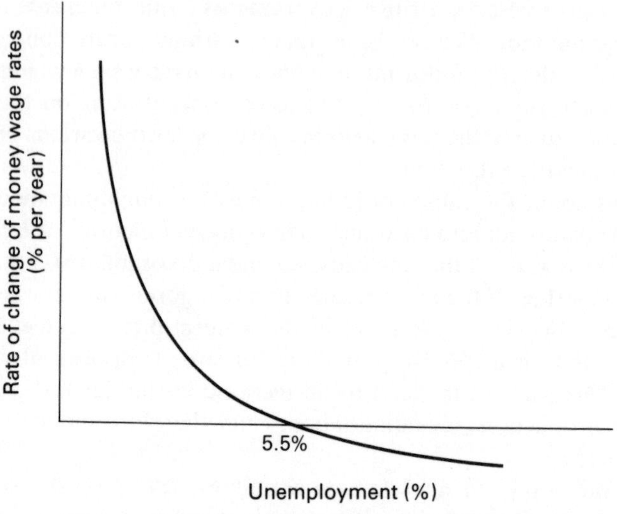

Figure 14.12 *The Phillips curve*

kept to a level consistent with stable wage rates the associated level of unemployment would be about 5.5 per cent.

The analysis seemed to present the authorities with a trade-off between lower unemployment at the cost of higher inflation or vice versa. It provided the stimulus to a great deal of further theoretical and empirical work, and Phillips interpreted his findings as providing strong support for the demand-pull view of inflation. Then in the late 1960s and the 1970s the traditional Phillips curve began to be inconsistent with stagflation – the persistent combined high levels of unemployment and inflation which were experienced in the UK.

One of the first to highlight the theoretical deficiencies of this model was Milton Friedman. He formulated an expectations-augmented Phillips curve which related the rate of change of money wages not only to the level of unemployment but also to expectations of the future level of inflation.[27] This suggested that the higher the expected level of inflation at any given level of unemployment, the higher the rate of increase in the wage rate. Thus in figure 14.12 there would be a whole family of Phillips curves above the one shown, each corresponding to a different expected level of inflation. These would show the short-run trade-off between unemployment and inflation, but, suggested Friedman, in the long run there is only one level of unemployment – the natural rate – which is consistent with the absence of inflation.

More recent work by Layard and Nickell[28] has suggested that real wages in Britain are a function of a number of factors including the level of unemployment, union power, the extent of the mismatch between vacancies and available workers with appropriate skills, the level of unemployment benefit, import prices, taxes, the effectiveness of incomes policies and the ratio of the capital stock to the size of the labour force.

Figure 14.13 shows the central features of their approach which assumes that pay and the number of jobs are determined simultaneously. The two curves in the diagram describe separate relationships between unemployment and the real wage rate. The labour demand curve shows the link between pay and jobs. The higher the real wage rate is, the greater is the level of unemployment. The wage bargaining curve shows the link from jobs to pay; as unemployment rises, so wage demands tend to fall. The intersection of the two curves defines equilibrium in the labour market. This approach depicts the determination of the equilibrium wage level (not the rate of change in wages as the Phillips curve does). Furthermore, the two curves in figure 14.13 are not independent. If the demand for labour changes, so too might the bargaining wage curve.

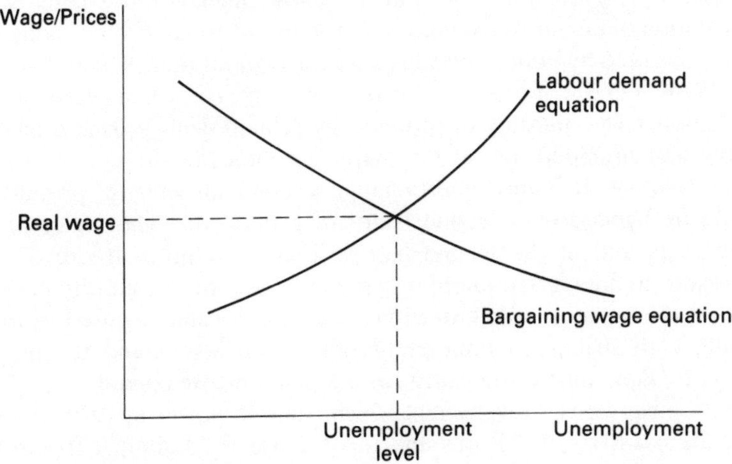

Figure 14.13 *The Layard–Nickell model of the determinants of the real wage rate and unemployment*

Recent work has re-invoked Phelps's concept of hysteresis.[29] The general concept involved is the idea that the course of recent history and the experience of various shocks to the economic system may have an impact on the equilibrium levels of unemployment. A rise in unemployment of itself may increase the natural rate of unemployment.

Government policy in practice has taken a number of forms in recent years.

Incomes policies of various types have been a regular feature of post-war government. They could be interpreted either as attempts to deal with cost-push inflation or as a method of trying to shift the Phillips curve bodily to the left so that the inflation – unemployment trade-off is made available on more favourable terms. The term *incomes policy* covers a whole gamut of proposals from voluntary measures such as Cripps's 1948 wage standstill through to statutory policies.

In the early 1960s the Conservative Government of the period set up a National Incomes Commission as an alternative to demand management methods of dealing with inflation, but it was abolished in 1964 by the incoming Labour administration. That government tried to introduce a 'voluntary' incomes policy – a tripartite statement of intent was signed by the government, the Confederation of British Industry (CBI) and the TUC. The idea was to have a target norm for wage increases of 3.5 per cent. There are various political problems involved in setting the norm at an appropriate level, since once established it tends to be regarded as the minimum acceptable settlement. It could be argued that it distorts the price-allocatory mechanism in the labour market. Because of the perceived failure of a 'voluntary' policy the National Board for Prices and Incomes was set up to reinforce it, but to allow higher settlements where reallocation of labour was required. (In short, a formal incomes policy was in fact accepted by both political parties throughout the 1960s and much of the 1970s despite protestations to the contrary when each was in opposition.) The question of productivity-related deals proved difficult to handle and provided one of the major loopholes in the policy over the period 1964–9. It is also questionable whether all gains in productivity should be handed over to one factor of production. The policy proved fairly weak and in the second half of 1966 a statutory freeze of wage increases was adopted followed by a period of severe restraint. In the latter part of the Labour administration attention became focused more on dealing with strikes, and the resolution which lay behind the incomes policy, by then aimed at a ceiling of 3.5 per cent, weakened.

The Conservative Government which came to power in 1970 abolished the National Board for Prices and Incomes (as the Labour Party in 1964 had done with the National Incomes Commission). Unemployment was allowed to rise, though it did nothing to moderate the size of wage settlements; and in the public sector a 'nil' policy involved an attempt to reduce the size of each successive wage settlement, but this foundered on the miners' strike of 1972. A statutory incomes policy was then, reintroduced with three stages. Stage 1 was a statutory freeze. Stage 2 was a norm of £1 plus 4 per cent, and a Pay Board and Price Commission to enforce it. Finally, stage 3 involved a threshold subject to various gateways, plus the promise of extra inflation-related adjustments should the rate of inflation exceed 7 per cent. Inflation did exceed this figure when stage 3 came into operation and resulted in wage promises which had to be kept by the incoming Labour administration in 1974.

The next government's approach was to initiate a 'social contract' between the government and the TUC which involved a commitment to moderation in wage claims. In its early years it was ineffective and though it was later stiffened there are numerous grounds for criticism. It would be more likely to succeed if bargaining were undertaken in the UK at a national or industry-wide level, but this is not the case. Individual bargaining units at single-employer level are much more likely to persuade themselves that they are a special case and are unlikely to be interested in the macroeconomic consequences of their actions.

Conditions are different in the public sector, where industry-wide agreements are more common and extremely visible. Governments are here faced with the difficult task of reconciling the requirements of their macroeconomic policy with the need to maintain an equitable and realistic pay structure within the public sector. Some sort of guidance on pay comparability was seen to be required. The government thus set up the Standing Commission on Pay Comparability which made several recommendations on public sector pay. These recommendations, made in 1978 and 1979, were honoured by the incoming Conservative Government. As with its Labour predecessor in 1974, the keeping of such promises posed a considerable macroeconomic embarrassment to the administration. The Commission was also duly abolished. The new government provided for free collective bargaining in the private sector, and subsequently attempted to impose a blanket 6 per cent cash limit on public sector awards. The problem here is that this leads to further inequities; groups with industrial muscle may have no trouble in exceeding the prescribed limits, whereas other groups, such as the nurses, are left standing on the sidelines. On the other hand, comparability claims can be used to justify leap-frogging wage increases.

The general efficacy of incomes policies thus remains in doubt. The attitude of the political parties appears to be totally ambivalent. It is frequently argued that incomes policies are temporarily successful in their stronger forms, but that as soon as they are relaxed a ‘catching-up’ phase undermines all that they have achieved. Yet some form of wage moderation may be required if it is conceded that the free labour market is inadequate because of the monopoly powers of trade unions and the non-market responsiveness of the country’s biggest employer, namely the state.

These difficulties have been greatly reduced by the massive privatization programme recently carried out by the Thatcher administration, which has returned numerous public sector operations to the private sector. Some of the more notable of these include various National Enterprise Board holdings, British Petroleum Ltd, British Rail Hotels, British Aerospace, the National Freight Corporation, parts of British Steel Corporation, British National Oil Corporation, British Transport Docks, British Telecom Corporation, British Shipbuilders, British Gas Corporation and British Airways.

References

1 A. Smith, *The Wealth of Nations* (1776), book 1, chapter 10, Penguin, 1970.
2 K. Marx, *Capital: A Critique of Political Economy*, vol. 2, part 2, chapter 10, Penguin, 1978.
3 P. Sraffa, *The Production of Commodities by Commodities*, Cambridge University Press, 1960.
4 A. Marshall, *Principles of Economics*, vol. 1, book 6, chapter 1, Macmillan, 9th edn, 1961.
5 A. Marshall, *Principles of Economics*, vol. 1, book 5, chapter 6.
Sir John Hicks, *The Theory of Wages*, Macmillan, 1968, p. 241.
6 A. C. Pigou, *Economics of Welfare*, 4th edn, Macmillan, 1962, book 4, chapter 5.
7 Ibid.
8 '1990 labour force survey preliminary results', *Employment Gazette*, (April 1991), pp. 175–96.
9 For a discussion of projections of the labour force see Department of Employment, *Employment Gazette* (April 1989). See also note 8.
10 For further discussion of pay differentials and pay bargaining see F. Blackaby (ed.), *The Future of Pay Bargaining*, Heinemann, 1980.
11 *Report of the Royal Commission on Trade Unions and Employers' Associations 1965–68*, Chairman Lord Donovan, Cmnd 3623, HMSO, June 1968, p. 207.
12 *Employment Gazette* (January 1981), p. 22.
13 A. M. Ross, *Trade Union Wage Policy*, University of California Press, 1948.
J. T. Dunlop, *Wage Determination under Trade Unions*, Kelley, 1950.
14 R. B. Freeman and J. L. Medoff, *What Do Unions Do?*, Basic Books, 1984.
15 A. J. Oswald, 'Efficient contracts are on the labour demand curve: theory and facts', Working Paper 178, Industrial Relations Section, Princeton University, 1984.
A. J. Oswald, 'Wage determination and recession: a report on recent work', *British Journal of Industrial Relations* 24 (July 1986).
16 Hicks, *The Theory of Wages*.
17 N. W. Chamberlain, *Collective Bargaining*, McGraw-Hill, 1951.
18 W. Brown (ed.), *The Changing Contours of British Industrial Relations*, Basil Blackwell, 1981.
19 G. Palmer 'Donovan, the Commission on Industrial Relations and Post-Liberal Rationalisation', *British Journal of Industrial Relations* 24 (July 1986).
20 *Employment Gazette* (April 1991), p. 543.
21 See 'Large industrial stoppages 1960–79', *Employment Gazette* (September 1980).
22 H. A. Clegg, *Trade Unionism under Collective Bargaining*, Blackwell, 1976, p. 82.
23 S. J. Prais, 'The strike-proneness of large plants in Britain', *Journal of the Royal Statistical Society* 141 (1978).
24 P. K. Edwards, 'The strike-proneness of British manufacturing establishments', *British Journal of Industrial Relations* 19 (1981), pp. 135–48.
25 J. Kelly, *Trade and Socialist Politics*, Verso, 1988.
26 A. W. Phillips, 'The relationship between unemployment and the rate of

change of money wage rates in the United Kingdom, 1861–1957', *Economica* 25 (1958).

27 M. Friedman, 'The role of monetary policy', *American Economic Review* 58 (1968).

28 R. Layard and S. J. Nickell, 'The causes of British unemployment', *National Institute Economic Review* 1/85 (1985).

R. Layard and S. J. Nickell, 'Unemployment in Britain', *Economica* 53 (1986), pp. 3121–69.

29 E. S. Phelps, *Inflation Policy and Unemployment Theory*, Macmillan, 1972.

See also R. Cross (ed.), *Unemployment, Hysteresis, and the National Rate Hypothesis*, Basil Blackwell, 1988.

15

Government Policy towards Industry

In this chapter we discuss current government competition policy, regional policy and policies towards public goods and externalities.

Competition Policy

The traditional rationale for competition policy is as follows. Suppose that an industry is perfectly competitive (price takers). Then in figure 15.1, where for simplicity the average cost is horizontal and so equal to marginal cost (MC), market price would be bid down to P_C. As explained in chapter

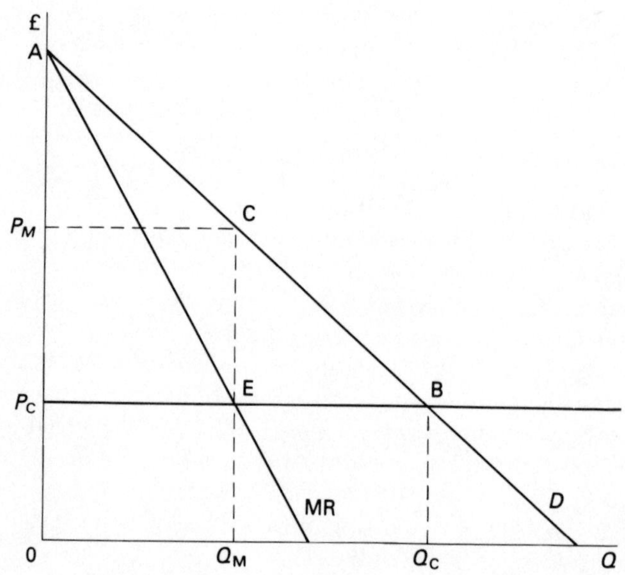

Figure 15.1 *The deadweight loss of monopoly*

2 the area AP_CB represents consumers' surplus, i.e. the amount of money consumers were willing to pay for the first unit plus that for the second unit (slightly less than the first) and so on, indicated by the height of the demand curve, over and above the amount they have to pay – given by P_C. Now suppose that all the firms merged to form a profit-maximizing monopoly and so produced the output where marginal revenue (MR) is equal to MC, i.e. Q_M, and set price at P_M. Consumers' surplus is now just AP_MC. The area P_MCEP_C is the amount which producers receive (OP_MCQ_M) above the minimum amount they require (OP_CEQ_M, where P_C = MC for each unit) to produce this quantity. This is therefore a surplus to producers or 'producers' surplus'. But the area CBE which was formerly a surplus to consumers is now received by no one and is called the 'dead weight loss' of monopoly. Since this money amount could have been spent on goods and services to give utility, the dead weight loss corresponds to a certain amount of utility which is lost by society.

Further, a high degree of rivalry between firms where at least one aims for maximum profits may force firms to be as efficient as possible, for otherwise their average costs may exceed their price and they would be forced to leave the industry. Thus in a price takers' market firms would opt for the profit-maximizing location, number of employees, plant size, advertising spending, organizational structure and so on.

However, the larger firm size resulting from the merger may enable economies of scale to be gained which were not possible in the case of a price takers' market. This could be represented by lower costs to the monopoly than for the perfectly competitive industry and so greater producers' surplus which may outweigh the dead weight loss. Alternatively, the lack of rivalry facing a monopoly (if entry is impeded) may reduce its stimulus to be as efficient as possible – it may spend too much on staff, locate suboptimally or not operate the most efficient plant size etc., a phenomenon known as *X*-inefficiency. A further relevant issue which, as shown in chapter 5, is unresolved is whether a monopolized or highly rivalrous industry would be the faster to invent and innovate.

So far we have considered the effects of a merger, but the elevation of price above marginal costs may result if a single firm has sufficient brand loyalty and entry is impeded or if entry is impeded and a group of firms agree to set similar (high) prices. Even if entry is not impeded, such price distortions may occur in the short run. Hence competition policy covers the behaviour of single firms and also of groups of firms.

The above arguments suggest that in some cases the social benefits of monopoly power may exceed the social disbenefits whereas in other cases they may not. Therefore the British and European approach to competition policy is to investigate each situation separately to see whether firm conduct is against the 'public interest'.

UK policies

A number of statutes detailing UK policy have been passed as follows.

Restrictive practices

Current legislation is a consolidation (in the Restrictive Trading Practices Act 1976) of the Restrictive Trading Practices Acts of 1956 and 1968.

Restrictive Trade Practices Act 1956

This Act set up the Restrictive Practices Court, composed of High Court judges helped by lay experts. The Court has to decide whether manufacturers' agreements are against the public interest or not. All such agreements between persons carrying on businesses in the UK in the production or supply of goods or services where the restrictions are accepted by two or more parties with regard to prices, charges, terms or conditions, quantities or descriptions, persons supplying or to be supplied had to be registered with the Registrar of Restrictive Trade Practices (a role now performed by the Director General of Fair Trading), and all are to be referred to the Court unless they are thought by the Secretary of State to be so insignificant as not to warrant this. In passing judgement on any agreement the Court *presumed* that these are against the public interest unless it was persuaded that one of six gateways and the 'tailpiece' applied. The gateways were as follows.

1 The restriction is necessary to protect the public where the use of the goods requires special knowledge or skill.
2 The removal of the restriction would deprive buyers and users of substantial benefits.
3 The restriction is a necessary defensive measure against other restraints imposed on the trade by persons outside it.
4 The restriction is a necessary defensive measure against an outside monopoly.
5 The removal of the restriction is likely to have an adverse effect on the general level of employment in some area, or is likely to cause a substantial reduction in the export trade in the UK.
6 The restriction is necessary to maintain another restriction which the Court finds to be not contrary to the public interest.

There is an additional 'general' gateway through which all agreements must pass. The Court must be satisfied 'that the restriction is not unreasonable having regard to the balance between those circumstances and any detriment to the public or to persons not parties to the agreement resulting from, or likely to result from, the operation of the restriction'.

The pervasiveness of restrictive practices in industry can be gauged by the fact that, by June 1963, 2450 agreements had been registered. But most were subsequently abandoned by the firms concerned or were amended so as to be excluded from the Act. By June 1972, 35 cases had been contested in court; 11 were found not contrary to the public interest. Only a handful of agreements remained on the Register where the course of action had still to be decided.

Although the 1956 Act prohibited collective enforcement of *resale price maintenance* (RPM) it effectively increased the powers of manufacturers to enforce individual RPM (namely the practice whereby the manufacturer stipulates the resale prices by withholding supplies from retailers who do not adhere to his terms).

Restrictive Trade Practices Act 1968

Experience since the 1956 Act, especially the possibility of operating unwritten price agreements, resulted in the Restrictive Trade Practices Act 1968, which amended the 1956 legislation in three ways. First, price exchange information, not registrable under the 1956 Act, can have much the same effect as a price-fixing agreement, although only the latter was registrable (and usually declared illegal). The 1968 Act empowered the Board of Trade to call up any such information agreements for registration (i.e. this would still not be compulsory). Second, an additional 'gateway' was added. A restriction can now be defended on the grounds that it 'does not directly or indirectly restrict or discourage competition'. Third, the government is permitted to make orders providing exemptions of certain agreements from registration, provided only that the agreement is necessary to promote efficiency in the national interest.

Monopolies

The earliest monopoly legislation was passed in 1948 but the current legislation is the Fair Trading Act 1973.

The Fair Trading Act 1973

The Fair Trading Act 1973 replaced all previous legislation. A Director General of Fair Trading (DGFT) was appointed. One of his main duties is 'to keep under review commercial activities with a view to becoming aware of, and ascertaining the circumstances relating to, monopoly situations or uncompetitive practices'. In most instances the DGFT has the right (previously confined to a government minister) to make references to the (renamed) Monopolies and Mergers Commission (MMC). The DGFT has also assumed the functions previously carried out by the Registrar of Restrictive Trade Practices.

The definition of monopoly for purposes of investigation by the

Commission was widened from the 'one-third of a market' rule of earlier legislation to embrace those situations where one firm or group of firms controls one-quarter or more of a market. The MMC is asked whether the monopoly is acting against the public interest. In defining the public interest, the MMC is to take into account whatever they consider relevant and to include the desirability of the following:

1 maintaining and promoting effective competition;
2 promoting the interests of consumers, purchasers and other users of goods and services in respect of the prices charged for them and in respect of their quality and variety;
3 promoting through competition the reduction of costs and the development and use of new techniques and new products, and of facilitating the entry of new competitors into existing markets;
4 maintaining and promoting the balanced distribution of industry and employment in the UK;
5 maintaining and promoting competitive activity in markets outside the UK on the part of producers in the UK.

Competition Act 1980

The DGFT was given power to investigate any activity which appears 'anti-competitive', i.e. any activity which may have the 'effect of restricting, distorting or preventing competition in connection with the production, supply or acquisition of goods'. The DGFT can refer such cases to the MMC.

Mergers

Under the Fair Trading Act 1973 the DGFT can refer a merger where the value of acquired assets exceeds £30 million or the resulting combine supplies or buys 25 per cent of a market. The Secretary of State can refer such acquisitions to the MMC who will be asked whether the acquisition is likely to be against the public interest.

Assessment of restrictive practices

Various criticisms have been made of the appropriateness of the gateways and the procedures of restrictive practices legislation. Considering first the appropriateness of the gateways, it has been argued that the first gateway is redundant for most circumstances because other legislation exists to protect the public against injury and where it does not gateway 2 would do so. The second gateway has been criticized by Korah[1] for lack of precision, thus restricting the ability of the Court to make consistent decisions. Gateway 5 has been opposed on the grounds that employment matters should not be considered by a court of law. A Green Paper published in 1988[2] argued that the effects of a restrictive agreement on the regional distribution of employment should be included in the Act but should be considered by the Court as part of the tailpiece and not as a separate gateway. The Green Paper also criticized the sixth gateway on the grounds that it was not stated in a way which would enable the Court to improve the balance of payments – the objective of the gateway. For example, there is no reference to agreements which may reduce imports. Finally, the Green Paper noted that the 1956 and 1976 Acts provide no specific definition of the detriments which are to be compared with the benefits of the restriction, although no evidence was submitted to its authors to suggest that an amendment to the tailpiece was needed.

A second criticism of the legislation concerns the issue of 'justiciability'. For example, Stevens and Yamey[3] have argued that it is not possible to debate complex economic arguments in a court since many judges and the two lay persons who make judgement lack the technical knowledge to understand the issues fully.

In the Green Paper it was further argued that whether the Acts require registration of an agreement depends on its form and not whether or not it restricts competition. However, the intention of the government was to prevent only those agreements which restrict competition. Some types of agreement – where only one supplier accepts an agreement – are not registrable but do restrict competition whilst others are registrable but do not restrict competition. Nevertheless it was accepted that the legislation 'has generally proved effective . . . in terms of increased economic efficiency' (p. 58) and has led to the widespread elimination of cartels. However, it was recommended that the legislation be changed so that desirable agreements which the Act may have deterred became easier to make, that the legislation be simplified and that the means of enforcement be strengthened.

The Green Paper made further criticisms. The penalties for registration are not sufficiently severe to prevent the formation of secret cartels and the penalties for non-registration were not thought sufficiently punitive to deter secret formations. It noted that the change from a 'form'-based registration criterion to an 'effects'-based criterion was needed since it is the registration criterion that determines which agreements are evaluated. The Green Paper indicated that a large and increasing number of exemptions were being granted with no consistent procedures existing to investigate whether the exceptions remain justified. The decision as to whether registration is required in the light of the list of exemptions was complex and very time consuming for firms and the authorities. In practice, many restrictions become eligible for exemption under section 21(2) of the 1976 Act after negotiations with the Director General of Fair Trading. These negotiations are wasteful in terms of time, especially since the Act is rather vague as to the criteria under which exemption may be granted. (The average time between registration and a section 21(2) exemption in 1985 was 2 years and 9 months.) The 1988 Green Paper reiterated the criticism made in an earlier Green Paper[4] that the legislation was form and not effects based, i.e. that both pro- and anti-competitive agreements of the appropriate firm had to be registered, and it made several proposals for new legislation.

In July 1989 the government published a White Paper which stated its intention to replace the 1976 Act with a new law. It is proposed that the law should operate only against agreements which restrict competition provided that the total UK turnover of the parties exceeds £5 million (unless it is a price-fixing agreement). The new Act would control only arrangements which reduce competition 'in the relevant market taken as a whole' (p. 6). A list of prohibited practices is included such as (a) price fixing and fixing of terms and conditions, (b) information exchange agreements, (c) collusive tendering, (d) agreements to share the market or suppliers and (e) collective refusals to supply. The prohibition relates to agreements which have the effect or the aim of restricting competition. Agreements where the benefits outweigh the restrictive effects will be exempted. The registration requirement will be discontinued. Instead the DGFT will carry out an initial investigation of each agreement to see whether it is amongst the prohibited categories above and/or whether it is exempt. If the DGFT finds that the agreement infringes the prohibition then it is investigated by members of the MMC who will make up a 'restrictive trade practices tribunal'. If the tribunal finds against the agreement it is proposed that the tribunal could fine the parties involved, those adversely affected could claim damages and the restrictions would be unenforceable.

Assessment of monopoly policy

Monopoly policy has been criticized in a number of ways. Hay and Vickers[5] and many others have criticized the definition of 'the public interest' as too vague. For example, the Fair Trading Act 1973 included, as a preamble, the need to take account of 'all matters which appear . . . in the particular circumstances to be relevant'. This Act also contains, as one consideration to be included in the MMC's judgement, 'the balanced distribution of employment'. This guideline would seem to be more relevant to an Act relating to regional rather than monopoly policy. It might confuse the workings of the Commission, and in certain circumstances may place it in a position where there is a need to take a decision favouring either more or less competition subject to providing more regional assistance. It is debatable whether such questions of distribution should be left to policitians or to their non-elected, but specialist, advisers in unrelated areas. The consistency of the Monopoly Commission Reports has also been criticized by Sutherland.[6]

However, it is often claimed that the pragmatism and flexibility of the British policy (especially in comparison with the American system where market share alone is often regarded as sufficient grounds for an unfavourable judgement) is its strength.

Assessment of Mergers Policy

In the last four years intense interest has been shown in the appraisal of UK merger policy: conferences have been held, a government Blue Paper has been published and many academic papers have been written. Fairburn[7] notes that, since even before Norman Tebbitt's statement of July 1984 that competition would be the main grounds on which a reference to the MMC would be made, mergers were consistently referred and that subsequently most referrals focused on competition issues. In some cases if a reference was likely on competition grounds, e.g. Guinness's bid for Distillers, the bid was not referred if the acquirer divested such brands that led the DGFT to believe that competition was not likely to be adversely affected (Guinness sold off Whyte and Mackay). Fairburn notes that this marked a change in policy, since prior to the early 1980s such bids would probably have been referred.

The 1978 Green Paper argued that merger policy was biased towards mergers since it assumed that few would be referred. There is evidence that only a small percentage of those eligible are referred. Fairburn[8] estimates that for 1965–86 the proportion was 3 per cent. By examining the shares of referred and non-referred mergers during 1965–77, Fairburn concludes: 'in a substantial number of cases mergers creating a strong presumption of danger of monopoly abuse were not even before the Commission.' Fairburn further criticizes the referral process by arguing that it is the duty of the DGFT to keep the degree of competition under surveillance and hence to be keen to detect reductions in it, but that by 1986 in ten cases the Secretary of State had not referred mergers which the DGFT suggested he should. Moreover, the justification for non-referral in the Canon/Owens Coming case suggested either that the Secretary of State felt that MMC inquiries were too slow or that he was able to replace their inquiry by his own judgement. In the first case the obvious policy is to boost the resources of the MMC; in the latter his degree of knowledge is suspect.

Fairburn[9] has summarized the MMC position on various issues which enter the Commission's view of the public interest. The Commission has objected to mergers thought likely to reduce management efficiency, e.g. House of Fraser/Lonhro. It has acted to protect employment and career prospects in Scotland (Standard Chartered/Royal Bank of Scotland, Charter Consolidate/Anderson Strathclyde). It has found foreign ownership in certain industries undesirable, e.g. Hong Kong and Shanghai Banking Corporation/Royal Bank of Scotland, but we must note that this is not always the case, e.g. Nestlé/Rowntree. The Commission has also taken into account whether the nature of the financing of the merger would result in financial weakness of the new group. In terms of deciding to what extent two products compete the MMC has to consider the similarity of various technical characteristics – price, geographical dispersion of outlets, similarity of purchases etc. – and then come to a value judgement. Surveying 18 reports, Fairburn argues that, beyond saying that mergers involving less than 30 per cent of a market are likely to be allowed and those over 60 per cent are likely to be prevented, no general statements can be made about the MMC's attitudes towards market share.

In the 1978 Green Paper it was argued that merger policy operated in favour of mergers because a merger is allowed if the MMC does not find that it is against the public interest rather than if the MMC finds that it operates in the public interest. Much evidence suggests that, on average, mergers result in reduced profitability. Hence supporters of the above argument have suggested that policy should be changed. The 1988 Blue Paper stated that government intervention should be kept to a minimum because commercial decisions in competitive markets lead to the most 'desirable outcomes for the economy as a whole'. Reversing the burden of proof would distort this outcome and weaken the stimulus to managerial performance presented by the threat of take-over. Additionally Borrie[10] reports that some argue that the currrent policy is biased in favour of conglomerates because the main criterion for a referral and for being found against the public interest is a reduction in competition which is unlikely to occur if two firms in non-overlapping markets merge.

Finally Hay and Vickers[11] have argued that the Secretary of State should not have the power to decide which company or merger is referred and whether to accept the MMC's recommendations. They argue that this arrangement concentrates power on a politician, it reduces the independent standing of the MMC and encourages lobbying such as in the British Airways/British Caledonian merger.

The Blue Paper announced the Government's intention to change legislation in two ways. First, firms can be told whether a referral is likely by completing a questionnaire, thus speeding up this decision. Second, in place of an MMC reference the DGFT will be able to accept legally binding undertakings by parties to a merger to act in ways thought by the DGFT to be in the public interest. Both changes were included in the Companies Act of 1989. Companies can now voluntarily notify the Office of Fair Trading before an acquisition takes place by completing a questionnaire (called a Merger Notice). In the light of the information supplied by the company the DGFT advises the Secretary of State whether or not an acquisition should be referred to the MMC. The Secretary of State has 20 working days after receipt of the pre-notification in which to make public his decision as to whether referral will take place. In addition, the DGFT can now accept undertakings in lieu of a referral.

European policy

European legislation towards restrictive agreements is contained in Article 85 of the Treaty of Rome. This states that all agreements 'which may affect trade between Member States and which have as their object or effect' the reduction of competition in the Common Market are incompatible with the Common Market. The Article gives, as examples of the behaviour which is outlawed, price-fixing restrictions on output, restrictions on technical development, market sharing, price discrimination and contracts contingent on supplementary obligations. Agreements are exempt if they are found to improve 'the production or distribution of goods' or to promote technical or economic progress while allowing consumers a fair share of the benefit, provided that they do not severely reduce competition. Companies party to an agreement are encouraged to notify the European Commission. Notification validates the agreement until it is investigated by the Commission.

As regards dominant positions, Article 86 of the Treaty of Rome states that 'any abuse of a dominant position' within the Common Market is outlawed in so far as it may affect trade between member states. Examples of such abuses are similar to those relating to restrictive agreements.

Finally, the European Council of Ministers agreed for the first time on 21 December 1989 on the details of a regulation concerning acquisitions (prior to this acquisitions were evaluated against Article 86 as if the acquisition created a dominant position). This will come into effect on 21 September 1990. The Regulation (no. 4064/89) applies to all acquisitions whereby control of another company is obtained where (a) the combined world turnover of the firms involved is over 5 billion European currency units (ECUs) and (b) the individual turnover of at least two of the companies is over 250 ECUs within the European Community unless each of the firms has over two-thirds of its aggregate Community turnover in one state (it is intended that these thresholds will be reviewed in December 1993). All such acquisitions must be notified to the Commission not later than one week after they take place or the bid is announced (whichever is earlier). If the Commission decides that the acquisition comes under the Regulation it will begin an investigation to see whether it is incompatible with the Common Market. In making its appraisal the Commission will take into account the economic and financial power of the firms concerned, the position of suppliers and users, supply and demand trends for the relevant goods and services, the rate of technical and economic progress and any barriers to entry.

Assessment of European policy

Restrictive practices

First, note that whilst Article 85 relates to competition *within* the Common Market, the European Commission believes it can impose (and has imposed) penalties, e.g. fines, on companies registered in countries outside the Common Market if they are found to act with member firms in ways which infringe the Article. Second, the Article relates both to actions which do distort competition and to those which may do so at some time in the future. Third, Article 85 is phrased in the same terms as the proposed UK legislation. That is, it prohibits agreements with the *aim or effect* of restricting etc. competition and is not a regulation which could be criticized as only applying to agreements of a specific *form*. Fourth, cases considered by the Commission show which competition-distorting behaviour has been criticized. These include the following.

1 *Price fixing agreements.* The Commission imposed fines on Fabbuca Pisana SpA, an Italian flat glass company, for, amongst other things, fixing prices and conditions of sale for flat glass for use other than in the motor vehicle industry and fixing prices and quotas for flat glass for the motor vehicle industry.
2 *Application of output or sales quotas.* Following investigations in 1983 and 1987, producers of PVC (polyvinyl chloride) and LDPE (low density polyethylene) were found to be agreeing at regular meetings to sharing the Western European market on the basis of annual volume targets, in addition to other behaviour.
3 *Exclusionary practices.* The Commission ordered the clause in an agreement made between Nutrasweet and Coca-Cola and Pepsico Inc., whereby the last two companies agreed to buy all their aspartance (a food sweetener) from the former, to be removed.
4 *Sole or exclusive distribution agreements.* The Commission prohibited an agreement whereby Grundig appointed Consten as the sole dealer of its products at the importer/wholesale stage in France. The agreement was upheld on appeal.
5 *Information exchange.* Certain manufacturers in the Dutch and Belgian Paper Industry Federations exchanged information which included notification of relevant prices giving individual company's names, general terms of supply, and sales and payments received including details of discounts to particular customers. The information exchanged was so detailed that it enabled members to plan their export sales policy knowing exactly the prices charged by local manufacturers. The European Commission decided that the practice infringed Article 85.
6 *Prevention of parallel imports within the European distribution system.* Pioneer, a hi-fi equipment supplier, was fined for operating, effectively, export bans.

Assessment of dominant positions

Article 86 refers to a 'dominant position . . . in a substantial part' of the Common Market but does not state what market share constitutes 'substantial'. Case law suggests that this could be a proportion of the market within a single state and the size distribution of the other firms in the industry is relevant. Market shares as low as 40 per cent (IBM case) have been taken as 'dominant'.

Notice that it is not dominance but its *abuse* which is incompatible with the Common Market. The Article gave examples of such abuse and the following cases give examples of practices which have been considered abuses.

1 *Action to restrict the development of a new entrant.* British Sugar was fined 3 million ECUs for abuse of its dominant position (market share 58 per cent of the British market for granulated sugar) because it had tried to force Napier Brown – a new entrant into the market – to withdraw. British Sugar, for example, discriminated against Napier Brown by refusing to sell it pure beet sugar, whilst supplying beet sugar to other customers.
2 *Inducements to deal exclusively with supplier.* British Plasterboard Industries PLC abused its dominant position in two ways, one of which was through its subsidiary British Gypsum, to put pressure on importers to stop imports of Spanish plasterboards.
3 *Charging different prices in different parts of the European Community for the same product.* The Commission found against United Brands for selling bananas at higher prices in Denmark and Germany and lower prices in the Benelux countries.

Assessment of merger policy

No agreed regulation applied to acquisitions before September 1990. Prior to this date, acquisitions were considered under Article 86, the seminal case being that of Continental Can Company Inc. Continental Can bought a majority shareholding in Schmalbach-Lubeca Wercke AG and then transferred these holdings to a holding company. The holding company then made a successful bid for a Dutch can producer. Thus the holding company controlled Schmalbach and the Dutch can producer. The European Commission argued that the removal of the Dutch company's competition was an abuse. This decision was revoked on appeal, the Court noting that competition was still offered to Schmalbach by glass and plastic containers and other metal producers.

The Philip Morris case suggests that Article 85 may also be applied to acquisitions. The undertakings given by Philip Morris concerning its use of a minority shareholding in Rothmans International were considered by the

European Court. The deliberations of the Court indicate that if shares are bought through public offers to shareholders then an agreement exists – as required by Article 85.

Since the new merger regulations only came into effect on 21 September 1990 an assessment of its operation is not possible. However, certain points can be made. First, the Council Regulation, like Article 86, does not define what is meant by a substantial part of the Common Market when stating the domain of activities in which competition is affected. Second, the factors to be considered by the Commission when considering each case are very similar to those of Article 85. Third, that the criterion which determines whether the Regulation applies is the turnover of the two firms and not their market share seems slightly inconsistent with outlawing acquisitions which restrict competition. Surely market share is a better guide to the degree of rivalry than turnover since the latter could lead to the consideration of diversifying acquisitions? Fourth, the requirement that acquisitions may be notified to the European Commission in advance of completion will be a considerable improvement on the previous situation whereby Articles 86 and 85 were applied, the former requiring a dominant position *to exist* before investigations can begin.

Regional Policy

Regional economic disparities have been observed in the UK since before the beginning of the twentieth century. They are often measured in terms of three variables: net migration, unemployment and output per head. Table 15.1 shows that in 1966 the less prosperous regions were the north, Wales and Scotland, these areas having low gross domestic product (GDP) per head, high unemployment rates and net outward migration relative to Britain as a whole. By 1976 the differences had marginally narrowed but by 1987 the differences had widened again with the least prosperous areas now being Wales, the north, West Midlands, Yorkshire and Humberside, the northwest and Scotland.

Various explanations for these disparities have been suggested. In the structural approach it is argued that certain regions have a higher proportion of employment provided by industries for whom demand is declining than do other regions. When such decreases in demand occur, the former regions suffer a proportionately greater decrease in employment, income per head etc. than do others. Industries which are concentrated in certain regions and for which demand is declining include coal, heavy engineering and shipbuilding.

One technique which has been used to isolate the effects of industrial structures from other factors in a region is the shift share approach.

Consider table 15.2. A hypothetical region is postulated. Employment change between years 1970 and 1980 is the indicator used. Assume a region

Table 15.1

	Per capital GDP at factor cost (UK = 100)			Unemployment rates (GB = 100)			Population change in annual growth rate (%)			New civilian migration as per cent of population			Net output per employee in manu-facturing (UK = 100)	
	1966	1976	1987	1965	1975	1989	1961–71	1971–81	1981–7	1966–7	1975–6	1986–7	1971	1981
North	84.1	94.8	88.9	179	144	163	0.1	−0.1	−0.2	−0.21	−0.02	−0.23	96.9	104.5
Yorkshire/Humberside	96.7	94.7	92.7	79	98	123	0.5	0	−0.1	−0.023	−0.12	0	90.9	911.5
East Midlands	96.5	95.1	95.1	64	88	92	0.9	0.5	0.4	+0.02	+0.10	+0.48	89.4	87.4
East Anglia	96.0	92.5	99.8	93	83	57	1.3	1.2	1.0	+1.02	+1.02	+0.16	103.1	107.2
Southeast	114.7	112.9	118.5	57	68	63	0.6	−0.1	0.3	−0.05	−0.19	−0.32	110.2	111.2
Southwest	92.0	91.0	94.0	107	115	70	1.0	0.6	0.8	+0.31	+0.73	+0.10	100.8	102.7
West Midlands	108.2	98.4	91.6	50	100	105	0.8	0.1	0	+0.04	−0.36	−0.04	93.3	87.6
Northwest	95.7	96.6	92.8	114	129	138	0.3	−0.3	−0.3	−0.23	−0.25	−0.44	98.8	99.5
Wales	84.2	90.3	82.4	179	137	179	0.4	+0.3	0.1	−0.09	+0.20	+0.50	101.6	97.6
Scotland	89.1	97.3	94.5	207	127	153	0.1	−0.1	−0.2	−0.87	−0.09	−0.27	102.8	104.8

Sources: *Regional Trends*, 1989; *Business Monitor*, *Census of Production*, 1981, vol. PA1001; *Business Monitor*, Census of Production, 1971, vol. PA1001; *Abstract of Regional Statistics*, 1969, table 7

Table 15.2 *A hypothetical application of the shift–share technique in a given region*

Industry	Actual employment growth 1970	1980	net	Attributable to national growth (10%)	Attributable to industry growth (structure)	Change due to region-specific factors
A	1000	900	−100	100	−100 (−10%)	−100
B	500	150	−350	50	−250 (−50%)	−150
C	100	100	0	10	10 (10%)	−20
Total	1600	1150	−450	160	−340	−270

is composed of only three industries A, B and C and that total employment nationally rose by 10 per cent. If industries A, B and C grew in the nation as a whole by 0, −40 and 20 per cent respectively, then, of these figures, −10, −50 and 10 per cent are due to growth or decline uniquely attributable to these industries themselves after deducting the national 10 per cent growth rate (the structural explanation). Any remaining difference is due to region-specific factors. Thus in our hypothetical region 450 jobs have been lost in the decade. This is 160 more than would have been expected if the region had grown at the same rate as the national economy. Because the region is heavily reliant on declining industries A and B, 340 jobs have been lost. But there are other peculiar factors in the region which are responsible for a further reduction in employment of 270. Had the economy as a whole not grown as it did, the region would have been still worse off than it actually is, namely by 160 jobs.

Studies which have used this type of methodology have varied in the importance attributed to structural differences. Fothergill and Gudgin[12] compared 1952–66 with 1966–79 to find that structural differences had little impact on employment changes in the latter period. In a paper by the Department of Trade and Industry[13] it is noted that Moore et al.,[14] on studying groups of regions (Development Areas, Intermediate Areas and Non-assisted Areas rather than individual regions), found differences in manufacturing structure to be important in 1966–71, of little importance in 1972–5 and more important in 1976–81. The same study by the Department of Trade and Industry, which included services as well as manufacturing, found that over the period 1975–81 the southeast and southwest had relatively favourable structures whilst Yorkshire and Humberside and the West Midlands had relatively poor structures.

Another school of thought is that the problem is structural in origin but other factors exist which handicap development. One such factor is the long distance between the regions concerned and large urban centres. This is said to lead to above-average transport costs leading to higher prices, risk of delays due to poorer quality transport links, less information about markets and less contact with customers and business services. But evidence suggests that only in the most remote areas, e.g. the Highlands and Islands of Scotland, and in only a small number of industries are transport costs a significant proportion of total costs.

A second argument is that the physical infrastructure, e.g. transport facilities, premises, and the social infrastructure, e.g. schools, recreation facilities, dereliction, are less attractive in the depressed regions. Empirical evidence suggests that such environmental factors are less important than, say, suitable labour and government incentives as a factor attracting firm location.

A further factor has been said to be that a greater proportion of establishments located in the depressed areas are owned by companies located elsewhere and this means that fewer professional and managerial jobs and less decision-making autonomy than would otherwise be the case are available. It has been suggested that such plants take less of their inputs from local companies, although there is little evidence to support this assertion.

Regional differences in the rate of innovation have also affected regional growth rates. In 1968 the southeast had 49 per cent of research establishments and 28 per cent of manufacturing employees. A study by Townsend et al.[15] found that, over 1965–78, while the southeast had 34 per cent of significant innovations it had 25 per cent of manufacturing employment. Yorkshire and Humberside and the northwest had 20 per cent of innovations but 25 per cent of manufacturing employees.

Current policy

British regional policy dates from around 1934 when the Special Areas (Development and Improvement) Act was passed which designated four Special Areas as regions suffering from considerably above average unemployment and to receive aid and loans. Subsequent policies have altered (a) the areas to receive assistance, (b) the nature and magnitude of financial incentives to firms to locate in such areas and for workers to move to more prosperous areas and (c) development controls which have restricted growth in the more prosperous regions. Following Moore, Rhodes and Tyler[16] the post-1945 period can be divided into six periods.

1 *1945–1960*. The Special Development Areas were renamed Development Areas and extended. The Board of Trade was given responsibility for regional policy including powers to build and lease factories and to give grants and loans to firms to locate in Development Areas. During this period building controls were extended to include the need to obtain an Industrial Development Certificate (IDC) if a manufacturing

firm wished to build a plant of over 5000 square feet. Assistance was given to unemployed workers moving to find work.

2 *1960–1966*. The 1960 Local Employment Act replaced Development Areas by Development Districts: areas where unemployment exceeded 4.5 per cent. These were redesignated annually as the unemployment rate of certain areas rose above or fell below 4.5 per cent. The government factory building programme intensified and more grants and loans were made.

3 *1966–1970*. The 1966 Industrial Development Act replaced the Development Districts by five Development Areas. Investment grants of up to 40 per cent of capital expenditure were made available. In 1967 firms in Development Areas could receive a Regional Employment Premium – a payment per worker per week – and the areas of severest unemployment were designated Special Development Areas with additional incentives, rent-free premises and 35 per cent building grants. IDCs were retained.

4 *1970–1975*. The 1970 Employment Act established seven Intermediate Areas in which government-built factories were available as were building grants. The 1972 Industry Act reintroduced Regional Development Grants (20 per cent in Development Areas; 22 per cent in Special Development Areas) and IDCs were abolished in Special Development Areas and Development Areas.

5 *1976–1979*. The area for which an IDC was required was increased so much that they became ineffective. Regional Employment Premium was abolished.

6 *1979–1990*. During this period Special Development Areas and Development Areas were at first reduced and in 1984 Special Development Areas were abolished. Development Areas and Intermediate Development Areas were drastically changed to cover 15 per cent and 20 per cent respectively of Britain's working population. The rate of Regional Development Grant was reduced and no application was accepted after 31 March 1988. It was felt that many investments would have occurred in the assisted areas regardless of whether or not grants were received. In the absence of an automatic grant facility a firm in a Development Area or Intermediate Area can only apply for Regional Selective Assistance for which the firm has to demonstrate that its project is viable, will produce 'significant benefits' and requires government support to proceed. A number of business incentive schemes were introduced with higher levels of grant in the Assisted Areas. For example, under the marketing initiative the Department of Trade and Industry will pay 67 per cent of the cost of 5 to 15 man-days of consultancy for firms in Assisted Areas.

In addition, from April 1988, new incentives (Regional Enterprise Grants) were introduced to help small firms in Development Areas. For example, subject to limits, firms with less than 25 employees can apply for investment grants of 15 per cent towards the costs of fixed assets and for a grant of up to 50 per cent of the costs of product and process development. In 1982 the IDCs were abolished.

Moore, Rhodes and Tyler[17] have established the government's real expenditure on regional incentives (table 15.3). This table shows that in terms of real expenditure the policy was at its zenith in the early 1970s. But the figures ignore the effects of IDCs and do not necessarily indicate accurately the perceptions of the businessman as to the strength of the policy.

Table 15.3 *Direct exchequer costs of regional policy (£million)*

	1961/2–1963/4	1964/5–1971/2	1972/3–1975/6	1976/7–1980/1	1980–1	1981–2	1982–3	1983–4
Investment incentives (investment grants, RGD, free depreciation, RSA, factory building, other)	20	118	276	559	703	854	917	643
Labour subsidies (REP, other)	1	69	157	67	29	0	0	0
Total (current prices)	21	187	433	626	732	854	917	643
Total (1975 prices)	55	383	578	407	361	389	394	261

Source: calculated from Moore, Rhodes and Tyler, 'Effect of government regional economic policy', table 3.1

Work to the workers or workers to the work?

Those who favour taking the workers to the work stress mainly the loss of economic growth which is caused by interference with the location of industry. Only when businessmen are given a free choice will they select an optimal location. Choice restriction will lead to the plant not being established at all, or an inferior or overseas location being chosen. The result would be productivity losses and a lower national growth rate. Labour mobility does not incur such costs.

Supplementary arguments are based upon the practical difficulties of devising a policy to influence capital movement without encouraging inefficiency. For example, grants do not distinguish between the efficient firm and the inefficient. Moreover, both grants and tax allowances may be given to those who had decided to expand any way.

Conversely, others argue that growth is little affected by locational interference. First, many industries' costs may vary very little by location. Second, if left alone firms may not choose optimum sites in any event. Third, the discussion should be about social costs, not pure economic or private costs, so the growth–productivity argument is not a relevant one.

Such costs include diseconomies such as congestion, and over-utilization of existing social capital and infrastructure and the disappearance of local cultures. This last (cultural) reason is possibly the most honest and least disputable of all the reasons for having any type of regional policy.

The 'work to the workers' school goes still further and argues that labour migration is not only socially undesirable but also economically inefficient. First, migration depresses the donor region and has an expansionary effect on the host region. (Donor regional income is reduced; less is demanded of and so spent on social capital; the migrant tends to be the younger more enterprising type.)

Most regional policy in the UK is of a 'work to the workers' type. However, it can be argued that both equipment grants and tax allowances on capital expenditure encourage capital- rather than labour-intensive industries to move towards the labour force. Moreover, while firms must be making profits to qualify for a tax allowance, any firm, efficient or inefficient (as measured by profits), can obtain a grant.

Growth points

The most that can be claimed for regional policy is a very modest degree of success. Critics of past policies argue that this may be because it was too piecemeal (from 1958 to 1966 it was essentially a 'fire-fighting' policy applied to all employment exchange districts with 4.5 per cent unemployment) or because the aid provided was spread too widely over the country (as after 1966) to make a really perceptible impact on the problem areas.

As a consequence, the 'growth point' school of thought has attracted considerable support in recent years. Essentially, it implies that aid should be distributed not indiscriminately to whole regions but to those few critical points within them where it can do most good. Artificially stimulated growth points, like naturally occurring ones arising through the operation of market forces, will of course entail the costs of still further enhanced stagnation and decline in the other parts of the problem region.

As with all planning, a badly chosen growth point not only will require subsidies to establish itself but also may never grow up. The need for subsidies may never disappear. Several examples of the misguided application of growth point philosophy are the motor and lorry assembly plants of Rootes (subsequently Chrysler, then Peugeot) and BMC (now British Leyland) at Linwood and Bathgate respectively. The hopes that these would generate a plethora of supporting ancillary component industries were never realized.

Planning or laissez-faire*?*

The case for abolishing regional policy rests on the belief that in the long run a perfectly competitive market will lead to the optimum location of individual activity. 'Optimum' means the maximum production of goods and services desired by consumers. Any regional imbalances are corrected though the price mechanism. Where resources are scarce, their prices rise, demand falls and supply increases. The converse occurs if resources are under-utilized. But this situation need not hold in reality. Why?

First, factor prices need not reflect relative scarcities. For example, national wage negotiations may result in (relatively) uniform wage rates within the same occupational group. Second, even if prices truly reflect scarcities, factors may not be mobile and may not move to the high reward area. Workers are deterred from moving from a low wage area and unemployment to a high wage area with a job because they lack knowledge of the opportunities available elsewhere, because of the high costs of moving and because of mismatches between their skills and those required in areas of excess demand. Similarly, businessmen may have objectives which rank a pleasant environment and lower profits more highly than less sociable areas with higher profits. They may also lack knowledge of the relative costs in two locations. Moreover, even if the free market could be relied upon it is essentialy a long-run solution; short-run disequilibria will exist.

The case for regional planning is that sensible planning will solve the regional problem. But first, it is not at all obvious that civil servants or politicians know better where to locate a factory or a labour force than the factory owner or worker, whose full-time occupation it is to make such decisions. Second, the question must be raised as to how wise it is to encourage a belief in the population that industrial structure and location is static. Third, unless one postulates omniscience, it cannot be argued that planners can always take account of the fact that points of growth are constantly altering, new industries arising and new consumer needs developing. The benefits of the railway system would never have been realized had the canal, stage coach and land-owning interests had the power that such analogous lobbies possess today. Similar commercial misfortunes occurred with the British Aluminium smelter at Invergordon and the government-owned oil rig construction yard at Portavadie which was still not complete long after the oil rig construction boom was over and privately sponsored yards such as those at Ardyne had been put on a care and maintenance basis.

One of the few things that can be said with certainty is that the arguments for and against regional policy, its alleged success or failure, and the reasons for its paucity or plethora of achievements will continue for some time to come.

Public Goods and Externalities

To this point we have restricted our discussion solely to private goods (i.e. goods which are scarce, or (which is the same thing) economic goods).

When a good does not suffer from reduced availability due to consumption it is called a *public good*. As consumers increase in number the same given amount is available. National defence is a classic example; so too is the Thames flood barrage, a television broadcast or a football game. In addition, people often cannot be excluded from the benefits provided by the good. Thus if the author's houses are saved (or not saved) from nuclear extinction by the effectiveness (or ineffectiveness) of Britain's defence forces the same result will also occur for our next-door neighbours. Similarly the Thames flood barrage provides flood protection equally to all inhabitants of that area. However, it becomes ever more possible to exclude outsiders as human ingenuity grows. In the simple case of the football game, the match is a public good until the point when someone decides to erect enclosures and stadia with only a few gates at which would-be spectators must pay. Similarly, cable-transmitted television (as opposed to wireless transmission) not only permits a wider choice of programmes but provides access to those programmes only if the viewer pays for the rental of the cable, or alternatively has a meter built into the set which registers the amount owing by the viewer to the broadcast company.

Another assumption we have made so far is that whenever a trade occurs all the costs and benefits from the exchange accrue only to the transactors. This need not be the case. For example, one consumer may heat his house with oil and pay the fuel company for the oil consumed. But the cost of his central heating may not be fully reflected in his fuel bill if the oil refinery produces a large amount of air pollution.

In effect, part of the cost of heating the consumer's house is being borne by others. They are subsidizing him. They may not use oil-fired central heating themselves but are involuntarily consuming dirty air. This is an external cost or *negative externality* (since it is external to the transaction which resulted in it). External benefits or *positive externalities* arise if, for example, a householder goes to his local garden nursery, purchases flowering shrubs for his garden and makes his own property pleasant and appealing to look at.

Externalities only occur if property rights do not exist. When private property rights are well defined and easily enforced there is no cause for concern about externalities. We shall examine this situation first, and then the problems of government policy when externalities persist.

The former proposition was first advanced by Ronald Coase and is now known as the *Coase theorem*.[18] The theorem states that efficiency will always be realized in the absence of transaction costs no matter how property rights are assigned. Consider an example used by Coase himself. There is a strip of unfenced unowned land between the property of a grain farmer and that of a cattle farmer. The grain farmer would like to plant grain but the cattle would inevitably damage it in whole or in part, so he does not cultivate the land. This may or may not be socially optimal. If society values grain at the margin more highly than cattle it is certainly not optimal, since the grain farmer cannot or will not use the land, while the cattle farmer can graze more cattle at zero grazing cost (zero cost to himself: he gains an external benefit). Nevertheless society would prefer the land to be used for grain.

Now assume that we do not know which use is more efficient from society's point of view. But assume the grain farmer takes a chance that he can plant grain and get a profit from the sale or at least some undamaged portion of it. He also decides to sue the cattle farmer for damages to his crop. The law court will, of course, find it very difficult to decide whether or not to award damages. Both farmers had equal rights (i.e. no rights or only squatter's rights) to the land. The judge must make a value judgement. Let us assume that he decides to award full private ownership of the land to one party or the other.

The important factor emerging from the Coase theorem is that once this award is made, irrespective of the direction of the judgement (in favour of the grain farmer or the cattle farmer), the land will now be put to its most efficient, most socially highly valued use. Table 15.4 explains why, showing the outcome if the judgement is (a) in favour of the cattle farmer and (b) in favour of the grain farmer. It also considers the increased profits of each farmer if he secures legal access to the land relative to his profits if he had no such access.

Thus the Coase theorem is proved, and efficiency is realized no matter to whom the land is assigned by the legal authorities (albeit the wealth of the farmer to whom the land was awarded will increase). However, there are

Table 15.4 *Property rights awarded to the farmer of (a) cattle (b) grain*

(a) Cattle	(b) Grain
1 *Additional profits per annum from use of the land*	
Cattle farmer £1000: the cattle farmer will farm cattle on the land and earn £1000 extra profit	Grain farmer £600: the cattle farmer will farm cattle on the land, earn £1000, but pay a rental to the grain farmer which must be above £600 (or grain will be farmed) and below £1000 (or it will be unprofitabe to graze cattle)
2 *Additional profits*	
Cattle £600: the grain farmer will grow crops, paying the cattle farmer a rent of over £600 but under £1000	Grain £1000: the grain farmer will use the land, the profit of £1000 indicating that this is its most socially highly valued use

always transaction costs in real life. The Coase theorem, boldly stated, assumes them away. Rental agreements must be entered into between the farmers.

Negotiation expenses must be incurred; most obviously, in this example, fencing costs are necessary to keep the cattle off the grain. We see that, if transaction costs (on a yearly basis) amount to £400 or more then, even if situation (a)2 occurs, cattle will be farmed. This is because the profits on farming grain less the transaction costs will be below £600, leaving no positive net profits with which to pay a rental to the cattle farmer. (Which party actually incurs the cost of fencing and other transaction expenses is not really relevant – it is the amount which matters. Once the property rights are assigned the grain farmer will always be able to claim damages from the cattle farmer if the land is assigned to him and he uses it for grain growing and not rental. Thus the cattle (grain) farmer will be motivated to fence in (out) the cattle to avoid paying for (losing) any grain. What it will affect obviously will be the upper limit to the rental the grain farmer is willing and able to pay.)

The first main lesson from the Coase theorem is that externalities can often be 'internalized' if property rights can be established and means of charging devised. Thus public goods may not be so common as supposed. The classic lighthouse example is not necessarily a public good. In America it is provided by government. But in Britain, Trinity House in England and the Commissioners for Northern Lights in Scotland, plus other bodies, built substantial numbers of lighthouses in the nineteenth century, collecting tolls from ships when they entered the harbour. Cable television has already been mentioned.

Another textbook example is that of beekeepers whose bees receive nectar free of charge from fruit tree owners (an external benefit) but provide cross-pollination services without charge (a negative externality to the beekeeper). In fact Steven Cheung has also dismissed this example.[19] He discovered that in California there were three groups of fruit orchards: those which provided nectar with a high honey potential; those with a moderate honey potential; and those which provided little or no honey potential. All, however, required pollination and cross-fertilization by bees and other insects. Cheung found a well-developed market, contrary to the textbook writers. Orchard owners with fruit trees of the first type charged the apiary owners a site rental to leave their hives in the orchard. Those of the third type paid apiary owners to leave their hives in the orchards during the relevant seasons. The middle grouping came to more or less no-charge agreements because the respective alleged externalities cancelled out.

The second lesson from the Coase theorem is that externalities can still occur, and if property rights cannot be established or transaction costs minimized then market failure will arise. How can it be minimized? What does the demand curve look like for a public good? Unlike the market demand curve for a private good (obtaining by adding each individual's demand curve horizontally), to obtain the market demand curve for a public good the addition is vertical. For private goods if one extra unit was made available only one individual could consume it (so we moved along the Q axis of the demand diagram) and this consumer would value the good at its market price (so we remained at the same position on the P axis). With public goods, however, everyone benefits if one extra unit is provided, so the value of that unit is the sum of the values that all consumers place on it. To reflect this we must move up the P axis.

With this tool-kit we can now look at some of the problems of public good provision. What is the optimal provision of the public good? Figure 15.2 shows a three-citizen community where the demand curves D_1, D_2 and D_3 represent their relevant marginal valuation curves. Curve D is equal to $D_1 + D_2 + D_3$ added vertically at any given Q. MC is the marginal cost of providing the good. At output Q' social marginal benefits received equal social marginal costs; Q' is consequently the optimal output.

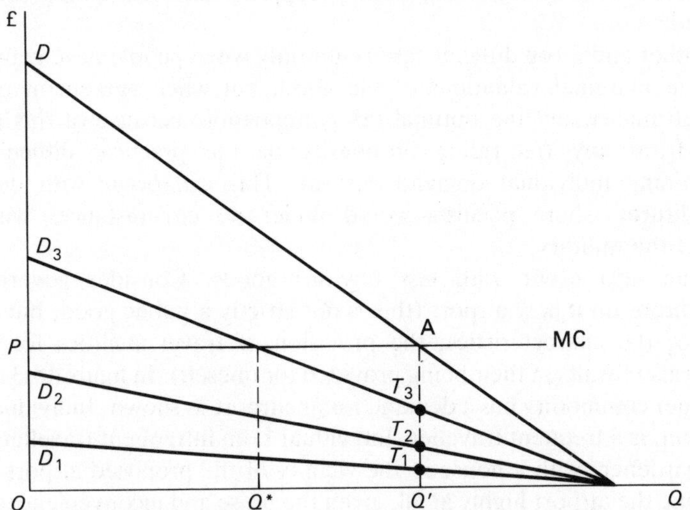

Figure 15.2 *Optimal provision of a public good under conditions of different marginal valuations*

But here we encounter the next difficulty. Although output Q' is socially optimal, only one individual values the good sufficiently highly to pay a price for the first few units which will cover the marginal cost. This is individual 3. He will buy to Q^* and then cease purchasing. In short, with public goods, everyone wants them but few, and sometimes none, are prepared to pay for them.

In addition, if individual 3 does pay for Q^* units then the other two members of the community are *free-riding* at his expense. They are obtaining the benefits without incurring any costs. All three members of society would prefer Q' units, which would increase their net benefits to equal the area DPA, the maximum net benefit they can collectively obtain.

With three individuals a collective agreement could possibly be hammered out to ensure that Q' units were produced. With a large nation the solution to the problem is usually obtained by handing the task over to government who will fund the provision through taxation. Again figure 15.2 can be used to show the difficulties arising from this approach. People will still wish to free-ride, if they can. So they will attempt to conceal their preferences (in a private good situation the act of purchase reveals them). Thus although at Q' the optimal solution is to raise marginal taxes of T_1, T_2 and T_3 from each individual respectively (where $T_1 + T_2 + T_3 = P$), and although Q' is the desired goal of all, it is clear that if people believe their share of total taxes will be based on their desire for the good then they will understate that desire to minimize their tax bills and hope, again, to free-ride. This difficulty may be viewed as real but practically insurmountable unless somehow the good can be privately supplied and the Coase theorem invoked.

Another and more difficult case is not only when people have genuinely different marginal valuations of the good, but when agreement on the optimal quality and the optimal tax is impossible because of this (quite apart from any free-riding propensity or the practical difficulty of determining individual demand curves). This can occur with defence expenditures where pacifists would under no circumstances willingly support the military.

It can also occur with less obvious goods. Consider government expenditure on a new airport (this is not strictly a public good, but it has some of the characteristics; the provision of travel facilities for other people also results in their being provided for oneself). In figure 15.3 a two-consumer commodity has a demand for an airport as shown. Individual 2, a salesman, is a frequent traveller. Individual 1, an infrequent traveller but a keen gardener, with a house in the vicinity of the proposed airport, does not value the airport highly at all, given the noise and inconvenience it will cause him compared with the slight benefits which might accrue to him. Moreover, individual 1 has a much higher income than individual 2 and knows that, in reality, his marginal tax rate is related to his income and not to his preferences for public goods of whatever nature. If their marginal tax rates are T_1 and T_2 respectively then, given the two marginal valuation curves, the marginal values of the new airport to individuals 1 and 2 exceed their marginal costs up to Q_1 and Q_2 units of airport (or flight arrivals or other subdivision).

Unfortunately, an airport is indivisible and both individuals must benefit from and pay for the chosen size of airport. With normal tax structures disagreement is inevitable, irrespective of preference distortion for public relations purposes. Moreover, neither party would be satisfied with the social optimum, Q^*, albeit that is the only output that both individuals

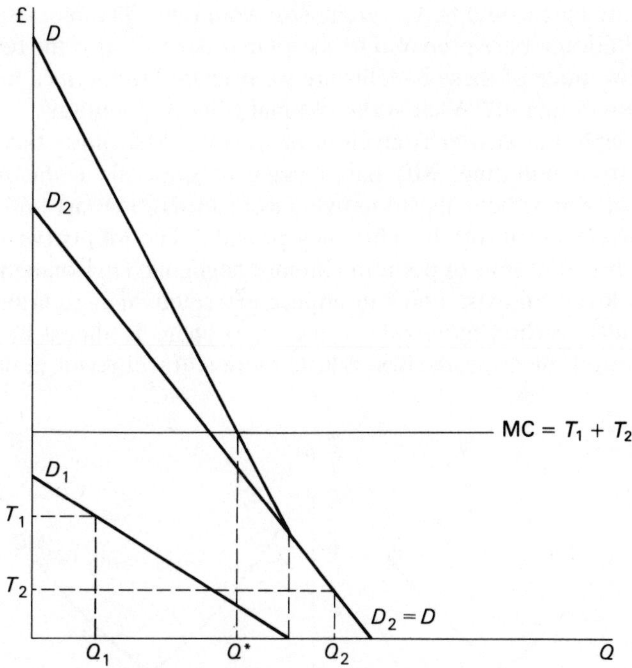

Figure 15.3 *Optimal provision of a public good under conditions of lack of agreement on quality and tax*

could desire and still collectively pay a tax covering the cost of the good. Thus individuals 1 and 2 would desire the public good – airport, national defence, industrial subsidies or whatever – up to the apparently, and probably factually, irreconcilable levels Q_1 and Q_2. This is a major advantage of private goods and attempts to internalize so-called externalities: that polarization of opinions and social disharmonies are minimized and individual diversity is permitted and accommodated.

Environmental Pollution

With these basic principles about externalities and public goods in mind, what can we learn about economic policy problems in issues such as pollution? Private motorists pollute the atmosphere with their exhaust emissions; farmers do so with insecticides and weed killers; firms in heavy industry produce sulphur dioxide and other fumes from their factory chimneys.

Every activity we engage in, from breathing to steel production, generates a by-product discharged into the atmosphere. The pollution 'problem' could thus be easily solved by banning all these activities, but the opportunity cost would be too great. We would die. The real issue is how much pollution we are prepared to accept in order to obtain the benefits we want. How much of these benefits are we prepared to sacrifice to obtain a cleaner environment? What is the optimal level of pollution?

In principle the answer is given in figure 15.4. MB shows the marginal benefits from polluting. MB has a negative slope since the first units provide enormous benefits (to individuals or firms); the last few units are near to irrelevant in the benefits they provide. The MC curve slopes up since the first few units of pollution impose negligible environmental costs; at higher levels an extra unit can impose extremely high additional costs. (Thus a little carbon monoxide in the atmosphere is almost harmless; a little more produces headaches; a little more still will result in death.)

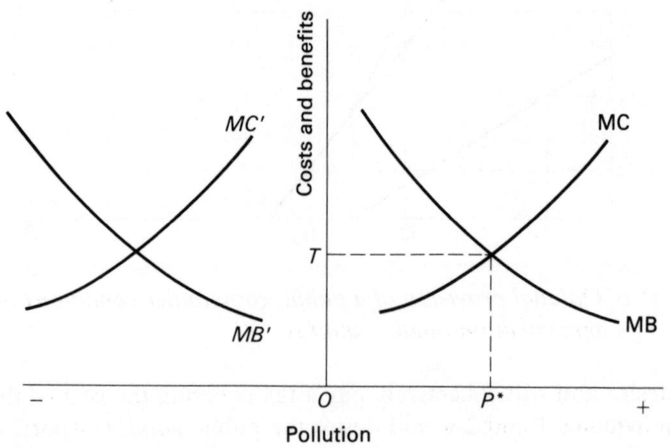

Figure 15.4 *Optimal level of pollution under a taxation system*

The optimal level of pollution to society is P^*. This is positive, and will be so for most products. However, in some cases it either is or is presumed to be negative, as with curves MC′ and MB′. When this occurs the government may ban the polluting activity altogether. Examples of such bans are the use of the drug thalidomide; the use of cyclamates, a very popular food additive in the 1960s as a sweetener; and the dumping of nuclear power station waste in unprotected heaps.

However, although the concepts of figure 15.4 are useful, they are difficult if not impossible to use. Moreover, the MB and MC schedules are society's valuations of the costs and benefits, and very few individuals in society are likely to agree over any average outcome even if it could be shown to be 'correct' in that statistical sense. What we can infer, however, is that pollution is likely to be in excess of the social optimum P^*. Why? The reason lies in the frequent absence of property rights and resulting negative externalities.

A firm with a factory chimney emitting noxious fumes will move (in figure 15.4) from the origin rightwards. As the factory emits more and more pollution it earns more and more profit (represented by MB) but the firm will not stop at P^*. Other things equal, it could continue until MB hits the horizontal axis. Although MC is rising the firm itself is bearing none of the costs of the polluted air. The community as a whole is (hence the rising MC) but the firm is only one small part of the community. If the firm introduced pollution abatement procedures, the benefits to the community would be large, but the firm would bear the total cost of this abatement and there is thus a positive externality for pollution abatement. From our discussion of public goods we know that pollution abatement is a form of public good and as such is unlikely to be purchased.

What then is the appropriate policy response to the pollution problem? There are three alternatives. First, and probably best, is to bear in mind the Coase theorem, and look for ways to permit *trading between the polluter and polluted.* If the individuals or groups of individuals who suffer from the negative externalities can agree with the polluter on a price they should receive in compensation, or alternatively a price they will pay to make him cease or reduce polluting activities, then the optimal level of pollution is likely to be reached. Certainly this requires assignation of property rights in the atmosphere and a mechanism whereby the damaged can sue the damager (or pay the damager depending on how the courts assign the rights) but this permits variation in individual evaluation of the costs and benefits of pollution.

This flexibility is not so readily present in the second alternative, namely *taxation of the polluter.* Thus, in figure 15.4 a tax of T, levied on the polluter, would ensure that he did not move down the MB curve beyond P^*. But the heights of the MB and MC curves can vary. Thus the demand for pollution (MB) is likely to be higher in cities and towns than in the country. (There are more people wishing to drive more cars; there are more firms wishing to be located close to their labour force and to their market.) Similarly the demand for a clean environment (i.e. the costs of pollution represented by the MC schedule) will be lower in country areas. This is because (a) there are fewer people anyway, and so the vertical aggregation of the curves results in a lower total schedule, and (b) the intensity of each individual's demand for anything, the height of the curve at a given quantity, is less the lower is his income. Country dwellers have a lower average per caput income than town dwellers, and so the MC curve is again lower.

In short, even if the situation of figure 15.5 existed, where P^* is the same in both town and country, varying taxation levels (T and T') would be required to attain it. Given the extremely large numbers of alternative situations, it is unlikely that any one tax, or even any range of taxes, could possibly cover all the different situations in the way that individual contracting, under the Coase theorem assumptions, could.

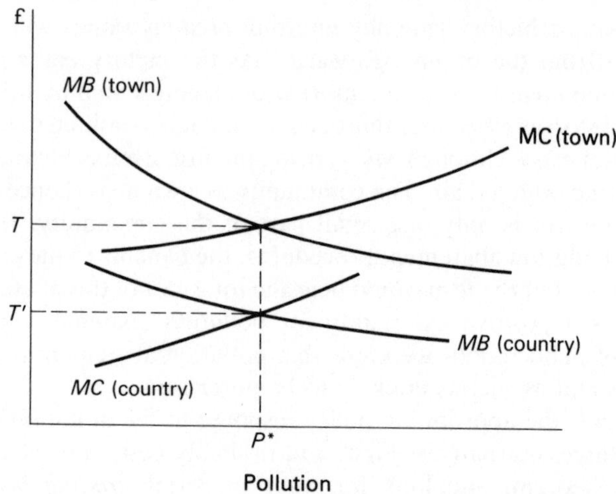

Figure 15.5 *Pollution and taxation in town and country*

Taxation, however, is probably a better policy tool than the third alternative, which is that of *setting standards*. Taxation will motivate the polluter to reduce pollution as cheaply as possible and to do so until the MB schedule equals the marginal tax rate. Even if the tax rate is not optimal or variable there are still significant advantages over the standards approach. The reason is due again to varying situations and therefore lack of complete information by the standard-setting authority.

For example, the typical anti-pollution law requires all polluters to reduce their emissions by a given percentage. Thus in figure 15.6 firms 1 and 2, which before the standard was set were polluting at P_1 and P_2 respectively (where their MB schedules equal zero, since they themselves

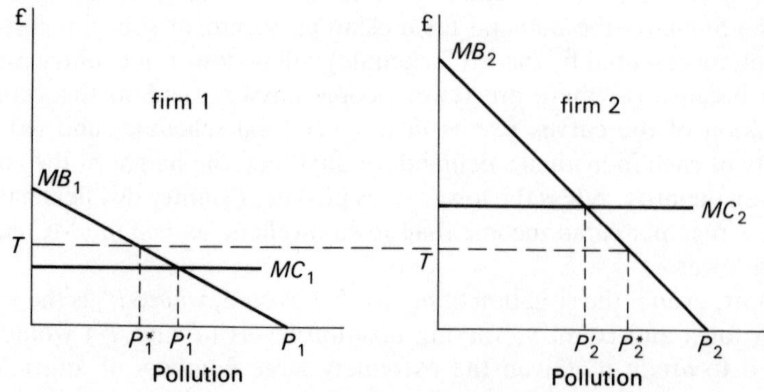

Figure 15.6 *Pollution under a standards system*

assumed none of the costs of pollution), reduce their pollution levels by the same percentage to P_1' and P_2' after the law is passed. To do this each must incur a cost. This cost is represented by the sacrificed MB of the polluting activity and is achieved by installing pollution abatement machinery, adopting new processes, or most simply by reducing output. In any event the cost is still the opportunity cost of the sacrificed MB. These costs are represented by MC_1 and MC_2 respectively. For whatever reason, firm 1 is more efficient than firm 2 in reducing pollution levels ($MC_1 < MC_2$). Thus the same amount of pollution reduction could have been achieved at less social cost than it has been by the imposition of standards. For example, say $MC_1 = £5$ and $MC_2 = £8$, then if firm 1 is asked to restrict its output of pollution from P_1' by one further unit, the cost is £5. If firm 2 is permitted to produce one further unit of pollution above P_2' then the total pollution is unchanged, but £8 of pollution abatement expenditure has been saved, a net social gain of £3.

A uniform tax, for all its faults, is thus better than uniform standards. It encourages the lowest-cost pollution abaters more than the high-cost ones to reduce pollution. This is seen in figure 15.6 where a uniform marginal tax rate is imposed on both firms at T. Firms 1 and 2 will now alter output to P_1^* and P_2^* respectively. The total pollution reduction remains the same but the total cost of pollution abatement has been lowered.

Not only does a tax motivate reduction of pollution more cheaply than do standards, it also encourages still further reductions by motivating a search for new technologies, and does so in a way that the setting of standards fails to do. If the long run is important, this is a major advantage of the taxation approach. Consider figure 15.7. The MB schedules are identical in each. The pollution produced by the firm in figure 15.7(a) is identical with that in figure 15.7(b). The only difference is that in the first

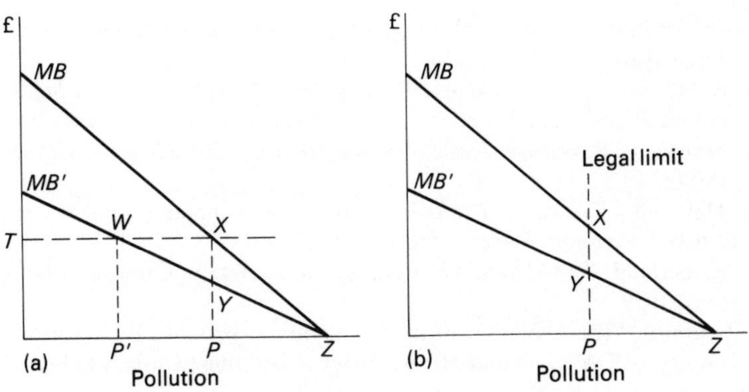

Figure 15.7 *Pollution and the search for new technology under systems of (a) taxation and (b) standards*

case the level of P achieved is accomplished by virtue of a tax, whereas in the second it is the result of a legal standard.

Now assume that a new technology becomes available which lowers the marginal costs of pollution abatement (i.e. it reduces the marginal benefits sacrificed by reducing the polluting activity). Diagrammatically MB shifts to MB′. In case (a) the firm subject to the tax is further motivated to reduce pollution to P'. There the MB of pollution (MB′) equals the marginal cost (T) of pollution abatement. Any other position is not one of profit maximization. In case (b) the firm will continue to pollute up to the legal limit of P and any costs saved by the introduction of the new technology (XYZ) will simply be additional profits to the firm. (Furthermore, experience indicates that legislative changes are relatively infrequent and often lag behind technological improvements.)

But, of course, not only does the tax result in reduced pollution; somehow research into the new technology itself must be encouraged. The incentive to do such research is greater in (a) than case (b). In case (b) the incentive to introduce the new technology is the additional profit XYZ. In case (a) the savings from introducing cheaper pollution abatement also include XYZ, but since the tax bill of the polluter is also reduced (by P' WXP) this must be added to XYZ; moreover, of course, the benefits forgone by reducing pollution from P to P' (WYPP') must be deducted. Thus the tax-paying polluter is better off by WXY as a consequence of introducing technology, *vis-à-vis* the regulated polluter. The tax-paying polluter thus has the stronger incentive to search for and introduce the new technology.

References

1 V. Korah, *Competition Law of Britain and the Common Market*, Elek Books, 1975.
2 *Review of Restrictive Trade Practices Policy*, Green Paper, Cmnd 331, HMSO, March 1988.
3 R. B. Stevens and B. S. Yamey, *The Restrictive Practices Court: A Study of the Judicial Process and Economic Policy*, Weidenfeld and Nicolson, 1965.
4 *A Review of Restrictive Trade Practices Policy*, Green Paper, Cmnd 7512, HMSO, 1979.
5 D. Hay and J. Vickers, 'The revolution of UK competition policy', *National Institute Economic Review* (August 1988).
6 A. Sutherland, *The Monopolies Commission in Action*, Cambridge University Press, 1969.
7 J. Fairburn, 'The evolution of merger policy in Britain', in J. Fairburn and J. Kay (eds), *Mergers and Merger Policy*, Cambridge University Press, 1989.
8 Ibid.
9 J. A. Fairburn, 'British merger policy', *Fiscal Studies* 6 (1) (1985), pp. 70–81.
10 G. Borrie, 'Competition, mergers and price fixing', *Lloyds Bank Review* (April 1987).

11 Hay and Vickers, 'The revoltuion of UK competition policy'.
12 S. Fothergill and G. Gudgin, *Unequal Growth: Urban and Regional Employment Change in the UK*, Heinemann, 1982.
13 Department of Trade and Industry, *Regional Industrial Policy*, HMSO, 1983.
14 B. C. Moore, J. Rhodes and P. Tyler, 'The effect of government regional economic policy', University of Cambridge Report to Department of Trade and Industry, unpublished, 1983.
15 J. Townsend, F. Henwood, G. Thomas, K. Pavitt and S. Wyatt, 'Science and technology indicators for the UK: innovations since 1945', Science Policy Research Unit Occasional Paper 16, 1981.
16 B. C. Moore, J. Rhodes and P. Tyler, *The Effects of Government Regional Economic Policy*, HMSO, 1986.
17 Ibid.
18 R. H. Coase, 'The problem of social cost', *Journal of Law and Economics* 4 (1961), pp. 1–49.
19 S. Cheung, *The Myth of Social Cost*, Hobart Paper 82, Institute of Economic Affairs, 1978.

Further reading

H. Armstrong and J. Taylor, *Regional Economic Policy*, Philip Allan, 1984.
Commission of The European Communities, *18th Report of Competition Policy*, Office of Official Publications of the European Communities, 1989.
Department of Trade and Industry, *The Department of Enterprise*, White Paper, Cmnd 278, HMSO, January 1988.
European Commission, 'Council Regulation (EEC) 4064/89 of 21 December 1989 on the control of concentrations between undertakings', *Official Journal of the European Communities* 32, L395 (30 December 1989).
M. Fleming and D. Swann, 'Competition policy – the pace quickens and 1992 approaches', *Royal Bank of Scotland Review* (June 1989).
D. C. Goodyer, *EEC Competition Law*, Oxford University Press, 1989.
Opening Markets: New Policy on Restrictive Trade Practices, White Paper, Cmnd 727, HMSO, July 1989.

16

Concluding Thoughts

Throughout this book we have emphasized a number of themes. One is that in the businesses which produce the overwhelming majority of UK output the identities of the owners of the firm and suppliers of capital differ from those of the managers. The managers act as agents on behalf of the owners or principals and may do so in a way which results in an agency loss. Managers are constrained to various degrees by several factors from implementing policies which differ from those which give results desired by the principals. Competition in the inputs (capital and labour) markets and in product markets yields observable performances with which those of agents can be compared.

A second theme is that new products and processes are introduced by entrepreneurs who perceive a profit opportunity and then seek funding and labour to fulfil it. The entrepreneurs may be the managers of large corporations or an individual performing experiments in his garden shed. Entrepreneurs may deliberately search for these opportunities (the ability to pay less to those who rent their services – suppliers of labour and capital – than is expected to be received in revenue) or they may be spontaneously perceived, i.e. they may not have been pursued not because of prohibitive costs nor even because of search costs but simply because no one has noticed them. Some have argued that the spontaneous perception of profit opportunities is the ultimate source of all entrepreneurial activity. Even if an innovation is introduced as a result of a long and deliberate analysis of market conditions, someone has first to decide to initiate the analysis. But this comes close to making the term 'spontaneous perception' a tautology.

However, this process may result in prices very significantly different from marginal costs with a welfare loss to society. The anticipation of gaining such profits encourages entrepreneurs to enter an industry, unless established firms act strategically to deter entry or barriers to entry exist. In these situations the social welfare loss of monopoly may persist for a rather longer period of time and a need for competition policy arises. Of course the prospect of earning supernormal profit must remain open to those innovating new products and processes and UK competition law enables this to be taken into account by the investigative authorities.

Some have argued that reductions in marginal income tax rates and the removal of regulations concerning prices and product characteristics would encourage greater innovation and employee motivation by increasing the profits or wages received and in the long run would result in an optimal resource allocation, i.e. of labour and capital to activities and of goods and services to consumers. However, there is evidence that reducing income tax rates does little to increase motivation. Furthermore, the level of human suffering which may take place over this period of temporary disequilibrium may be very great indeed. For example, without regulations covering the safety of medicines, some unsafe drugs may be marketed before consumers decide which drug companies to avoid purchasing drugs from. Without taxation it is unclear how public goods would be provided. Finally, on political grounds many adhere to the belief that the distribution of income in a highly competitive economy devoid of transfer payments (such as social security payments) or taxes is rather undesirable. But economists are not politicians!

Index

The Economics of Modern Business
Second Edition

W. D. Reekie, D. E. Allen and J. N. Crook

Outdated management techniques cannot be expected to cope with the complex problems of modern business. Today's managers must have a better understanding of the internal structure of the firm and a clear picture of the firm's place within the economy as a whole.

In the thoroughly revised and updated second edition of this highly original textbook for business students, W. D. Reekie, D. E. Allen and J. N. Crook examine contemporary management issues in an objective and well balanced fashion. A special feature of the book is its successful integration of introductory financial analysis with microeconomic theory. It includes extensive sections on financial markets, distribution channels, industrial relations and government policies and stresses the overriding importance of market forces in business decision-making.

The second edition incorporates all the changes created by 'big bang', new accounting standards, the EC and the harmonization of reporting requirements as well as a completely revised discussion of taxation systems, industrial relations, pricing, small firms, privatization and monopoly policy.

It is an essential text for students and provides an up-to-date and complete introduction to the economics of modern business.

W. D. Reekie is Professor of Business Economics, Department of Business Economics, University of the Witwatersrand. **D. E. Allen** is Senior Lecturer, Department of Accounting and Finance, University of Western Australia. **J. N. Crook** is Lecturer in Business Economics and Director of the Part-Time MBA Programme, Edinburgh University Management School.

Jacket design by Miller, Craig & Cocking
Design Partnership
Printed in Great Britain

ISBN 0-631-17215-7

BLACKWELL
Business